How to
Draw & Paint
What You See
RAY SMITH

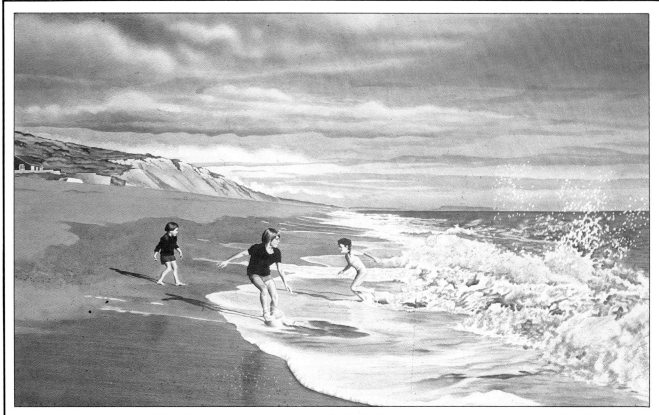

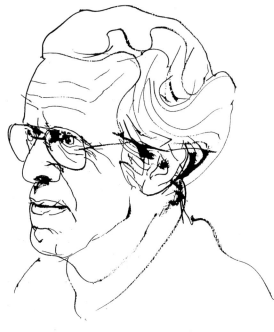

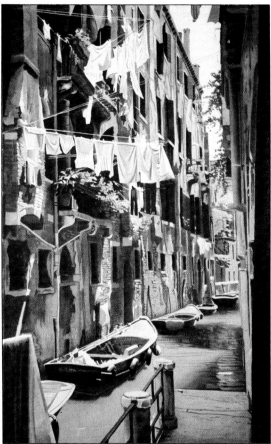

How to
Draw & Paint
What You See

RAY SMITH

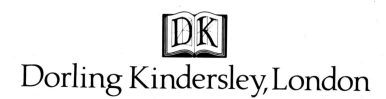

Dorling Kindersley, London

For my parents

How to Draw & Paint What You See
was edited and designed by
Dorling Kindersley Limited,
9 Henrietta Street,
London WC2E 8PS

PROJECT EDITOR
Phil Wilkinson
ART EDITOR
Neville Graham
EDITOR
Joanna Godfrey Wood
DESIGNER
Julia Goodman
MANAGING EDITOR
Alan Buckingham
ART DIRECTOR
Stuart Jackman

First published in
Great Britain in 1984 by
Dorling Kindersley Limited,
9 Henrietta Street,
London WC2E 8PS

First published as a Dorling Kindersley paperback 1989
Reprinted 1991
Copyright © 1984 by
Dorling Kindersley Limited, London
Text and illustrations copyright © 1984
by Ray Smith

British Library Cataloguing in
Publication Data

Smith, Ray
   How to draw and paint what you see.
   1. Drawings
   I. Title
   741.2
ISBN 0-86318-357-3

CONTENTS

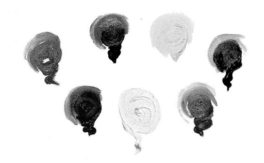

INTRODUCTION

MAKING IMAGES with pencil or brush is as basic to everyone's make-up as eating or sleeping. We are all artists and we each have our own individual style that is as unique as our handwriting. But for many people the problem is that the fluent self-expression of their early childhood has been cramped and inhibited by education and by self-consciousness. Artists seek to regain their early confidence, so that eventually they learn to speak with their own voice once more. This voice is what we respond to when we look at a great work of art. We recognise that despite the social, domestic, economic, political, or artistic pressures, or even perhaps because of them, the artist comes through clearly and authentically, presenting a uniquely individual vision.

The best artists may present us with a unique vision but this does not mean that they dwell in some separate and inaccessible realm. Most of them have their feet planted firmly on the ground. They tend to be practical people. And yet even today, a fog of romantic mythology seems to envelop the figure of the artist. This may be because people do not normally think of the artist as an artisan working directly and straightforwardly with tools and materials. The artist's use of these materials seems somehow mysterious, a gift from on high rather than the down-to-earth and practical art that it is. One result of such misconceptions is that some of those who wish to take up painting buy a set of colours and wait for inspiration. It is not surprising that their initial enthusiasm evaporates and the colours are passed on to family or friends who may have better luck. But painting need not be such a chancy business as this: the practical side of the art can be learnt in a similar way to any other manual skill.

The language of painting is built on the materials of the craft, and familiarity with the range and use of painting materials is the first stage of becoming a painter. The best way to discover your own voice as an artist is by practising the language of painting so much that you become fluent in it. At some point, you may wish to break all the rules of grammar in an attempt to extend the language itself, but at least you will be doing so from a firm base. The way we naturally learn a language is by imitation and repetition and this applies equally well to painting. Very often books that set out to explain the materials and techniques of painting do so by encouraging you to imitate a method of working or a way of producing an effect in complete isolation. The reader is somehow expected to make a connection between this isolated activity and a real painting. In this book, the method is to show all the techniques in the context of real paintings. All the images that you are encouraged to copy have been made expressly for this purpose and have been photographed at every stage of painting. This allows each part of the image-making process to be clearly set out and explained. Since I have written the text as well as painting the pictures, there is a close link between words and images, with all the special problems of each painting explained in detail.

The basic approach of this book arose out of a series of oil-painting classes that I began some years ago. I found that by giving people a carefully pre-selected image with specially drawn outlines which they traced on to their canvases, they were able to concentrate initially on all the practical aspects of painting. They did not have to worry about what to paint or how to draw it accurately. As we explored the use of materials—first of all in black and white and later in colour—the students quickly became experts in handling paint. The transition from pre-selected images to those of their own choice was made smoothly since, by then, they had the confidence to tackle almost anything.

The first two sections of this book are designed to get you painting. The first, "Black and White Techniques", starts with simple line work. In subsequent drawings and paintings, tone is introduced and techniques such as blending and modelling are demonstrated, first with simple subjects and later in more complex paintings. Many of these exercises show you how to paint the images in oils, acrylics, and watercolours. In addition there are often drawn versions of the subjects in this section.

In a similar way, the section on Colour Techniques introduces many basic aspects of colour including mixing, complementary colours, and colour contrasts. The latter include the contrasts between warm and cool colours, hard and soft, and transparent and opaque. These are all shown in the context of specific images.

The third section focuses a little more clearly on the basic formal elements of making a painting. These have been dealt with to some extent in the first two sections, but now they are explored more fully in the context of more finished paintings and drawings.

The book's fourth section brings the elements of painting together in a series of paintings arranged according to their subject. Still life, landscape, portrait, and nude sections are included. Within each of these categories the paintings are varied in style, medium, and subject. In the still life section, for example, a simple oil painting of apples, painted in a direct and loose style, is contrasted with a very controlled and tightly painted watercolour of an arrangement of glass. As with the paintings in the first two sections, each has an outline drawing on a grid and each stage of the picture's making is illustrated and described. In addition, the introduction to each work discusses its particular challenges and problems, showing you the kinds of decisions you will have to make when you come to do paintings of a similar type.

In order to make the book as practical to use as possible, I have kept to a minimum the range (though not the use) of colours, brushes, and painting mediums. This means that you will not have to buy a complete new set of items for each picture. For this reason it is worthwhile buying good quality materials at the outset.

If by making the paintings in this book you gain confidence in the use of artists' materials, then the book will have achieved its main purpose. But there is another theme that runs through it. When you no longer have the support of a set of instructions and a particular image to work towards, you will be faced with the question of exactly what to paint and how to paint it. The book has, of course, shown you that you can tackle successfully almost any subject in any number of styles and media. But it also helps you to understand yourself enough as a painter to gain the confidence to recognise and exploit your own individual ideas and enthusiasms.

Ray Smith

MATERIALS

SUPPORTS

THE MATERIAL THAT you paint on is called the support. It may take the form of a flexible substance, such as paper or stretched canvas, or an inflexible material, such as a panel of hardboard or plywood. The best quality canvas, which you should use if you can afford it, is pure, closely woven linen. But many artists use cotton, and in particular, cotton duck. If you use cotton, avoid the cheapest grades. For example, the 9 oz grade, used for painting scenery in the theatre, is too loosely woven for fine-art painting. It is worth paying a little extra for the 10 oz, or better still the 12 oz or 15 oz varieties. The best watercolour papers are hand-made from pure linen rags. Papers of the next grade have a certain amount of cotton in them. Wood-pulp paper discolours and turns brittle with age, but pure rag paper is permanent. If you do not want your watercolour paintings to deteriorate, choose an acid-free (or "neutral pH") paper. There are generally three types of surface available. Rough paper has a heavily textured surface, not (that is, not-pressed or cold-pressed) paper has an intermediate grade of surface texture, and hot-pressed (or "HP") paper is relatively smooth.

Paper generally needs no preparation before you paint on it apart from stretching (see p. 10). However boards and canvases require sizing and the application of a ground or primer. The purpose of sizing is to isolate the support from the potentially harmful oils in the paint. The ground or primer makes a surface that acts as a reflector for the paint and provides a surface of the right degree of absorbency. Because of their flexibility, canvases must be painted with grounds which, when dry, are also fairly flexible. In addition, the paint film applied on top must be more flexible than the ground. For this reason, you can use an acrylic ground for an oil painting on a rigid board, but not for an oil painting on a canvas.

You can buy canvases that are already stretched and primed. These are reliable and allow you to start painting without a lot of preparation. But they are expensive and it is quite easy to prepare your own. Also, you may want to experiment with different types of ground and surface, to see which suits you best.

PREPARING INFLEXIBLE SUPPORTS

Good quality hardboard is one of the best forms of wooden panel for painting. Large panels require battening at the back to stop the board from bending, but if you use the quarter-inch thickness and keep to smaller sizes, battening is not necessary. You can do most of the oils and acrylics in this book on board without battening.

The simplest method for rigid panels is to buy acrylic primer and apply it straight to the board. You can use either side of the board, but the smooth side is probably best. If the hardboard is a little greasy, try rubbing the surface with acetone before priming. Two thin coats of primer, well brushed on, will give a satisfactory surface. Each coat takes half an hour to dry and, since no sizing is required with this type of primer, you will be ready to paint in an hour. For studies and exercises, it is possible to use good-quality household vinyl emulsion paint as a substitute for the more reliable purpose-made primer. Sand the surface lightly between coats for a smooth painting surface.

If you use an oil-based oil-painting primer or a traditional gesso ground, you will also need to size the board. The best material for this is rabbit-skin glue size, which you can buy at most art stores. For rigid panels, use $1\frac{1}{4}$ oz of size per pint (75 g per litre) of warm water. When it is dissolved you brush it on to the board. It is advisable to paint the edges and back at the same time. This will protect the board and prevent it from warping.

You can combine the sizing with a simple method of giving your board a cloth texture. Do this by putting a sheet of muslin over your board and "painting" it on with the size. Pull out the wrinkles as you go and tuck and glue the muslin neatly round the back of the board. This is a well known and inexpensive way of producing your own canvas board. You can, of course, use acrylic primer on the resulting surface.

When the size has dried thoroughly, apply the ground. Two thin coats of oil-painting primer should be enough to give an even, white surface for your painting. You should allow the first to dry thoroughly before applying the second. With oil-based primers this takes several hours. Make the brushstrokes for the second coat at right-angles to those for the first.

Oil-based primers make the least absorbent painting surfaces. Traditional gesso grounds are the most absorbent. They are generally made from a mixture of whiting with about ten per cent Titanium White or Zinc White. Use just under $1\frac{1}{2}$ oz of size to a pint (90 g per litre) of water for the glue mix. You pour hot (but not boiling) glue over the powder and stir it thoroughly until the mixture is brushable. Gesso is applied thinly with a flat, wide brush over the whole panel. After the first coat is dry, you apply further coats (sometimes as many as four or five) at right-angles to the previous ones, allowing each to dry. Finally, you should sand the surface finely to a smooth finish and polish it with a damp cotton pad. Gesso grounds are excellent for the thinner type of painting, which uses the reflective qualities of the ground.

PREPARING FLEXIBLE SUPPORTS

Canvases for painting are held on wooden stretchers. Unless you have the special tools required for all the jointing involved in making these, you should buy them ready-

STRETCHING A CANVAS

To keep the tension even, ensure that your staples or tacks are equidistant, and follow the order shown below. Start with a row of staples in the middle of one edge, balancing it by attaching the opposite edge (steps 1 and 2). Do the same with the other two sides (steps 3 and 4), and then start to work towards the corners in the directions indicated (steps 5 to 12). On steps 5, 6, 9, and 10, leave gaps of about 3 ins (8 cm) at the corners, to allow you to fold them over. A neat and effective method for dealing with the corners of the canvas is shown in the photographs at the bottom of the page.

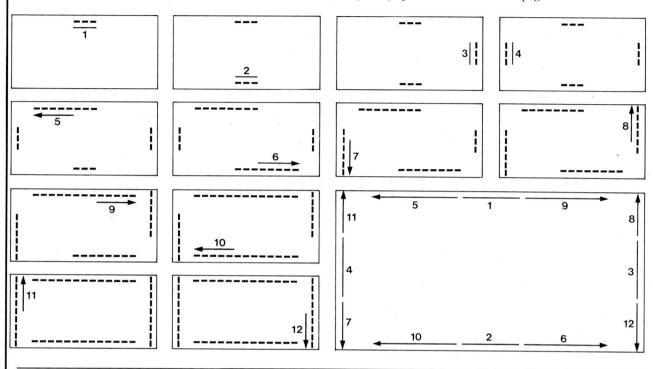

1 You can use your hands, rather than specially designed canvas pliers, to get the right tension.

2 A staple gun can be used to attach the canvas to the wooden stretchers.

3 For a neat corner, make folds in the canvas at each edge of the stretcher.

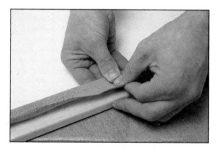

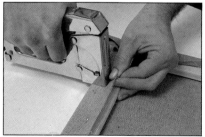

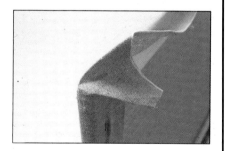

4 Pull one corner fold over the other and round the back of the stretcher frame.

5 Keeping the canvas neatly folded, staple the corner in position.

6 The finished corner, neat and effective, gives even tension at all points on the canvas.

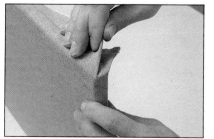

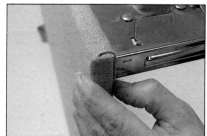

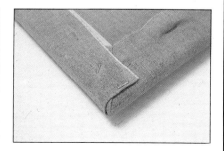

made from a specialist firm or buy prepared stretchers from an art store and make your frames with these. In stretcher frames, the flat edges that touch the canvas are recessed so that contact is only made with the canvas around the outer edges of the frame. In addition there are spaces in the corner joints for wooden wedges that can tighten up a slightly loosely stretched canvas, so it is not advisable to stretch a canvas on a flat or rigid home-made frame. To stretch your canvas, make sure that the frame is square by checking the corners with a set square or measuring each of the diagonals (these should be equal in length). Lay the frame flat on the floor over a piece of canvas that has been cut to a size two or three inches larger than the frame all round. To fix the canvas to the stretchers most artists use a staple gun, though traditionally, a hammer and tacks are used. With staple guns, it is best to avoid thin staples. The order in which you insert the tacks or staples is very important.

If you use an acrylic primer for an acrylic painting, you do not need to size the canvas. With other primers you do. You should use a slightly thinner mixture than for panels: a ratio of a little under 1 oz of size to a pint of water (56 g per litre) is satisfactory. You can scrape the size on to the canvas when it is cold, when it has a puree-like consistency. Use a plastic spatula or the broad side of an old credit card. If you warm the size up a little you can brush it on. But do not apply it hot to the canvas. If it is too hot, the size will soak right through the canvas and it will not provide a good seal from the ground layers.

For oil painting on canvas, an oil-based oil-painting primer is best, because of its flexibility. Similar primers based on synthetic resins are also available. Some artists use oil-based undercoats, but these can turn yellow with age. Household emulsion paints are not suitable. They absorb too much of the oil from the paint leaving a brittle, matt surface. Generally, two coats of primer will give the even, white surface required for painting. Brush the first well in and leave it to dry thoroughly. You can use a very fine sandpaper to give a smooth surface for the second coat. Do not begin your oil painting until the second coat is completely dry.

WATERCOLOUR SUPPORTS

All watercolour papers have been sized during the manufacturing process — without size they would be as absorbent as blotting paper. Different manufacturers use different amounts of size, so that papers vary in the way that they respond to paint. The weight of the paper also influences how it responds. The lightest papers are 72 lb (the weight of a ream of paper) while the heaviest are rated at 555 lb, and there is a range of weights in between. The more you wish to work the surface, the heavier the weight of the paper should be. With the very heavy grades, no stretching is required, but, generally speaking, watercolour paper should be stretched to keep it flat while washes of colour are applied and dried. If it were not stretched it would buckle and lose its shape.

To stretch a sheet of watercolour paper, use the following method. Run some cold water into the bath and immerse the paper for about half a minute, so that it gets wet but not sodden. Then, after letting the excess water run off, take the water from the back of the paper with a large sponge and lay the sheet on to a horizontal drawing board. Push it out from the centre with the sponge so that it lies flat, and take off the excess water at the same time. Then stick wet gummed paper tape around the edges, making sure that the adhesive has been wetted all along. Take off any remaining puddles of water and leave the paper to dry in a horizontal position. As it dries, the paper will stretch flat ready for use. Some manufacturers supply watercolour blocks that are bound on all sides so that the paper does not need to be stretched. It is not as reliable as stretched paper but is useful for outdoor work.

PAINTING MEDIUMS

As their name suggests, oil paints are dry pigments ground in a drying oil. Traditionally linseed oil, obtained from the flax plant, is used, though some manufacturers use poppy oil or safflower oil. The linseed oil dries by absorbing oxygen to form a flexible and insoluble film. The flexibility of this film makes it very suitable for painting on canvas and its insolubility when dry makes it suitable for various kinds of overpainting.

TURPENTINE

If you want to thin paint to facilitate handling, you can use a solvent such as turpentine. This dilutes the paint, but has no lasting effect on the paint film (unless used excessively) since it evaporates soon after doing its job. It is made from the resin of pine trees, but the manufacturing process removes all the resinous compounds and you can buy the resulting liquid as "pure distilled turpentine", "rectified turpentine", or "pure gum turpentine".

Turpentine deteriorates in the light, so store it in a brown bottle, or keep a clear bottle in a dark cupboard or protect it with a cardboard sleeve. To avoid contact with air it is best to keep the bottle full by adding glass beads, or to transfer the liquid to smaller bottles. Turpentine that has partially oxidised is useless for painting since it results in a sticky surface which never seems to dry. A number of the paintings in this book use only turpentine to dilute the paint, and this allows a wide range of techniques.

MEDIUMS FOR OIL PAINTS

Some approaches require you to add a painting medium. For example, glazing is made easier if you can use a different consistency of paint, and the "fat over lean" rule requires that successive layers of oil paint should be more flexible (and therefore contain more oil) than the ones beneath. These approaches require the use of a medium.

For the paintings in this book I have used a painting medium that includes a small amount of resin varnish. The advantages of resin varnish are that it provides increased brilliance of colour, gloss, ease of manipulation, and quicker drying. The disadvantages of resin are that its dried film is brittle and also resoluble. These problems can be counteracted by including in the medium a heavy-bodied form of linseed oil such as stand oil. Where I have used a painting medium in this book I have used the mixture recommended by the distinguished chemist, Ralph Mayer. This consists of 1 fl oz (28 ml) stand oil, 1 fl oz (28 ml) damar varnish, and 5 fl oz (140 ml) pure gum turpentine. In addition, Mayer recommends 15 drops of cobalt dry, but I find the medium quite satisfactory without this ingredient. For work other than glazing, it is best to make the mixture slightly thinner, by adding a little more turpentine. When you are building up layers of paint, you will need to add one or two more drops of stand oil for each layer, in order to increase the flexibility of the paint film. If you wish, you can use a straight mix of stand oil with turpentine, or even a ready-prepared painting medium.

MEDIUMS FOR ACRYLICS

With acrylics most effects, ranging from thin, transparent watercolour-type techniques to the use of thick impasto, can be achieved simply by mixing the paints with water or using them as they are. But there are useful mediums that can increase the texture or gloss of the paint, wetting agents that can increase the flow of the colour, and retarders that slow down the drying rate.

Acrylic colours are available in tubes or in pots (below). Acrylic paints bought in this way are ready for mixing with water or an acrylic medium. Alternatively they can be used as they are. A small selection of the available colours is shown.

MEDIUMS FOR WATERCOLOURS

There is also a range of gums and mediums produced for watercolour painting, but most artists prefer to accept the balance of ingredients in the best watercolour paints and dilute them with water alone. Strictly speaking, you should use distilled water, but tap water is normally pure enough not to affect the surface of the painting. Adding a wetting agent such as ox gall can be useful in improving the flow of colours on the paper, especially when you have to cover large areas.

COLOURS

THERE ARE TWO main types of pigment. The first, known as inorganic pigments, traditionally includes those made from natural earths (such as Yellow Ochre and Burnt Sienna), and colours made from hard minerals (such as azurite and lapis lazuli). The second type are known as organic pigments. These were traditionally prepared from vegetable sources (for example, root madder), or animal materials (for example, cochineal).

Both types of pigment are now available in synthetic form and it is possible to buy superior artificial versions of many of the traditional colours. Artificial ochres, known

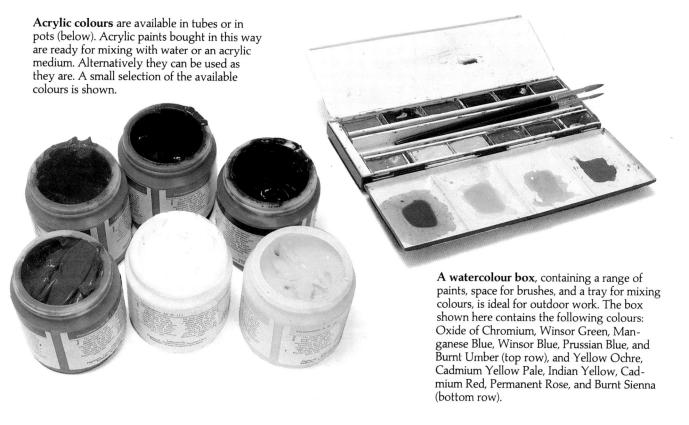

A watercolour box, containing a range of paints, space for brushes, and a tray for mixing colours, is ideal for outdoor work. The box shown here contains the following colours: Oxide of Chromium, Winsor Green, Manganese Blue, Winsor Blue, Prussian Blue, and Burnt Umber (top row), and Yellow Ochre, Cadmium Yellow Pale, Indian Yellow, Cadmium Red, Permanent Rose, and Burnt Sienna (bottom row).

as "Mars" colours, provide a range of permanent and consistent ochres, browns, and reds. The synthetic "Azo" pigments incorporate a useful range of colours, including permanent reds like Winsor Red, and colours such as Hansa Yellow, valued for its light-fast quality. Another useful synthetic pigment is copper phthalocyanine. This provides a permanent and reliable blue (available as Winsor, Phthalo, or Monastral Blue) and an intense green with a hue similar to Viridian. More recently, the appearance of the equally permanent Quinacridone pigments has given a new range of more permanent pinks, reds, and magenta colours.

Ideally you would only require three of these pigments. The three primary colours, magenta, yellow, and cyan theoretically enable you to mix all the other colours. Some of the paintings in this book use only three primary colours plus white, and tackling these paintings should increase your skill in colour mixing. But no set of three artists' colours forms exactly the three primaries and to limit your palette in this way is to deny yourself the enjoyment of using the rich variety of pigments available. It can also be tedious to have to go through many stages to mix a colour that is available directly from the tube.

Two or three different reds, yellows, and blues will give you a useful range and enable you to mix a wide variety of colours. Choose one red that is nearer to orange (such as Cadmium Red or Winsor Red), one that is nearer to violet (such as Alizarin Crimson or Permanent Rose), and perhaps an iron oxide red (such as Indian Red or Mars Red).

For the blues Manganese Blue and a phthalocyanine blue (such as Monastral, Phthalo, or Winsor Blue) will give you a wide range of possibilities for colour mixing. A combination of Permanent Rose and Winsor Blue will allow you to mix a good range of violets.

With the yellows, Cadmium Yellow Pale, Hansa Yellow, or Azo Yellow are durable colours, while for glazing the warmer Indian Yellow has marvellous transparency. The latter is not completely light-fast in its modern synthetic form, so it can be useful to add Transparent Gold Ochre or Raw Sienna to the palette.

As far as greens are concerned, Phthalocyanine green (available as Monastral or Winsor Green) is an intense, permanent, transparent colour that is particularly useful for mixing. A combination of this colour with Transparent Gold Ochre will provide an acceptable and permanent approximation to Sap Green. This is itself a very useful colour, but one that in its present form is not completely light-fast. At the other end of the scale of intensity, Oxide of Chromium is a very useful opaque green.

Other useful colours include Burnt Sienna. This provides a warm brown that you can easily cool down by mixing towards Burnt Umber or even Raw Umber. Titanium White is a good substitute for the poisonous Flake White, though the latter is highly regarded for its covering power. Many artists prefer to mix their darkest colours with blues and browns. For the paintings in this book that use a black paint, Ivory Black has been chosen.

Most of the oil paintings in this book were made with a selection from these oil colours. They are illustrated squeezed from the tubes on to a white palette. The paints were then worked with a brush to show the colours in a less saturated and more recognisable form.

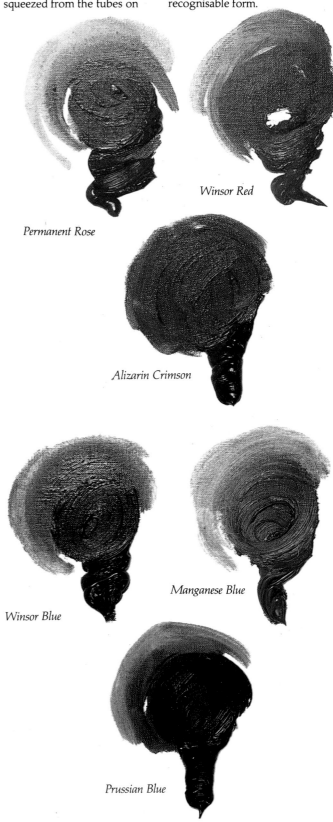

Permanent Rose

Winsor Red

Alizarin Crimson

Winsor Blue

Manganese Blue

Prussian Blue

BRUSHES

*Cadmium
Yellow Pale*

Indian Yellow

*Transparent
Gold Ochre*

Winsor Green

Sap Green

Burnt Sienna

Titanium White

BROADLY SPEAKING THERE are two types of brush. The first is the soft-hair type, which includes red sable, squirrel, and ox-hair brushes. The second is the stiff-hair or bristle type. Both traditionally use animal hair and bristles, but there are also synthetics made of nylon and other synthetic fibres. Watercolour painting, with its thin, aqueous approach, employs soft-hair brushes almost exclusively. Oils and acrylics use both types: stiff brushes for manipulating thick paint and brushing it well on to the canvas and soft brushes for more detailed work or very thin paint mixtures. Within each category there are two basic shapes, round and flat, with variations on these including the short flats known as brights and the flats with rounded ends called filberts. The type and shape of brush dictates to a large extent the style and appearance of your work.

BRISTLE BRUSHES

Among the bristle brushes, hogs'-hair types are the most frequently used. They come traditionally with long, cream handles. Of these brushes, the round, particularly in the larger sizes, always feels full and rich with its long bristles loaded with paint. It encourages you to treat the canvas generously. The bright's square shape fosters a more planar approach with short, stabbing brushstrokes. The longer bristles of the flat make for smooth strokes, while the edges of both flat and bright are useful for lines and details. The filbert is a particularly useful bristle brush, combining the best features of the round and the flat. You can use it freely and generously, making vigorous brush-strokes. These strokes do not have the ridge on either side that the square edges of the flat and bright can make. The filbert can also be used with a great deal of precision, especially when you hold it side-on, painting with the edge of the tip (or "toe") of the brush. The hogs'-hair filbert is used extensively for the paintings in this book.

SABLE BRUSHES

The finest brushes for watercolour work are the round red sables made from the tail hair of the kolinsky. They are traditionally made with black handles. No other brush can match them for the resilience of the hair, its capacity to take up paint and release as much or as little as you want, and for the sharpness of the tip, which enables you to paint fine details with even quite a large brush. To make a wide range of watercolour paintings you will need only a very small number of these brushes. Although they are expensive, they are a very good buy, for the quality of your work will depend to a large extent on the quality of your brushes. In the very large sizes required for broad areas of wash, however, the best red sables tend to be either unobtainable or prohibitively expensive. Most artists use wash brushes made from squirrel or ox hair. These come as "mops", flats, or "single-stroke" brushes and are very useful for the broad strokes across the paper that such areas require.

The sables used for oil painting come in roughly the

Bristle brushes, used for oil painting, come in a variety of shapes. For each shape, two sizes are shown, No. 3 and No. 8. The round is ideal for covering large areas. The flat and bright allow you to paint lines and details with the edge of the brush, but you can also make broad, stabbing strokes with the bright and smoother strokes with the flat. The filbert is a versatile brush. Its strokes do not have the ridges that you can get with the bright and flat.

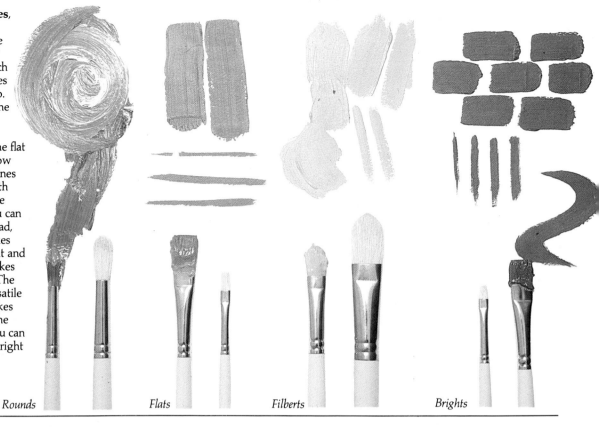

Rounds   *Flats*   *Filberts*   *Brights*

Nylon and sable brushes are used in watercolour and acrylic painting. The shapes are generally the same as for bristle brushes. Sables are shown, together with some of the nylon equivalents. Riggers are particularly useful for fine work, while the fan blender, as its name implies, is designed for blending colours together.

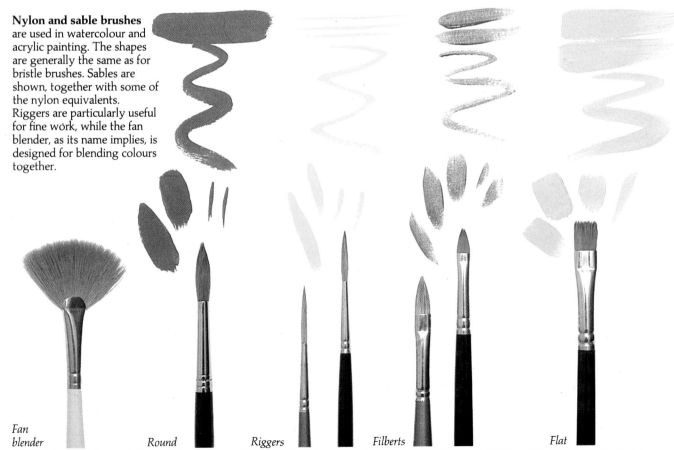

Fan blender   *Round*   *Riggers*   *Filberts*   *Flat*

same shapes as the bristles and with similarly long handles, although the sable flat is not so spade-like as the bristle. When damp, it forms a chisel-edged point that is very useful for precise work. More like the bristle flat in appearance is the "long" sable which is, in fact, a long-haired flat.

SYNTHETIC BRUSHES

Synthetic-fibre brushes are produced in the same shapes and sizes as the traditional soft-hair and bristle brushes and are much less costly. They can be very useful in certain areas. For watercolours, in my opinion nothing has yet been found to replace the feel of the finest sable brushes, though among the large flats used for this medium, the nylon ones work well. For oil painting, however, nylon brushes come into their own as substitutes for sables. They are a little firmer than sables and, in a way, better suited to the consistency of the paint, unless you are using very thin mixtures. With acrylics, too, the synthetic brushes work perfectly well, although there is a tendency for the acrylic to accumulate quite quickly in the heel of the brush around the metal collar (or "ferrule"). This causes the hairs to splay out and the brush to lose its point. This can happen even if you are scrupulous in

rinsing out your brush after every application and it can even occur to a lesser extent with oil paint. So you must keep these brushes as clean as possible at all times.

CLEANING BRUSHES

While you are painting you should always keep two jars of water (for acrylics and watercolours) or white spirit (for oils) to rinse brushes and keep them clean while you are painting. Use one for the first rinse to remove most of the paint and the other for a cleaner second rinse. This will have the effect of keeping your colours pure and fresh.

When you have finished painting you should clean your brushes thoroughly. First wipe off the excess paint with a cloth or tissue and rinse the brush. Use water for acrylics or watercolours or white spirit for oils. Then repeat the rinsing with clean white spirit or water and then, for oil brushes, wipe off all traces of the white spirit in cool, running water. The next stage, for all brushes, is to wash them with soap and water, using ordinary household soap, working up a lather with the brush on the palm of your hand. The soap will remove all residual traces of pigment and you should rinse and repeat this process until there is no sign of any colour in the lather. Finally, rinse the brushes to remove all traces of soap,

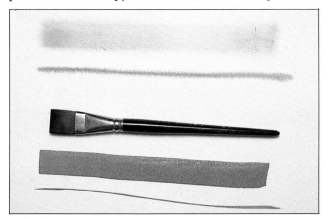

The one-stroke nylon flat, used on both wet and dry paper, with both edge and face, gave these strokes.

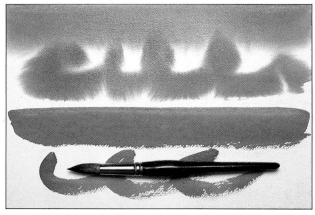

A No. 16 squirrel brush, used on both wet and dry paper, produced these results.

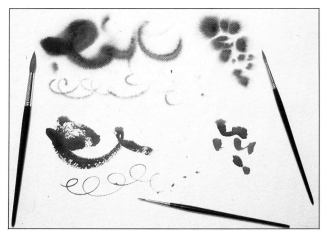

Sable brushes (No. 8, left, No. 4, right, and No. 1, bottom) make fine strokes with the "toe" (or tip) and broad strokes with the "heel" (where the bristles join the handle).

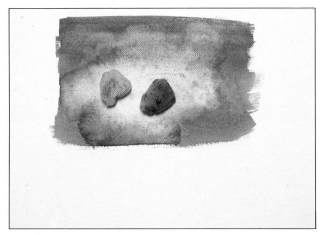

A sponge can be useful in watercolour painting to remove tone once you have laid an overall wash. You can also use it to pick out smaller highlights.

shake them, and restore their shape between your finger and thumb. Store your brushes in jars with their hairs uppermost. Do not use hot water to clean brushes — it will expand the metal ferrule and can disturb the shape of the brush. Hot water can also have a tendency to make acrylic paint set in the hairs and ruin the brush.

SPECIALISED ITEMS

There are several specialised brushes that you can use for particular ways of manipulating the paint. Among those used in this book are the badger blender, used for working oil glazes, and the fan blender or duster, generally used for the fine, smooth blending of tones during the final stages of a painting.

You can use other equipment for applying and manipulating paint. With watercolours, natural sponges are useful to dampen surfaces, apply washes, and take out colour. With oil paint, you can use painting knives when the paint is being worked thickly. Do not confuse these with palette knives, which are used for mixing paint and scraping it off the palette. Painting knives are more delicate instruments that come in a variety of shapes. The thin, round metal shaft that connects the blade to the handle always has a bend in it, so that the blade is lower than the handle. This keeps your hand away from the paint surface while you are working. The different shapes, such as trowel, pear, and diamond, as well as the different available lengths, allow for a wide range of manipulations. Store painting knives carefully — the blades are very vulnerable and are quite useless if they get bent and lose their springiness.

An airbrush is another useful tool for applying paint. It uses compressed air to atomize the paint, enabling you to spray it finely, in a controlled way, on to any part of

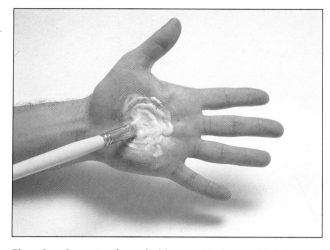

Clean brushes using household soap. Work up a rich lather in the palm of your hand. Rinse and repeat the process until all traces of pigment have been removed.

a painting. The most common use of the airbrush is in graphic design and illustration, where it is employed for artwork and photographic retouching. But it can be useful in "fine art" painting too. It is particularly suited to applying very controlled, uniform or graduating tones to particular areas, for softening edges or rounding out shapes, for applying highlights, and for specialised applications such as painting the glow around a light. Airbrushes are expensive, so you should only get one if you think you are moving towards a style of painting that would often incorporate its effects. If you do use an airbrush, you must keep it absolutely clean. This is particularly important when you are using oil or acrylic paints.

A painting knife can be used expressively to apply bold dabs of pigment, but you can also paint more finely with it, working with the tip of the blade. It also allows you to mix colours on the painting itself. You can use it for both oil and acrylic colours. For fuller instructions on painting knife technique, see p. 76.

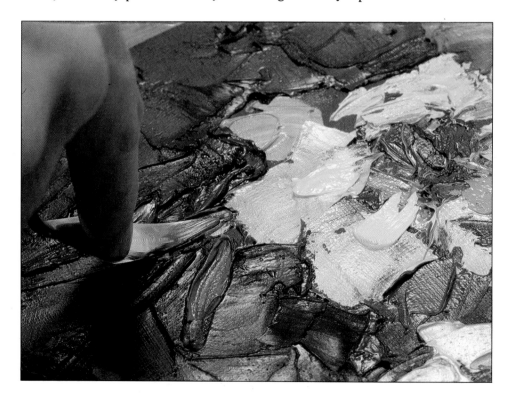

OTHER EQUIPMENT

PENCILS, CRAYONS, AND ERASERS

Apart from regular drawing pencils that are available in degrees of hardness (from extra hard to extra soft), there is an enormous range of crayons, charcoals, and pastels on the market that each have their own special characteristics. There is so little preparation required for work in any of these media that it is worth making a selection from the range and trying out their effects, from the soft greys of natural charcoal to the black strokes of compressed charcoal or the crisp, dry lines of a sharp, hard lead pencil. The more you experiment, the more sensitive you will become to their particular kinds of mark-making and the more you will know which to use in a particular situation.

From the variety of erasers available, two in particular seem to me the most useful. The first is the white plastic eraser that does a more efficient job and is more versatile than the traditional rubber type. The second is the kneadable putty eraser. This can be moulded to any shape and has a range of uses including lightening areas of tone and picking out highlights.

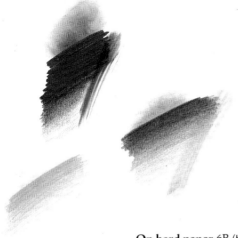

On hard paper 6B (top), B (above), and 4H (left) pencils were used. The effects of finger and eraser work are also shown.

On soft paper, the same range of pencils gave lighter results, with the texture of the paper showing through.

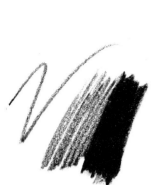

Chinagraph (left) gives a hard, waxy appearance, while conté pastel produces a softer surface (above).

Compressed charcoal (above) makes an intense black mark, while willow charcoal produces a lighter, softer surface (left).

PALETTES

The well-known oval mahogany palette with its thumb hole was developed during the late-nineteenth-century impressionist period largely for outside work. Few painters use such a palette in the studio. It is preferable to keep both hands free and use a small desk or trolley beside the easel, with a sheet of glass or similar material on top, on which to mix the paints. Some painters put a sheet of white paper underneath the glass to give a clearer sense of the colours. Others use white china plates. I use a piece of very pale grey formica. A clear, white, or off-white surface gives you a far better picture of the precise tone and colour you are mixing, and it is particularly useful if you are working on a pure white ground. For transparent work, which uses the white of the ground so positively, it is essential to mix the colours on a similar, reflective surface to ensure colour accuracy.

When oil painting, you should clean your palette thoroughly after each painting session unless you are planning to return to your painting within an hour or two. This involves a certain amount of paint wastage, but it will prevent you applying half-dried colours to your painting. These could prove disastrous to the strength and adhesion of the paint film. Remove the excess paint from your palette with a palette knife and swab the palette with a piece of cloth or tissue dampened with white spirit to get the surface clean.

Acrylics dry so quickly that you have no choice but to clean your palette each time. For acrylics, it makes good sense to mix on surfaces such as white china plates or glass slabs. You can lift these up and hold them under warm running water. Even after the paint has dried completely, it will peel away very easily if you use this method. With watercolour you mix your colours in the lid of your painting box or in saucers. You can safely leave dried mixed colours there. Simply add water to them when you want to use them again. They will be as reliable as they were when first mixed.

It is convenient when you are working outside to use a well-balanced palette with a thumb hole. There are several lightweight versions on the market with surfaces lighter than the traditional dark wood. But if you are working on a canvas with a tinted ground, a dark wooden palette of the traditional type can be useful – it gives you fewer problems with glare.

EASELS

When you begin painting it is perhaps best to buy a sturdy sketching easel that can double as a studio easel for indoor work. It should be reasonably stable and light, it should be able to take a moderately large canvas, and, most important, it should allow you to tip the canvas or drawing board both forward a little (to avoid reflections) and back to a horizontal, table-top position. Unless it can do this it will be useless for watercolour work.

One problem with even the sturdiest sketching easel is that when you are working outside the wind can quite easily catch the canvas and blow it over. To avoid this, take three meat skewers with you. Push one into the ground beside each leg of the easel and then tie skewers and easel together.

If you want to work on a very large canvas without having to buy a heavy-duty studio easel, simply rest the canvas against the wall. Keep it off the floor by using two wooden blocks or paint cans. If you need to raise it to work on the lower part, put two screws in the wall and suspend the stretcher from these.

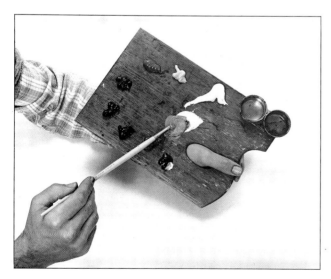

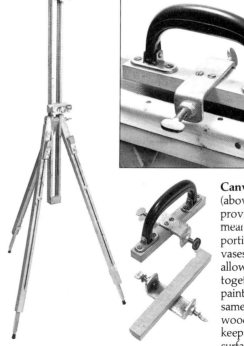

A wooden palette (above) can be useful when you are painting outdoors. The best colour depends on the ground on which you are painting, but it should be well balanced when you hold it.

A sketching easel (right), small but sturdy, is most useful for the beginner. Make sure it offers a full range of adjustments.

Canvas carriers (above and left) provide a simple means of transporting wet canvases. The brackets allow you to clamp together two paintings of the same size, and a wooden block keeps the canvas surfaces apart.

BLACK AND WHITE TECHNIQUES

Trees In Silhouette

Media OILS, ACRYLICS, or WATERCOLOURS

THE BRANCHES AND leaves of a winter tree silhouetted against the sky make a perfect subject for practising delicate line work with a small sable brush. In these exercises the linear tracery of a tree is set against a sky which is tonally blended from white on the horizon to light grey at the top of the picture. The tree I chose for the oil painting had been bent and shaped by the prevailing wind. Its twisted branches have direction and movement which you can express in your brushstrokes. The painting is made in two stages — the sky first and then the tree. The sky must be completely dry before you tackle the tree. You can use either oil or acrylic paint for this exercise. If you paint on a board or a rigid support rather than a canvas, you can use acrylic for the sky and oil paint for the tree. Acrylic dries quickly, so you can work on the tree almost immediately. Oil paint takes a day or two to dry.

It is a valuable exercise to make similar paintings using watercolours. The most important difference between the watercolour and the oil and acrylic versions is that however well controlled your use of watercolours, the wash you apply will be different every time, depending on how well-loaded with paint your brush is, how wet it is, what the precise angle of the paper is, or whether the paper is dampened before you apply the wash. Watercolour is a direct way of painting, and has a life of its own that makes it an exciting medium.

Another idea for this kind of subject is to reverse the tree silhouette and paint a light tree against a dark sky. There are many natural atmospheric situations in which the tree will be lighter in tone than the sky. It may be picked out by the sun against a deep blue summer sky, or against a dark grey cloud. In either case you will find it almost impossible to paint a wash around such an intricate shape. So the solution is to paint the tree in rubber masking fluid before applying the sky wash.

MATERIALS AND EQUIPMENT

Oil and acrylic versions
Support
Canvas or board 14 × 10 ins
(35.5 × 25.5 cm)

Oil or acrylic colours
Ivory Black, Titanium White

Brushes
No. 5 hogs'-hair filbert, No. 2 round sable, No. 2 sable rigger

Other items
Charcoal or pencil, painting knife

Watercolour version
Support
Good quality (140 lb) watercolour paper
14 × 20 ins (35.5 × 25.5 cm)

Watercolour paints
Paynes Grey

Brushes
No. 14 round squirrel, No. 3 or No. 4 round sable

Other items
Masking fluid, old round sable or nylon for applying masking fluid, hairdrier

METHODS

For the oil or acrylic versions a band of white paint is applied across the bottom of the canvas, then a light grey one is added above it, followed by a mid grey one above that. The bands are then blended so that they are smoothly graded. The tree outline is then sketched in charcoal or pencil and the tree's skeleton is painted using fluent but controlled "S" shapes. The tree is then built up from the outer twigs inwards. Finally the ground beneath is filled in.

For the watercolour version a graded wash is laid on dry or damp paper. If it is to be dry the paper should be inclined slightly to accumulate paint along the brushstrokes' lower edges. If the wet-paper method is used, the paper is entirely dampened first so that the colour runs freely. The tree is then painted in.

Masking fluid can be used to reverse a silhouette of a tree. This is drawn in pencil and then masking fluid is painted over it. The background wash is applied and then the fluid is rubbed off to reveal a light silhouette set off against a dark background.

1 Preparing your paint
On one side of your palette mix a reasonably large quantity of Titanium White to a creamy consistency using painting medium. Do the same on the other side of the palette with a smaller quantity of black. Use either a painting knife or a hogs'-hair brush to mix the paint. Save a little of the white paint on one side of the palette.

2 The white background band
Using the hogs'-hair brush, apply a band of white paint across the bottom 3 ins (7.5 cm) of the canvas. Brush it on finely and smoothly with horizontal strokes.

3 The lower grey band
Add the smallest touch of black to the white on your palette and mix it to a very light grey. The difference in tone between this and the white should be only marginal. If you find you have put too much black into your mix, add the white that you put on one side. Apply the grey above the white in a band about 2 ins (5 cm) wide. Wipe the brush off, or use a clean brush, and blend the two tones together by brushing along the join. Your brushstrokes should be firm at the beginning, lighter in pressure as the tones blend.

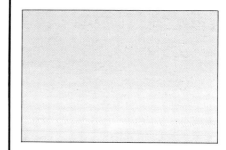

4 The upper grey background band

Add a touch more black to the light grey on your palette and, after mixing, apply it in a similar band of tone above the first one. Repeat the blending procedure until you have a light to mid grey tone at the top of the canvas. The tones should now all be smoothly gradated.

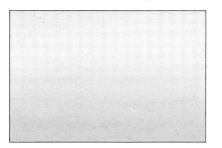

5 An alternative blending method

Rather than following the horizontal layers of tone when you are blending, you can use the brush at various angles. These more random brushstrokes give a less smooth, but equally convincing, lightening of tone towards the horizon. They suggest cloud cover rather than clear sky.

6 Sketching the tree outline

Once the sky is dry, draw in the main lines of the tree roughly. You do not have to be particularly accurate — a few charcoal or pencil strokes will be enough to act as guidelines for your initial brushstrokes.

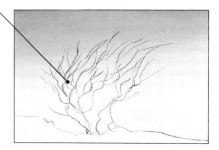

7 Starting to paint the tree

Mix the black on your palette to a thinner consistency than for the sky. This will enable it to flow smoothly from the sable brush. If the mixture is too thick you will not be able to paint a fluent line; if it is too runny it will be difficult to control. Practise a few squiggles on a piece of spare paper to see if it feels right. Then paint in and build up the main lines of the trunk. Notice how the tree consists broadly of a series of "S" shapes. Hold the brush at the end of the handle so that there is some distance between your hand and the painting. You will be able to make more controlled and fluent marks by using this method.

8 Building up the tree shape

Build up the shape of the tree with smooth, careful strokes. Work into the tree towards the centre from the thin outermost twigs. This process will take some time to complete and it is important not to rush it.

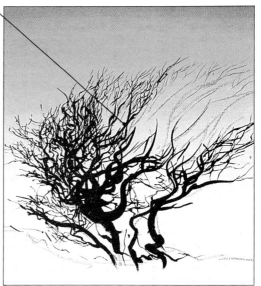

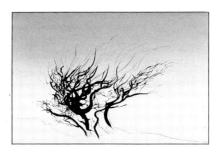

9 The land

Using my finished version as a rough guide, continue to build up the outer branches of the tree. When you are satisfied with the tree, paint in the land beneath. Use the hogs'-hair brush, but add some details of the grass and plants with the sable.

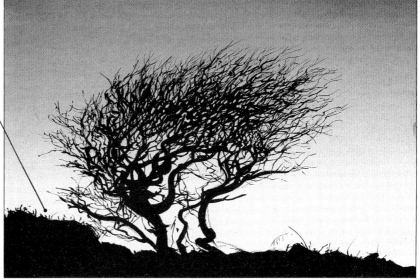

ACRYLIC VERSION

If you make separate acrylic and oil versions of this exercise you will begin to get an idea of the particular properties of each medium. Oil paint cannot compete with the fast-drying characteristics of the acrylic, but for smooth, fluent application and covering power, I think that oil paint is a particularly satisfying medium to use.

So make your own versions of this exercise. Use tree silhouettes that you have sketched or photographed. This acrylic study is based on a photograph, and, as with the oil study, I painted the trunk and main branches first to establish a structure and then gradually built up the tree by adding the smaller branches and the twigs.

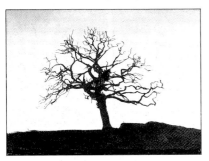

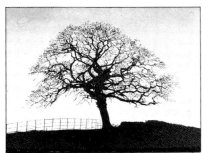

WATERCOLOUR VERSION

1 Preparing the paper
First stretch your watercolour paper on a drawing board. If you are using a reasonably heavy paper, this stage will not be necessary.

2 Preparing to lay the wash on dry paper
Put a generous dessertspoonful of clear water in a saucer, add paint, and mix until you have a dark tone. Try out the mix on a scrap of paper since it is difficult to tell how dark it really is until you get used to it. You will also have to allow for the fact that it dries considerably lighter than it looks. Mix a similar amount of lighter tone and put it in a separate saucer. Do the same with an even lighter tone. Make sure that you have a jar of clear water to hand.

3 Applying the wash to dry paper
Put the paper on a slight incline, so that after each horizontal stroke of the brush the paint tends to accumulate along the bottom edge of the brush-stroke. You can take up the accumulated paint on the next stroke. If the paper is too steeply inclined the paint will run on to the bottom edge too quickly, and may even run in rivulets down the paper. Load your No. 14 brush with paint from the first saucer and make a brushstroke right across the top of the paper from left to right. Do this smoothly so that the paint fills the indentations on the paper. If you do it too quickly you will tend to leave white holes in the paint surface. Make a similar brushstroke below the first, joining up the edges so that the paint runs into the next tone.

When you have done this three or four times use the lighter tone and repeat the procedure for the next 2 ins (5 cm) of paper. Then change to a third, lighter tone and do the same again. For the last few inches of paper use clear water — a certain amount of light grey will blend into this. Let the wash dry. You can speed this up by using a hairdrier.

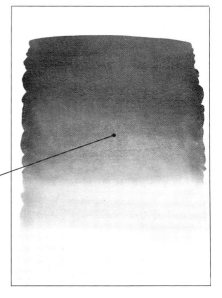

4 An alternative way of laying a wash on dry paper
Another way of making a similar effect without using separate saucers is simply to add water to your first mix at each stage during the painting process. You may also find it useful if you make your first brushstroke from left to right, the second from right to left, and then alternating again, continuing the process down the painting.

REVERSING THE SILHOUETTE

1 Drawing and masking
Begin by drawing the shape of the tree in soft pencil on your paper, and then apply the masking fluid. This is usually a yellow colour, so that you can see what you are painting. Use a thin, round sable or nylon brush — preferably an old one — and work from the thin outside twigs to the larger branches, and then the trunk. Then wash the brush thoroughly in warm, soapy water.

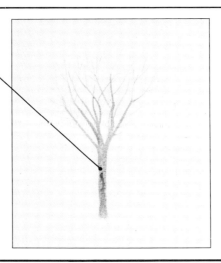

2 Applying the background wash
When the fluid is dry, apply a wash over the whole picture. When this is dry, peel off the masking fluid by gently rubbing it with your fingertips.

5 Laying the wash on damp paper
The method for this is identical to that described above, except that before you start painting you cover the whole paper surface with clean water. Allow this to soak in a little and make sure that you have removed any excess water before you apply the wash. The trick is to make sure that the paper is damp uniformly. You can use a brush, a sponge, or you can spray the water on. A sponge is particularly effective since you can control the amount of water on the surface more easily. Having damp paper will allow the colour to blend and run more freely. So it is worth experimenting with degrees of wetness and dryness in conjunction with various intensities of pigment to discover the range of effects you can get.

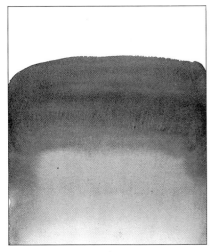

6 Painting the tree
Now paint in the tree. In my version I drew the main lines in pencil when the wash was dry and then painted the tree using a No. 4 round sable. You can either copy this tree or sketch one of your choice. Or you can find a suitable reproduction in a book or magazine and trace it on to your paper. The effect of painting a silhouette like this is to make you look at the background wash in terms of three-dimensional space. This simple juxtaposition transforms the flat background into an arching sky.

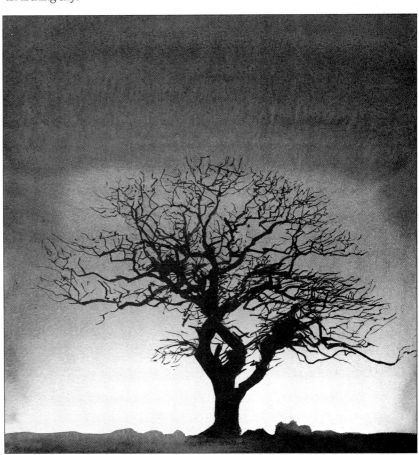

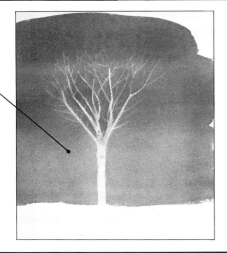

3 The finishing touches
If your background is intended to be a deep, blue summer sky, or a grey, threatening storm cloud, the edges of the trunk and branches should be in shadow. So if you want to, you can add appropriate shadow areas.

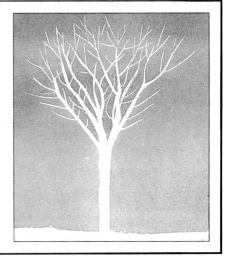

CLOUD STUDIES

Media OILS, WATERCOLOURS, CHARCOAL, or PEN AND INK

CLOUDS HAVE ALWAYS fascinated painters because of their infinite range of dimension, texture, and mood. They can dominate a scene, or be insignificant, and in their role as filters of light they modulate the tones and colours of things around us. They are also transient and this affects the painter in two ways. Firstly, cloud effects must be recorded very quickly if you are working from life – or they can be photographed for later reference. Secondly, because clouds are insubstantial the painter can, within limits, get away with a great deal of formal inaccuracy. This can generate a sense of freedom which enables you to relax and, often, to produce good work as a result. The negative side of this is that it can make a lazy painter fall into the habit of repeating a personal formula for a cloud stereotype.

Clouds are endless sources of inspiration and can even form a complete "landscape" in themselves. Our experience of air travel gives us a totally new perspective on clouds – we can see them from a viewpoint that painters have never been able to before. Anyone who has flown above heavy, low cloud at sunset knows that there is little to equal it as a visual experience.

As technical exercises these studies are designed to encourage the free handling of brushes and paint, charcoal and pencil, to practise mixing and blending tones, and to demonstrate how easy it is to get a realistic effect. The first two exercises are in oils. This is an excellent medium for making cloud studies. Edges can be easily softened and the wet paint surface can be modified and adapted as you go along. The first oil study is simple, showing you the basic techniques, while the second oil study is more complete, employing the same techniques as the first but with more control. Then follow several different techniques for watercolour, and finally, some ideas for drawing clouds in charcoal, and pen and ink.

MATERIALS AND EQUIPMENT

Oil versions
Supports
Boards 9 × 12 ins (23 × 30.5 cm) and 12 × 18 ins (30.5 × 46 cm)

Oil colours
Ivory Black, Titanium White

Brushes
No. 6 and No. 1 hogs'-hair filberts (first oil study), No. 7, No. 6, and No. 1 hogs'-hair filberts (second oil study)

Other items
Turpentine

Watercolour versions
Support
Sheets of watercolour paper, any size

Watercolour paints
Ivory Black or Paynes Grey

Brushes
No. 7 round squirrel, one old round sable for applying the masking fluid

Other items
Artist's sponge, rubber masking fluid, fine sandpaper or domestic sponge, scourer

Drawn versions
Support
Sheets of paper – any size

Other items
Charcoal, pen and ink

METHODS
For the first cloud study, in oils, the outlines are drawn and the paints mixed. First the "blue" sky area is painted, leaving gaps for white clouds. Next cloud edges and white areas are added, followed by the cloud base, painted in three grey tones. Then the tones are blended in. Lastly white highlights are added to the edges. For the second cloud study, also in oils, the method is similar to that for the first study, except that the painting is divided into three distinct sections. These are painted separately according to the nature of the cloud masses in each.

The watercolour studies demonstrate the use of a sponge, rubber masking fluid, sandpaper, and mixing techniques to achieve different cloud effects. Lastly, two drawn studies show the possibilities of using charcoal and pen and ink.

CLOUD STUDY I

1 The outlines
Draw the outlines on to your board. No guideline sketch is provided because you can afford to be flexible and inventive with all these shapes.

2 Mixing the paints
Mix a reasonable quantity of white paint with the painting medium to a thick creamy consistency. Then mix a smaller amount of black to the same consistency. Use separate palette knives to take the white and black to your palette's mixing area.

3 The sky
Mix a mid to deep grey tone and paint the "blue" sky with the No. 6 hogs'-hair brush. Leave two gaps large enough for the clouds.

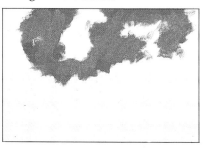

4 The cloud edges
Mix a light tone for the edges and apply with light touches of the No. 6 brush. Do not stray too far into the clear sky since you want to retain tonal uniformity at this stage. Now clean your brush thoroughly.

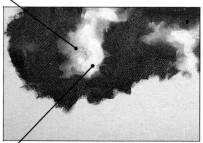

5 Applying white
Apply white to the inner to right-hand areas of the clouds with the No. 6 brush. Wipe your brush off and blend the white in with the grey at the edges with light circular strokes of the brush. Wipe the brush off once more and add more white if necessary.

6 The cloud base structure

Mix three mid-grey tones on to your palette — one light, one darker, the third darker still. Sketch in the structure of the cloud base using these three tones, leaving a larger area than you need for the shape of the white clouds — their shapes will diminish as you start blending in. Wipe your brush off and blend the tones in carefully where necessary.

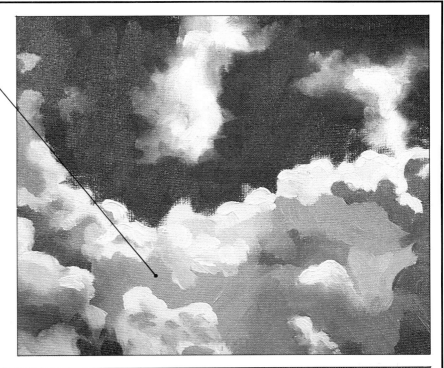

7 Adding highlights

Using the smaller brush add the white highlights to the cloud edges or the places where they are lit by sun. Blend in and add more white where necessary.

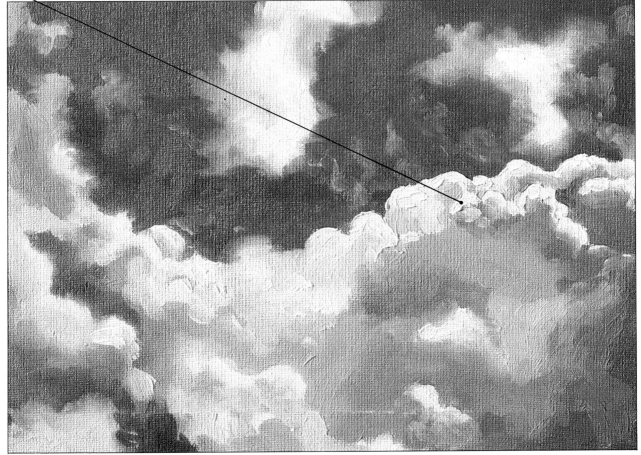

CLOUD STUDY II

1 Tinting the board
Tint the board a mid to light grey, using a thin mix of black and white oil paint and turpentine. Painting on a toned ground enables you to work towards both light and dark tones. Alternatively you could apply a very thin coat of black plus turpentine with a large hogs'-hair brush and then wipe it off with a rag so that the ground is simply stained. This is a good method, and the surface dries quickly.

2 The outline shapes
Draw the outline shapes on to your board and work on the study section by section, matching your tones as closely as possible to my version. It is useful to divide your study into three separate sections as I have done in the following steps.

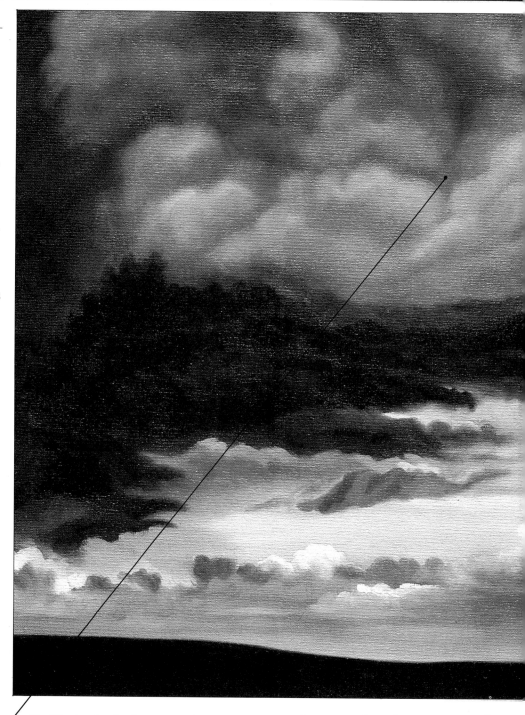

3 The top bank of clouds
The first section is the top bank of clouds which dips into the picture in the centre. These are the clouds closest to you — the foreground clouds. They have a thin, grey rain-soaked quality, so you should try to reflect this when you are painting them. It is important to understand the form and structure of what you are painting. Here you can see four "lines", like lines of perspective, which take the clouds into the dip to the left of centre. Follow a similar method of painting to that used for the first cloud study. In this case it is a good idea to begin by painting the cloud structures in mid-grey tones, so that you know the shapes you are dealing with. The blending should be smooth and the paint thinner than for the first cloud study. This is to reflect the nature and quality of the cloud.

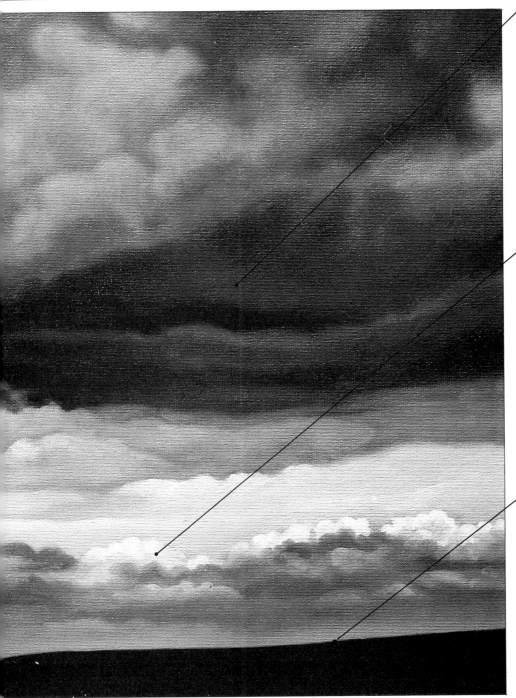

4 The dark grey cloud area
The second section is the very dark cloud area which forms an elongated shape separating the upper and lower clouds. This is the "middle ground", and the quality of the painting here is smooth with little tonal variation. The tones are very dark here, especially on the left, so match them as closely as possible with those shown in the illustration.

5 The distance
Below the dark cloud the low horizontal cloud recedes into the distance. This forms the third section. The accumulating cloud masses have edges which catch the sunlight through a gap in the intervening layers of cloud. The technique for this section is similar to the top bank of clouds, except that you should use smaller brushes. If you wish, you can use small round sable brushes here.

6 The finishing touches
The land mass at the bottom is almost black. Soften the edge so that the transition from light to dark is not too abrupt. With the original study, I returned to the painting when it had dried to make final adjustments to the tones. I made the clouds at the top deeper in tone so that the eye is drawn into the picture. The middle section has also been clarified and deepened a little.

WATERCOLOUR TECHNIQUES

Using a sponge

This is a very good way of isolating one or two clouds drifting in a clear sky (below). You will want to lay the dark sky wash evenly, without having to paint around awkward cloud shapes. The method is to lay your wash for the sky and immediately dab the cloud area with a wet sponge. Your sponge should be wet, but not too wet. After one or two dabs wash it in clear water, squeeze it slightly, and repeat the process.

Using masking fluid

This method gives you pure white cloud shapes (below right), since no paint can penetrate the rubber masking fluid. You can use this method on its own, or in conjunction with other methods. Paint the parts of the paper with masking fluid where you want the cloud shapes to be. Do this before you lay your wash. The method of painting the masking fluid on is to dip the brush in the fluid right up to the ferrule and to use it at a very shallow angle to the paper, using the heel of the brush as much as the toe. This will give the half-tone effect where the masking fluid just brushes against the raised parts of the paper's surface. You must let the masking fluid dry before you paint over it, and you must let the paint dry before you rub off the masking fluid with a soft eraser or your clean fingertip.

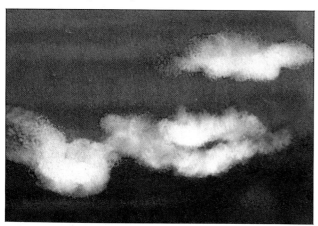

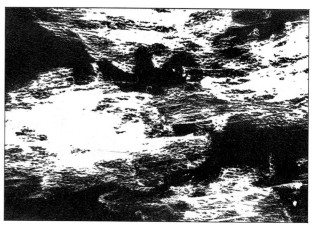

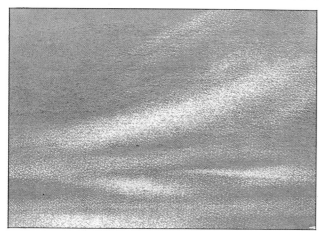

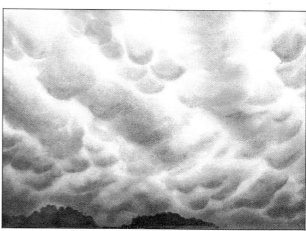

Using sandpaper

This is a very straightforward method and simply involves rubbing the surface of the picture with fine sandpaper to bring out lighter tones and highlights. You do this after you have laid the wash and allowed it to dry thoroughly. Use a hairdrier to speed up the process. I find that domestic square sponges with fine abrasive coatings are very useful for this. The thinner shapes on my example (above) were made with the edge of one of these. They are useful for achieving a wide range of shapes.

Mixing techniques

This study (above right) is based on a photograph and employs a range of techniques. The sky has a "cotton wool" feel, with its plump, semi-circular shapes, forming a soft overall texture, and darkening towards the lower edge. I tried to create a painting in which the pattern of the sky gave the picture surface itself an interesting texture, which could also give the illusion of being an arching space. To create this kind of effect you should tackle one shape at a time on a small section of the paper that you have already dampened to avoid making harsh edges. Where the tones are darker repeat the process. Working on a small area at a time can make it difficult to create a uniform image. You may find that you have to rub the surface lightly with sandpaper, so that the texture of the paper acts as a structure for the shapes and tones. The final step is to soften this effect by airbrushing.

CHARCOAL DRAWING

This charcoal drawing shows the kind of cloud formation that can give the sky a real sense of spatial recession. The ridges of cloud retreat into the distance. If you look at the drawing upside down they look like ridges of hard sand left by the receding tide. We rarely see such a consistent pattern in the sky, and on this occasion I was lucky enough to have a camera with me to provide an accurate reference for the drawing. To create this effect, draw the clouds with small, light strokes of the charcoal. You can soften them a little by rubbing with your index finger. The best way to pick out highlights is to use a soft eraser.

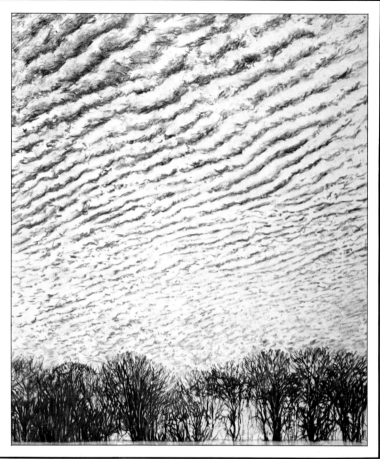

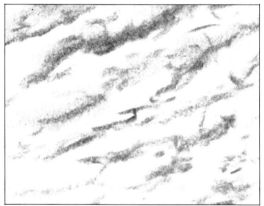

Actual-size detail

PEN AND INK

The twentieth century has offered artists artificial cloud formations — the marvellous condensation trails that aircraft leave across the sky. They have the purity of a single gesture — as if a brush dipped in white paint had been swept lightly and confidently across the sky. If you use pen and ink, the contrail can provide you with a means of making a drawing which is actually about the texture of the sky itself — cross-hatching gives the sky's surface richness and depth. Tones and shapes are gradually brought out and the surface reflects the busy energy of the shading.

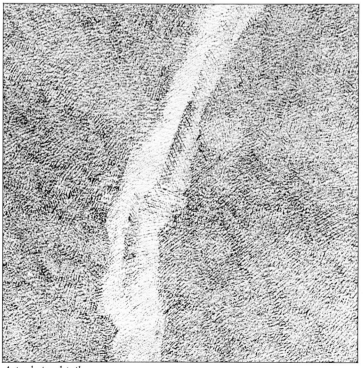

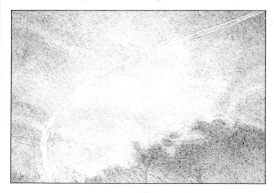

Actual-size detail

TONAL LANDSCAPE

Media OILS or WATERCOLOURS

THIS EXERCISE DEMONSTRATES an important pictorial idea — that of tonal recession in a landscape. This means that, as the lines of trees and hedgerows recede in the mist, their tone becomes lighter and a beautiful atmospheric effect is produced. Look for it next time you are in the countryside or on a high vantage point in a city. The effect is quite easy to demonstrate in black and white, when it looks obvious, yet it is often forgotten by artists beginning to work in colour. The outlines can be sketched in a matter of minutes since unnecessary detail is abstracted out naturally.

In terms of technique, the exercise is designed to give you more practice at mixing paint — so you can get the consistency and tone you need — and also to give you some experience with both sable and hogs'-hair brushes. The sable brush is used for the detail in the edges of the shapes, and the hogs'-hair for the broad strokes and the blending of tones.

You can also try this exercise in acrylic paints, and doing it in both oils and acrylics will demonstrate the advantages and disadvantages of each medium. The advantage of using acrylics is that as each "layer" of the landscape is painted it dries quickly, enabling the next layer to be painted over the top clearly and freely. The disadvantage of acrylics is that you need to work quickly and confidently to blend the tones, whereas oil paint gives more flexibility in this respect.

MATERIALS AND EQUIPMENT

Support
Board or canvas 14 × 19 ins
(38 × 48 cm)

Acrylic or oil colours
Ivory Black, Paynes Grey, Titanium White

Brushes
No. 7 and No. 4 sable rounds, No. 10 hogs'-hair filbert

Other items
HB pencil, painting medium (see p. 10)

METHOD

First the lines of trees are drawn in pencil. Then a band of white is painted above the distant line of trees, followed by a band of mid tone above it. The tones are blended together. The process is continued to the top of the picture. Next the land is tackled, starting with the distant trees. The method is to paint to the edges of the trees, then a lighter tone is mixed and painted below this. The two tones are blended. This procedure is repeated for each row of trees.

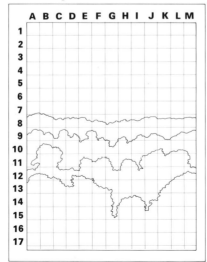

The guideline sketch on its grid. See pp. 226–7 for instructions.

OIL VERSION

1 Drawing the image
Trace the lines of the trees on to your board. Keep your pencil sharp and the lines thin. You must be able to see the lines clearly, so, if necessary, go over them again.

2 Mixing the paint
On one side of your palette, mix a reasonably large quantity of white paint to a thick, creamy consistency by adding painting medium to the pigment. Use a palette knife or even a hogs'-hair brush to mix the paint, but don't use a sable brush. On the other side of your palette, mix a smaller quantity of black paint to the same consistency. Put half the white in the middle of the palette.

3 The white area above the distant trees
The sky should blend gradually from white at the horizon to mid grey at the top of the picture. So using your hogs'-hair brush, begin by painting a band of white over and above the most distant line of trees. The band should be about 3 ins (7.5 cm) wide, and you will still be able to see the pencil line through it.

4 The mid-tone area of the sky
Now add a touch of black to the white, mix it in thoroughly and apply another band of paint above the white, overlapping it by about 1 in (2.5 cm). Wipe any excess paint off your brush with a rag, and, using light horizontal brushstrokes, blend the tones together so that there is a smooth transition from the white to the light grey.

5 The darker bands of grey sky
Add a little more black to the light grey on your palette and continue the process to the top of the picture, using increasingly darker bands of grey and blending them in as you go.

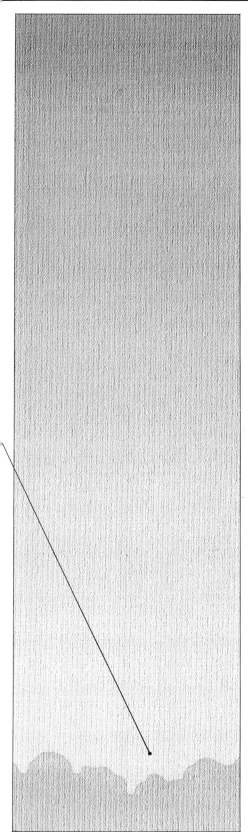

Actual-size detail from the finished painting showing the full tonal range of the sky.

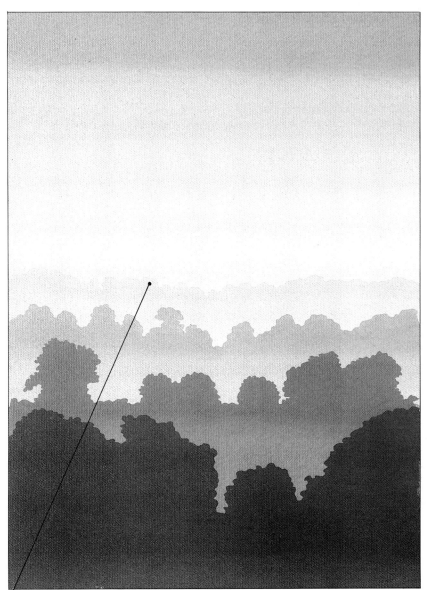

6 Painting the land
Clean off the dark grey left in the middle of your palette and bring most of the rest of the white to the middle. Mix a light grey and, using your No. 4 sable brush, paint to the edge of the most distant line of trees. Keep the tip of the brush quite well loaded with paint so that you can paint over the white from the sky that went over the line. Switch to your No. 7 sable and paint down about 1 in (2.5 cm) from the edge of the trees. Now use the rest of the white to mix a lighter grey, apply it as a band below the first, and blend the two tones together. Repeat this procedure for each row of trees, every time adding more black to the grey.

WATERCOLOUR VERSION

You can also paint a watercolour version of this image. In this medium the painting appears looser and more spontaneous – though it is, if anything, more difficult to paint effectively. The first step is to dampen the area of sky with clear water. You then lay down a graduated wash with confident, horizontal strokes of a well-filled sable brush. As you work downwards from the top of the picture to the horizon, use less pigment (in this case, Paynes Grey) in your mix. You should wait for each stage of the painting to dry before you go on to the next.

When the sky is complete, mix enough grey for the first line of trees and put this to one side. Then, using clear water, apply a uniformly damp wash up to and along the edge of the first tree line and down below the second. Fill your brush with the prepared colour and draw it across the top of the dampened area. The paint will run into the contours of the first tree line and also down below the second line.

When this area is dry, repeat the procedure for each subsequent row of trees, deepening the tone of the paint each time. As you do this you will find that, however controlled is your use of watercolours, there is always a delightful unexpectedness in the paint's movement on the dampened paper.

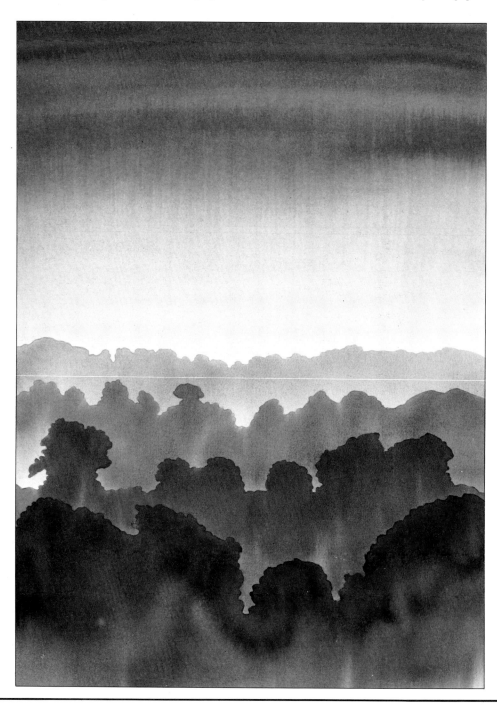

OLD COINS

Media OILS, WATERCOLOURS, or PENCIL

IN THESE EXERCISES we begin to explore modelling and look at that aspect of painting which sets out to create the illusion of form, volume, and space on the surface of the canvas. A good way to work towards this effect is to choose a subject with low relief. This could be a front door key or a detail from a relief carving. When lit from a shallow angle by a single light source, the surface texture of these objects will be picked up, and the shadows will fall in the same direction. If the subject is straightforward and can also tolerate a certain amount of inaccuracy, it is not difficult to create a convincing effect. This is because the eye identifies the subject's flat base with the surface of the picture itself so that the modelling seems to stand out above the picture surface. I chose two coins from the fifth century BC, one Persian, one from Eretria. The Persian design is a mixture of straight lines and flowing curves. The spear virtually bisects the coin, like the spokes of a wheel whose hub is the warrior's right hand. The feet touch the edge of the circle as if treading a wheel into motion, and the curving lines of the tunic reinforce the sense of movement. Scaling up something as small as this to many times its own size enables you to make pictures that are bold, avoiding too much fiddly detail.

MATERIALS AND EQUIPMENT

Oil versions
Support
Board or canvas 10 × 12 ins
(25.5 × 30.5 cm)

Oil colours
Ivory Black, Titanium White

Brushes
No. 2 hogs'-hair filbert (first version),
No. 8 and two No. 4 long pointed sable or nylon flats (second version)

Other items
Turpentine, pencil or charcoal

Watercolour version
Support
Rough watercolour paper (140 lb)
10 × 12 ins (25.5 × 30.5 cm)

Watercolour paints
Paynes Grey

Brushes
No. 8 and No. 5 sable rounds, No. 14 squirrel

Other items
Hairdrier (optional)

Pencil version
Support
NOT-surface drawing paper
12 × 10 ins (30.5 × 25.5 cm)

Pencil
2B

Other items
Plastic eraser, pencil sharpener, fixative

METHODS

The first oil version is made with quite thick paint and a single hogs'-hair brush. The second is more finely worked, using thinner paint and nylon or sable brushes. For the watercolour, the figure is built up accurately, but freshness is maintained as you apply the pigment to a wet surface. The pencil drawing is made with light, diagonal shading.

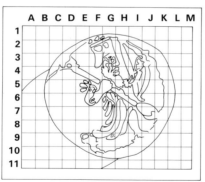

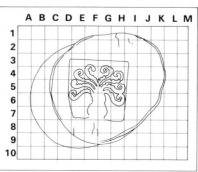

The guideline sketches on their grids. See pp. 226–7 for instructions.

OIL VERSION 1

1 Preparing the surface
Give your canvas or board an overall thin tone of light grey. Do this by applying black paint thinned with turpentine all over with a large bristle brush. Then wipe it off with a clean cotton rag. This will leave a uniform grey tone which will dry quite quickly. Another method is to mix black with white thinned by turpentine and paint on a coat of this mix. If you are using an inflexible board rather than canvas you can paint it grey using acrylic paint. This will dry almost immediately and enable you to begin your painting more quickly. Then draw the outlines according to the guidelines provided.

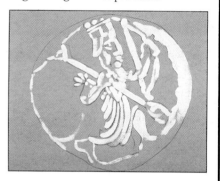

2 The lightest parts
Squeeze out a fair amount of white on to your palette and mix it with a few drops of turpentine to make it a little more workable. It should still be quite thick. Using the No. 2 hogs'-hair filbert, paint in the lightest parts of the coin. These are the prominent features on the figure itself and the front and back edges of the coin. For most of this use the brush "flat". Use the "toe" of the brush to dab in the light tones above the helmet or on the face, and the "heel" for the large areas such as the front right-hand edge of the coin. For other areas, such as the left-hand edge of the coin and the foot, you will have to use the thin edge of the brush. When you paint, try not to be too mechanical. For example, when you are painting the flowing curves of the tunic, try to make your brushstrokes reflect the movement of the curves in single, lively strokes.

Continued over

3 The mid-toned areas

Add Ivory Black to the white on your palette, a little at a time, until you have a mid-grey mix. Using the No. 2 hogs'-hair filbert, paint all the mid-toned areas such as the right-hand side of the profile and the space inside the bow. In both these areas you should leave room for the deep black shadows of the edges. Then use this mix to paint the area beside the feet, along the bottom right of the coin, and up the left-hand side of the figure. Leave a space between the figure and the grey area where the deepest black tones will go. There is also some mid-grey detailing for which you will have to use the thin edge of the brush. This includes areas such as those between the folds of cloth and in the face (beside the nose, the line of the mouth, and the areas under and beside the helmet).

4 The deep shadows

Next mix Ivory Black to the same workable consistency as before and use the same brush to paint in the deep shadows. These are cast along the edges of the bow and spear, the arm, the leg, the tunic, the side of the head, under the nose, and the eye. Use the thin end of the brush where the shadows are thin. This is particularly important where you use black between the tunic folds. Notice how the shadows cast by the tunic each belong to one particular fold, rather than being just one solid block of tone. Also paint the large shadow to the left.

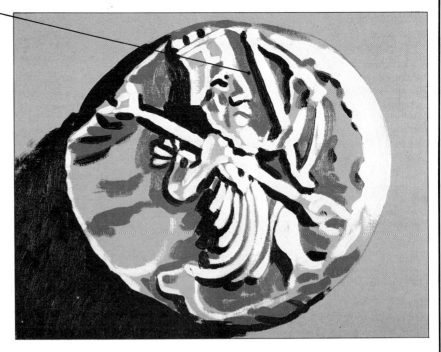

5 Adding body

Your painting now consists of black, white, and one mid tone, and you will see how successful it already is in creating the effect of relief. Next mix grey tones on your palette that are lighter and darker than the mid grey you have already used. Use these greys to add body to the painting. Fill in the areas where the ground colour still shows through. This will make the painting look more finished. Notice especially the work on the "flat" area of the coin to the left of the figure and to the right of the bow. And pay attention to the figure itself, particularly the very light grey on the helmet, beard, arm, and both feet. Next paint around the coin above, below, and to the right, using a light to mid-grey mix. This will help the highlights stand out. Finally trowel in highlights using thick dabs of white paint.

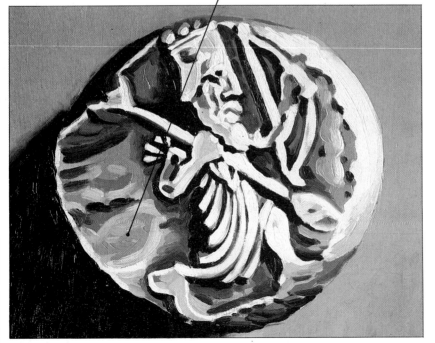

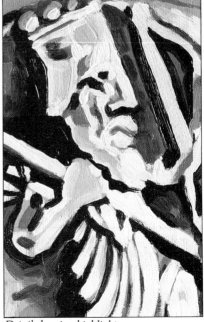

Detail showing highlights

OIL VERSION 2

1 Preparing the surface
This is a more finely worked version of the same Persian coin. Paint your canvas or board in a thin overall grey tone in the same way as for the first version. When this is dry draw in the guidelines.

2 The lightest tones
Mix a good amount of white on your palette with turpentine to make a creamy consistency thinner than for the first version. Paint in the lightest tones using the No. 4 brush, but as you paint soften the edges by using the No. 8 dampened with turpentine. Where the white is thinner you will get light grey tones where the background shows through. The brush you use for softening edges and diluting the white must not be too wet.

3 The darkest tones
Next, mix up black to a slightly thinner consistency than the white and paint in the darkest tones, beginning at the top left and working round the painting. Use a clean, damp brush to soften the edges and work outwards. Use first dark and then lighter grey tones by thinning the paint down further with turpentine. Again, make sure that the brush is not too wet. Work on a small section at a time.

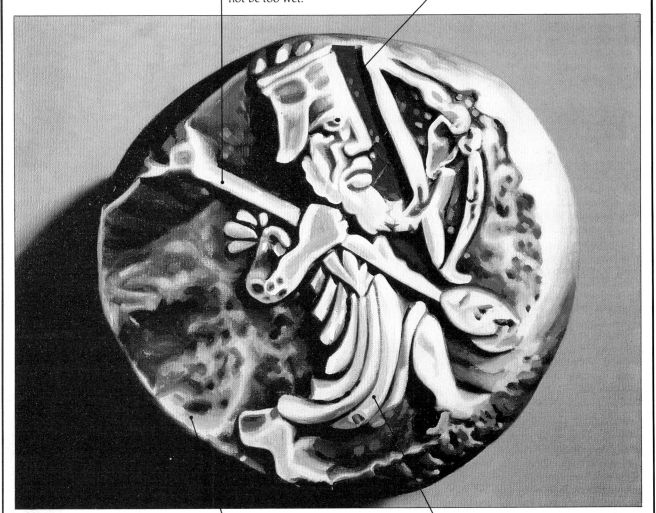

4 The background and shadow
Once you have painted in the black and white, you will find that you have a very credible image with a range of half tones. Now paint the background, making sure that you mix up enough light grey to cover the whole area. Then use the No. 8 brush to paint in the black shadow. Blend the join to soften the edge of the shadow.

5 Building on the image
Now build up the image, working slowly and carefully, a section at a time. You can mix white with black for greys at this stage, but use the paint thinly – almost as a wash – especially over the unmodelled parts of the coin where the texture is indicated by the brushwork.

6 Working up the figure
When you get to the figure, you will find that painting thin greys over much of the original white will give the modelling more dimension. Work carefully on one small section at a time, such as a tunic fold, an arm, or a foot. Look closely at my finished version and work yours up to a similar level. Finally, you should add any highlights that are necessary, using a slightly thicker white paint than you did before.

WATERCOLOUR VERSION

1 Watercolour techniques
The two most important factors to concentrate on are the degree of wetness of the paper and the amount and density of the pigment on your brush. You can only really learn these by trial and error. After drawing in the outline of the figure faintly, begin painting the shadow on the edge of the coin, just above the spear on the left. Paint the shape of the shadow in water with the No. 8 sable. The paper should not be swimming in water, but it should be very damp. The colour you apply will run anywhere the paper has been wetted, so when you paint the shape with water, do so carefully.

4 The area to the left of the body
Paint the whole of the area in shadow below the spear and on the left-hand side of the tunic in exactly the same way as before, painting the area in deepest shadow first. Let the paint run where an edge is not crisp. Modify tone and your control over the paint by varying the wetness of the paper and the density of the pigment. In areas where tone needs to be lightened or where you want to remove some pigment, you can use a clean, slightly damp brush to pick up the paint while it is still wet. In places such as the "flat" area to the left of the figure, where contours do not have to be precise, the method is to touch the toe of the brush, well-loaded with pigment, into a large wet area. Then let the natural reaction of the pigment with water do the rest.

5 Lessening contrast
Work your way around the whole figure, dealing with large or small sections of the painting in the same way as before. Then lessen the contrast between the very light and very dark tones by introducing mid-grey tones. Do this by diluting the pigment with water to the required density. Areas such as the hand and arm gripping the spear require an even light grey tone with no harsh edges. For these, you must make sure that each area is evenly damp, but not wet. When you introduce the paint, make sure the brush is also damp with paint, but not too wet. Keep a clean brush close at hand to mop up any paint that goes astray. When you come to the shadow of the coin itself, use the No. 14 squirrel after dampening the paper.

2 Painting the shadow shape
Mix some Paynes Grey on your No. 5 brush. Do not overload the brush with paint or let it get too wet. Paint over the shadow shape with a couple of smooth brushstrokes and the paint will run evenly around it. At the top edge of the shape, soften the end with a damp No. 8 sable so that there is no harsh edge where the shadow continues to the right. Soften the shape edges nearest the figure in the same way. Dry your work with a hairdrier.

3 The area to the left of the head
Now tackle the area in shadow between the left-hand side of the head and the spear. Paint the whole area with water and then, with the No. 5 sable quite well loaded with pigment, paint along the edge of the head and the spear. Let the paint run freely in the rest of the area. Dry the section thoroughly.

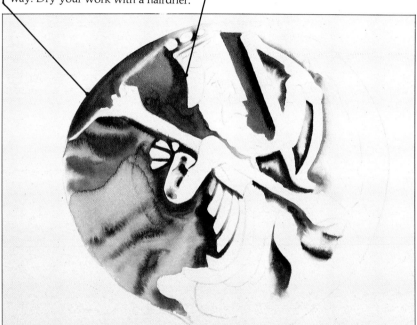

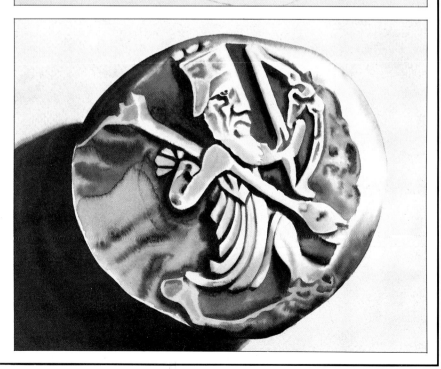

PENCIL VERSION

1 Drawing the outline

This is a different coin, treated as an exercise in pencil drawing. Though it is not essential to reproduce the shape of the coin exactly, you should try to draw in the tentacles as accurately as you can, concentrating on their flowing lines curling up and out of the body. Use the eraser to get rid of your rough pencil lines and to guide the lines of the curves. These lines are important since they provide a framework on which to build the shape and tone.

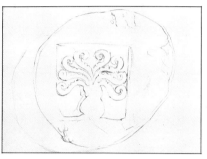

2 The shading technique

Begin shading at the top left-hand corner, starting with the shadow of the coin. Shade lightly on the diagonal, using the natural movement of your hand and arm with your elbow resting on the table or drawing board. Shade very lightly at the edges of the shadow and more strongly where the tones are very dark. But do not try to match the depth of the darkest tones with a single shading or you will ruin the surface of the paper. Build up tone by shading on top of areas that you have already shaded. The drawing should not give the effect of being laboured over. The "relaxed" appearance of the drawing is the result of light, confident pencil strokes all running along roughly the same diagonal axis. To soften the tone, lightly rub the area with the top of your index finger. Once you have done this you may have to tidy up edges with the eraser and do a little more shading.

3 The highlights

When you come to the places where the coin catches the light, try not to stop your shading too abruptly but make the transition from dark to light as smooth as you can. Shading of this kind is quite a slow business, so work carefully across the drawing.

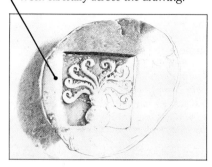

4 The top of the coin

For the large flat area above the octopus motif, vary the angle of your pencil strokes slightly in each small section of shading. This will give the effect of a surface that is not perfectly smooth.

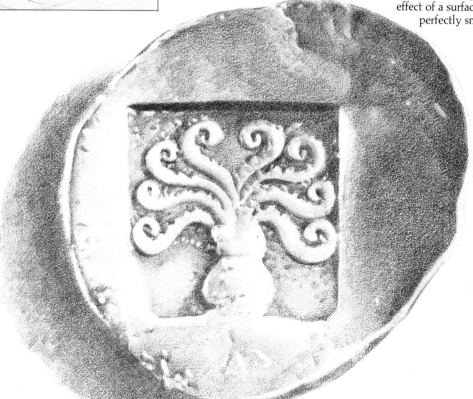

5 Finishing the drawing

Follow the various ridges and indentations on the coin with your shading and use the erasers to soften a sharp edge or pick out a highlight. Also, continue to use your fingertips to soften overall effects of shading where necessary. When you feel that you have brought all the shading to the correct depth of tone, clean up the drawing with a rubber where it has been smudged particularly around the edge of the coin and in the shadow areas. When you have picked out the highlights once more and you are fully satisfied with the drawing, give it a coat of fixative. Remember that this will have the effect of deepening the tones a little.

Windmill

Media ACRYLICS, OILS or WATERCOLOURS

THE PREVIOUS PAINTING showed an object in shallow relief. This picture shows you how to develop your skills further, to depict a free-standing, three-dimensional object lit by a single strong light source. The sides of the windmill, with their flat planes, make it perfect for this type of painting, because the important thing here is to show accurately the differences in tone between the well-lit facets and those that are in deep shadow.

It is quite easy to achieve a realistic image. The techniques required are straightforward and you will get a good result provided that you mix your tones reasonably accurately. The picture incorporates most of the techniques covered so far, including creating smoothly gradated tones, doing line work, and making cloud studies.

You may also find it interesting to use these techniques to make your own studies of simple three-dimensional objects such as matchboxes or bricks. Vary the direction and quality of the lighting for each study. You will see how these changes of lighting dramatically transform the atmosphere and "feel" of even a very simple object.

MATERIALS AND EQUIPMENT

Acrylic and oil versions
Support
Board or canvas 18 × 14 ins
(46 × 35.5 cm)

Oil or acrylic colours
Titanium White, Ivory Black

Brushes
No. 8 hogs'-hair round, No. 4 hogs'-hair filbert, No. 4 sable flat, No. 1 round rigger

Other items
Water (acrylic version), turpentine (oil version), HB pencil

Watercolour version
Support
90 lb rough watercolour paper
14 × 10¼ ins (35.5 × 26 cm)

Watercolour paints
Paynes Grey

Brushes
No. 8 and two No. 4 round sables

Other items
Sponge, masking fluid

METHODS

For the oil and acrylic paintings the method is similar, but with acrylics you do not have to wait so long for the paint to dry. Because of this quick-drying quality, it is often best not to premix tones when using acrylic paint, but to mix each one as you need it. The sky is first painted as a tone that gradates smoothly from light mid-grey to white. When this is dry, the clouds are overpainted. The next stage is to draw on the shape of the mill and paint each of its facets in turn, finally adding the windows, the three visible sails, the silhouetted trees, and the vegetation at the base of the mill. Lastly, the details in the foreground (the path and the grass) are filled in.

For the watercolour, the method is to paint the shapes of mill and path with masking fluid before tackling the sky. The sky itself is a gradating tone and the clouds are picked out using a wet sponge. When this is dry and the masking fluid is rubbed off each shape is dampened with water and painted in, following the tones of the original.

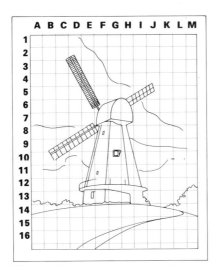

The guideline sketch on its grid. See pp. 226–7 for instructions.

The guideline sketch on its grid. See pp. 226–7 for instructions.

ACRYLIC VERSION

1 The background
Beginning about a fifth of the way up the board paint a tone that gradates smoothly from near white at the bottom to light mid-grey at the top. Do this in the same way as you did for the tree painting (see p. 20) and use the No. 8 brush.

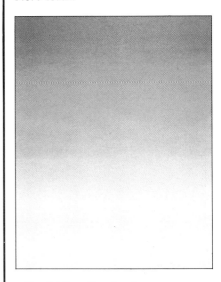

2 Adding the clouds
When the background is dry, paint in the clouds using Titanium White and the same No. 8 brush. Use a thin mix of paint and circular movements of the brush. Build up the clouds in layers, so that they gradually grow more opaque, and allow each layer to dry before continuing. Do not let the clouds become too light. If you look at the finished painting (see p. 40) you will see that the top of the windmill is much lighter than any part of the cloud.

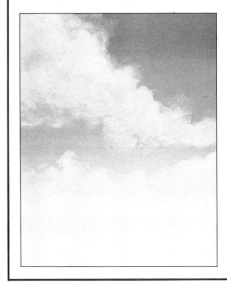

3 The white areas
After drawing the image on to your canvas by tracing, you can start to paint the windmill itself. Start with the white top of the mill and the white left-hand edge, using a No. 4 sable flat. Paint these areas a couple of times to get the opaque quality that is necessary here.

4 Blending the shadow tones
Now paint the next facet of the mill with the No. 4 hogs'-hair. If you need to, you can use the No. 4 sable for the corners. Paint the lighter grey right-hand edge first and paint about two-thirds of the way across with this colour before painting the slightly darker left-hand edge. Then wipe off your brush and blend the tones, so that there is a smooth transition from one side of the facet to the other. Do this on the lower part of the mill also.

5 The third facet
Now paint the next facet on the right, using the No. 4 hogs'-hair brush in the same way as before but with two slightly darker tones. Paint the part of the top of the mill that is in shadow using the same tones — the darker one around the edge and the lighter one in the middle. Use the sable brush to make the corners neater.

6 The darkest facet
You should now paint the darkest facet and the shadows at the top and above the base of the mill. These shadows are the darkest tones in the painting, but they are not pure black, so use a touch of white in your mix. The central part of the facet is a slightly lighter tone, which you should blend with the darker tones at the sides. Use the No. 4 sable or even the No. 1 for the corners and difficult edges, and the No. 4 hogs'-hair for the rest.
Continued over

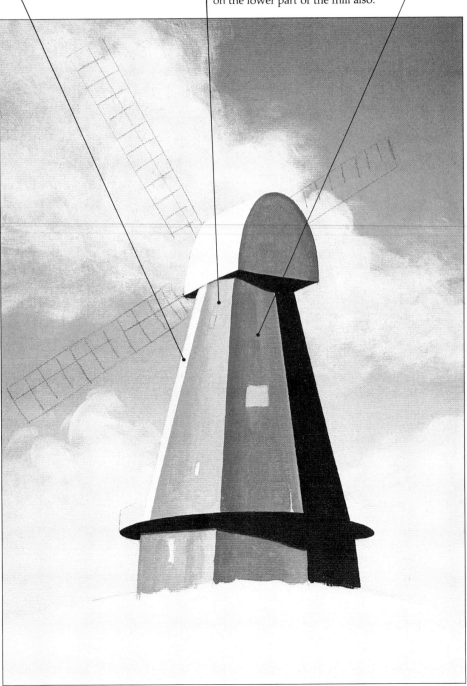

7 Painting the sails

Now you have painted the main body of the windmill, you can tackle the sails and smaller details. For this use the No. 1 round or, if you prefer, the No. 1 rigger. (The latter is useful for the long, thin lines of the sails.) The sail at the top left of the picture has two basic tones, one for the central spar and the stronger cross-bars, the second for the thinner cross-bars and the long outer lines. Use slightly lighter versions of these tones for the sail just beneath this one. The sail on the right is in shadow, so paint in the spaces between the cross-bars with the appropriate grey and the No. 4 sable. Put in the windows and give a hint of the rail around the walkway.

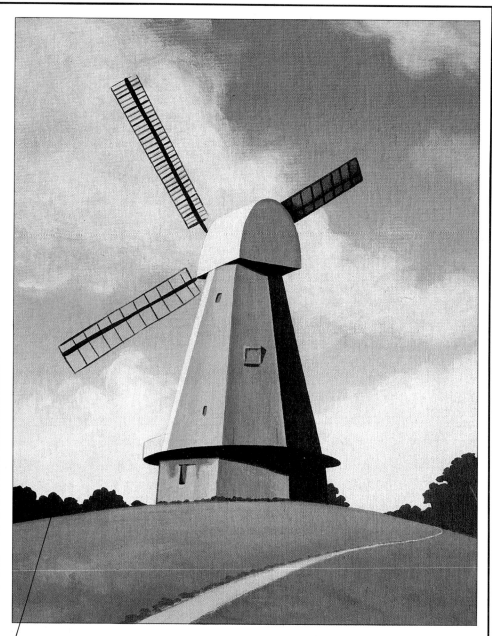

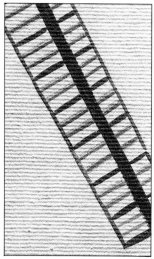

Actual-size detail

8 Adding the trees

Next take the No. 4 sable and, with a slightly lighter version of the grey you used for the darkest facet, paint the silhouetted tree line. This forms an important compositional device, framing the mill and giving an idea of distance. At the same time, indicate some vegetation at the base of the windmill.

9 The foreground

You can now paint the foreground. Begin with the light grey path and then go on to the grass. Use two dark grey tones similar to those in the third facet of the mill, painting the lighter tone at the top and the darker one below. For this work, use the No. 4 hogs'-hair. Finally add a trace of darker tone above the line of the path and make any adjustments that you feel are necessary.

OIL VERSION

For the oil version (below), follow a similar method to that used for the acrylic painting. However, you will have to wait far longer for the sky and clouds to dry before you can continue with the windmill. There are two ways you could speed up the process. You can paint the sky and clouds in one go, so that you only have to wait for one layer to dry. Or, if you are painting on rigid board rather than canvas, you can do the sky and clouds in acrylics and paint the windmill itself in oils. This way you can practise the most important aspects of the exercise sooner.

One advantage of oil paint is the fact that the tone you put on is the tone you will see when it is dry. Oil paint is also highly flexible, making it easier to blend tones and edges. With oils you can therefore soften the joins between the mill's facets (below). You do this by stroking the chiselled end of a sable brush along the join, wiping accumulated paint off the brush, and continuing down the join. The effect is to soften the abruptness of the painted edge, in contrast with the angular acrylic version.

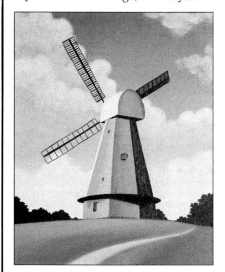

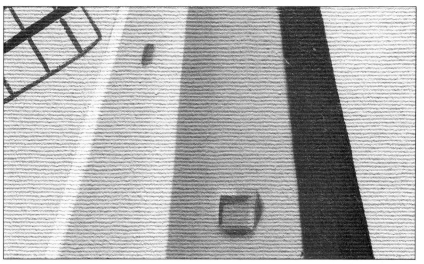

WATERCOLOUR VERSION

To produce a watercolour painting (right), begin by drawing the windmill's outlines. Then paint the shape of the mill and the path in masking fluid (below left). When it is dry give it another coat. Paint the sky by applying a graded wash and pick out the clouds with a piece of wet sponge. When this is dry, rub off the masking fluid (below right) and paint the mill in sections. You can rub the masking fluid off easily with your fingers. Before the paint is applied, dampen the particular area to be painted with water.

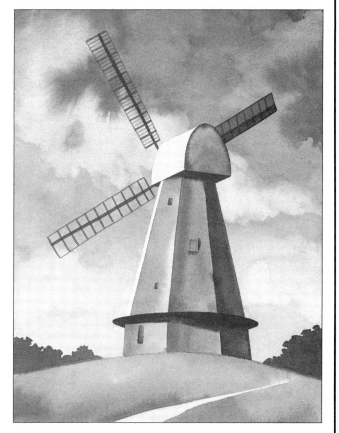

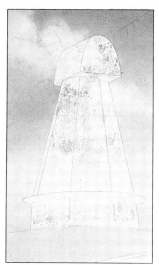

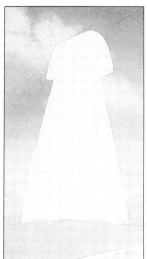

CHILD'S EGG CUP

Media OILS, PENCIL, or WATERCOLOURS

THIS EXERCISE is designed to extend your manipulation and control of tone. It can be drawn in pencil or painted in oil or watercolours. I have taken a simple object that is lit directly from a single light source, creating a strong contrast between light and shadow areas, with a wide range of intermediate tones. There are broad areas of tonal modelling to deal with, such as the shape of the egg itself, and there are more intricate areas such as the wooden rabbit. If you wish, you can leave out the rabbit, but if you take it slowly and carefully you will find it much easier than it looks. Go on to choose your own simple subjects to paint or draw in this way, but stick to things with fairly simple shapes, so that you can easily plot the progress of light across the surface. I have explained how to do this exercise in oil paints, pencil and watercolours, so that you can learn how to achieve surprisingly similar effects using very different media and techniques.

MATERIALS AND EQUIPMENT

Oil version
Support
Prepared board 10 × 14 ins
(25.5 × 35.5 cm)

Oil colours
Titanium White, Ivory Black (any black will do)

Brushes
No. 1, No. 4, and No. 7 hogs'-hair filberts, No. 1 nylon or sable round

Other items
Painting medium (see p. 10)

Pencil version
Support
90 lb drawing or watercolour paper
10 × 14 ins (25.5 × 35.5 cm)

Pencils
1B or 2B

Other items
Plastic eraser, fixative

Watercolour version
Support
90 lb drawing or watercolour paper
10 × 14 ins (25.5 × 35.5 cm)

Watercolour paint
Ivory Black

Brushes
No. 2, two No. 4, and No. 7 sables

METHODS

For the oil painting each area is painted quite separately. The method is to work from the lightest to the darkest tones, and then blend in along the lines where they meet. The principle is the same for all the areas but it is best to start on the simpler parts of the painting. It is important not to rush this painting, so take it slowly and in sequence, keeping the brushes clean and colours pure. If you are in doubt as to which of two brushes to use, choose the smaller.

For the pencil drawing the tones are built up by overshading. This is achieved by shading as much as three times over the same area with the pencil. An eraser can be used to redefine shapes, soften tones, and tidy edges.

The watercolour version is painted in stages, building up tone by overlaying washes. The most important thing is to make sure that one coat is completely dry before laying on another. With large areas it is worth dampening the whole area before putting on the first wash. This will make it easier to avoid tidemarks and unsightly edges.

The guideline sketch on its grid. See pp. 226–7 for instructions.

OIL VERSION

1 Outline and background
Draw the outlines of the picture on to your board. For the original I painted the background with a very light grey up to the edge of the shape, just to have a background against which to assess the tones of the object. This should really be done in oil paint, but to speed up drying I used thin acrylic, which is acceptable on an inflexible support like the prepared board I used. If you decide to use oil for the background, make sure it is quite dry before you start working on the subject, so that you can rest your hand. If you use acrylic you can repaint with oils later.

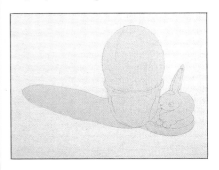

2 Mixing the paints
Begin by mixing up a good quantity of Titanium White. Since you will be painting the picture in one go, use the painting medium to reduce the paint to a thick, creamy consistency. Mix a smaller amount of Ivory Black to a similar consistency. Keep these two colours quite separate on your palette, or mix them in separate containers. All the grey tones will come from a mixture of these two, so it is important to keep both black and white pure. For this reason use a palette knife, painting knife or brush that you keep for that purpose to bring the paint to the mixing area on your palette.

3 The egg

Beginning with the egg, work from the lightest tones to the darkest areas. Apply pure white for the highlight, then mix a little off-white by adding a tiny touch of black and paint that around the highlight. Add a little more black to the mixture and paint this darker tone around the lighter one. Continue in this way, working round and out to the darker tones, following the natural shape of the egg with your brush. I used a No. 6 hogs'-hair filbert for the egg and a No. 1 for the edge. If you wish, you can also use a round sable for the edge.

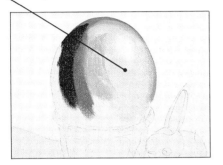

4 Blending the tones

When you have laid the tones down, wipe the paint off the brush with a rag and blend them on the board with smooth strokes of the brush along the lines where they meet.

5 Working procedure

Use the method I have explained in this step and Step 4 for the whole painting. You paint and blend all the larger areas with your hogs'-hair brushes and use round sables for the smaller areas and detailing. Simply mix the tones to match what I have done in my painting. Apply them to the area to be painted, paint in the adjacent tones, and blend them in. Where you have a dark and light tone adjacent to each other and you need to soften the edge, as in the perimeter of the shadow, chisel the tip of a damp sable and stroke it along the join. Wipe the brush off every time you take it off the board.

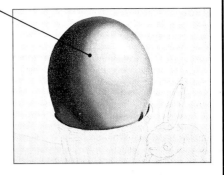

6 Repainting the background

At the end you may find that the background needs repainting. This is a little unorthodox, but entirely legitimate here — where a relatively simple shape is enclosed in light tone. It may be a useful way of tidying up some of the edges, too. If you do repaint the background, mix enough paint to cover the whole area and paint up to the edges carefully with a round sable. You can paint the rest with the No. 7 hogs'-hair. Remember to soften the join between background and object or shadow where necessary.

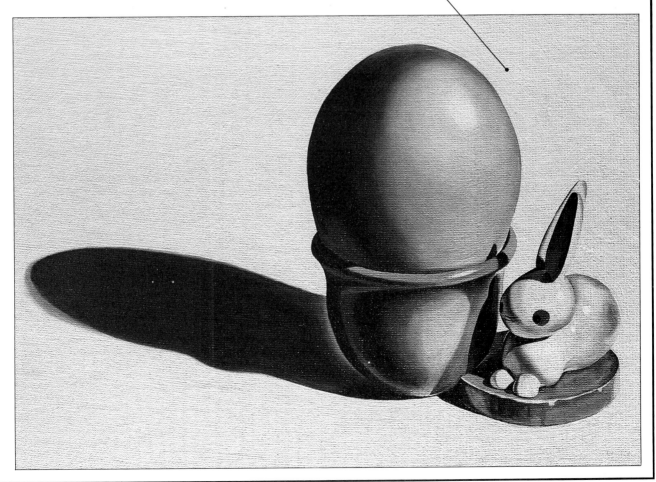

PENCIL VERSION

1 Drawing tips

First draw the shape of the egg cup on to your paper, using the guide-line sketch. Then start the drawing by working down from the top of the egg to the rim of the egg cup, shading on a diagonal approximately from top right to bottom left. Rest your forearm on your drawing board and shade lightly using the natural movement of your wrist. It is a good idea to protect the part of the paper your hand or drawing arm may be resting on by placing a thin sheet of paper between it and the drawing. Keep your pencil at a shallow angle to the paper so that there is a light and sensitive contact between the pencil and the paper. Aim to reproduce the tones as accurately as possible. Keep your pencil long and sharp for the whole drawing. This will give it a satisfactory uniformity.

2 Overshading

Shade up to the left-hand edge of the egg, building up tone gradually by overshading. Don't try to achieve great depth of tone immediately – you will only dig the pencil into the paper. The knack is to continue to make fast, relaxed pencil strokes while staying within the contours of the shapes you are defining.

3 Using the eraser

If you do go over the edge of the outline with your rapid pencil strokes, you can always redefine it with your eraser. Cut off a corner of the eraser with a scalpel to give you a sharp edge to work with. You can also use the eraser tip to tidy up edges, soften tones, and pick out highlights.

4 The egg's right-hand edge

If you are right-handed, the right-hand edge of the egg will be difficult to shade up to. You can either turn the drawing upside down (so that it is as if you are shading to the left-hand edge), or define the line of the edge more clearly, then shade over it, and use your eraser to "redraw" the edge when you have finished.

5 The shadow

The dark shadow to the left of the egg cup is even in tone – apart from the edges and the area where it touches the egg cup. You will find that keeping your shading even is just as difficult as it is to graduate your shading from light to dark. The essential thing is to keep the same pressure on the pencil tip, and your shading will be even. You will need to go over the whole area two or three times to achieve the correct depth and evenness of tone.

6 Softening the tone

You can soften tone by smudging gently with the tip of your index finger. For the egg, use a circular movement to echo the curve of the object.

7 The egg cup

Work next on the egg cup itself. Begin by shading in the darkest tones. This will give you a sense of the object's three dimensions. Build up tone and if necessary use the eraser to pick out highlights or soften edges. Try to imitate the tones in my version as closely as you can.

8 The rabbit

Begin with the dark shading on the left-hand side of the rabbit and move to the very light tone on the right. Here your pencil's pressure must be very light indeed, barely touching the paper. Use a light circular movement of the tip of your index finger to soften any shading lines. Deal with all the small areas of light or dark tone in much the same way as you did the larger ones, bearing in mind the source and direction of the light. Fix the drawing as soon as you have finished. This has the satisfying effect of slightly deepening the tones.

WATERCOLOUR VERSION

1 Watercolour tips
This painting involves overlaying colour to build up tone. So it is useful to have a small hairdrier beside you to speed up the drying process at each stage. It is also very useful to work with two brushes — one filled with paint for applying the tone, and the other damp and clean for taking tone out, or softening the edges while the paint is still damp.

2 The shadow
First draw the shape of the egg cup using the guideline sketch provided. Then apply the paint to the dampened shadow shape with a well-filled No. 7 brush, and where the tone lightens towards the egg cup use your No. 4 to soak up excess paint and lighten the tone.

3 The egg
Treat the egg in a similar way, but in this case leave an area larger than the white highlight dry, and then, when the paint has covered the rest of the egg, soften the edges with a damp, clean brush. Dry this area (you can use the hairdrier), and then apply more colour to deepen the tone of the shadow and the left side of the egg. Here again, use the second brush to soften the edge of the colour. The brush should not be so wet that the water runs back into the colour you have just applied or so dry that the colour does not lighten smoothly.

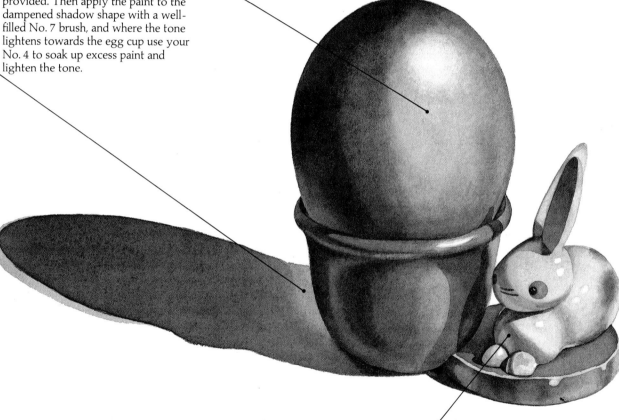

4 An alternative method
Another method is to dampen the area where you want the tone to lighten before applying the paint. If you are doing this on top of colour be careful not to use too much water.

5 The rabbit
Treat the rabbit in the same way, and build up the painting gradually until you have reached the depth of tone in the illustration.

MADONNA

Media PENCIL or OILS

THIS IS A PAINTING of a Michelangelo sculpture. It shows you how to reproduce the effect of light falling over a smooth but very irregular surface and how accurate use of tonal modelling and blending can create the almost tangible impression of a three-dimensional object. The particular image is the tender face of Mary contemplating the dead Christ in one of Michelangelo's most moving works, the *Pietà* of 1501. The highly finished, almost polished surface of sculpted marble lends itself well to an exercise of this kind. This is because the surface texture's overall uniformity necessitates a similar uniformity in the way tones are blended in the picture.

You will have to be prepared for both oil and pencil versions to take some time. There is a good day's work in the drawing, while the oil painting will have to be made over a period of two or three days. But they are well worth attempting, and if you take them slowly and carefully, stage by stage, you will find how straightforward it is to make an apparently complicated and advanced image. The image will also be useful because it will give you some experience of the kind of modelling used for portraits.

MATERIALS AND EQUIPMENT

Pencil version
Support
Good quality NOT watercolour paper at least 16 × 12 ins (40.5 × 30.5 cm)

Pencil
4B

Other items
Plastic eraser, putty eraser, cotton buds (optional), fixative

Oil version
Support
Canvas or board 16 × 12 ins (40.5 × 30.5 cm)

Oil colours
Ivory Black, Titanium White

Brushes
No. 8 and two No. 4 sable (or nylon) pointed flats, No. 1 sable round, No. 11 and two No. 4 hogs'-hair filberts

Other items
Turpentine, painting medium (see p. 10)

METHODS
The drawing is made with a thick, black, bonded lead pencil. The technique is to shade with the pencil and then soften the tone by rubbing with the fingertips or with a cotton bud. A plastic eraser is used to pick out highlights and a putty rubber to modify tones.

The oil painting is first sketched in with thin, transparent tones of black pigment. The grey tones are added later, working carefully on one small section of the painting at a time. The paints are mixed with turpentine only.

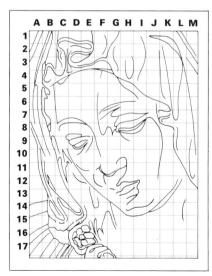

The guideline sketch on its grid. See pp. 226—7 for instructions.

1 Sketching the outlines
Sketch in the main features in outline using the guidelines provided. Even at this stage you should aim for fluency in your line, to reflect the poise of the subject. Although you need very few lines to establish the main features of the picture, it is important to make them as precise as possible. The accuracy of the whole drawing will depend on them.

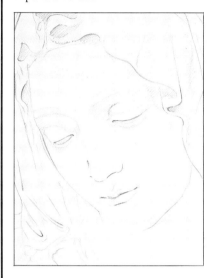

2 The folds of the headdress
Begin at the top left. There are quite dramatic contrasts between light and dark in this part of the drawing and it is important to represent them as accurately and boldly as possible. If you fail to do this you will have a lot of reshading to do at the end. Do not dig your pencil heavily into the paper to create the darkest tones. Build them up by reshading. As you work, soften the tones with your fingertips or a cotton-wool bud. Then pick out areas of lighter tone that have been smudged with the sharp end of a plastic eraser. Pay particular attention to the edges, especially the vertical strip which is situated an inch in from the left next to the first big loop of the headdress.

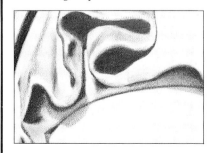

3 Fabric and forehead
The area towards the right-hand side of the headdress is less detailed. Work up the lighter tones by smoothing with your fingertips and taking out the highlights with the plastic eraser. The forehead is a similarly broad area with a little detail. These areas look simpler than they are, since it is quite difficult to control an even and light tone over such an expanse of paper. The important thing is to begin shading very lightly indeed, because it is considerably easier to darken tone than to lighten it. The paper surface and soft pencil will help you in this. The paper surface gives a fine overall texture, while the soft pencil lead is more easily smoothed to a consistent finish than a harder one would be.

A putty rubber is very useful for removing tone from a surface if you have made part of the drawing too dark. Work a piece of the eraser into a ball between the palms of your hands. Then push it down on to the area you want to lighten. As you pull it up it will take some of the shading with it.

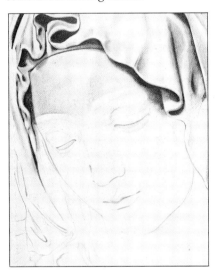

5 Completing the face
Work down the rest of the drawing in the same way, so that it is almost complete. You should now have a good overall look at the picture and adjust any areas that seem to be receding or protruding too far, pick out the highlights once more, and make any further alterations that seem necessary. It is advisable not to fix your image immediately. Leave it for a day or two, to give yourself time to make a more objective judgement on anything that may need further attention.

4 The eyes
First shade these loosely, then carry out once more the process of smoothing, reshading, erasing, and redrawing to bring them to their finished state. As you do this, work diagonally down the drawing, so that everything in the picture above the point you are working on has been taken to roughly the same stage. This means that your hand or arm will always rest on a part of the paper that has not been intensively worked. This way you will avoid inadvertent smudging. The danger of this method is that you may get so caught up in a small part of the picture that you fail to see it as a whole. So it is very important to keep referring to the whole drawing so you see each small section in its context.

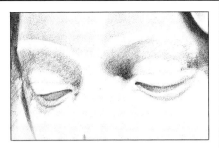

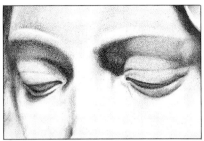

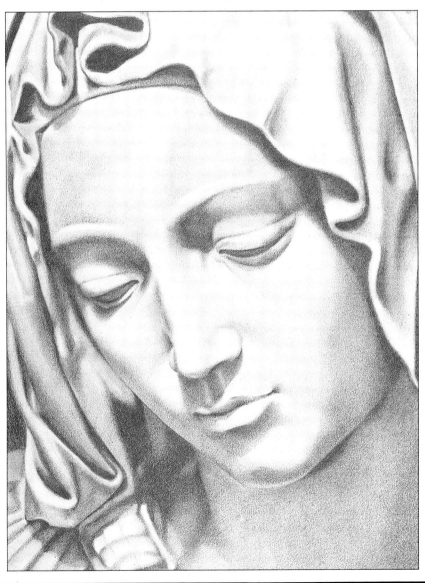

OIL VERSION

1 The tint and outline sketch

Give the canvas a light grey tint by mixing a little black with a lot of turpentine and applying the mix with the No. 11 hogs'-hair brush. First cover the canvas with horizontal brushstrokes, then use vertical strokes. You should next wipe the canvas with a clean cotton rag or an absorbent paper kitchen towel. This will remove the excess turpentine and pigment, leaving your canvas with a uniform light grey tone. Once this has dried, draw the outline sketch. If you have already made the drawing of this subject, you can make a tracing of the features from that.

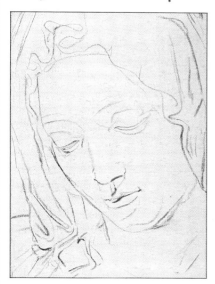

2 The broad areas of tone

Rough in the tones using a very thin Ivory Black mix diluted with turpentine. Use the No. 4 pointed flats to apply it. Start with the top left of the painting, where the shadows are most intricate. The method is to fill the dark-tone areas with paint, and sketch in the half tones lightly, simply stroking the brush over the surface of the canvas. As you do this, the pigment adheres only to the raised parts of the canvas, giving

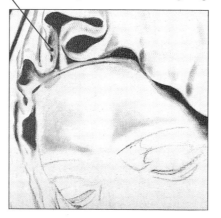

4 Preparing for the overpainting

For this you will need Titanium White on one side of your palette and Ivory Black on the other. From these you can mix a wide range of grey half tones. Do not mix too much of any one tone — by the time the painting is finished your palette will be a mass of very small areas of mixed tone. The reason for this is that you should work on the painting slowly and carefully, a small section at a time.

the appearance of half tones. An alternative method is to dilute the pigment further where the tone is lighter. Do this by using a clean brush dampened in turpentine, stroking pigment from the edges of the darker areas into the lighter parts. In both cases, do not allow your brush to be wet with paint — it should only be damp. For larger areas of half tone use a hogs'-hair brush with very little pigment on it, and brush it lightly over the area.

3 Underpainting the face

Continue the underpainting in the same way that you did for the corner of the hood, using a very thin mix. Paint economically — you need very little painting to rough in an image that is quite realistic. As long as the features are in approximately the right places it is not vital to aim for very smooth gradations of tone at this stage.

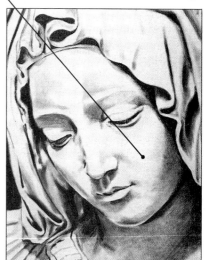

5 Beginning the overpainting

Start with the top left-hand side of the hood, painting in the two dark parallel strips with the No. 4 flat and the light grey stripes next to them with the other No. 4 brush. Keep one brush for the dark tones and one for the lighter ones. Apply the paint thinly and brush it in well. Blend with a clean brush, running it smoothly along the join. Notice how some areas (such as parts of the hood, the cheeks, and the neck) have very smooth gradations of tone, extending over a considerable area of

canvas. In other places the transitions are more abrupt. This is the case with the eyes and eyelids, the lips, and some parts of the hood. For the latter, you should soften the abrupt transitions to avoid harsh edges. Use the No. 4 sable brush. For the former, the transitions can be worked more vigorously using a No. 4 hogs'-hair or the No. 8 sable. The headdress incorporates both intricate and broader areas of blending, and painting it should give you the confidence that you require in order to tackle the face.

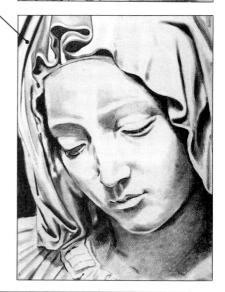

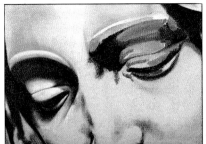

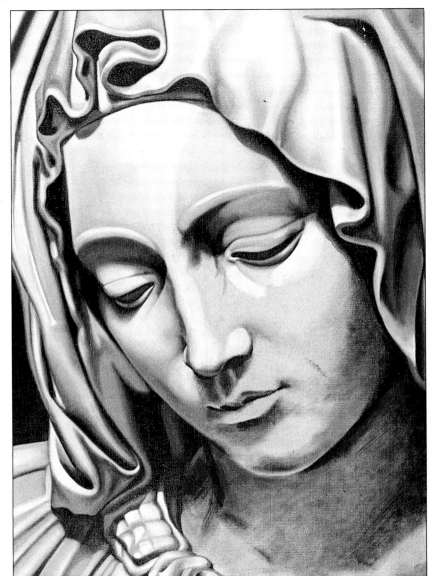

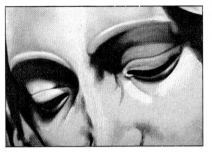

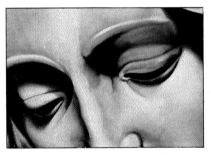

Building up details The three details of the eyes show how you can build up tones to the required smooth finish. Start by painting broad areas of tone (top). Then blend these and add further tones such as the white patch beneath the eye on the right (centre). Finally, as you paint the rest of the face, blend the white area with the grey of the cheek as in the finished picture (detail above).

6 The face

First paint in the tones of each area as flat shapes close to each other but not overlapping. Then blend and repaint until you achieve the smooth finish of the final state. As you do this, try to avoid the danger of painting according to a visual stereotype – in other words of assuming that the nose should look like this or the lips like that. The best solution is to look very closely at the illustration of the finished painting before tackling a particular section. You might even find it helpful to think of each area as a completely abstract area of light and shade. However you approach the painting, work slowly and carefully, letting the work dictate its own pace. When you come to the smooth, broad areas such as the cheek on the right and the neck, mix your tones with particular care, since almost imperceptible changes in tone can have quite dramatic effects on the appearance of the face.

Continued over

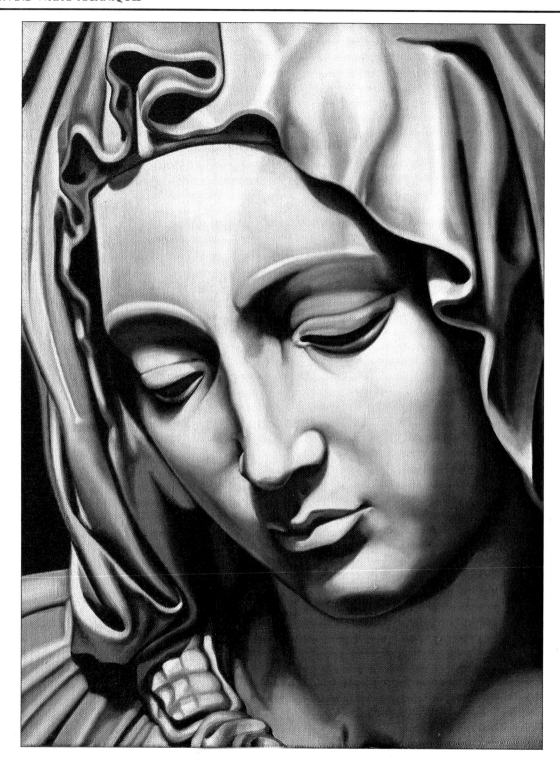

7 Reworking the picture
When you have painted the whole face, make any obvious adjustments to make the tones more accurate. For example, if a highlight is too bright, work the surrounding tones over it with a clean, almost dry brush. If it is too dark, mix some white and paint it on, working it smoothly into the surrounding pigment. There must be a uniformity of surface over the whole painting. If one area looks more roughly painted than another, rework it, blending and smoothing the tones. Put the painting aside for a day or two and look at it again. It may need adjusting.

COLOUR
TECHNIQUES

SUNSETS

Media OILS or WATERCOLOURS

THE FIRST PAINTINGS in black and white showed how you can paint a sky with tones that gradate from light at the horizon to a mid tone at the top of the painting (see pp. 20–3). In these colour pictures you make similar transitions. But this time the basis for the background of each picture is the colours of a sunset. Once you have painted these colours, you can turn each image into a complete painting with the addition of a simple silhouette. Several different versions are shown but the subjects for the silhouettes are only suggestions – you can easily incorporate ideas of your own.

MATERIALS AND EQUIPMENT

Oil versions
Support
Canvas or board 10 × 14 ins
(25.5 × 35.5 cm)

Oil colours

Winsor Red		Transparent Gold Ochre	
Winsor Blue		Burnt Sienna	
Manganese Blue		Permanent Rose	
Cadmium Yellow Pale		Titanium White	

Brushes
No. 6 and No. 4 hogs'-hair filberts, No. 2 sable (or nylon) round, No. 0 sable round rigger, No. 4 and No. 8 sable pointed flats

Other items
Turpentine, painting medium (see p. 10).

Watercolour versions
Support
Good quality, rough-surface watercolour paper approximately 9 × 12 ins (23 × 35.5 cm)

Watercolour paints

Cadmium Red		Burnt Sienna	
Winsor Blue		Burnt Umber	
Cadmium Yellow Pale		Permanent Rose	

Brushes
No. 8, No. 7, No. 4, and No. 2 sable rounds, No. 14 round squirrel

METHOD
For the oil paintings, the method is to paint in adjacent colours in horizontal bands and blend them in by brushing along the joins. A hogs'-hair brush is used for the initial painting and blending. An alternative method is to paint all the colours and subsequently blend them with brushes that are dampened in turpentine.

For the watercolours, two methods are used. The first is to build up colours by overlaying washes on those that have already dried. The second method is to work wet-in-wet, introducing new colours into the wet paint already on the paper, to make a complete background in one go.

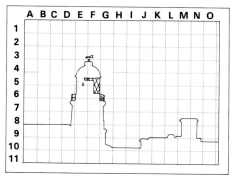

The guideline sketch for drawing up the lighthouse. See pp. 226–7 for instructions.

LIGHTHOUSE IN OILS

1 **Beginning with the background**
Mix a fair amount of Titanium White with a little turpentine to a creamy consistency and add a touch of Cadmium Yellow Pale. Paint this in a horizontal band along the bottom of the canvas using the No. 6 hogs'-hair brush. Add a little Cadmium Yellow Pale to your mixture and paint another band above the first. Wipe the brush off on a clean rag or paper towel and then blend the colours together by brushing along the join.

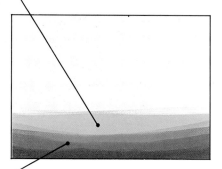

SEABIRDS IN OILS

1 **The background**
Paint this with the No. 6 hogs'-hair brush. Begin with a band of Cadmium Yellow Pale about 3 ins (7.5 cm) up from the bottom.

2 **Blending the colours**
Below the Cadmium Yellow Pale paint a band to which you have added a little Winsor Red. Increase the amount of red in the mix as you add two more bands of colour below this. Then blend these colours as before but paint along the joins with a bristle brush. Wipe off the excess paint as you blend and if necessary dampen the brush with a little turpentine. Clean the brush thoroughly.

2 Building up the sunset

Add more Cadmium Yellow Pale to your mixture and paint another horizontal band above the last. Wipe your brush as before and blend the colours together. Add a little Transparent Gold Ochre and paint in another band of colour, blending it again. Then repeat this process with another band of Transparent Gold Ochre. Next add a small amount of Winsor Red to the mix. Paint a band of this colour, above the last, blending as before. By this time you should be about two-thirds of the way up your painting.

3 Finishing off the sunset

Add Winsor Red to Cadmium Yellow Pale and Transparent Gold Ochre and continue to paint horizontal bands of colour up the painting. Add more Winsor Red as you go along and add a little Burnt Sienna by the time you get to the top. Let the painting dry thoroughly before attempting to paint the silhouettes.

4 The silhouette

You can paint in any shape you wish, basing it on your own observations, on a sketch or on a photograph. If you want to paint the lighthouse draw the shape on to your painting using a sharp pencil and a ruler. Paint the intricate grille and the rail round the light chamber with the No. 0 long-haired pointed rigger. Use a mixture of Winsor Blue and Burnt Sienna thinned down with painting medium. Finally paint up to the other outlines using the No. 4 flat and fill in the shape with the No. 4 hogs'-hair.

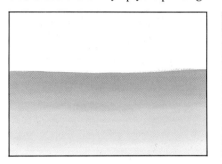

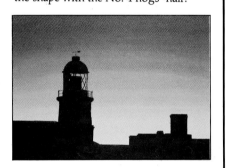

3 The upper section

Mix some Titanium White on your palette, add a little Cadmium Yellow Pale, and paint a lighter band above the yellow. Blend the colours as before and clean your brush. Add a little Permanent Rose to your mix and repeat, blending as you go.

4 Finishing off the sunset

Add a touch of Winsor Blue to the mixture and paint in the last two or three bands adding a little more blue each time. Blend in each band and continue until you reach the top of the painting. Then let the paint dry thoroughly before you add the silhouette of the birds.

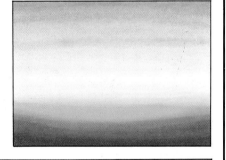

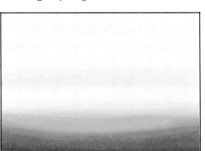

5 The silhouette

Make a mixture of Winsor Blue and Burnt Sienna for the silhouette. Use the two round sable brushes for the birds and the No. 4 pointed flat for the land.

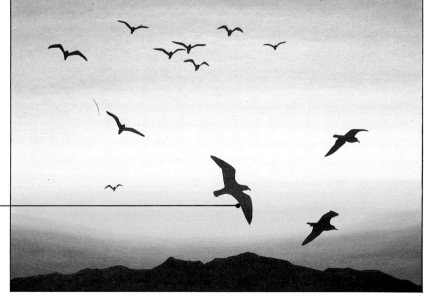

FIGURES IN WATERCOLOURS

1 The blue wash
Dampen the paper with the No. 14 squirrel brush. Mix Winsor Blue with water; the mixture should not be too dense with pigment. Apply a graded wash with the No. 14 brush, adding water to the mixture to lighten it as you go. By the time you get just over halfway down the paper, the blue should be almost invisible. Dry the paper before continuing.

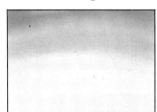

2 The yellow wash
Turn the paper upside down and dampen the surface again. Wet it right over the blue with light confident strokes of the No. 14 brush. If you start scrubbing the water in, you will disturb the blue. Mix Cadmium Yellow Pale to a similar density of tone as for the blue and paint a graded wash down the paper. The yellow should overlap the blue in the middle, but here the tone (as with the blue) should be very light. This combination of colours will make the sky look greenish.

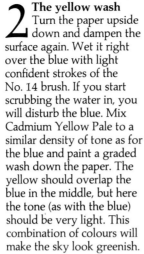

3 The pink wash
Turn the paper round so that you are working down from the blue edge. While it is still damp introduce a Permanent Rose wash over the blue. Take this to about halfway down the blue, lightening it as you go.

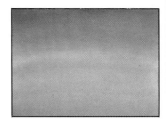

4 The red wash
Dry the paper and turn it round so that you are working down from the yellow. Wet the paper once more. Then mix and paint in a graded Cadmium Red wash as you did with the Permanent Rose. Again, take it halfway down the yellow, lightening it as you go.

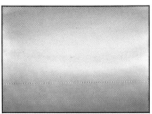

5 The silhouette
Dry the paper before drawing the outlines of the figures and hill top with a sharp HB pencil. Paint the silhouette in a mix of Burnt Umber and Winsor Blue. Use the No. 4 sable for the figures and a larger sable for the land.

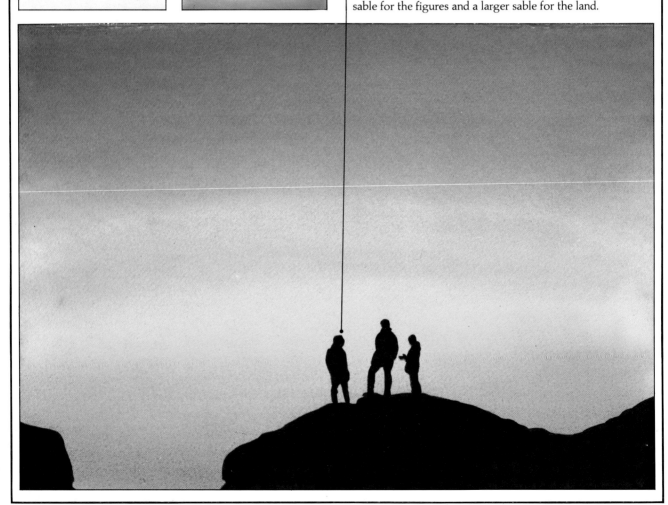

INDUSTRIAL LANDSCAPE IN WATERCOLOURS

1 Working wet-in-wet
After dampening the paper, give it an overall wash of Cadmium Yellow Pale. Use the No. 14 squirrel brush. While the wash is still wet introduce Cadmium Red into the yellow with a No. 8 sable. Make single, confident horizontal brushstrokes and let the movement of paint and water across the paper do the rest.

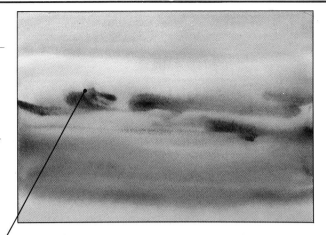

2 The sky details
At the top paint a line of thin Winsor Blue with the No. 14. Then above the orange use a No. 7 sable and a mix of Burnt Umber and Burnt Sienna to sketch in the wispy cloud shapes. It is essential that your brushstrokes should be confident. The best movement to use is a touch of the toe of the well filled brush followed by a smooth driving stroke with its heel.

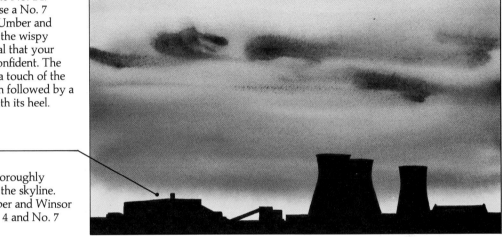

3 The silhouette
Dry the painting thoroughly before you draw in the skyline. Paint it with a Burnt Umber and Winsor Blue mix and use the No. 4 and No. 7 sable brushes.

TREE IN WATERCOLOURS

Use the same technique for this more dramatic version of a similar sky, but apply the pigment more densely with additional bands of Cadmium Yellow Pale laid into the original overall wash. Then add Cadmium Red: use it quite fiercely in one horizontal band. The cloud shapes are Burnt Umber with Permanent Rose added near the horizon and Yellow Ochre below that. All these colours are painted with the No. 7 sable. As before, you paint the silhouette in a mixture of Burnt Umber and Winsor Blue after the background has completely dried. You should begin with the trunk and the main branches using the No. 4 sable and finish with the twigs, using the No. 2 round sable or the No. 0 rigger for these details.

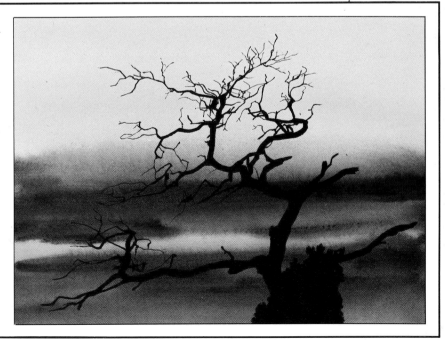

BALLROOM DANCERS

Medium OILS

THE "NEW TECHNOLOGY" of the last few decades has given artists a wide range of new visual material. Most of this material is in colour and much of it is presented in ways that are unique to our century. The kind of imagery produced by film and television and by innovations in lighting, printing, and visual display combines to present a new world to us, a world that has already been processed and packaged.

A great deal of our visual experience is vicarious. We absorb images that are only partially related to what they are meant to represent. The screen or filter that the new technology sets up between the viewer and the "real" world may affect us in different ways. It may alienate us from the imagery, or it may create a sense of security. But what we are concerned with in this painting is how this type of imagery has transformed our experience of colour. As artists we can react against its artificiality in favour of a more direct relationship with the natural world, preferring to paint straight from life. But on the other hand we can choose to enjoy and exploit this imagery as an entirely new source of inspiration unavailable to artists of earlier generations.

This painting was inspired by the extraordinary effects of colour produced by the television. It is based on the image of a pair of ballroom dancers, and it shows how you can use images from the television as a way of enjoying pure colour for its own sake in your paintings.

MATERIALS AND EQUIPMENT

Support
Canvas or board 10 × 14 ins
(25.5 × 35.5 cm)

Oil colours

Winsor Red		Winsor Green
Winsor Blue		Permanent Rose
Cadmium Yellow Pale		Titanium White

Brushes
Three No. 4 hogs'-hair filberts, No. 4 sable pointed flat

Other items
Turpentine

METHOD
First the canvas is tinted and the figures and spotlight drawn in. The white highlights are painted in using fairly thick paint. Then the colours are added one by one using vigorous, dabbing brushstrokes — the lightest tones are painted first, working through mid-tones to the darkest shades. It is better to mix the colours loosely so that the various tints are obvious. The paint should be kept thick. The patterns of colour are built up according to the original. First the figures and reflection are painted in, followed by the spotlit area. Lastly the background is filled in.

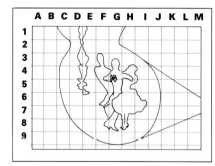

The guideline sketch on its grid. See pp. 226–7 for instructions.

1 The white highlights
Tint the canvas with Permanent Rose and draw in the figure outlines. Take the No. 4 hogs'-hair and apply Titanium White to the highlight areas. You may need to add a little turpentine to the paint, but you should apply the paint quite thickly — both here and throughout the painting. The large highlight area to the left of centre at the top of the painting does not have to be particularly accurate, but it is important to paint some of the other areas carefully. Pay special attention to the man's hair and collar, the woman's hair, her left arm, and the left side of her body, including her dress. If necessary, use your No. 4 sable brush for these areas. It will help you to be more accurate.

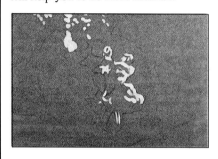

2 The yellow areas
Now mix Cadmium Yellow Pale loosely with Titanium White. Apply this with quite vigorous brushstrokes to create the woman's dress and hair. Then paint in the other patches within the spotlit area where tones are light — to the left of the man's shadow, near his legs and above his head.

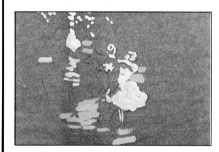

3 The orange colours

The next stage is to mix Cadmium Yellow Pale with Winsor Red and paint in the orange colours of the spotlit area. It is not necessary for you to mix the colours to an absolutely uniform orange to get the required effect. The finished painting will be much more interesting if you use colours that are loosely mixed, producing varying tints. So modify the tones of the orange as you paint it on. You should make horizontal, dabbing brushstrokes, using the No. 4 hogs'-hair brush.

4 The dark pinks and browns

Mix Permanent Rose with Titanium White for the dark pinks adjacent to the reflections on the dance floor. Use a deeper Permanent Rose mix towards the centre. Then mix a range of orange-brown colours using Cadmium Yellow Pale, Winsor Red, and a little Winsor Green. Again, mix the colours loosely. Apply these to the areas to the left of the man's shoulder and over the spotlit area of the dance floor. Then clean your brushes.

5 The greens

Add a touch of Winsor Green to Titanium White for the front edge of the woman's dress. Then mix Cadmium Yellow Pale with a touch of Winsor Green for the light greens that break up the orange in the spotlit area. Add a small amount of Winsor Red to some of these to bring them slightly closer to the orange colours.

Continued over

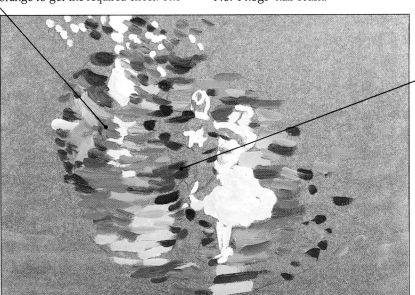

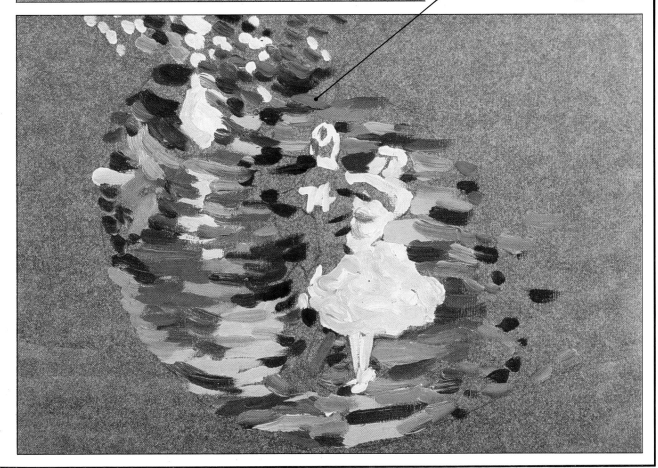

6 The man

Paint the man's suit using a mix of Titanium White and Winsor Blue. Use lighter and darker tones. For the part of the suit nearest the woman add Winsor Green and Titanium White to the light blue mixture. Apply this mix across the man's shoulders in two diagonal strokes near his waist and down the middle of his trouser leg. Use a mix of Winsor Green and Cadmium Yellow Pale for the upper part of his right arm and close to the two diagonal strokes. Then indicate his feet with a mix of Winsor Blue and Permanent Rose. This is the main colour for the shadow on his left. This also has touches of pink, orange, blue, and brown.

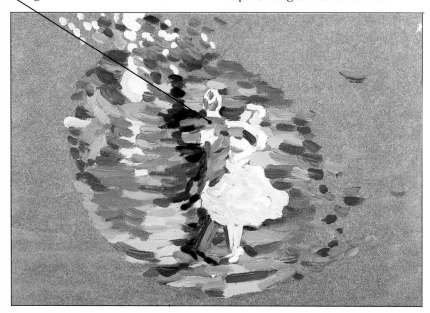

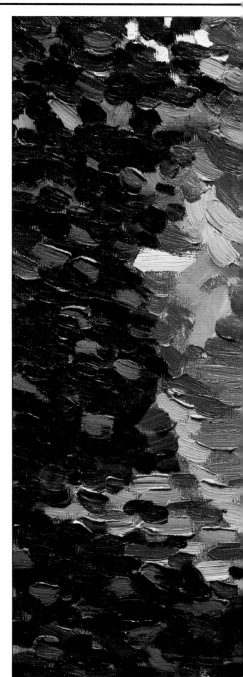

7 Painting around the spotlit area

The next stage is to paint the areas to the left and right of the spotlit circle and around its circumference. Use dabs of Winsor Blue plus Titanium White in a light and dark version. Use Winsor Red on its own, Winsor Red and Cadmium Yellow Pale for the orange, Winsor Green and Cadmium Yellow Pale for the green. And use Permanent Rose with a touch of Winsor Blue and Titanium White for the violet. Use these colours for the triangular areas on either side of the spotlight and for the light itself. Apply them with short, horizontal strokes of the brush.

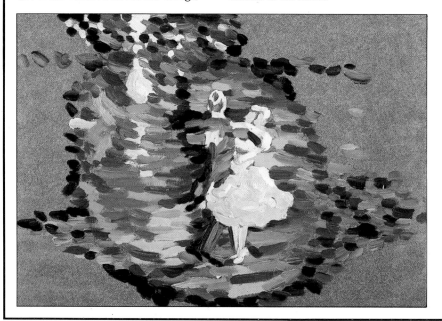

8 The background

For the background mix three colours: Winsor Green plus Cadmium Yellow Pale for the green; Permanent Rose plus Winsor Blue with a touch of Titanium White for the violet; and Winsor Blue with a touch of Titanium White for the blue. Use a separate No. 4 hogs'-hair for each colour to keep each one pure, and paint the background with horizontal dabs of colour. It does not matter if some of the pink shows through.

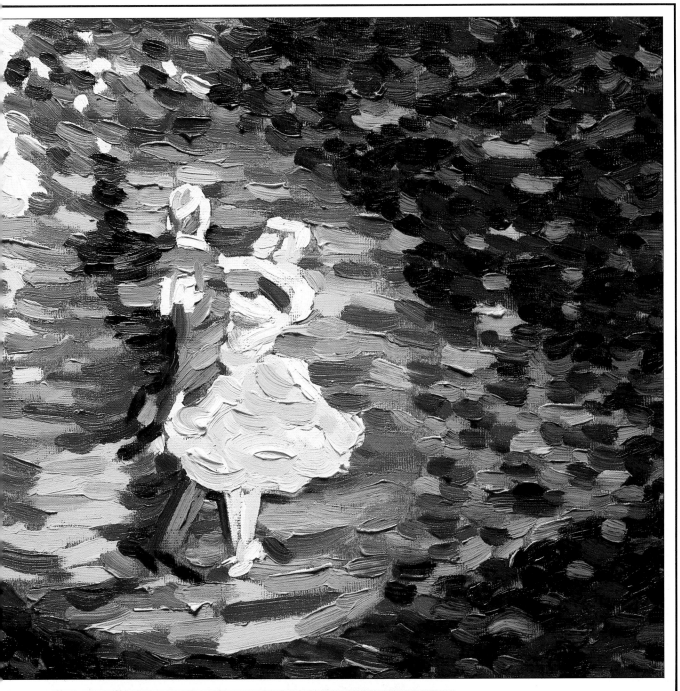

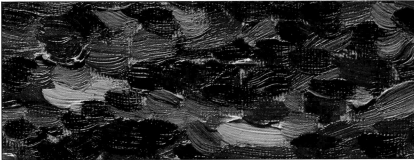

Actual-size detail taken from the top right-hand corner of the picture.

SPRING WOODLAND

Medium OILS

WHERE THE PREVIOUS exercise explored colour in an artificial context, this one takes a similar set of colours and applies them to a more natural situation where their effect is quite different. Here you can practise the technique of blocking in the main underlying areas of colour in a painting before working in more detail with touches of opaque colour on top.

This technique is particularly appropriate to the kind of image treated here, where what is conveyed is not so much a precise rendering of recognisable plants and foliage as the impression of a scene of fragmented light, shade, and colour. If you applied your touches of colour directly to a white canvas, your painting would probably become overworked and yet still look thin. As it is your touches of colour can be applied quite economically over flat underlying colours of the background. Because of the presence of these background colours, your painting will still give a solid and rich impression.

MATERIALS AND EQUIPMENT

Support
Canvas or board 10 × 14 ins
(25.5 × 35.5 cm)

Oil colours

Winsor Red	Burnt Sienna	
Winsor Blue	Transparent Gold Ochre	
Manganese Blue	Permanent Rose	
Cadmium Yellow Pale	Titanium White	
Winsor Green		

Brushes
No. 6, No. 4, and No. 2 hogs'-hair filberts, two No. 4 sable or nylon point- ed flats, No. 2 sable or nylon round, No. 0 long-haired rigger

Other items
Turpentine, painting medium (see p. 10)

METHOD

After the guidelines are sketched in, the method is to block in the broad tonal areas using thin oil paint mixed with turpentine and a No. 6 hogs'-hair brush. It is best to leave the painting for a day or two before continuing. This will allow it to dry completely. When it is dry, the overpainting is worked up using small touches of colour mixed with painting medium. Smaller hogs'-hair brushes and sable or nylon flats are used for the whole of the overpainting.

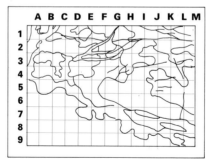

The guideline sketch on its grid. See pp. 226–7 for instructions.

See pp. 226–7 for instructions.

1 Underpainting the bank
After you have pencilled in the broad areas of tone, start to under- paint the bank. Use turpentine to mix your paints. For the deep shadow area mix Burnt Sienna, Permanent Rose, and Winsor Blue to a dark brown colour and paint in the whole triangular section with the No. 6 hogs'-hair.

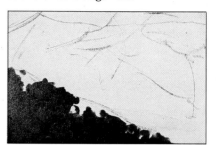

2 The background colours
Use your dark brown colour for the tree trunk in the top left-hand corner. Then with a clean brush mix Burnt Sienna, Winsor Green, and Titanium White to the dark green colour immedi- ately above the bank. Paint this along the top edge of the brown and use the same colour for the top right-hand corner of canvas. Mix a lighter green colour us- ing Transparent Gold Ochre, Winsor Green, and Titanium White, and paint the shape that extends from the bank to the left centre, and up to the top of the painting. Use the same colour below the dark green area in the top right-hand corner. Next add a little of this colour to Titanium White and a touch of Winsor Blue for the light blue-green shapes next to the colour you have just applied.

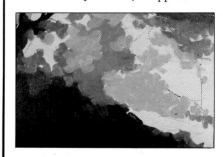

3 Finishing the underpainting

First paint in the gap above the bank on the right. The lightest tone here is a mix made from Titanium White and Winsor Blue, while the slightly darker tone is the same mix with a touch of Burnt Sienna and Permanent Rose. With a clean brush mix Titanium White with a little Cadmium Yellow Pale for the lightest tones of all. These conceal the rest of the ground colour and complete the underpainting. You will find that it is much easier to continue with the details of the overpainting if you leave the picture for a day or two to allow it to dry out completely.

4 The tree branches

Now start to mix your oil paint with painting medium to give a workable consistency. Start the overpainting by putting in the branches of the tree. Use a mix made of Burnt Sienna and Winsor Blue and apply the paint with the No. 2 round or the rigger.

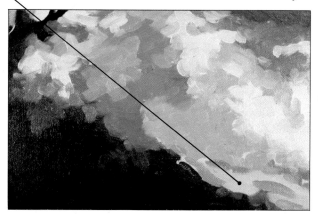
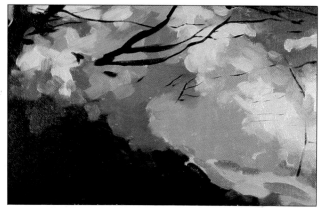

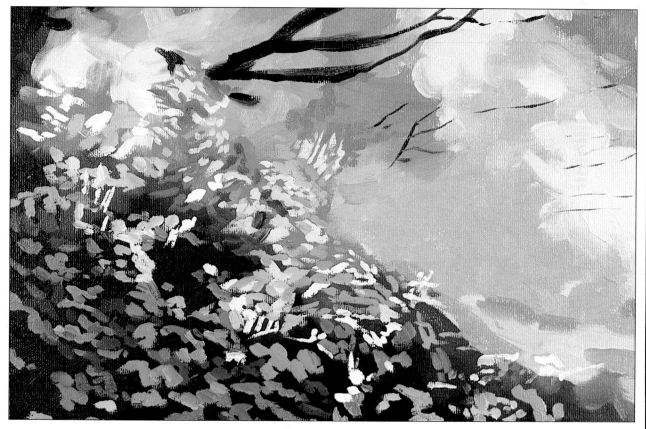

5 The details of the bank

Pick out the detailing on the bank using your two No. 4 pointed flats, one for the lighter and one for the darker tones. Use the following colours: Transparent Gold Ochre, Cadmium Yellow Pale, Titanium White, Manganese Blue, and Winsor Green. The dark brown of the underpainting will hold together the range of colours you have superimposed. The main colours are a range of blue-greens mixed from these colours. Since they are in shadow, they should all be quite dark in tone. For the line of foliage running down the bank that catches the light, you should incorporate some red-orange colours, for which you will have to add Winsor Red to your range of paints.

Continued over

6 Adding the highlights

Next, working from the top of the painting down, add the white high-lights. Using absolutely clean brushes, dab Titanium White on to the under-painting in those areas where it is light in tone; add one or two touches in the dark areas too. The effect of this is to open out the composition, introducing space and distance to it. Continue this process with a slightly darker mix of Cadmium Yellow Pale and Titanium White and then add a touch of Winsor Green, continuing to add touches of colour to the lightest areas. This will break up the large underpainted areas with small touches of pigment in various colours and tones. The underpainting will hold together all the separate patches of colour, giving the painting unity.

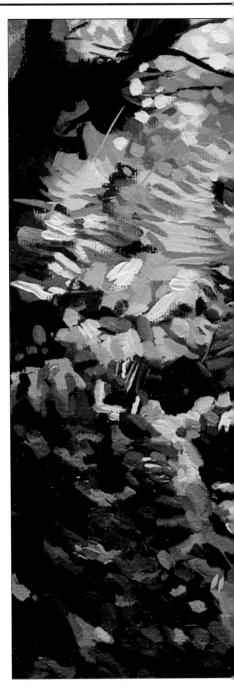

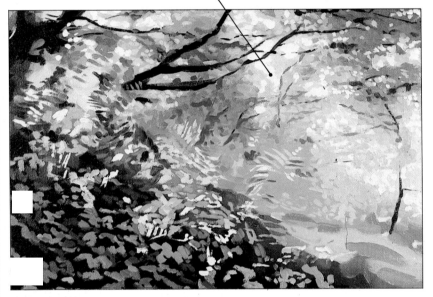

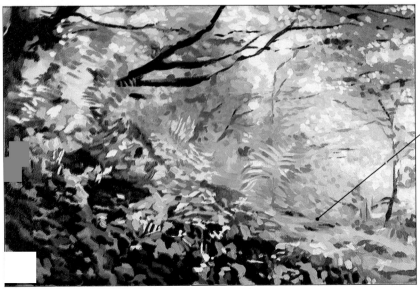

7 Building up the foliage

As well as the very light yellows and greens, there are pure, very light blues (Manganese Blue plus Titanium White), various blue-greens (Manganese Blue, Titanium White, and Winsor Green), and darker yellow-greens (Cadmium Yellow Pale plus Winsor Green). Work round the painting, building up a mosaic of these colours that echoes the effect of the light shining on the foliage.

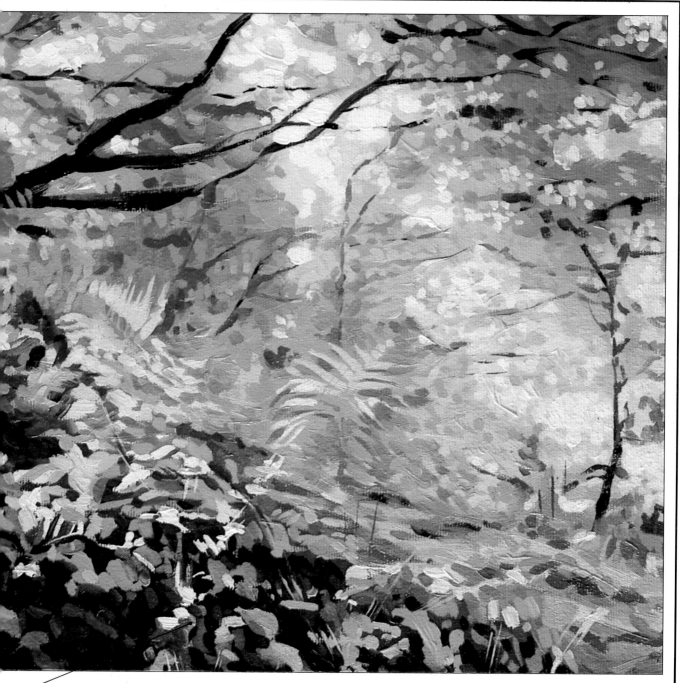

8 Refining the foreground

Turn your attention once more to the foreground and give the area the overall continuity of tone and surface that it needs. At this stage its tonal transitions are still rather abrupt. Make them more subtle by applying dabs of intermediate tone between dark and light areas. Make sure that you also soften the orange-red colours in the foreground at this stage. This process continues the move from solid blocks of tone in the underpainting to the more active patterns of smaller brushstrokes that replace them. Keep your colours clean. Since you are working "wet-in-wet" you will only be able to apply one stroke at a time before wiping your brush and starting again.

9 Making the final adjustments

If you have overpainted any of the white highlights in the picture, you should replace them at this stage. In addition use the thin side of one of the No. 4 sable or nylon flats to add a few plant stems in the foreground. This should give some sense of movement to the ferns on the bank.

FRUIT

Media WATERCOLOURS or COLOURED PENCILS

THESE SIMPLE EXERCISES show how the juxtaposition of two complementary colours has the effect of making each look more vivid than it would on its own or when set against another colour. I have taken a "magenta-red" pepper, an orange, and a lemon and incorporated the complementary colour of each into the shadow cast by the fruit. I chose fruit for these pictures because they have simple shapes that give you practice in modelling, and so that, if you wish, you can make your studies from life.

Artists have long recognised that placing complementary colours close to each other is a particularly useful technique for creating optical effects and for enlivening and enhancing the colours in a painting. Although these pictures show only primary and secondary colours, it is worth pointing out that every colour, however light or dark and however intense, is complemented by an opposite colour of equal tone and intensity. So for practical purposes you can apply the effects of complementary colours just as well to soft and subtle colours as to loud, dramatic ones.

For the exercises to be as effective as possible, you should match the true primary and secondary colours as closely as you can. But you will be at the mercy of your materials manufacturer in this respect, so for the drawn versions especially, your colours will probably have to be approximations.

Before you make the painted versions, it is helpful to experiment with the effects of colour juxtaposition in simple drawings. Make a chart in which you contrast each piece of fruit with its own complementary and also with those of its neighbours. You will be able to make your own colour comparisons.

The watercolour studies present more finished versions of these images. The enhanced colour effects are clearer, because the colours you use are more controlled and better balanced, with only two colours used for each image.

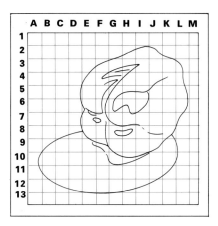

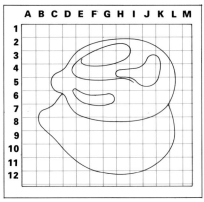

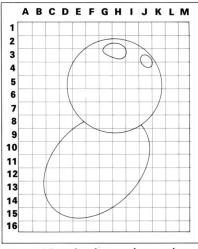

The guideline sketches on their grids. See pp. 226–7 for instructions.

MATERIALS AND EQUIPMENT

Watercolour version
Support
Three small sheets of rough-surface watercolour paper (e.g. 185 gsm or 90 lb weight)

Watercolour paints

Cadmium Red

Winsor Blue

Cadmium Yellow Pale

Winsor Green

Permanent Rose

Brushes
No. 7 and two No. 4 sable rounds

Other items
HB pencil

Drawn version
Support
NOT surface drawing paper A4 size ($11\frac{3}{4} \times 8\frac{1}{4}$ ins/29.7 × 21 cm)

Coloured crayons
One darker and one lighter tone of: Red, Orange, Blue, Violet, Green, Yellow

Other items
HB pencil

METHODS
For the drawing, coloured pencils are used. Two tones of each colour are required, for drawing the lighter and darker areas of each fruit. When all the fruits are completed, the shadows are added beneath.

For the watercolour studies the form and tone of each fruit is built up in a series of washes of the same colour, finishing with an overall wash. In the case of the orange and lemon, surface texture is then added by pulling a brush of dry paint across the surface of the paper. The final step is to paint in the shadows, again using several washes of the same colour.

CRAYON VERSION

1 Drawing the peppers
First divide your paper into nine equal squares and draw in lightly the outlines of the fruit. Arrange them in vertical rows. Then sketch in the dark red tones of the peppers. Next sketch in the lighter tones on the peppers and then start to paint the darker tones of the other fruit.

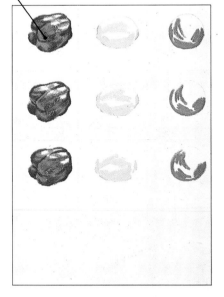

2 Drawing the other fruit
Continue to draw the lemons and oranges, putting in all the darker tones before filling in with the lighter ones. In each case, you should leave a little white paper showing through at the top right of the fruit. This represents a highlight.

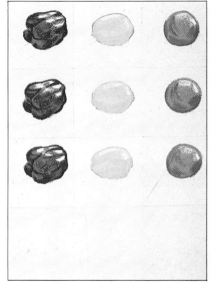

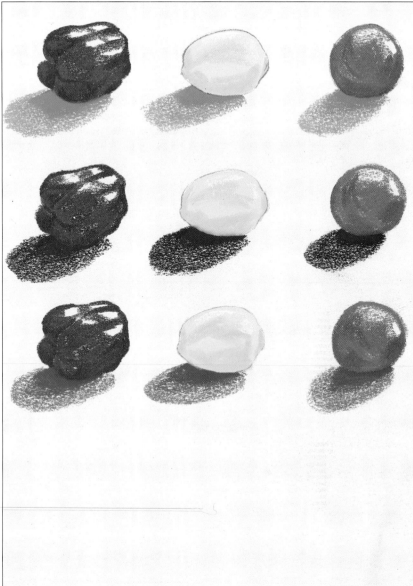

3 Putting in the shadows
Underneath the top three pieces of fruit draw a green shadow. Under the next row shade in violet and under the bottom row shade in blue. If you wish, you can lightly shade round the whole image in a lighter tone of the colour used for the shadow. Compare the effects you have made. The red pepper should look most vivid against the green, the lemon against the violet, and the orange against the blue.

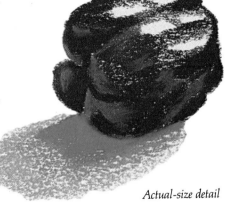

Actual-size detail

WATERCOLOUR VERSION

1 Starting to paint the orange
First draw the shape of the orange faintly. Fill the No. 7 sable with water and paint the whole shape of the fruit, taking off any excess water with your brush. The whole orange should be damp but not too wet when you apply the colour. Mix Cadmium Yellow Pale with Cadmium Red until you have a deep orange. This is the colour for all the painting of the orange. Using a No. 4 sable, paint round the sides and bottom edges and faintly around the top, allowing the paint to run with the dampness of the surface. Do not put too much colour on your brush. If you find the paint is running into areas where the highlight should be, take it out with the clean No. 4 sable while it is still wet. Touch the central part of the orange with the brush where the tones are deep and then let the orange dry.

2 Repainting the orange
When the orange is completely dry, repaint it with the No. 7 sable using clear water. Do this gently and smoothly. If you scrub the water too fiercely into the surface, you will affect

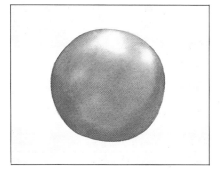

the layer of paint you have just dried. When the fruit is damp give it an overall orange wash, leaving out the two highlights as you paint and keeping any paint out of these areas with a clean, slightly damp sable. Let the orange dry.

3 The pitted surface
To give an idea of the surface of the orange, load the No. 7 brush with fairly dry paint and pull it very lightly across the darkest areas at a very shallow angle to the paper. This will allow the ridges of the rough grain of the paper to pick up the paint, giving the right kind of surface texture to the orange. Then clean your brushes thoroughly and change your water when you have done this.

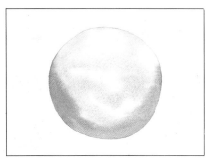

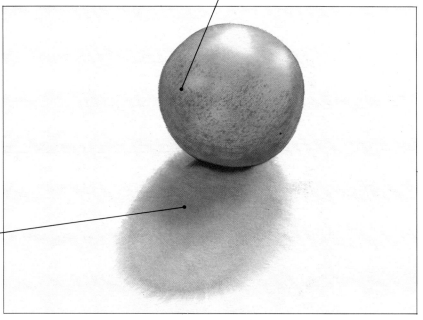

4 Painting the shadow
Use Winsor Blue on its own for the shadow. Apply a little clean water under the base of the orange and then use a No. 4 sable to paint a fairly deep Winsor Blue tone around the bottom edge, allowing the paint to run down into the shadow area. Dry this thoroughly and then wet another larger area under the orange into which you paint a slightly thinner blue with the larger brush, allowing the edges to soften into the damp paper. Let this dry. Finally, wet the area again and paint in another slightly darker elliptical shape immediately below the base of the orange. You should let the edges soften as before.

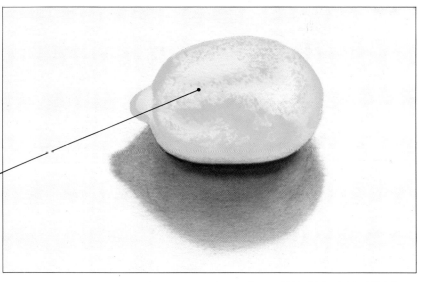

5 Painting the lemon
The method is exactly the same for the lemon as it is for the orange, except that the colours used are Cadmium Yellow Pale for the fruit itself and a mixture of Winsor Blue and Permanent Rose for the shadow.

6 Sketching the pepper

The pepper is a more complex shape than the other two fruits, but by the time you come to paint it, your experience with the other two fruits will enable you to tackle it successfully. When drawing in the outlines, do so as lightly as possible. If you do this, both colours and paper will look purer when you come to the painting.

7 Starting to paint the pepper

Next dampen the shape of the pepper with clean water, so that all the paint applied within will have soft edges. It is important that this shape should be no more than damp when you apply the colour, since your first areas of colour will be smaller than those on the orange and lemon. Here there are four bulbous shapes on the left to which you have to give dimension by the correct application of colour. Use one No. 4 sable with Permanent Rose for the painting, keeping the shapes in control with the other sable, which you should keep clean and damp. Dry this thoroughly before you build up tone and shape following the same method as with the other fruits, overpainting until you reach a point where you feel that the form of the pepper is defined.

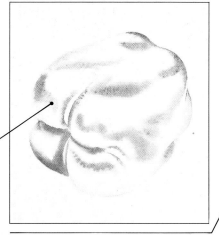

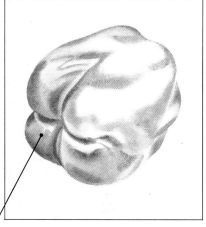

8 Applying the pink wash

Next give the pepper an overall pink wash. Before this dries, pick out the highlights by dabbing the appropriate areas with cotton buds or small plugs of absorbent paper. You will find that you have to do this two or three times until the area is dry enough not to let any more paint run into the highlighted areas. Because the surface of the pepper is quite smooth it is not necessary for you to apply any textured effects as you did in the case of the orange and the lemon.

9 Painting the shadow

When the pepper is thoroughly dry, you should paint the shadow. Use the same method as for the orange and lemon, but use a mix of Cadmium Yellow Pale and Winsor Green.

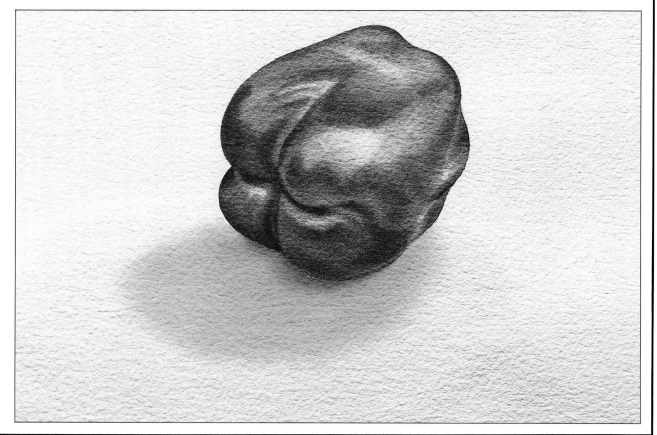

ROSE

Medium OILS

THIS OIL PAINTING demonstrates the use of a black and white underpainting over which transparent coloured glazes are applied. The rose is much larger than life, so the modelling does not have to be too intricate. The lower leaves do not necessarily have to be painted in as much detail as they are here.

For this technique, the underpainting, and especially the highlights, must have considerable body to work with glazes. Many manufacturers produce a special "underpainting white" which is recommended for such techniques. Painting coloured glazes over a monochrome underpainting is a system of working which can produce a very resonant painting. Its methodical nature may not appeal to everyone, but it has been a successful method for centuries. One aspect of the method is that it enables you to concentrate on accuracy of form and tone before thinking about colour. This is very useful if you find it difficult to judge tone correctly when you start to paint with a wide range of colours. You can ensure that your image is accurate far more easily by painting it monochromatically first, and then "colouring" it. Your grey tones can be the result of mixing white with black, or you can use any colour provided that you are aware of the effect of glazing a colour over it. If you want to check the effect of a certain transparent glaze, try out different coloured sheets of cellophane or gelatine over your underpaintings.

MATERIALS AND EQUIPMENT

Support
Canvas or board 16 × 12 ins
(40.5 × 30.5 cm)

Oil colours

Winsor Blue	Transparent Gold Ochre	
Manganese Blue	Permanent Rose	
Winsor Green	Underpainting White	
Burnt Sienna		

Brushes
No. 6 and two No. 4 hogs'-hair filberts, No. 4 sable round, No. 6 badger blender or shaving brush, sable fan blender (optional), large soft sable or nylon round

Other items
Turpentine, painting medium (see p. 10)

METHOD
First the canvas or board is tinted and the guidelines sketched. Then the rose petal highlights and darker tones are painted in to provide a tone guide for the underpainting. The rose and leaves are then painted in opaque body colour and the separate tones blended in. Careful attention must be paid to uniformity of light and tone over the whole painting. The underpainting must be dry before the glazes are applied. If oil paint is used, this means leaving the painting for a day or two at the midway stage. The next stage is to apply the correct colour by glazing. The painting is placed on a flat surface and the glaze is mixed to the right consistency. The glaze is painted over the whole area to be in that colour. A badger blender is used to smooth and blend the surface to make the surface uniform.

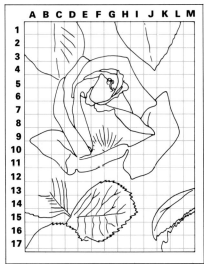

The guideline sketch on its grid. See pp. 226–7 for instructions.

1 The sketch
Tint your canvas or board with Manganese Blue and let it dry. Then draw in the outline of the rose according to the guidelines provided.

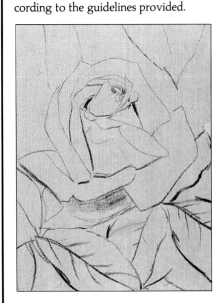

2 The petal highlights
Use Underpainting White with your No. 3 hogs'-hair to sketch the highlights in the rose petals. Dilute the paint with turpentine for the less bright parts of the flower. It helps to squeeze excess paint from the brush with absorbent paper. This is because you are not filling the canvas with paint, but merely providing a tone guide for the real underpainting. You may need to use a smaller sable for the highlights in the central part of the rose.

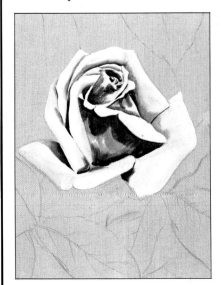

3 The darker tones

Mix Burnt Sienna with Winsor Blue and turpentine for the darkest tones, using a thinner mixture for the less dark ones. Keep as closely as possible to the tones and shapes shown, and work up the leaves.

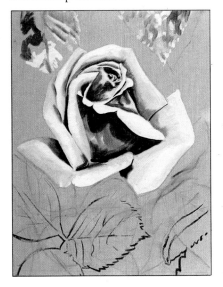

4 The underpainting technique

Now paint the rose completely in opaque body colour mixed only with turpentine. Make the pigment densest at the highlights. Work on a small section at a time, for example a single petal. You should begin with the lightest tones and move towards the darker ones by mixing Underpainting White with the Winsor Blue-Burnt Sienna mix. Paint in the separate tones side by side and then blend them together by stroking along the join with a wiped-off brush. Don't be tempted to rush this part of the painting.

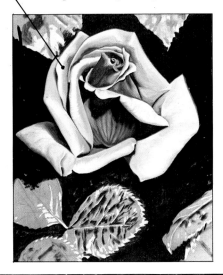

5 The individual petals

Each petal will take some time to complete, and as you move from one to the next you should be aware of the overall look of the flower so that you achieve uniformity of light and tone over the whole image. Make the darkest tones as dark as I have painted them, and if you lose tone depth when you are blending, you should always repaint the area to the strength of tone required. This also applies to the white highlights, which may lose a little of their whiteness during the process of blending. If this happens you should reinforce them with pure white pigment.

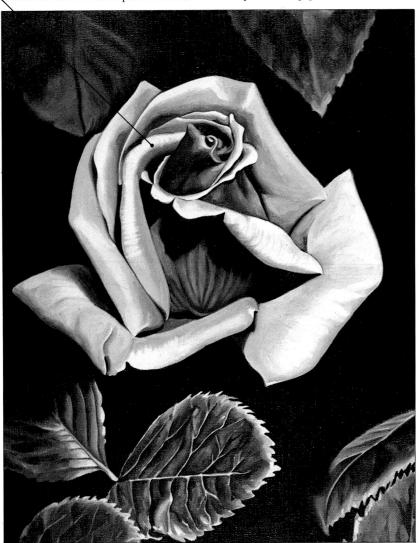

6 The background

The background is a mix of Winsor Blue and Burnt Sienna, and you should apply it with a No. 4 hogs'-hair. Paint up to the jagged sawtooth edges of the leaves. Use a small sable brush for this intricate work.

7 The top leaves

Repaint the top leaves, deepening their tones so that they recede into the background. There should be little definition, and you should blend tonal contours well.

8 The lower leaves

For the lower leaves, especially the central one, there is a lot more definition, so use small sable brushes to pick out detailing such as the veins. Pick these out in white and they will provide a useful framework that allows you to tackle the leaf section by section. Each segment between the veins has its own three-dimensional qualities, and the process of painting them is the same as for each petal, except that the sections are smaller and need smaller brushes.

Continued over

9 The glazing process
Make sure your underpainting is completely dry before you apply the coloured glazes. For the glazing process you should place the canvas in a flat, horizontal position — on a table, for example. The most important points about glazing are to get the mixture of paint and medium to the right consistency and to build up the glaze in thin layers. If this is the first time you have tried glazing, you may try to mix too little paint in the painting medium. This will mean that your mixture will be too runny and difficult to control. Beginners often feel that all their careful underpainting will be obliterated if the mixture is not thin. In fact, this is not so. A feature of glazes is that they can, to a large extent, be manipulated on the painting itself, to the density you require. Also, if you work entirely with transparent colours, your underpainting will inevitably show through.

10 Glazing the flower
Use single colours for the rose, leaves, and background. For the flower, mix Permanent Rose with the painting medium to a soft mushy consistency. Paint this over the flower with a large, soft round sable or nylon brush. You can paint over the edges since the background is so dark and will also be repainted later. Colour the whole area and don't worry about unsightly brushstrokes or ridges of paint. Cover the flower, but don't overload it with paint when you do this.

11 Smoothing and blending
Now use a dry badger blender brush (or a shaving brush) to smooth or blend the glaze by dabbing it gently over the surface. Work across and down the shape. If the brush gets clogged up with excess paint, dab it on to an absorbent kitchen towel to remove the excess paint. This is easier than cleaning and drying the brush. The badger blender will have the effect of removing all the ridges of paint and making the whole surface of the glaze a uniform tone. If you want a deeper-toned glaze, you can use the sable fan blender brush instead of the badger to dust the surface to a uniform density. This brush will remove less glaze.

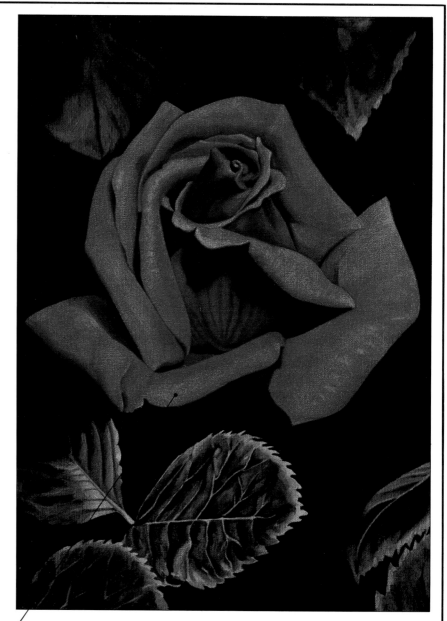

12 Lightening the glaze
At this point your rose should resemble the one in the finished painting. If you wish you can lighten the glaze over the highlights by stroking them with a small, dry sable. This will pick up paint and lighten the colour in these areas.

13 Glazing the leaves
For the leaves, mix Transparent Gold Ochre with the painting medium and add a little Winsor Green to the same consistency as for the rose. Paint this in the same way and smooth it with the badger blender.

14 The background
For the background, mix Winsor Blue and Burnt Sienna to the same consistency. Paint up to the sawtooth edges of the leaves, and any other intricate edges, with a small round sable. Paint in the rest of the background with a larger sable. Leave the painting to dry thoroughly.

THE ELEMENTS OF PICTURE-MAKING

LINE

LINE IS THE BASIS of all picture-making. When, as young children, we use crayons for the first time, we make a linear journey over the paper, producing an apparently random series of lines. These very quickly turn into zigzag patterns that correspond to the natural swing of the arm from the elbow, or circular patterns that use the movement of the whole arm from the shoulder. Such patterns reveal a natural spontaneity and fluency of gesture that adult artists have to work hard to achieve.

The next important stage is the discovery of outline, when children begin to impose boundaries on the chaos of the world around them. Very often their first explorations of outline drawing show embryonic tadpole shapes with eyes and mouths added. Later, arms and legs are included, as an unending series of permutations on the human figure is explored. These drawings usually have carefully defined outlines which are in turn filled with exuberant, chaotic scribbling.

Children use line with natural fluency, but there is another, more controlled way of working with line. This is the use of line as diagram. Both children and adults use diagrammatic conventions for representing particular features of the world around them. At the simplest level, a child will use a triangle for a girl's body and a rectangle for a boy's. Such conventions are continually modified as the young artist observes and assimilates new material. What they do — and this is an aspect of the economy of line — is to enable young artists to say what they want to say in a picture much more quickly than if they had to start afresh each time. They work out new diagrammatic conventions for each new situation that arises, and this enables them to make immediate and highly perceptive drawings of the world they inhabit. These drawings may show no attempt to reproduce the actual shapes of things. They show line in its analytical and objective role — used as a way of recording the contours of an object. And they reveal a great deal of intuition and keen observation that goes beyond mere resemblance.

THE NATURE OF LINE

One of the most important aspects of line — and one that is especially clear in the drawings of children — is its fluent and expressive nature when used as a natural extension of hand and arm movement. In children, decisiveness and lack of hesitation in the use of line generate a freedom and fluency that can give their line drawings real strength. For children this comes naturally; for adults it has to be relearnt. One way of recreating the effects of immediacy is to repeat a line or gesture many times until one finally emerges that really works successfully.

Allied to the idea of fluency is that of economy. A single line, as children understand, can represent a complex object. It is important to know when one line will be enough, and to keep your drawings simple, without a slavish dependence on truth to appearances. Both these things, often obvious to children, must be relearnt by the mature artist.

Another feature of the child's use of line is the unselfconsciousness with which children can set up a unique and credible representation of their experience of the world. Their evident commitment to what the pencil is doing exists because, for young children, drawing is a natural activity. For most people, the process of education and growing up distances them from this innate skill and introduces the selfconsciousness that prevents them from giving true expression to their ideas and feelings. By looking at the drawings and paintings of children, we can remind ourselves of the truly unselfconscious condition to which most artists aspire. As Picasso said, "It took me a lifetime to learn to draw like them".

TREES IN CHARCOAL

The first tree study (below) shows a loose, flowing use of line, with twigs curling up like ribbons across the paper. This use of line gives the image an active and dynamic feel. The main stems were drawn with thick charcoal, pushing it up along the line of the central stem with a single movement. The thinner lines were drawn with correspondingly thinner charcoal, holding it flat on the horizontal and pushing it along the paper in a quick, vigorous movement. The hand was lifted at the end of the stroke, to make the line thinner and lighter. The method of drawing the very thin, light twigs was to hold a complete stick of thin charcoal at the end furthest from the drawing tip and to make light strokes back towards the branches. All these charcoal strokes were made quickly and confidently.

The second tree study (bottom) is much tighter and more tense. The lines of the charcoal are like short, heavy punches, giving a solid character to the drawing. The main branches, as before, were made by pushing the charcoal up the paper. Here a heavy staccato action was used, in an angular, rather than flowing, curve. Medium-sized charcoal was used towards the head of the tree, and thin charcoal at its extremities. The whole drawing comprises short, stabbing strokes of the charcoal, echoing the scrubby, angular feel of both tree and land. I used a rubber to "shave" the curve of the top of the tree, and to reinforce the dynamic line that runs from the base of the tree towards the left, up, round, and out at the top right.

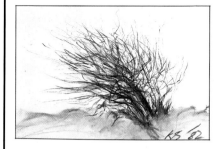

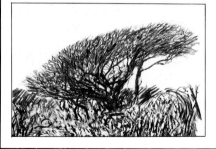

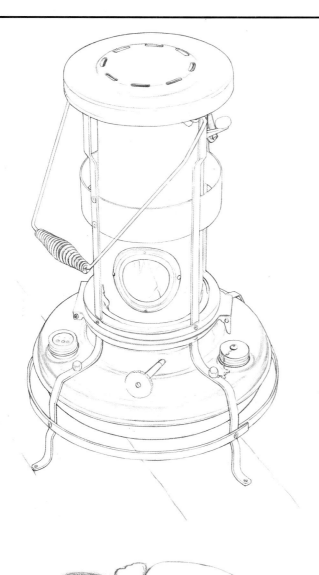

STUDIO HEATER

This drawing was made by working carefully and precisely with a pencil. It shows how you can use line to draw a three-dimensional object with precision. Making this type of drawing normally involves a lot of very soft, rough pencil work before the defining lines begin to emerge. You gradually erase the rough drawing, and redraw the thin, clear outline with a sharp pencil. The varying thickness and density of this line helps to define the object clearly and give it more character.

If you want to make your own version of this drawing, begin softly and carefully, using the pencil quite blunt. Work from square to square on your grid, until the various elliptical shapes reveal themselves, allowing you to draw them as complete curves. For the straight lines, use a ruler to draw them in softly so that you can redraw them freehand later.

As you start to redraw the lines with a sharpened pencil, some edges are more clearly defined than others. For example, the outline around the top of the heater is quite sharp and dark at the back where it is silhouetted against the floor, while its counterpart at the front is very much softer. This distinction works for the whole drawing: a more clearly defined edge has a stronger outline than a less defined one.

NUDE

Drawing the human body is an excellent way to explore the special qualities of line. The body's gentle contours can find expression in the soft curves of pencil or charcoal. This simple example will present no great difficulties in transcribing on to your paper if you use the grid system – there are no tricky fingers or toes to draw in. But it is not simply a question of putting the lines in the right place. It is the feel of the line that must be right if the drawing is to succeed.

The model had curled up on top of a number of large cushions and, having made a nest, went to sleep. The lines had to reflect the feel of sinking into the cushions, and the gently arching curves of the buttock, side, and calf. I also wanted to show something of the vulnerability expressed in the pose.

If you copy the drawing, begin with the central triangle of legs, arm, and back. Then work down towards the feet and up towards the head. This way you will be starting with the main structure. Work softly with the pencil at first. Gradually, as your lines emerge, make them crisp and fluent with the sharp edge of an eraser. You may have to do a fair amount of drawing, erasing, and redrawing to get the main contours of the figure right.

LINE PORTRAITS

Heads make good subjects for line drawings. If you want to practise with various media, but lack the confidence to work with a model, work from your own reflection or from a photograph. A simple, strong line drawing of a head can be just as effective as a tightly worked realistic treatment. It often takes thirty or forty attempts to get an image that really works. If you make such a series of drawings, put them aside for a day or two – you will often fail to recognise a good drawing when you make it.

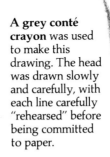

A grey conté crayon was used to make this drawing. The head was drawn slowly and carefully, with each line carefully "rehearsed" before being committed to paper.

The quality of line given by charcoal is demonstrated by this drawing (above). It ranges from dense, vigorous strokes to much softer, light-toned lines. The darker line implies a greater tonal contrast between areas on either side of it than the lighter line.

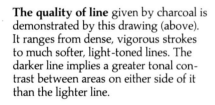

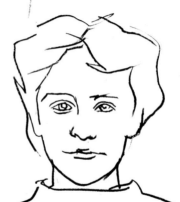

These two drawings demonstrate different approaches to the same image. Both were made with a chinagraph pencil, but one shows a bold and free use of line (left), while the other (above) uses a more precise and gentle approach.

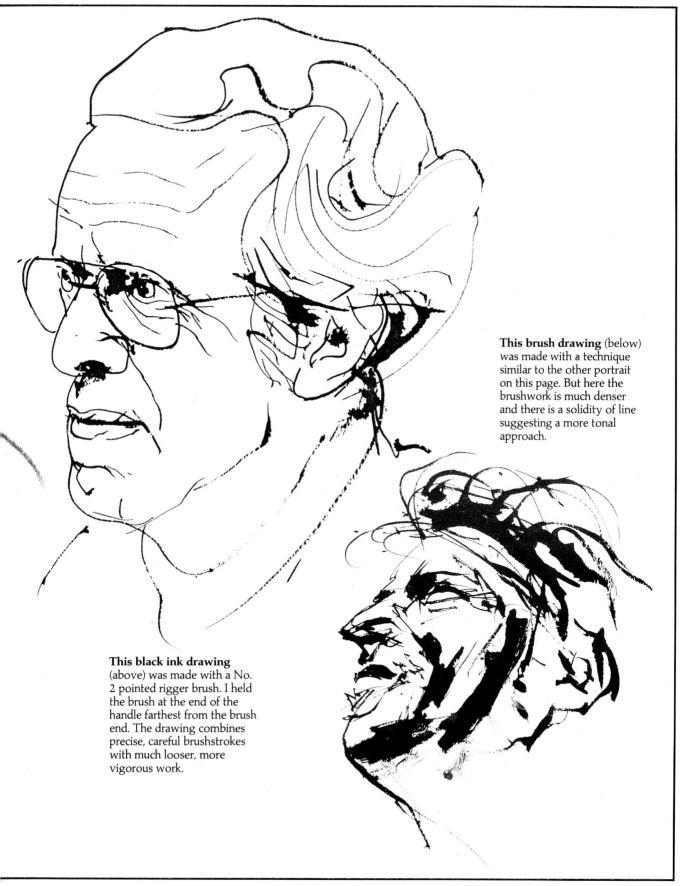

This brush drawing (below) was made with a technique similar to the other portrait on this page. But here the brushwork is much denser and there is a solidity of line suggesting a more tonal approach.

This black ink drawing (above) was made with a No. 2 pointed rigger brush. I held the brush at the end of the handle farthest from the brush end. The drawing combines precise, careful brushstrokes with much looser, more vigorous work.

TONE

ALL THE EXERCISES in the Black and White Techniques section were connected in some way with tone. The tree paintings (see pp. 20–3) showed how you can create a gradation of tone from light to dark, exploring the tonal variation that occurs in the sky from light at the horizon to a much deeper tone above. The cloud studies (see pp. 24–9) showed that, however formless clouds may appear to be, with their lack of well defined contours, you can give them dimension by applying the tones correctly. The tonal landscape (see pp. 30–2) demonstrated how the atmosphere softens the tones of the countryside as the land recedes towards the horizon — an effect known as aerial perspective. And the last four black and white exercises (see pp. 33–50) showed, with objects of varying complexity, how it is tone that accurately defines form in particular lighting conditions.

Accurate representation of tonal values is vital for the success of any painting that sets out to recreate the three-dimensional reality of what you see. Whereas line provides a kind of diagrammatic shorthand, tone gives body and form to your subject.

LIGHT AND TONE

Objects appear to be intrinsically light and dark — I have dark hair and pale skin. But it is the effect of light striking objects that creates the tones we want to represent in paintings. As I write, light from a lamp falls on to one side of my face, and the other side is in darkness. In these shadows there is little tonal difference between my hair and my skin. When the light is very bright, tonal contrasts are accentuated, giving light, bright shapes and dark shadows. Objects in intense sunlight have a harsh clarity, and their colour is bleached out by the light. In soft, uniform light, on the other hand, a whole range of half tones is revealed, and because the tonal contrasts are not so glaring, you have to look harder for them and to beware of confusing colour with tone. To see tonal values more accurately, you can try half-closing your eyes while looking at a scene. Blurring the focus a little will remove confusing details and enable you to see the differences between tones.

It is useful to compare images in black and white and colour. If you have a colour television, try turning the colour right down, so you can compare a black and white image of the same subject with a colour one. You will be considerably more aware of the fine distinctions of tone while watching in black and white than you are when the colour is turned up. Subjects in black and white seem clearer and more resolved and therefore easier to represent than they do in colour.

Subdued lighting conditions give the most resolved experiences of tone. This is because in these conditions we are using the rod cells in the retina, rather than the cone cells, and it is the latter that distinguish colour. There have been schools of painters who have exploited such subdued lighting, creating the so-called "tenebrist" paintings that exploit the atmospheric effects that tone can produce in low light.

You can try making experiments with tone by turning almost all your house lights off at night. A single lamp or candle can produce a wide variety of very dramatic tonal effects if you put it in different places. Art schools often use black mirrors (to make similar effects) for exercises in tonal drawing. If you look at your reflection in a train window at night, you will see the same sort of tonal image.

TONE AND ATMOSPHERE

This charcoal drawing (opposite, top) shows how the use of broad, simple areas of tone can convey a particular atmosphere. It shows a view looking forward at the bow of a ferry boat on a very dull, grey morning. There is nothing to see all around the boat and there is nobody on deck. A morning like this might appear to offer little scope for drawing or painting, yet this sort of atmosphere can have a positive effect on a drawing. It can remove the clarity of detail, enabling the work to proceed on its own terms.

The charcoal in this drawing has been extensively "worked". It has been rubbed

USING A PAINTING KNIFE

This tonal study of a fourteenth-century eagle lectern (opposite) was made with a medium diamond painting knife. It is a satisfying, though expensive, way of working, to trowel on slabs of paint that correspond with areas of tone. Here, a solid shape emerges from the shadows and there is very little detailing, making it a good image for this technique.

The painting knife is not limited to bold and vigorous slashes of pigment, though it is very good at these. You can also use it with great sensitivity and precision, depending very much on the way you hold it. For a bold touch, grip the handle firmly. For a lighter touch, hold it like the bow of a violin, with the four fingers on one edge and the thumb counterbalancing them on the other. The tip of the blade can be controlled for fine work by holding the knife at the metal stem — you should press the wooden handle against the back of the palm, leaving the index finger free to push the blade up and down. This technique was used for the dots of white on the shield.

After sketching in the eagle's shape on a grey-toned ground, the method for this painting was to work from light to dark tones. With a painting knife you can mix tones on the painting itself and transitions from light to dark were made by mixing loosely on the palette and applying the paint with bold sweeps of the knife, to give the streaked effect. The painting knife is also useful for applying a pure new tone over an old wet one. This must be done with one confident stroke of the knife, which should be wiped off after each stroke.

in with the fingers, erased, and redrawn until the overall effect seemed right. The structure of the drawing, with the chevron shape of the bow and upper deck forging towards the strong horizontal of the horizon, helps to contain the soft shapes and surface of the charcoal within a rigid composition. The central vertical of the small mast on the bow, with its echo on deck, also has an important compositional role. As well as bisecting the drawing, it links the ship to the sea and sky, and helps to emphasise the ship's forward movement. The thin white line that represents the lower two-thirds of the mast and the edge of the hull and the deck were picked out using the sharp edge of a plastic eraser.

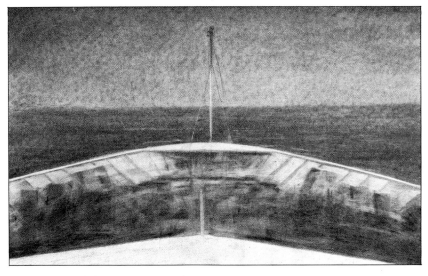

TONE AND SPATIAL QUALITY

The main tonal contrast in this charcoal drawing of a lion in the Musée Cluny (below) is between the figure and the ground. The drawing shows how one dark, almost flat area can enclose a lighter one and project it towards the observer. It is tone that pushes the stone lion into the foreground and gives the drawing its spatial feel. It shows a very controlled use of charcoal, which is worked heavily in the background and lightly in the foreground to show the crumbling relief of the stone. Once the contours of the lion were lightly sketched in, the surface was worked on from left to right. This ensured that there was no smudging to interfere with the sharp-edged clarity of the lion shape.

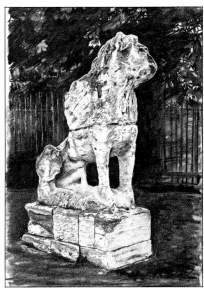

TONE AND COLOUR

In most paintings tone is linked closely to colour. The painting of dancers (below and bottom) is concerned with the effects of light and shade particularly in the areas of spotlit and secondary lighting, in the shadows of the dancers, and in the surrounding areas of shadow. It therefore relies heavily on the correct use of tone. And yet it is a kaleidoscope of colour, without which it would lose much of its atmosphere. The picture demonstrates how tone and colour usually work together in a painting so that, unless you are working monochromatically, it is impossible to consider one without taking the other into account.

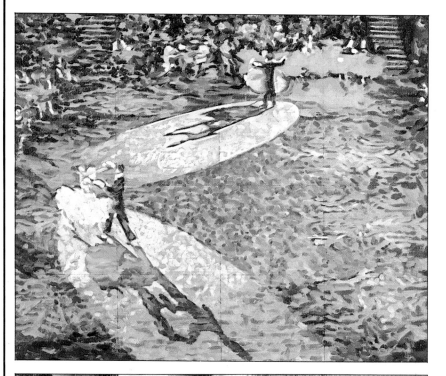

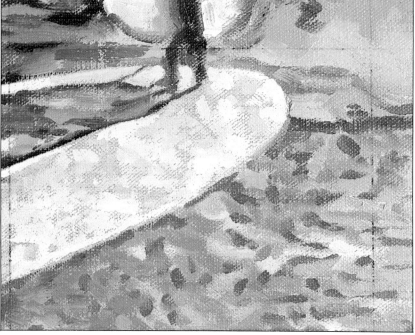

LINE AS TONE

This pencil sketch (opposite) shows how line can build up areas of tone. There are no single outlines—the forms are defined by cross-hatching. The main source of light comes from a window to the right of the drawing, but it reflects off a white wall on the other side of the room, providing secondary illumination, in particular to the right-hand side of the girl's face.

Although it would be possible to make a convincing outline drawing of this subject, the tonal treatment adds greatly to the atmosphere, especially to the figure of the mother who is almost entirely in shadow. The gentle atmosphere is reflected in the tonal range, which extends from white to mid grey with no dark grey or black tones.

In a drawing of this kind, there are areas, such as the heads and hand, that should be worked more intensively than others. Here you can miniaturise your technique—but it must be the same technique that you use elsewhere in the drawing. If you use a different method there will be no uniformity and no easy passage from one area to another. Where the cross-hatching is bolder you can make lively pencil marks to give the drawing a sense of activity.

This pencil drawing (below) shows the effect of strong side lighting on the tones of the subject's face. It turns her pale skin on the left into a very dark tone indeed. Tonal modelling is more apparent in the shadows than it is on the right-hand side of the face, where the strong light flattens the contours. The drawing was made on mould-made pure rag paper with a NOT finish.

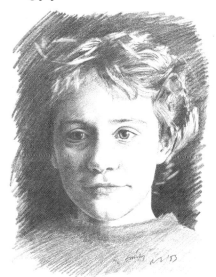

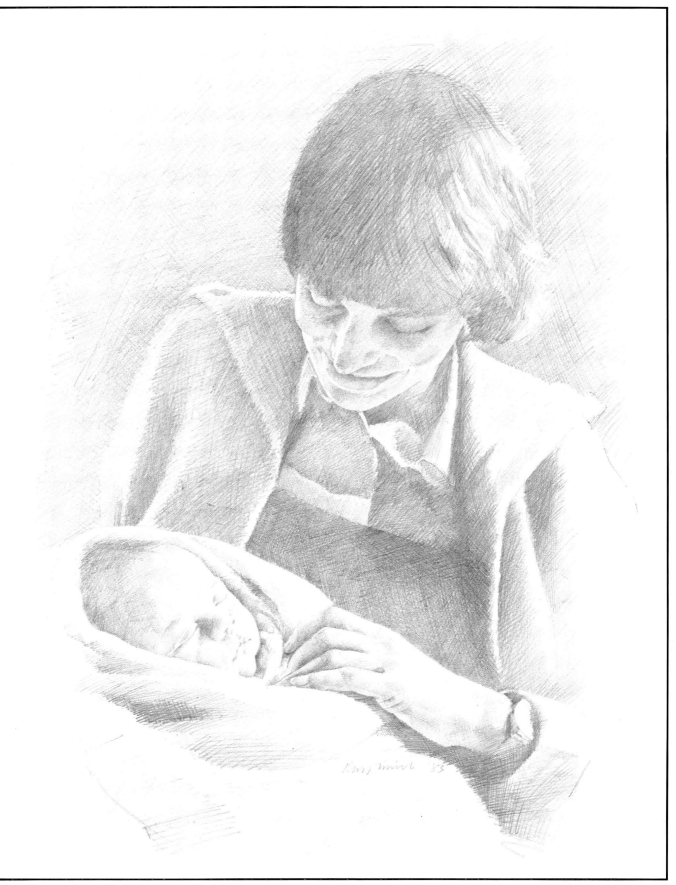

COLOUR

THERE IS NO COLOUR without light. Our perception of colour is entirely determined by the effect of light on the things that surround us. When rays of light strike the objects in front of us their effect produces a visual stimulus. This is what, as artists, we are concerned to represent.

The three primary colours of light are orange-red, green, and blue-violet. If you set up three white-light projectors, each with a coloured filter over the lens that corresponds to one of these colours, and direct the beams on to the same white surface, the combination of the three colours will produce white. This is known as additive colour mixing. Each time you *add* light you increase the intensity or brightness of the colour. But if you switch off the blue-violet beam and direct the red and green beams on to the same spot you will produce yellow. This yellow will be brighter than either the green or the red because it is made from two lights rather than one. Similarly, a combination of the blue-violet and orange-red lights will produce magenta, while green and blue-violet light will give cyan.

These three colours — yellow, magenta, and cyan — are the additive secondary colours. But as far as mixing pigments is concerned, they are the *primary* colours. This type of mixing is known as subtractive colour mixing, because by adding pigments together less light is reflected back to the eye. With the addition of pigment, light is increasingly absorbed into, or subtracted by, the pigment. So a combination of the three primary pigment colours will produce black, a colour in which almost all the incident light has been absorbed or subtracted. By adding yellow to magenta you make orange-red, by adding cyan to magenta you make blue-violet, and with yellow and cyan you make green. These three colours — green, orange-red, and blue-violet — are the subtractive secondary colours.

For artists, the subtractive mixing of pigments seems more important than the additive mixing of light. But we are continually observing the effect of white light on surfaces that absorb one or more of its primary constituents, and it is a useful exercise to work out which colours are being absorbed and which reflected. A yellow car, for example, would be absorbing most of the blue-violet light. It would be reflecting the green and red light, the two colours that additively produce the colour yellow. The blue-violet part of the light is the colour that represents the most complete contrast to yellow. Yellow and blue-violet are described as complementary colours, as are green and magenta, and red-orange and cyan. The combination of each pair of complementaries in light produces white. When you combine a pair of complementary colours in pigment, however, you produce black.

Complementary colours, therefore, create a satisfying balance. The colour we see is balanced or completed by the absorption of its complementary colour from the light source that illuminates it. There is a similar balance of opposites in adjacent lights and shadows. Here, a warm light has the effect of inducing cold complementary colours in its shadows and the reverse of this is also true.

The influence of adjacent complementary colours on the eye is very important for the artist. The optical effects of placing complementaries side by side can determine the liveliness and harmony of a painting. If the adjacent areas are large enough, the contrast between the two complementary colours can be enlivened. On the other hand, the contrast can be denied where small adjacent touches of complementary colours combine optically to form neutral greys. Such colour relationships, which extend beyond the complementaries to the influence of any colour on any other, are of course fundamental to the art of painting. They are dealt with in practical terms in every colour painting included in this book.

MIXING OIL COLOURS

For this oil paint chart (opposite) I used the primary colours, red, yellow, and blue. The specific colours were Winsor Red, Indian Yellow, and Winsor Blue, but you could use any similar set of colours. Cadmium Red, and Azo or Hansa Yellow could be substituted, though it is best to keep to a phthalocyanine blue (see p. 12), since it provides a very pure pigment for mixing.

The three primary colours have been mixed into their secondary and tertiary combinations. Each colour has been mixed with the painting medium to a creamy consistency, applied and further diluted to show it as a thin transparent wash. It has also been mixed with Titanium White as a light-toned, opaque colour. This particular chart, of course, presents only a very small number of the possible colours that can be mixed from these three basic ones. If you took many more stages to move from one colour to the next you would increase the range considerably.

Many colour combinations (below) produce mixes similar to commercially available colours. You can make most of the colours you will need with three basic pigments plus white.

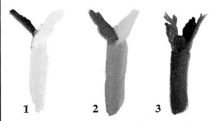

1 Winsor Green plus Cadmium Yellow Pale gives a similar green to Cadmium Green Pale. **2** Winsor Red plus Cadmium Yellow Pale gives a similar orange to Cadmium Orange. **3** Permanent Rose plus Winsor Blue gives a transparent magenta colour.

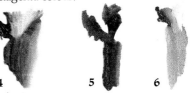

4 Winsor Green plus Transparent Gold Ochre gives a transparent green similar to Sap Green. **5** Winsor Blue plus Burnt Sienna gives a very similar colour to Burnt Umber. **6** Transparent Gold Ochre plus Titanium White gives a similar colour to Yellow Ochre.

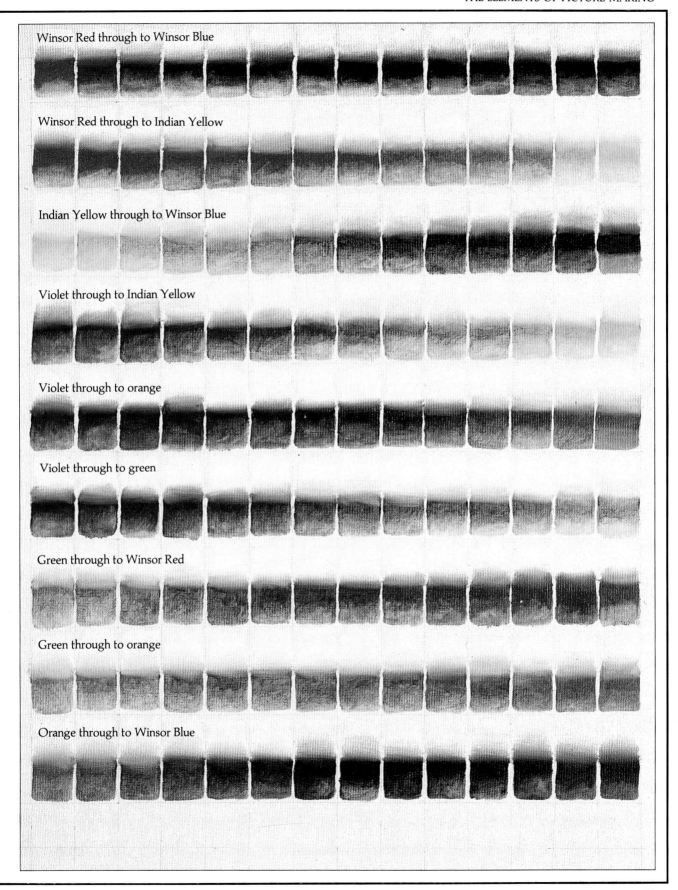

Winsor Red through to Winsor Blue

Winsor Red through to Indian Yellow

Indian Yellow through to Winsor Blue

Violet through to Indian Yellow

Violet through to orange

Violet through to green

Green through to Winsor Red

Green through to orange

Orange through to Winsor Blue

LAYING ACRYLIC WASHES

This chart shows the effect of overlaying thin washes of three tones of red, blue, and yellow acrylic paint. It shows the colour mixing that occurs as you superimpose transparent layers of pure colour. Although there are only two layers of paint on the white watercolour paper, you can see clearly how different effects are obtained with lighter or darker tones, and when one colour is laid on another.

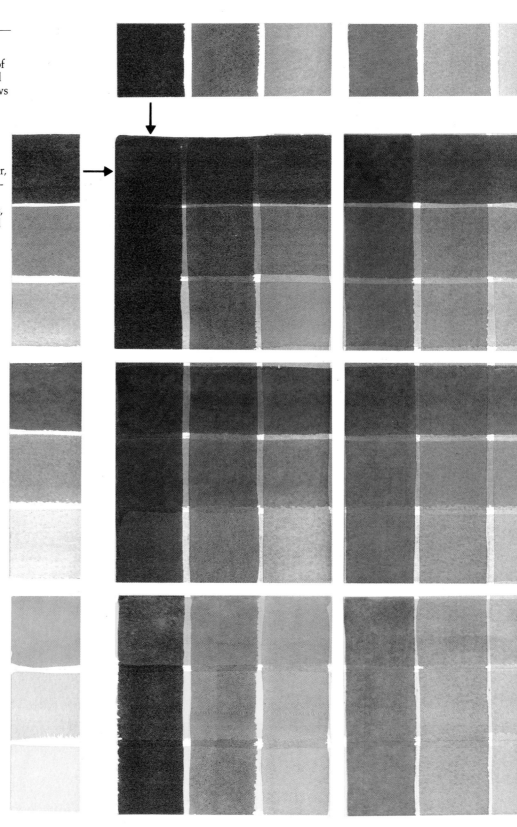

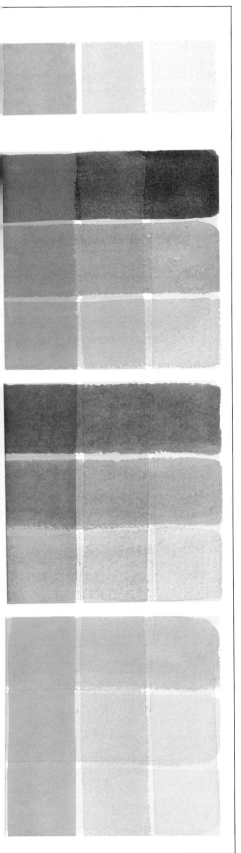

THE EFFECT OF LIGHT ON A PAINTING

Since it is light, and not any intrinsic colour, that enables us to see a painting, we should be aware of the effect of light on the surface of the painting itself. Paint consists of insoluble particles of pigment dispersed or suspended in a vehicle or medium. The medium, which can take many forms, binds the pigment together and attaches it to the painting ground. The pigment particles may be distributed thinly within the medium, so that the ground is visible through the paint, as in the case of transparent glazing techniques. In this case, the extent to which the rays of incident light are refracted will depend on the refractive index of the medium. They will become less intense, but they will also give the appearance of a deep luminous colour. But if the paint is used opaquely, less light is absorbed and more is reflected from the surface of the pigment particles. The colour appears light as a result.

HUE, VALUE, AND CHROMA

There are three ways of defining or attempting to measure the appearance of particular pigments. Firstly, you can assess the hue, that is the basic colour of the pigment in terms of its position in the colour spectrum. Secondly, you can speak of its value, in other words how light or dark it is in relation to the light that illuminates it. Thirdly, you can refer to its chroma or saturation. This is the degree of intensity of the colour itself, whether it is full of colour (fully saturated) or whether it is mixed with white, or made more transparent as a tint, or made mixed with black as a shade.

MIXING COLOURS

It is said that the better an artist is, the more limited his palette. It is certainly true that it is generally superfluous to acquire a huge range of pigments — most colours can be mixed from just a few. These charts show you the range of mixes you can make from a small number of colours. You will find this information particularly useful when making some of the paintings in this book, since I have deliberately limited the palette in certain cases.

Many artists rely on paint manufacturers to provide their colours ready-mixed. This saves time, but there are benefits in mixing particular colours. This is especially true during the early stages of learning the craft of painting. Mixing colours helps you towards a deep and practical understanding of colour and leads to a very real control in making the colour that precisely fits your need.

If you use these charts in conjunction with the written guidelines to the paintings in this book, remember that any of the colours mixed here can be mixed again with each other to produce yet more combinations. So if a colour is described but does not appear directly on the charts, find one that is close to it and choose another which, when added to it, will give you the nearest result. In other words, you should use the charts with a little flexibility.

COMBINING ACRYLIC COLOURS

This acrylic colour chart demonstrates clearly the wide range of colours you can make by mixing from a very limited palette. In this case, four colours were used: Cadmium Red, Azo Yellow, Phthalo Blue, and Sap Green. The reason that

I added Sap Green to the three primary colours was that the combination of Azo Yellow and Phthalo Blue produces a rather cool secondary green. This is not sufficiently intense for the purposes of colour mixing.

Cadmium Red   Phthalo Blue   Azo Yellow   Sap Green

Cadmium Red through to Phthalo Blue

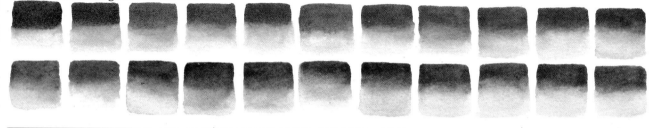

Phthalo Blue through to Azo Yellow

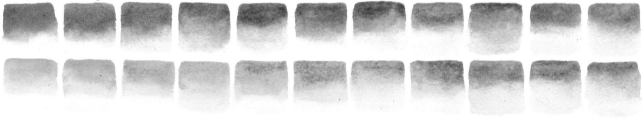

Azo Yellow through to Cadmium Red

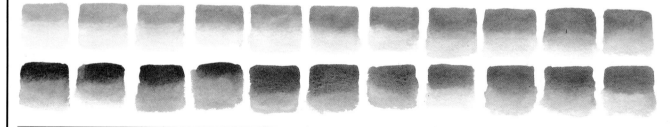

Orange through to Sap Green

Orange through to violet

Orange through to Phthalo Blue

Violet through to Azo Yellow

Violet through to Sap Green

Sap Green through to Cadmium Red

Sap Green through to Phthalo Blue

Sap Green through to Azo Yellow

Brown through to Phthalo Blue

Brown through to Azo Yellow

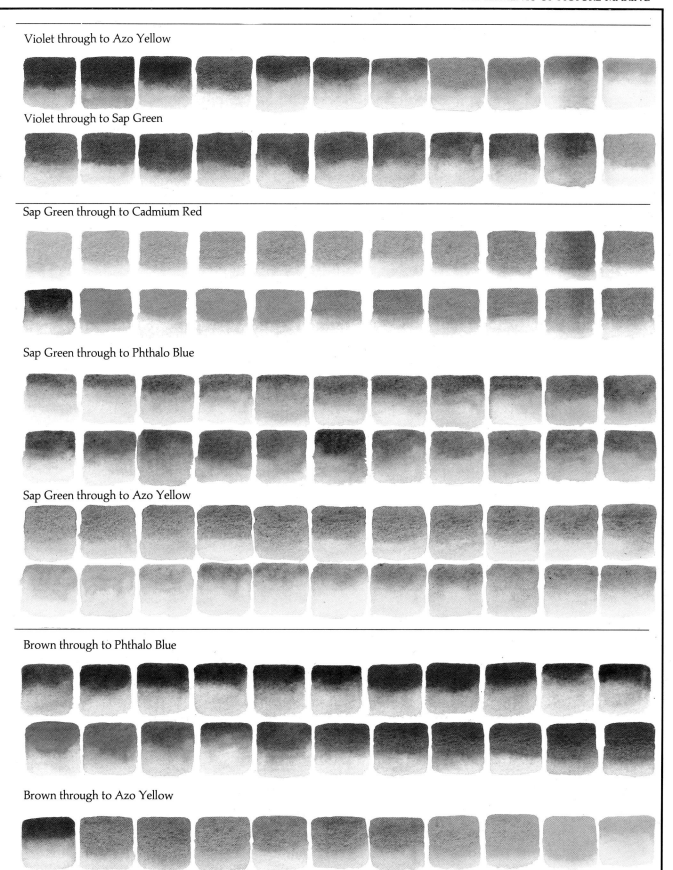

COMPOSITION AND PROPORTION

THE FIRST CRUCIAL decision to make when you are organising the composition of a painting is the ratio between the height and width of the canvas. Traditionally there are three picture formats, known as "portrait", "landscape", and "seascape". The portrait format is the one in which the height is greater than the width, and for the landscape format, the ratio is the other way round. In the seascape format the proportion of width to height is greater than for landscape. There are conventional sizes within these formats that are useful to the manufacturers of prepared canvases as a way of standardising production. But you can paint on whatever size canvas you like.

For a conventional single head-and-shoulders portrait or a full-length seated figure, the traditional ratio of height to width in the portrait format is a useful guide. The other two formats also provide useful guidelines on which you can base your compositions. The traditional horizontal landscape usually needs a rectangle that is less square than the one you would get by turning the portrait shape on its side. The seascape, often with a less obstructed horizon line, requires a proportion that suits a more panoramic view.

But broadly speaking, the ratio of height to width — especially if you are preparing your own canvases — will depend on the size and arrangement of your particular subject. For example, if you want to make a painting of eight carriages of a train seen from the side, your canvas should, very properly, be a long, thin, one. You can work on any shape that attracts you, and there are many painters who have worked very successfully on canvases of quite irregular shape. Although most of this work lies outside the scope of this book, it does demonstrate how positive a flexible approach can be.

If you have determined the precise shape and size of the canvas in order to accommodate a particular subject, the composition, in the sense of the arrangement of the subject matter, has already established itself. But when you are working on a standard-size canvas, you must adapt the composition to suit the proportions of the canvas. There is a wide range of alternative approaches to this problem. The first is simply to follow your instincts: if it looks right and feels right, then it probably is right. On the other hand, you may find it difficult to get a result that looks right. In this case, if you are working with a fixed subject such as a landscape, try changing your own position by taking a higher or lower point of view. By cutting a rectangular hole in a piece of card to the scale of your canvas and holding this at arm's length, you can try out the various alternative angles to see which seems the most effective. Try moving away from your subject or further in towards it. There may be some elements that disturb a potentially harmonious composition, in which case you can leave them out of the painting altogether.

DIVIDING UP THE CANVAS

A successful composition stems from the artist's ability to see the subject in broad terms, cutting out all the incidental detail in order to recognise the structural framework that holds it together. It is for this reason that a geometric approach to the problem is often recommended. This is a method whereby the artist experiments with a mathematical way of dividing up the rectangle of the painting. The Golden Section (or Golden Mean) is one well known method of dividing the canvas in a way that suggests harmonious proportions, and of producing a point of visual focus. If you take drawing paper with you that you have divided up according to the Golden Section, you can experiment with a method of composition that has, for centuries, provided artists with a useful guide to the harmonious arrangement of forms.

WORKING OUT THE GOLDEN SECTION

The Golden Section, which provides a pleasing way of dividing up a composition, is quite easy to work out. All you need is a ruler and a set square.

First stage To find the Golden Section for a given length (AB), first measure this distance and mark the mid point (C). Then from B draw a line up at right-angles to AB, and make a mark at point D, so that the distance BD is equal to the distance BC.

Second stage Now draw a line to join A and D. Then measure along AD from D the same distance as BD, and mark a point (E). The distances BC, BD, and DE will all be equal.

Third stage Next measure the distance AE, and mark a point (F) on the line AB at the same distance from A. The distances AE and AF will be equal.

Fourth stage Drop lines down at right-angles from A, F, and B. On the lines from the points A and B measure the distance AF, to give two points (G and H). These will mark the bottom corners of your rectangle. Measure the distance FB on the lines AG and BH, to give the points K and J. Joining KJ will give the Golden Section point L where this line crosses the line FI.

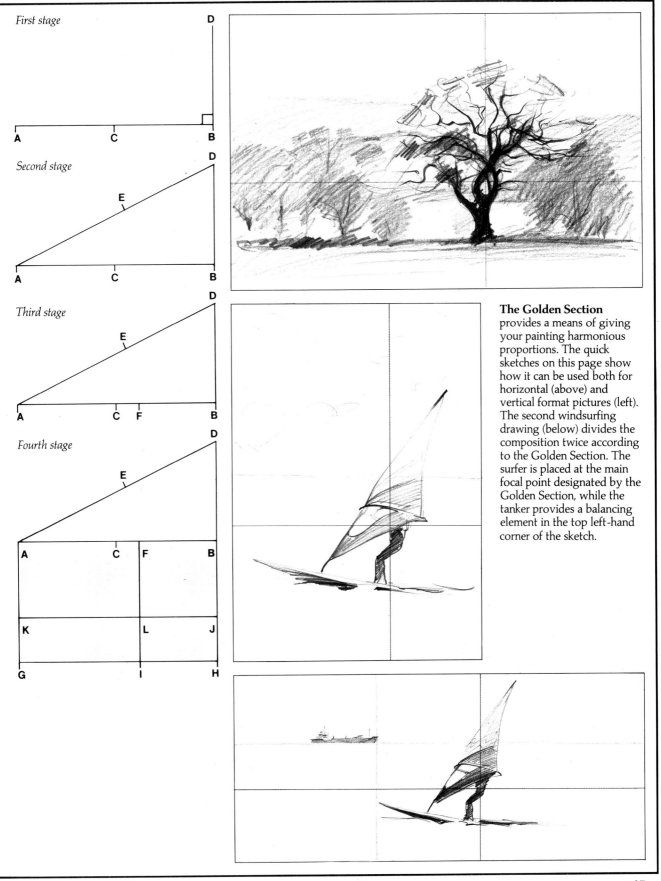

First stage

Second stage

Third stage

Fourth stage

The Golden Section provides a means of giving your painting harmonious proportions. The quick sketches on this page show how it can be used both for horizontal (above) and vertical format pictures (left). The second windsurfing drawing (below) divides the composition twice according to the Golden Section. The surfer is placed at the main focal point designated by the Golden Section, while the tanker provides a balancing element in the top left-hand corner of the sketch.

Another possibility is to work around simple geometric shapes, such as triangles, diamonds, and diagonals, which you have previously drawn on to your paper. If you are working in the landscape, you should aim to find imagery that sits happily within the framework you have devised. This is an interesting approach, but it is one that may prevent you from drawing what you actually want. If, on the other hand, you are setting up your own subject, as in a studio still life, you are free to move all the elements around.

Such methods make interesting and useful exercises in exploring the many ways in which you can divide up the canvas. But they do have a kind of abstract geometry as their starting point and this is often difficult to relate to the real world. This is because there is a large gap between a two-dimensional diagram and the three-dimensional complexity of the world itself. It could be said that by making your subject conform to an arbitrary set of geometrical rules, you are denying the richer possibilities for composition that the subject itself might suggest. But you can avoid this conflict if you neither stick rigidly to the rules, nor ignore them completely.

Another method of arriving at an understanding of the essential features of a composition is to learn by example, working from illustrations of paintings you admire. By laying tracing paper over them you can sketch in the main lines of their composition, working out the relationships between their forms.

For very large-scale paintings with a complex arrangement of forms such as a large number of figures, it is always necessary to make detailed compositional studies. You should then piece these together on a complex compositional grid. There is no other way of setting up and sustaining the credibility of such a complex painting without a great deal of compositional groundwork and experience. It would be absurd to embark on a large-scale task of this sort without working out on paper the problems of composition.

For smaller-scale paintings — a vase of flowers or a head-and-shoulders portrait, for instance — the problems of a major composition do not arise. There are, of course, angles to sort out, backgrounds to select, and colour relationships to assess. But these are the details of a composition that is, as a whole, predetermined, and you can usually get by without extensive compositional diagrams. But the composition is still important — it is often what tells the spectator which particular point you are making. If, for example, you filled your frame with a vase of flowers, your painting would be accepted as concentrating on the flowers themselves, particularly their form and colour. But if you put the vase on a shelf in one corner of a canvas that also depicts a wall with stained and torn old wallpaper, you will make a different point, one that relies for its effect on the way you have devised the composition.

OPEN AND CLOSED COMPOSITIONS

Another important decision you should make is whether to produce an open or a closed composition. Imagine the rectangle of the canvas as an enclosed space. The contents, like the fish in an aquarium (see pp. 130–5) can travel to the edges, but can go no further. You would call this a *closed* composition. This type of composition — more common than any other in easel painting — is one in which all the contents of the picture are designed to operate only within the area of the canvas.

But if you imagine the rectangle of the picture frame superimposed on a subject that clearly extends beyond the boundaries of the canvas, this would be called an *open* composition. An open composition exists when what we see on the canvas is clearly part of something larger that extends beyond the frame. If you were to cut a small rectangular hole out of a piece of card and hold it arbitrarily at arm's length, you would probably be looking at an open composition. Most paintings would be open compositions if the artist did not artfully compose them in ways that discourage the eye from travelling outside the area of the painting, giving the effect that we are looking at something complete that sits snugly within the bounds of the canvas.

A FRAME WITHIN THE FRAME

The small crayon drawing made in the insect house of a zoo (opposite page) illustrates quite dramatically the features of a closed composition. The boundaries of the drawing coincide with the sides of the container. The drawing was made from a photograph taken with flash lighting and the flash reflects off the front of the tank and off each of its

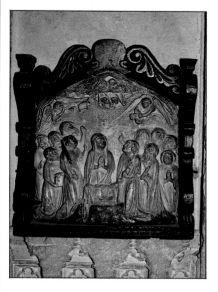

There is no reason, apart from convention, why artists should not explore open compositions. There are some excellent historical examples, such as this medieval carving from Wells Cathedral (above). In this example, the figure of the ascending Christ has already risen half-way out of the horizontal top edge of the carving. All the movement in the composition is upwards with the pointing hands and upraised heads. The platform, with its indented footmarks, creates a link through the carving to Christ's feet. Such a composition is all the more exciting for being unusual.

edges. This has the effect of making you more aware of the transparent glass surface which coincides with the surface of the paper. The shadows of the twig define the space inside the tank, making us aware of the confined space.

Although the subject of this drawing is unconventional and takes the idea of closed composition to its limits, you will see how similar it is in formal arrangement to a subject like a vase of flowers. If you substituted a vase for the cotton wool at the base of the stem and

flowers for the twig, then removed the sides of the tank, you would have a perfectly traditional closed composition.

The drawing was made with coloured pencils on good quality drawing paper with a hot-pressed surface. If you want to make a version of this drawing you should start by drawing the outlines of the image with a pencil. Use a ruler for the edges of the tank and surround, but modify these straight edges afterwards by working freehand. The twig need not be completely accurate – you can draw

your own freehand version. The method of shading is to work from top left to bottom right (or top right to bottom left if you are left-handed) making adjustments as you work your way down. All the shading is diagonal and reflects the natural movement of your wrist. Do not dig into the paper with the first strokes of the coloured pencil, but build up tone with layers of shading. These layers may be in one colour, or you can overshade in different colours to get the effect you want.

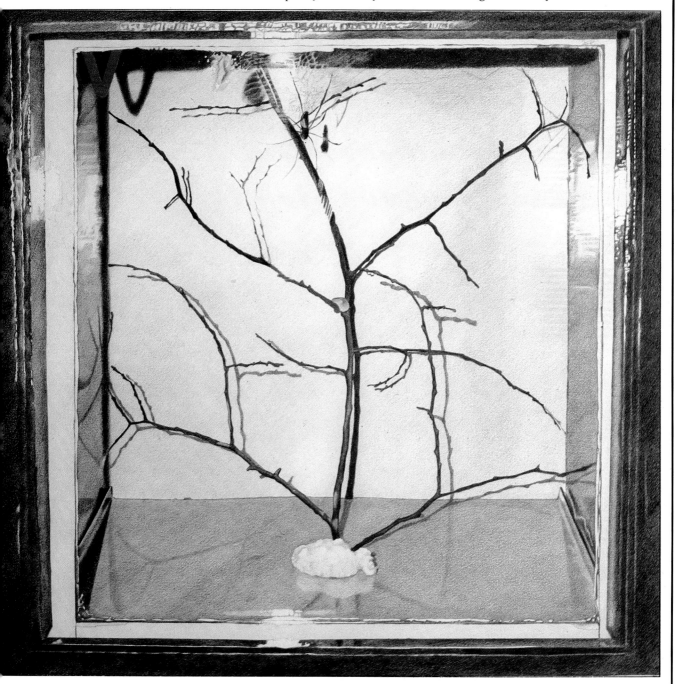

SCALE

WE CAN DESCRIBE every object we see in terms of its size. But objects in themselves have no scale — they can only be small-scale or large-scale in relation to something else. For example, huge ocean-going oil tankers look tiny when they are steaming along the horizon but enormous when you are standing on the quay below them at the docks. The scale of the tankers is perceived in terms of size relative to distance.

A familiar use of scale is in map-making. We talk of the scale of a map as being, for example, one inch to the mile or one centimetre to the kilometre. Maps represent the relative size of the features of the countryside diagrammatically by means of scale. When the countryside is scaled down in this way to put it on a map, you can see it as a whole — the vast size of the country has been made intelligible. When you do the same thing on canvas in the form of a painting, the effect is similar. By means of scale, the painter tries to create order and understanding out of the chaos of the visible world.

Every time you make a painting, you have to decide on its size in relation to the objects depicted. For example, if you paint a cup and saucer on a canvas 10 ins (25 cm) square the scale of the painting will be appropriate to the subject. But if you paint the same subject on a canvas 10 ft (3 m) square the transformation in scale will give the cup quite a different character. Its huge presence even transforms the scale of the spectators, who may be forced to reconsider their view of the subject by this new situation. (This is, in a sense, the effect all good paintings have — though not necessarily in such a dramatic and obvious way — of shifting and modifying our view of objects so that we can see them with the shock of fresh recognition.)

The scale of the painting itself should be appropriate in some way to the subject. But the scale of the various features within the painting should also be appropriate to each other. You can include small-scale figures in a large-scale painting, for example, but their relationship with each other and with their surroundings should be clear. It is this relationship that determines whether the aspects of scale have been successfully considered.

As a painter you are free to modify the scale of any subject, to increase or decrease the relative size of any part of a painting, in order to focus attention on a particular area of the work. This is no more than our eyes do when they are travelling round a room and focusing on one small part of it some distance away. If you took a photograph of the room the relative sizes of the objects it contained would be uniform. But if you looked at one of the objects alone, you would increase your awareness of that object so much that the rest of the room would diminish considerably in presence. Since painting is not like photography, the slave of the lens, you can use shifts in scale in your work to give particular parts of your subject the prominence you require.

SCALING DOWN

You will generally have to scale down the scene in front of you so that it will fit within the confines of your picture plane. When doing this you should concentrate on accurately transcribing the relative sizes of the components of the scene. You will have to be aware of the effects of perspective (see pp. 95–7). These are most visible in cities with their straight lines and right angles. If you are on a high vantage point in a city, and you look over the rooftops towards the horizon, the average height of most of the buildings will generate a flat plane. The biggest building will stand out above this plane and will appear, by comparison, especially large in scale. In medieval times, anyone approaching a city with its massive cathedral rising out of the small, huddled buildings beneath would have had this sort of experience of scale. Juxtaposing objects can enhance the effects of scale in a painting. You may,

SHOWING SCALE

This painting looks down on a rocky outcrop that towers out of the sea. The figure of the man sketching is painted to show the scale of the rocks that surround him. When doing the preparatory charcoal drawings for this painting (opposite, above and centre) I experimented with placing figures in different positions. Finding the correct position is not the only problem you face when incorporating a tiny figure in a composition that features large, bold shapes. There is a danger that the treatment of one will not tie in with the other. In particular, there often is a temptation to paint the figure too realistically using very small brushes. Unless you give the rocks the same painstaking attention, the painting will look unresolved since there must be an element of uniformity in the overall surface of the painting for it to work as a complete image. In the finished painting

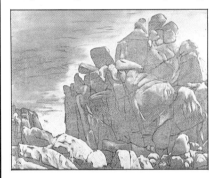

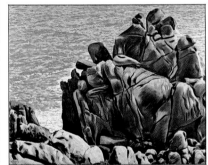

(below) the figure is painted more minutely than the rocks, but the difference is not great enough to seem odd. A similar problem arises with the sea, where a treatment that was too minute could undermine the style of the rocks. Like the figure, the sea is painted quite economically with bold strokes of the brush.

The method for this painting was to tint the background and draw in the outline. Then highlights were added to the rocks using the paint more thickly for the lightest tones and thinning it down where they were lighter (opposite, centre). Then the dark tones were added in a similar way and the area of the sea was painted in (opposite, bottom). When the rocks were dry they were overpainted with quite thick pigment using small hogs'-hair brushes. A mix of Transparent Gold Ochre, Burnt Sienna, Winsor Green, and Titanium White was used. The under-painting gave a guide to form and

tone—where the rocks are in deep shadow the tonal variations are quite subtle. In the places where the rocks are in sunlight, I enlivened their surface by adding Winsor Red and Cadmium Yellow Pale to the palette. I used bold brushstrokes and mixed the colours loosely so that some of the individual strokes are made up of two or three separate colours.

The figure was painted in thick colour using a small round sable. I dampened the brush first in the painting medium, wiped it off, and then used it like a trowel, scooping up colour from the palette and applying it in flat strokes with the paintbrush at a shallow angle to the canvas. If you want to make a version of this painting you may have a little difficulty in getting the figure to look right. You should practise copying it on scraps of cardboard before adding it to your painting. Even if you do make a mistake, it is easy to scrape the paint off with a painting knife and start again.

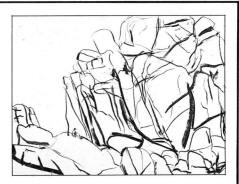

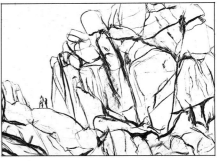

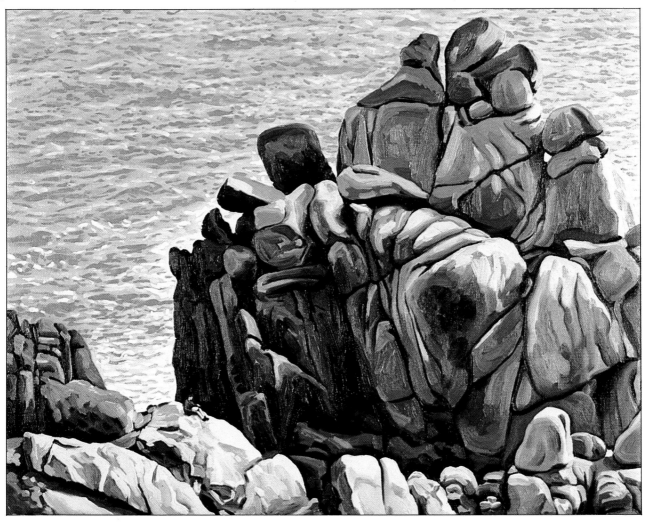

for example, be painting the huge boulders at the foot of a sea cliff that rises three hundred feet above you. We have all had the experience of somehow not being able to express the scale of such a visual experience. The painting seems tame in comparison with the reality and it is not clear how far you have scaled the subject down. But introducing a tiny figure, painted to scale, on one of the boulders (it can be anything of a recognisable size that enables us to comprehend the scale of the rock face) will transform the effect of scale in the painting and help to emphasise the monumental quality of the subject. On the other hand, you may want to paint a tiny and delicate flower. Here again, without introducing an element that enables the spectator to measure the flower's scale, it will not be seen as the small and fragile object you want to portray. These objects are at opposite ends of a spectrum that applies to a greater or lesser extent to all paintings. If you are aware of these effects of scale, you can begin to incorporate them positively in your work.

SCALING UP

When you want to enlarge a drawing, sketch or photograph in order to make a larger scale work, you use the process of scaling up. The straightforward techniques (but not the effect) of scaling up are described in the section on drawing up an image (see pp. 226–7). Apart from the sheer fact that the image is larger and perhaps more imposing, the effect of scaling up is to make especially clear the nature of the marks on the canvas or paper. It puts your style under a magnifying glass and enables you to dissect and analyse as you recreate your image. It also gives you much more scope in your technical exploration of the picture, since there is now more room for manoeuvre. In short, it gives you the chance to create a richer and more telling image.

It is worth making experiments using the grid system (see pp. 226–7) on a favourite drawing or painting. Try scaling it up to the size of a wall in a bedroom, for example. If you work methodically, square by square, the painting will emerge accurate and fresh. If you are used to working on a small scale, the experience of covering large areas with bigger brushes, of inventing new textures, and using new techniques in order to get the right effect, will be very exciting. If you do not want to work on a wall, use large separate sheets of paper for each section of your grid.

By making large paintings of very small objects you can explore the effect of transforming the scale of a surface. Very small sections of things like the grain of a piece of wood fabric, or the surface of a rock form suitable subjects. This type of work will encourage you to look closely at things that might never otherwise get such scrutiny, and to develop ways of recreating them.

SCALING UP A CHILD'S DRAWIN

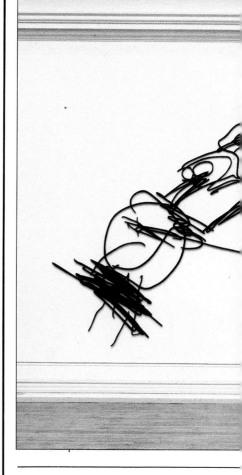

SCALING UP A LANDSCAPE

For this work I chose one of hundreds of tiny drawings in an old Italian phrase book found in a junk shop. I felt that the

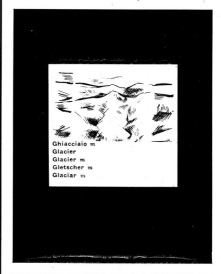

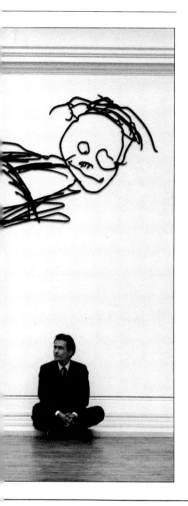

The early drawings of children show a natural fluency of expression (see p. 72). This scaled-up example focuses on this fluency. It shows how, by carefully scaling up this kind of image, we can encourage people to give it more detailed and deliberate scrutiny than it would otherwise have had. Enlarging an image in this way transforms the appearance of the original in a radical way. The light, scratchy quality of the pencil drawing becomes thicker and darker, so that a lightweight image on paper becomes a heavyweight image on the wall, looming large and sinister over the observer. But the essential framework of the child's drawing still remains.

In a work like this the choice of image and its relation to the medium of the recreation are very important. In this case I chose the original from a number of drawings my daughter had made some years before. The drawing was traced and re-worked in black ink. This was then enlarged on to plywood and the shapes cut out with an electric jigsaw.

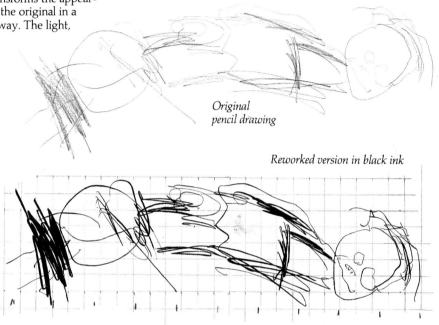

Original pencil drawing

Reworked version in black ink

drawing, showing a glacier, would be particularly effective when scaled up. The transformation makes the marks of the original more powerful in themselves. It also makes them more abstract, so that each tiny section of cross-hatching becomes a large and expressive piece of abstract calligraphy as well as being part of a complete image. The work was made in the same way as the scaled-up child's drawing, but in this case I produced a replica of the tiny original that was itself scaled-up before creating the large-scale version by cutting the shapes out of plywood.

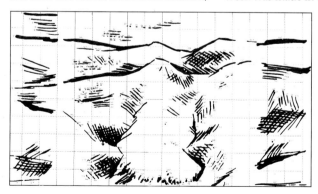

The original (opposite) was so tiny that I had to do an intermediate scaled-up version (above) before producing the final version (right).

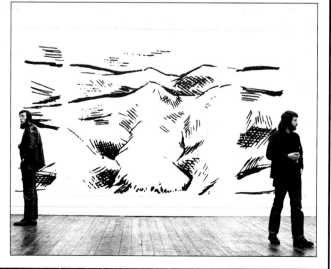

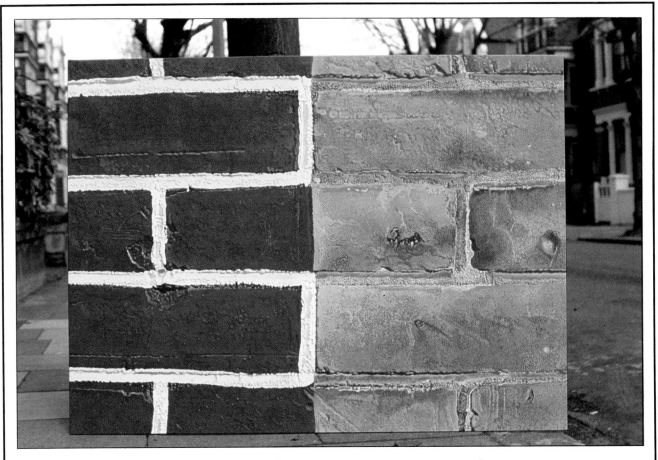

SCALING UP
FAMILIAR OBJECTS

By making large paintings of very small objects you can explore the effect of transforming the scale of a surface. Very small sections of things such as the grain of wood, a piece of fabric, or the surface of a rock form suitable subjects. Painting them will make you look really closely at things that might never otherwise get such scrutiny. You will also have the challenge of finding ways of representing these details in paint.

This acrylic painting shows the effect of transforming the scale of the surface of brickwork where two houses abut.

The painting itself is 6 ft × 4 ft 6 ins (183 × 137 cm), so each brick has been magnified to many times its normal size. This allows us to explore the complex geography of the brickwork's surface and to experience the subject in a new and unfamiliar way.

On the right, the bricks and mortar in their "natural" state show chasms, channels, and rocky outcrops, with bright sunlight creating deep, dark shadows. A shallow indentation becomes a crater and a tiny crack becomes a deep fissure. But on the left the original brickwork has been painted red and white so that the paint has created a skin that softens the sharp edges, presenting a surface that is

smoother and more bland. Because the original surface has been concealed in this way, our experience of it on this side of the painting is dulled.

The painting was made by first spraying each half of the canvas with an appropriate basic colour. Next the mortar was painted on both sides in white, and later overpainted using thin washes of acrylic colour. The next stage was to paint the details of the bricks themselves, using browns, reds, and oranges. Some overall tones were applied with an airbrush. Finally the highlights were picked out with opaque white and the surface was later modified where necessary to bring the painting to its finished state.

PERSPECTIVE

THE RULES OF linear perspective provide one method of representing on a flat surface the three-dimensional reality of the world. These rules can be particularly useful in helping the artist to solve problems of relative size, angle, and position — all you have to do is follow a series of quite simple geometric procedures. But you must remember that perspective is an artificial, mechanical system. It assumes that you are looking at your subject from a fixed point and it does not allow for the fact that we normally see with two eyes. So you should not always follow its rules to the letter.

Simple objects appear to get smaller and less clear the further away from you they are. At a basic level, perspective can help you represent this. At a more advanced level it can provide an accurate method of drawing very complex three-dimensional objects and their reflections and shadows.

THE PRINCIPLES OF PERSPECTIVE

Imagine that you are looking at a fixed object (a building, for example) through a rectangular window pane. The window pane can correspond to the surface of your painting or drawing. Rays of light from the object converge at your eye, passing through the glass at points that can be plotted. If you joined up these points you could make an accurate drawing of the object.

In perspective drawing the pane of glass is known as the *picture plane*. The base of the picture plane (the bottom of your picture) is called the *ground line*. This line also forms the nearest edge of another plane, called the *ground plane*, which travels at right angles to the picture plane towards the horizon. The *horizon line* represents the most distant edge of the ground plane and is parallel with the ground line. The height of the horizon line up the picture plane coincides with your eye level. So if you are looking from a high vantage point, the horizon line is correspondingly high.

The distance between the picture plane and your eye in front of it and the objects behind it determines the size and position of the objects in your drawing. If an object is in a fixed position, the closer the eye is to the picture plane, the smaller the object will appear in relation to the size of the picture plane. With the eye in a fixed position, the closer to the picture plane the object moves, the larger it seems.

The point that marks the position of the eye on a perspective drawing is known as the *station point* (or point of station). The point on the horizon line directly opposite the station point is called the *centre of vision*, and the line that joins these two points is the *central visual ray*. This ray is the central axis of the so-called *cone of vision*, which describes the convergence of light rays on the eye. This cone operates within a maximum angle of about 60 degrees.

In parallel perspective (below), the sides of a square converge towards the centre of vision (C). To locate the rear edge, draw a 45° angle at the station point (D) to give a 45° vanishing point (E 45°). The diagonal from here to the front of the square crosses the side where you should draw the rear edge.

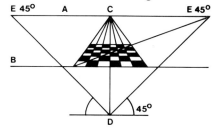

In oblique perspective (below), an ascending vanishing point (E) enables you to draw an object at an angle, like the lid of the box in the diagram. The ascending vanishing point is located on the vertical line drawn at right-angles to the horizon line (A) and the ground line (B). The sides of the box recede towards 45° vanishing points (E 45°) on the horizon line, located by drawing a 45° angle at the station point.

In angular perspective (right) you can draw a square with its diagonal at an angle to the ground line (B). The sides recede towards 30° and 60° vanishing points on the horizon line (A). To locate the corners of the square 60° and 30° measuring points on the horizon line (F 60° and F 30°) are used. The measuring points are found by drawing two arcs. The first has a radius E 45° D and centre at E 45°. The other has radius E 30° D and centre at E 30°. The two measuring points fall where these cross the horizon.

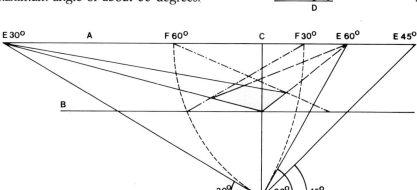

When you are working out how much to include in your picture on either side of the central visual ray, you should bear this 60 degree angle in mind.

The simplest perspective system is called *parallel* (or one-point) perspective. It deals with objects that are parallel or at right-angles to the ground line. Parallel lines travelling in the same direction towards the horizon appear to converge at the horizon. The point at which they seem to meet, the *vanishing point*, coincides with the observer's centre of vision.

If you are drawing a square in parallel perspective with one of its sides on the picture plane, you will need to know where to draw the fourth side. This will be parallel with the picture plane, but at what point will it meet the lines of its receding edges? To determine this, take the radius from the centre of vision to the station point, and draw an arc that cuts the horizon line on each side of the central visual ray. This will create two 45 degree *measuring points*.

From either of these measuring points you can draw a line to the corner of the square on the picture plane on the opposite side of the central visual ray. The far corner of the square will be where this line cuts the side of the square that recedes towards the centre of vision.

If an object is at an angle to the picture plane a single vanishing point is inappropriate. If the object recedes on either side of the centre of vision, *angular* (or two-point) *perspective* is used. With this system, vanishing points are plotted on either side of the centre of vision, on the horizon line. If the object also recedes in an upward or downward direction, an additional ascending or descending vanishing point is employed above or below the horizon line. This is known as *oblique* (or three-point) *perspective*.

THE USES OF PERSPECTIVE

The laws of perspective enable architects and designers to create three-dimensional drawings out of their plans and elevations. When they do this, they are creating hypothetical three-dimensional objects that do not really exist. The rules of linear perspective are invaluable for the process of making a "realistic" image out of a series of measurements or from an idea that has no tangible form. Perspective gives the resulting drawings a particular quality – a kind of antiseptic freshness that puts these images in a world of their own.

Artists usually work the other way round, starting with objects that already exist. They generally use the laws of perspective to solve a specific problem, such as drawing a shadow at the correct angle. As an artist working from life, you are unlikely to make a mathematical survey of a scene in front of you, taking accurate measurements and making ground plans in order to create a perspective drawing later. You are more likely simply to have the basic principles of perspective in your mind as you work.

But perspective can be useful to the artist. If you want to create a three-dimensional space as a setting for a particular subject you want to paint, perspective may be especially helpful. Many artists have used the conventional rules of perspective in an unconventional way. One way they have done this is to draw illusionistic spaces that encompass a wider cone of vision than the 60 degrees that the human eye can take in without distortion.

Movements in art during the last hundred years have shown that it is entirely possible and often stimulating to dispense altogether with traditional linear perspective. It has been abandoned in favour of a more individual approach to representing objects in three dimensions In fact, the anxious desire to "get it right" can sometimes ruin an image.

Few artists rely on a perfectly formulated perspective structure for their paintings, and although the basic rules can be helpful and are easily learnt, they can invariably be replaced by good observation and the rule of thumb system of measuring distances and angles with a pencil held at arm's length. Certainly, for the majority of complex objects, which do not conform to the toytown simplicity of the objects in perspective drawings, it would be a waste of time to work out the complex geometry involved.

PARALLEL PERSPECTIVE

This drawing of a single-track railway line illustrates the system of parallel perspective. The lines of the railway track recede into the landscape and if they did not curve round to the right they would appear to converge at a single vanishing point on the horizon. The drawing shows how, even at this simple level, the use of perspective enables you to convey the illusion of spatial recession.

The drawing also illustrates two other aspects of perspective. Firstly, the higher the eye level, the more ground is visible. To make the studies for this drawing I stood on a bridge over the track. This high vantage point meant that, with the horizon line two thirds of the way up the drawing, the recession of the track was gradual and more visually satisfying than it would have been if the eye level (and therefore also the horizon line) had been lower.

The drawing also shows aerial perspective. Although it is not subject to the same rigorous geometry as linear perspective, aerial perspective is of equal importance to artists. As its name implies, it deals with the effect of the atmosphere on objects as they recede towards the horizon. In general, objects lighten in tone and cool in colour as they recede. The prevailing atmospheric conditions determine the precise amount of change that takes place. In this drawing, the effect is exaggerated by the deep shadow of the embankment, but you can also see how the tones in the landscape become gradually lighter in the distance.

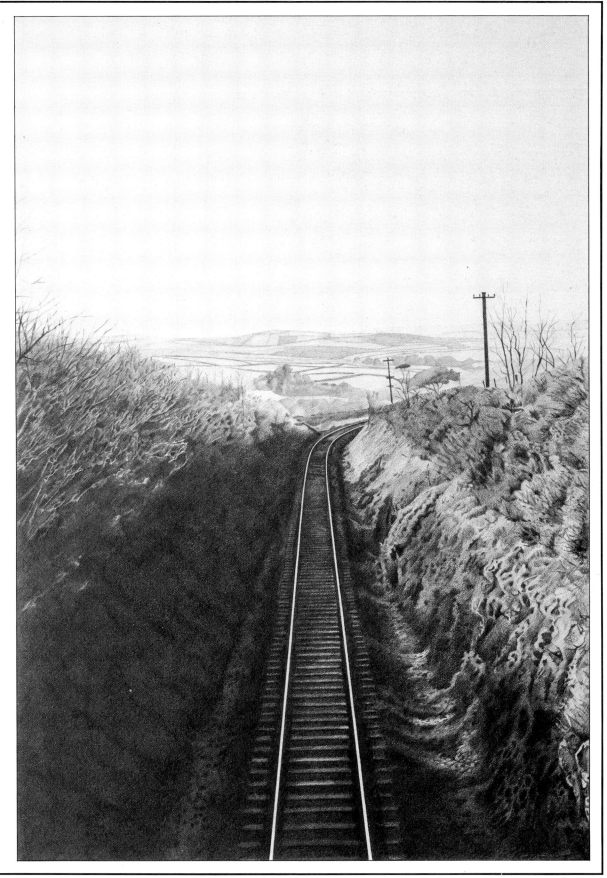

ILLUSION

THE FINAL coat of varnish on an oil painting is like the surface of a rock pool lit by the sun. If you look at it from certain angles, the reflection of the illuminating light source will dazzle you. You will be able to see nothing but the mirror finish on the flat, two-dimensional surface plane. But when you move a little to one side a three-dimensional world below the transparent surface is revealed. In both the rock pool and the painting, the world revealed is a limited one. The space beneath the surface of the pool is confined but tangible; the world beneath the varnish, while non-existant in fact, may be far less confined than the pool if the illusion of the painting is sustained. For the illusion to work, all the elements of picture-making are brought into play, so that the painting represents a credible and unique world of its own.

There are several broad approaches to the role of illusion in art. Some artists aim to conceal their artifice and recreate the illusion of a naturalistic space. Others delight in pointing up the artifice, inviting the observer to enjoy the mechanics of art with them. For a third group the illusion is less visually related to the real world. It belongs only in the unique space that the artist has created. All these types of illusion work only when they display their own separate truth. This is very important, since the real commitment of the artist creates an image with its own identity and which casts its own spell on the observer. This is true whatever the style or medium of the painting and however subjective or objective the artist's approach.

TROMPE L'OEIL PAINTING

Artists have often used systems of perspective to help create the illusion of a world that recedes beyond the picture plane. There are particular types of painting in which it is easier to create a naturalistic illusion than in others. If, for example, each of the four outside edges of the painting represent the nearest edges of the sides of a box, the illusion of spatial recession could be very effective. The eye would be led into the picture according to the laws of linear perspective (see pp. 95–6). If you made a painting of a shallow box

POND IN AUTUMN

This painting explores the idea of illusion in a very straightforward way—using illusion to represent depth on the surface of the canvas. If you think of the similarity between the surface of the painting and the surface of a pool, you can bring these two together by making a painting that shows the view

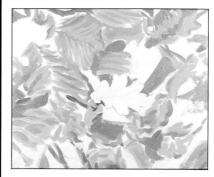

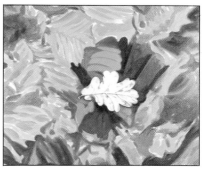

Since I had no mounted butterfly to paint from life, the subject of this water-colour painting was specially contrived. The elements I used were perspective, the separate image of a butterfly, and a frame that happened to be in the studio. By establishing the angle of the light rays from a fictitious light-source it was a simple matter to plot the lines of the shadows and produce a fairly convincing painting.

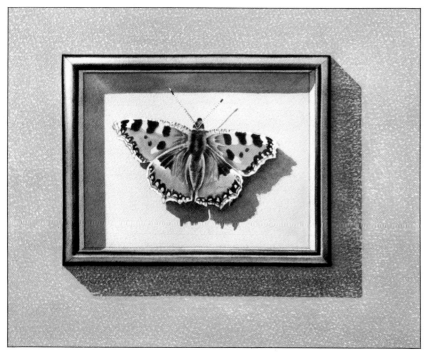

looking down on such a pool. An object on the surface of the water seems to be brought above the surface of the painting, out into space. In this painting the illusion works because the focus is blurred on the plane farthest away from the spectator, while the floating leaf is sharply delineated.

Oil paints were used for this picture, because, in my opinion, they provide the best medium for the controlled softening of edges. The method was to start by blocking in roughly the shapes and tones of the bed of leaves starting with the lightest tones and working down towards the dark ones. The range of colours was increased on the way (opposite, top). Next the highlights of the central leaf were blocked in, followed by the veins. They provided a grid for painting the small patches of yellow-orange and dull pink discolouration on the leaf. Then the background was filled in to the smooth overall finish needed to give the underwater effect. Three No. 7 round sable brushes were used, one for the light tones, one for the mid tones, and one for the dark tones. The area around the central leaf was tackled first (opposite, below). Green was introduced in the darkest shadows and to neutralise some of the mid tones – it acts as a useful foil to the warm browns and oranges of the background. The tones were generally deepened and the colours made more unified during this stage of the painting. When the background around the central leaf was finished the join was softened between the leaf and the darker part of the background. When the background was finished the central leaf was repainted to make it as realistic as possible, in contrast to the blurred shapes beneath. The technique was the same as for the background, but the work was on a smaller scale and smaller brushes were therefore used. Finally the spots of dirt and dust on the surface of the pool were picked out, to produce the finished painting (left). These were painted by picking up small blobs of white paint on the end of a small sable brush and simply dotting them on to the canvas in the appropriate places.

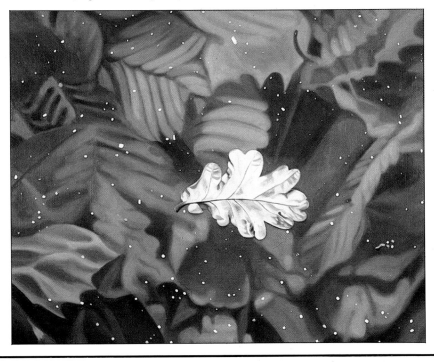

containing a mounted butterfly, the sides of the box would correspond to the sides of the painting, and the illusion of space would seem almost tangible if the butterfly and the shadow in the box were painted accurately.

This type of painting is known as "trompe l'oeil", painting that deceives the eye. In fact it tricks the brain into thinking that the objects depicted are real. Trompe l'oeil painting on a large scale usually relies for its effects on a mastery of perspective, especially of foreshortening. In some Italian Baroque buildings, for example, walls and ceilings seem to evaporate into space filled with the floating figures of saints and angels. These works were conceived and executed on a grand scale, but on a more basic level and on a smaller scale you can make a convincing trompe l'oeil painting using almost any small object. A useful rule to follow initially, as I have indicated above, is to relate the subject to a plane parallel to the picture plane. You should also pay particular attention to the accuracy of the shadows.

One subject that lends itself well to trompe l'oeil treatment is the household noticeboard with its reminders, favourite postcards, childrens' sketches, and other items. This provides a personal source of inspiration and is also a favourite subject for students of trompe l'oeil. It gives you the necessary shallow-depth composition, with objects protruding from the flat surface, and it is easy to set up and paint in stages. You can easily make a tracing of the shapes attached to the board to provide the framework for your painting. You should paint all the broad shapes first and then add detail. Notice particularly how the edges of the paper on the board curl up and cast shadows on the flat board. Try to copy these as accurately as possible.

FLOATING SAILBOAT

This painting shows a similar subject to that in the picture of a leaf floating on a pond (see pp. 98–9). But in this painting, instead of the blurred carpet of leaves on the bottom of the pond, there is a world that is sharply focused. The edges of the leaves are as well defined as the boat.

After stretching the watercolour paper the shape of the boat was painted carefully with rubber masking fluid. When this was dry, work was begun on the roots and leaves under the surface of the water. These were to be the lightest tones beneath the water. The long leaf that waves up on a diagonal from near the bow of the boat was painted by mixing two greens and applying them wet so that they ran into each other. The highlights were taken out with a damp, clean brush and the area dried quickly with a hairdrier. This method gives the granulated effect. The next stage was to paint over the leaves and roots with masking fluid to protect them from the colour washes with which the background was painted. To aid the

composition, the blue arc at the top left was also painted at this stage (below left). The next step was to dab the whole of the unpainted area with a sponge. This gives the texture of the rocky bottom of the pool. The method is to wet the sponge, squeeze it out, dab it into the pigment, and then dab it on to the dry surface of your watercolour paper. This was done several times with different colours and in varying degrees of pigment density. The sponged area was dried thoroughly before applying an overall wash of Winsor Green mixed with Yellow Ochre. This in turn was dried with a hairdrier and, when it was

completely dry, the masking fluid was rubbed off the leaves and roots. It was not removed from the boat. At this stage there was a great discontinuity between the two painted areas. The leaves and roots looked much too light and needed to be reintegrated with the background. They were therefore repainted, using the same colours as before, but being a little bolder with the depth of tone. Green washes were also built up on the leaves, (below right). The next stage was to remove the mask-ing fluid from the boat. It was then painted in tones that are generally lighter than those of the pool (bottom).

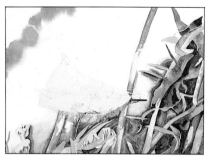

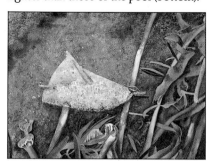

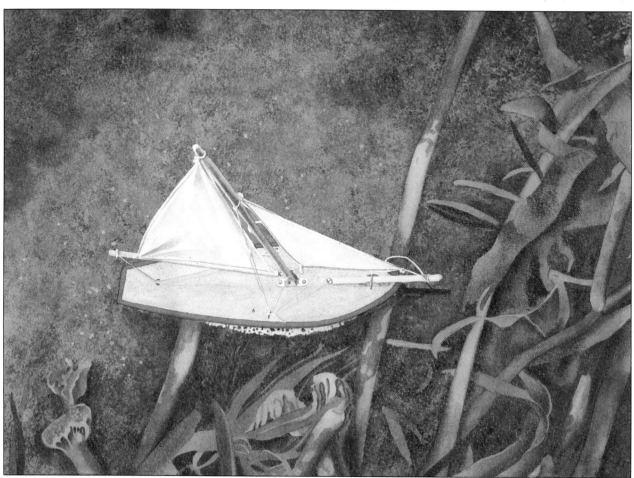

SUBJECTS
AND STYLES

DEVELOPING AN APPROACH TO PAINTING

UP TO NOW, this book has dealt with particular aspects of painting and drawing. This has meant separating elements that in practice are interrelated. Most paintings incorporate all the basic ingredients in a unique mix that reflects the individual personality of the artist. In this section of the book, the scope broadens, moving from the elements of picture making to encompass the subject matter itself. As before, the approach is to encourage you to acquire skills by producing actual pictures. The techniques introduced in the first two sections of the book and the basic elements of the third are all brought into play in these paintings. The range of subject matter is broad and the approach varied. For each painting, there is a full set of instructions so that you can make your own version.

To allow you to concentrate on the practical aspects of putting an image together, the subjects of these paintings have been preselected. But the results will have your own individual stamp, as my experience of working in a similar way with a group of students has shown. However, selecting subject matter and doing preliminary work for paintings is important. I have therefore included, at the beginning of this section, some examples of the kinds of source material used for particular images. I have also given some information about sketching and copying.

DEVELOPING A STYLE

Many people who are new to painting see it as an activity that is separate from the rest of their lives, something that is cleared up and tidied away with the brushes and paint box, only to re-emerge when the materials come out again. But the more you paint, the more you realise that both what you paint and how you paint it are inextricably bound up with every aspect of your life. You may assume that you are making disinterested decisions about what you paint or the arrangement of your subject matter, but these things arise out of the pattern of your work, your life, and your own individual vision. So as well as learning how to draw and paint what you see, it is essential to learn *how* you see, for each of us sees in a different way.

People often wonder how they can find out what constitutes their own personal vision. The answer is simply to begin by learning to recognise what really interests you and then making a note of it. We are all unaccountably struck by certain things at odd times. It may be an effect of the light, something read in a book or magazine, a picture in a newspaper, a remark someone has made, or an idea that seems to come from nowhere at all. Your experiences will provide you with all the clues you need to establish a pattern for your work. But in order to enjoy the full effect of these, you will have to be on the alert, to tune into your experiences and record them in some way. Cutting an image out of a magazine, making a quick sketch or written note, and taking a photograph are some of the ways you can do this. All the things you record will then be fixed. They are there to jog your memory even though they may not be used in a direct way in your work. You may come back to them years later, by which time you will probably have a clearer idea of why you were attracted to them in the first place. As these things accumulate, they will start to form patterns. In addition, the more paintings you make, the clearer will be your idea of exactly what to look out for.

All this activity shows that by taking the trouble to keep your eyes open, you will really begin to identify your likes and dislikes, in fact your own style. You will find out that to know what you really want to paint you have to discover your own personal imagery. To do this you must have the courage of your convictions.

GATHERING BACKGROUND MATERIAL

The second, and more straightforward, part of preliminary work surrounds the making of particular pictures. It involves gathering all kinds of visual or technical information, making sketches that explore the components of the composition, taking photographs, making notes, and researching any other material that is likely to be a useful source of reference. This type of extensive preliminary work normally only applies to large-scale paintings. For a smaller work a thumbnail sketch may be all that is needed.

For most painters the course of a painting is rarely smooth. The current painting is always going to be better than the last. You feel that it is the one in which you are going to find your true voice, and in which the gap between initial concept and finished picture is finally bridged. The early stages are all excitement. This is followed by a more straightforward "hard work" stage. During this, you have to solve most of the technical problems, and there is bound to be some anxiety about whether they could be solved by some happier method. Then, as the painting takes shape, there may be a problem about whether you have the courage to take those bold steps, which, though they seem to be needed, spoil the effect so far. As the painting develops, the feeling of imminent success is tangible. When you decide the painting is complete, there may be a few moments during which you feel that you have produced a successful painting. But not so long afterwards you will probably decide that there is a gap between the conception and what you have produced, that perhaps the next painting will be the one to come out right. And so it goes on, a process that perhaps never reaches a satisfying conclusion but that makes the artist go on trying.

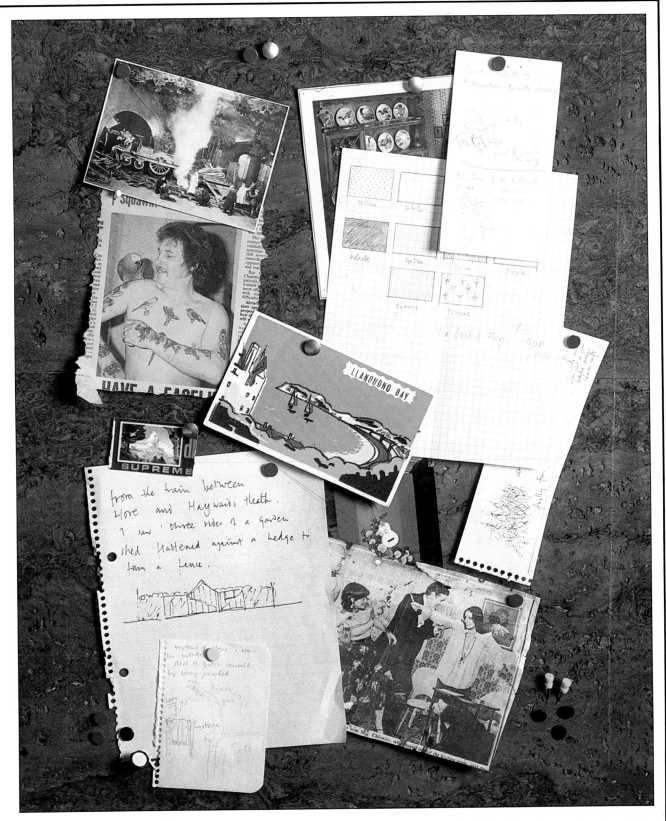

This noticeboard contains a selection of the items I keep pinned to my studio wall. Included are newspaper cuttings and photographs used as reference material for paintings, sketches and notes of things I wanted to remember, a brightly coloured postcard, and material copied from books. Items like these can help establish a pattern for your work.

COPYING

WHEN DRAWING OR painting from life, the artist is constantly aware of the mass of incidental detail in both the subject and its surroundings. You can see every twig and leaf on a tree clearly, the pores in a person's skin, and the wood grain on a chair leg. These details seem to chide you for not being accurately reproduced in your work, even though you know that the limitations of time and technique prevent you from doing so. Artists' versions of what they see have always been abstractions of the visual complexity that lies before them, a complexity that can be daunting even to experienced painters.

For this reason, it can be helpful to work from images that have already been processed in some way. Images in which the limitations of another medium, such as photography, printing, or video have filtered out much of this redundant detail are particularly suitable. They leave you with a subject that you can transcribe much more easily into painting terms. The subject's three-dimensional reality has already been presented in two dimensions on the page, the photograph, or the television screen, so that you can see it more clearly in the terms of the two-dimensional canvas surface.

This preliminary screening can be very liberating for the artist. By removing much of the anxiety of accurate representation, it seems positively to encourage a more relaxed approach and a more experimental use of materials. Another advantage of this way of working is that it presents you with an enormous range of new, and often inaccessible, subject matter. For example, a wildlife film of an exotic insect might suggest exciting possibilities.

This type of visual information, which we are constantly bombarded with, must contain germs of inspiration for every painter. The challenge is to recognise those images that could provide you with the basis for exciting paintings. It is an entirely personal choice and no two artists will make the same selection. But it is essential to be honest with yourself and not to work from images you feel you ought to use, but from those you really *want* to use. The exciting thing about painting is that you can paint anything you like, and paint it how you like.

VAN GOGH PORTRAIT

This head after Van Gogh is a detail from a portrait in the Jeu de Paume in Paris. In reproducing the image I have concentrated on the vigour of the brush-strokes and the juxtaposition of warm and cool colours. What is particularly striking about the original is that although the paint has created a vibrant, dynamic surface, there is real strength and solidity in the shape and form of the head itself. It stands out of its dark background with a striking three-dimensional effect. The sculptural aspect is emphasised by the close-cropped hair and by the fact that the beard is contained within the shape of the neck. This gives the whole head a taut, nut-like shape. There is a nervous, watchful anxiety in the eyes, which has its formal counterpart in the movement of the brushstrokes. In a letter to the painter Emile Bernard in 1888, Van Gogh said, "I hit the canvas with irregular touches of the brush which I leave as they are." Here the marks of the brush are forceful and direct but also, as in so much of Van Gogh's work, they tend to follow the form of the subject. In this painting they come across the cheekbone, round, and

down the side of the face to the beard. These "figure-hugging" brushstrokes hold the shape together as a solid but pulsating mass.

The use of complementary colours incorporates the simultaneous colour contrast effects that Van Gogh used so much. Tints and shades of oranges and reds are placed next to blues and greens against a light-toned neutral-to-warm background.

Making a copy of this head seems to recreate a sense of urgency, of having to get the image down as directly and intensely as possible. Together with this, there is clearly an enormous amount of control in the application of the right colour to the right place on the canvas. This combination of intensity and control gives one the feeling that no stroke of the brush can be weak: every dab of the brush seems to have its own force within the painting as a whole. This is strong, courageous painting and though we can see this by looking at the original, by actually making the attempt to copy it, the recognition will be overwhelming. This experience can only serve to strengthen your own resolve to focus more fully and completely on your own art.

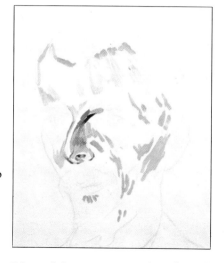

Most of this copy was made with small hogs'-hair filbert brushes, with the occasional use of a round sable at the end to define the edge of the iris or the nose. The three stages illustrated (above and opposite) show how the head was built up. In places where I overpainted wet-in-wet, the brushes, loaded with paint, were used very flat to the canvas. This made it possible to cover another colour without mixing into it. Such strokes must be made confidently, otherwise you get a muddy effect. The side of the brush was also used with a direct jabbing motion in the hair on the subject's left temple. When you make copies you will find that particular methods of using the brush will be suggested by what you have to represent.

COPYING THE WORK OF OTHER PAINTERS

Copying is an invaluable way of finding out about painting. It is much more helpful than simply looking at other painters' work. As with other forms of copying, you are transcribing an image that has already been processed. You are not faced with the problem of what to do with the reality of the subject in front of you — the original artist has already faced and solved this problem. What you have to do is to work backwards from that solution through all the technical problems of making the painting. You will find that this greatly increases your knowledge of technique. You will also discover something about the mind and attitude of the artist in question. In fact, copying the work of a great painter will probably tell you more about that artist's sensibility than any other form of study. It can show the real commitment required to paint a particular work, and demonstrate the skill and intuition needed to select a particular colour and apply it in a particular place in a particular way.

When you start to copy paintings it is best to choose an image that seems to be within your scope — a small oil sketch, for example, or a detail from a larger work. It is preferable to choose a work that has been painted directly, with little or no overpainting. You will obviously need more experience for a painting that incorporates several layers. In order to paint accurately it is best to begin with a picture in a gallery near where you live. You can then refer to the original or even, with permission, work in front of it. But whichever painting or detail you decide to work from, the most important thing is that it is by an artist you really like and admire.

Start by getting the painting's outlines on to your canvas as accurately as possible. One way of doing this is to buy a reproduction of the painting you want to copy — a postcard will be quite adequate. You can superimpose a grid on this (see pp. 226–7) and then draw up the image square by square. Alternatively, you may be able to buy a slide of the original and project this on to your board or canvas. This method will give you the correct image size very easily, and will also produce an accurate outline. When you have drawn the outline, you can concentrate on your main concern — imitating the way the painting was originally made.

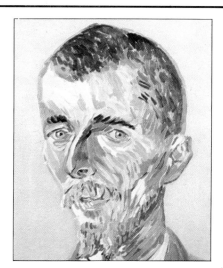

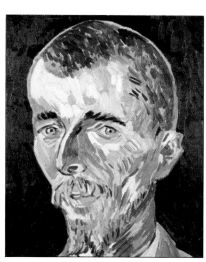

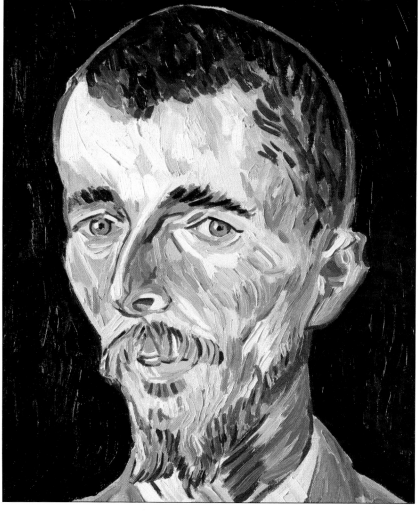

COPYING FROM BOOKS AND MAGAZINES

Sometimes you will come across an image in a book or magazine that ties in perfectly with an idea for a painting. It could be a scene that you are unlikely to find in nature, or something from the past that tugs at your memory. It could be a whole image or part of one. For example, you may find the perfect background for a painting you have already started, or even a reference for one small detail that has eluded you. This wealth of visual material can provide you with a source of inspiration almost as rich as the natural world itself. Useful images can crop up in the most unlikely places and you should keep your eyes open

and be prepared to recognise what you might use when you see it.

Whatever material you are copying, use the grid method to draw the outline (see pp. 226–7). Remember that you can scale your painted version up to any size. If you are working on a large canvas from a small original, there is great scope for your version to become more personal and experimental than a mere transcription. Aim to re-create what it was about the original that first attracted you. Remember that you are free to modify colours and tones, giving more weight to one aspect of the image than to another. In this way you are using the original as a starting point, as a means towards a more personal end.

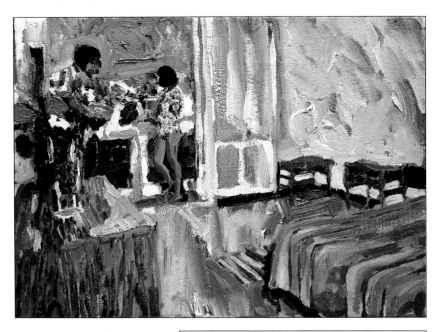

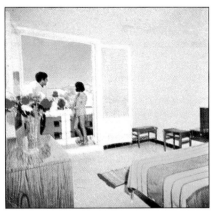

I cut this image (above) from a holiday brochure twelve years before using it to make a small oil painting (left). This work demonstrates how copying can transform an ordinary image. The original acts as a trigger for a painting that transcends it in several ways. Taking the image out of its context affects an initial transformation. In the brochure, the picture clearly illustrates a hotel bedroom — its purpose is to attract the consumer to a package holiday. But as a painting it becomes more mysterious. We wonder who the figures are and why they are there. Secondly, the treatment is completely different from the bland, mis-registered printing of the original. The brushstrokes are immediate and the paint is thickly applied. It suggests that a story is being told as urgently as possible. In addition, the shape of the image has been changed, concentrating the composition.

This painting (right) was based on a book illustration of a few decades ago. I painted it in red, blue, yellow, and green acrylic colours on 300 gsm watercolour paper, using round sable brushes. Looking back on this type of image, it seems to me to exist in a quite separate world. It was this sense of detachment that I wanted to create in my version, the detachment of a world that looks clear and recognisable, but one that exists outside time and there-fore only in the imagination. Such a world gives us a tug of recognition that is a form of nostalgia.

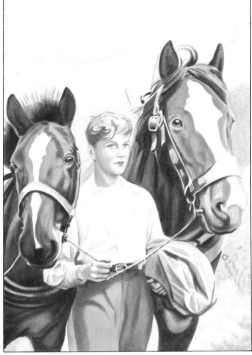

This landscape (opposite) was based on a tinted photograph from the same period as the illustration that inspired the painting of the boy with horses. For both paintings I used washes of acrylic paint (a medium not in use when the images first appeared) to recreate a watercolour effect. I chose acrylics for the control they give and to build up considerable depth of tone.

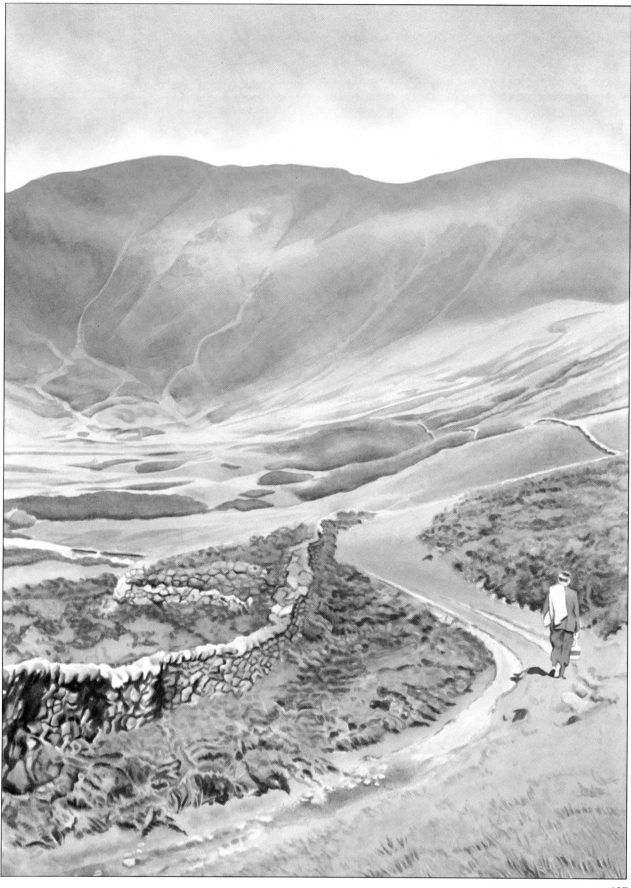

COPYING FROM TELEVISION

Television colour can be highly inaccurate. When you copy it, you often have to adopt a palette that takes you far from the naturalistic range of colours you may be used to using. This can introduce you to the joy of using colour for its own sake, showing you that the inaccuracy of television colour can be a positive advantage. When you are working from a television image the best method, if you have a video recorder, is to record the programme that interests you. You can then freeze the appropriate frame on the video, photograph the resulting image, and work from that. If you do not have a video recorder, take your photograph directly from the television. For the best results, darken the room, turn down the screen contrast, and set the camera shutter at around 1/30 sec.

TELEVISION COLOURS

This painting, which was copied from television, shows a group of actors rehearsing their flying for a production of *Peter Pan*. It was painted quite rapidly in oil colours on a canvas with a warm brown tint. The colours were all applied thickly and I kept them as clean as possible, to prevent the painting getting muddy. After tinting the canvas, the first stage was to paint the dark background around the shapes of the figures. This was followed by the white spotlit area around the shadow of the central figure. The other white areas — the stars, and parts of the figures themselves — were also painted at this stage. Next the violet semi-circle above the spotlit area, together with the adjacent blue colour, were added. The deep brown shadows on the clothes and hair were the next areas to be painted, and these were followed by the details of the actors' clothing. Finally, the green and blue edging on the figures, and the performers' hair were painted, together with the finishing touches to the stars in the background.

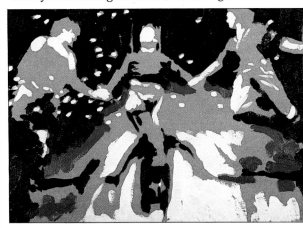

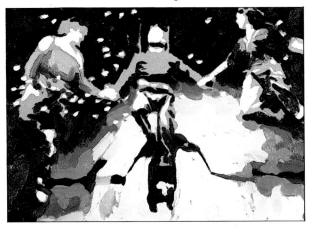

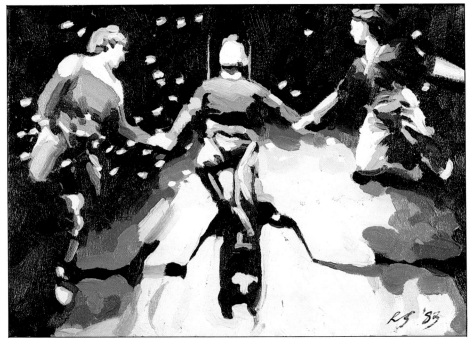

The dark background, the white areas, and the violet fringe around the spotlight were painted first (above left). Then the colours were added to the figures (above) before applying further details to figures and background to produce the finished oil painting (left).

DRAWING WITH A SKETCH BOOK

MUSEUMS ARE GOOD places in which to draw. They are full of interesting small objects that form very suitable subjects, especially for the beginner. Like libraries, they have a quiet atmosphere that can help concentration. If you have not done any drawing in museums, it may be because you lack confidence. You may feel that you don't want people looking over your shoulder and making unkind, if unspoken, remarks about your talent. But once you get into the habit of drawing in public places you will find that other people are not particularly interested and that once you have started your drawing, your concentration will be so strong that you will not notice what is going on.

You do not have to work on a large scale. A small drawing book, pencil, eraser, and sharpener are all you need. It is also advisable to take a small plastic bag that you can use for the pencil shavings. It is best not to leave a trail of wood shavings and graphite on the museum floor! Many museums provide stools and drawing boards and today museum authorities seem to have a more welcoming attitude to people coming in to draw and paint in their institutions. If you need any further encouragement you can do no better than to follow the example of the children who go into museums and throw themselves into the task of drawing what they see.

You must make your own decision about what to draw. Everyone is attracted to different items in a collection and you should recognise and follow your instinct however odd your choice of subject may appear to be. External factors, such as the amount of time you have, the

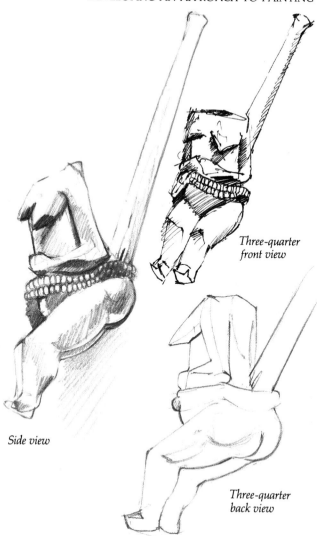

Three-quarter front view

Side view

Three-quarter back view

This wooden helmet mask from the Baga tribe of Guinea (left) is larger than the other objects that I drew. It was beautifully displayed in a darkened room with strong illumination highlighting its features dramatically. An empty attendant's chair gave me a perfect vantage point. The lighting dictated a tonal approach, with the vigorous shading contained by the strong shape of the mask. I used an eraser to keep the edges crisp.

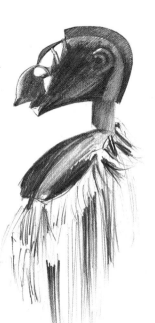

This pipe, showing a horse and rider (below), is from the Transkei. It is a very chunky carving, so I did the line drawing with a 6B pencil. The drawing was made quickly, vigorously, and as economically as possible. I did not modify any of the lines or rub any out. I wanted to create a bold, primitive effect that would reflect the character of the object being drawn. In a drawing of this type you should not worry too much about formal accuracy. It is the feel of the drawing that is important but you must still look closely at the subject.

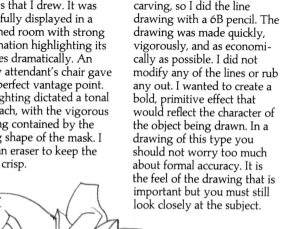

These three sketches (above) show the same pipe from Sotho Lesuto. Its bowl is roughly carved in the shape of a buxom woman. The side view was drawn first, using a 2B pencil and incorporating some tonal work. I then drew a three-quarter front view with a thin felt-tip pen, and finally a three-quarter back view, using the 2B pencil in an entirely linear style. In my opinion, the last is the most lively drawing. There seems to be more freshness and conviction in the quality of the line than there is in the first two. This demonstrates the importance of doing more than one drawing of the same item. The more you get to know your subject the more confidence you will gain.

USING A SKETCH BOOK

A sheet from your sketch book can contain a variety of material – odd drawings, quick sketches, or written notes to remind you of things that you have seen.

The Red Indian stone pipe bowl had to be drawn quite accurately to give a sense of its crisp carving.

The Hawaiian portable image of a god, unlike the pipe bowl, was jotted down quickly, to remind me later of these large, bizarre, carnival-type figures. I particularly wanted to remember their soft covering of tiny feathers, contrasting with their shining bone teeth.

I sketched the Asante wooden fertility doll to remind me of a certain sculptural quality.

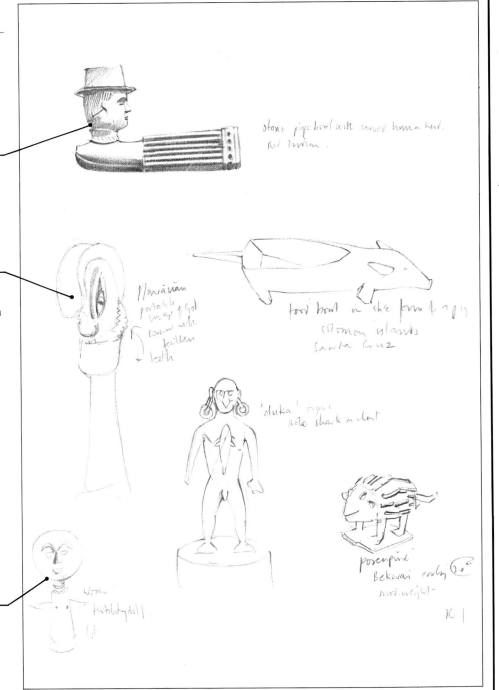

Between the extremes of the images on the left-hand side of the page are the drawings of the food bowl (centre right), the "Duka" figure from the Solomon Islands (bottom centre), and the modern Bekwai paper weight (bottom right). There is nothing to reveal the scale of these figures. In fact the big bowl was almost a yard long, while the porcupine was only a few inches across. Both pieces seemed to me to be very loving creations. The "Duka" figure has a very different appeal. Here the shark on the chest transformed a quite ordinary, though strong, figure into something stranger and more interesting.

paper size, and the medium will also influence what you draw and how you draw it. Many beginners start with drawings that are too complex. They end up with a sketchbook full of half-finished work. Thumbnail sketches can be just as satisfying as large, tightly worked drawings.

You will develop your own approach, but if you are faced with a small object in a museum case and you want to make a drawing of it, there are several guidelines you can follow. First, you should find the best viewpoint. Find out if the object looks best to you from one side or another, or when you are looking down on it or up at it. With small items in display cases, the vantage point given by a low museum stool often gives the least interesting angle. You will find that instead of looking up at the object from the stool, you will want to stand up to draw. The combination of holding your drawing board with one hand, balancing your body in order to control your drawing hand, and concentrating on both drawing and object can be extremely tiring. This too will influence the nature and scale of your drawing.

When you have decided on your vantage point, the second stage is to establish the object's shape. Do this by half-closing your eyes or blurring their focus a little to eliminate incidental detail. This will give you a unified impression of your subject. If you sketch this roughly and lightly, it will give a framework for your drawing.

The next decision will usually be whether you are going to tackle your subject in a purely linear way, in a purely tonal manner, or as a combination of both. This will depend both on the object you have chosen and on the lighting conditions. If your subject is dramatically illuminated, like the wooden helmet-mask (see p. 109), then a tonal approach will probably do it most justice. If there is soft overall lighting and the subject reveals interesting patterns, a more linear approach is probably desirable.

It is difficult to generalise about the part of the object where you start your drawing. But you will find that the more you draw, the more you will know instinctively where to begin. If you are right-handed, you will probably draw most comfortably if you follow the contours of your subject across the paper from left to right, and work down the paper rather than upwards. Left-handed people usually find it easier to start at the top right.

The examples shown here are the result of a couple of hours' work during a visit to an ethnology museum. The system I use is to look quickly round the exhibitions, making mental notes of all the things that interest me. Then I return to each one, spending some time looking before I begin to draw. All the drawings were made standing up (with the exception of the mask), using an A4 size ($11\frac{3}{4} \times 8\frac{1}{4}$ ins/29.7 × 21 cm) sketchbook.

These two drawings show how useful it can be to make a quick line drawing first. In the first example I used felt-tip pen to fix the shape in my mind before making a slower and more accurate pencil drawing. The attraction of this object was in how it was presented in the display case, the benign expression, the sculpting of the hair, and the overall scale. The pipe was suspended above a felt base as if sailing in mid-air, and cast a strong shadow.

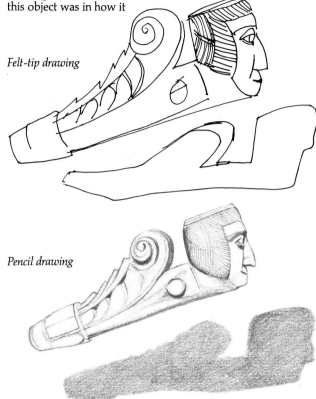

Felt-tip drawing

Pencil drawing

The twentieth-century Asante doll (right) that I drew at the end of my visit to the museum seemed altogether more homely. Teetering on its little legs with its huge rear, long body, and rather worried, prissy look, here was a character just waiting to be drawn.

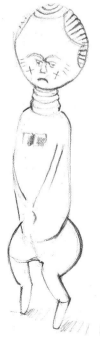

STILL LIFE

STILL LIFE PAINTING offers you a captive subject. Very often, lighting conditions are fixed, too. This enables you to concentrate on accuracy of form and colour since you have as much time to spend on your subject as you wish. When you are painting landscapes you are at the mercy of the light and the weather, and when you are painting a portrait you must fit in with your model. But still life subjects stay where you put them, giving you real freedom to explore and experiment with materials and techniques. You can also shut yourself away, so that, unlike when you are sketching out of doors, nobody will be looking over your shoulder and distracting you. All this makes still life painting a very liberating activity.

Still life usually deals with objects on a small scale and in a shallow space. This makes the subject easier to translate into painting terms. Visually you can take in your subject more easily than you can a large-scale subject such as a broad landscape panorama. It is usually far easier to create the illusion of three dimensions when working with a confined space than when dealing with infinity.

Because still life subjects are generally small in scale, a still life painting sets up a model of the world that is more easily grasped and absorbed than the world itself. This has positive, practical advantages for the painter. If you tackle a small piece of rock or mineral in the studio, you will be confronting precisely the same problems that you find when painting a mountain. You are dealing with the natural world in miniature and this gives you a solid foundation for full-scale landscape work. You can explore at your leisure the structure of natural things such as plants, flowers, and shells, and by doing this you will come to understand the separate components that make up the visible world.

It can be very useful to approach still life in a very formal way. Take an object out of its context and set it up in the studio to explore its texture, form, or colour. You can transform your subject by creating different lighting conditions. The differences you observe in these controlled conditions will help you to understand and represent them when you encounter them in the natural world.

PAINTING MAN-MADE OBJECTS

It is not only natural objects that you can explore in still life work. There is a vast range of man-made items that can provide invaluable subject matter and can expand your experience of surface, colour, and form. You do not

have to confine yourself to the traditional bowls and bottles. There are many other objects that provide similar transparent or translucent surfaces with hard-edged highlights and these objects may have a much more personal significance for you. We all surround ourselves with objects that we like, and it is to these that we should turn when looking for subject material. As with any painting, the best still life is one that reflects the artist's positive commitment to the image. This is only likely to arise when there is some attachment to the subject. But it can be surprising how complex even the most straightforward objects can turn out to be when you start to paint them, so do not be too ambitious in your selection of subject matter.

You can also emphasise the personal aspect of a still life subject by painting it in situ. Although you will not be able to alter the arrangement of objects or change the lighting you may be able to tell a story or create a portrait from your still life. Objects on a dressing table, on a shelf in a child's room, or in a garage could all be treated in this way and would all show something about the life of their owner. Such objects can create a portrait or even tell a story, since the things that surround us invariably reflect the drama of our lives.

STILL LIFE AND ILLUSION

The actual three-dimensional appearance of still life subjects on the canvas is just as important as what they are and how they are arranged. Because a still life painting represents a confined space with shallow recession, it is easier for the spectator to believe in the illusion of the work than it is with one that represents an infinity of space. The illusionistic effect of still life is enhanced because of concentration through scale. Most of the objects in still lifes are shown at about life size. There may be some alteration in scale, but this is small compared to the shift required to represent, say, a tree on a small canvas. This means that the painter can pay very close attention to the actual surface appearance of the subject. This gives you a very good preparation for the skills that are involved in portraiture. It is also the aspect of still life painting that has led to *trompe l'oeil* painting (see pp. 98–100). This is the type of highly realistic work that might show subjects ranging from notice boards, where the tangibility of the drawing pins and crumpled letters and postcards seems uncanny, to illusionistic drawings of drops of water on shiny surfaces.

This watercolour study (opposite) shows a vase made in 1973 by the artist Andrew Lord. The vase is not only a striking and witty object, with the aeroplane flying through the centre of the vase, but it is also delicately and beautifully glazed. The painting demonstrates that for still life subjects we should paint all the things we like that surround us.

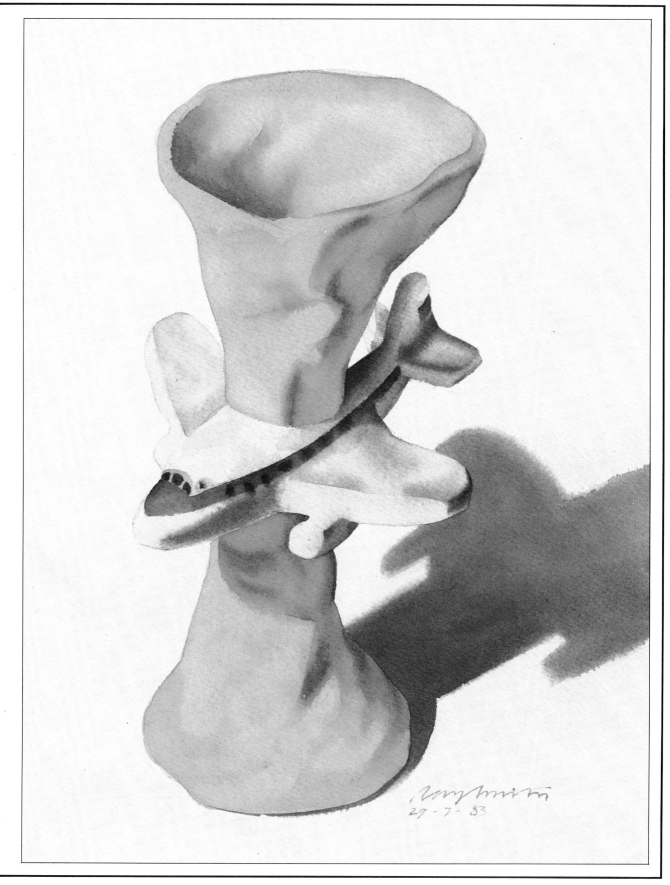

IRIS

Medium WATERCOLOURS

WATERCOLOUR IS a particularly suitable medium to use for painting individual flowers from life. With a watercolour box, pencil, rubber, brushes, and two small jars of water, together with a pad of reasonable quality watercolour paper, you are well set up to paint whatever you like. You may prefer to buy your flowers or pick them from your garden and paint them at home. Here you are free to establish your own fixed lighting conditions and the flower is not continually moving in the wind. When you work from a cut flower, you will find that it changes its appearance rapidly. In this painting I began work on the iris during one evening and finished the following morning. By morning it had opened out considerably. So if you plan to work on a complicated flower, you should use a plant growing in a pot.

But whether you work outdoors or inside, on a growing or a cut flower, the essential first step is to look at the flower carefully, to decide what its essential characteristics are. Copying the shape of a flower accurately is of course a challenge in itself. But doing so without knowing what particular quality of the flower appeals to you, or without some overall sense of its structure, will make your painting mechanical and far less interesting. To paint it because you like it is enough, but if you ask yourself why you like it, you might get some clue as to how to paint it.

This particular iris seemed to me to have great poise. Irises can look rather floppy when they are completely out. This one has symmetrical petals that are open and exposed, but it has only recently blossomed and its delicacy is combined with a certain firmness. In the centre at the top the vertical petals are cupped by the two leaves. This seems to give a real sense of the way the flower grows up from the stem. Opposite the central section, curving out and back towards it is a slim petal that seems to give a taut balance to the flower. These were the aspects of the flower that I tried to emphasize in the painting.

MATERIALS AND EQUIPMENT

Support
Watercolour paper A4 size
($11\frac{3}{4} \times 8\frac{1}{4}$ ins/29.7 × 21 cm)

Watercolour paints

Winsor Blue	Burnt Umber
Cadmium Yellow Pale	Yellow Ochre
Winsor Green	Permanent Rose
Burnt Sienna	

Brushes
Two No. 4 sable rounds

Other items
HB pencil, rubber

METHOD

After making the outline sketch, the petals are underpainted in pink. The violet colour is made by adding a thin blue wash. The colour of the stalk and leaves is built up in stages, by adding three different green shades.

For the guideline sketch on its grid see p. 234.

1 Underpainting the petals

After drawing the outline according to the guideline sketch, paint the yellow centres of the two side petals using pure Cadmium Yellow Pale. Then paint all the petals in Permanent Rose. Work with both brushes, one for the colour, the other clean and damp. Start with the darkest tones around the middle of the central petal. Draw in the tone with the first brush and soften the edges with the second. Use quite thin colour at first — you can build it up with later layers. When you come to apply the overall wash to the flower's central petals, make sure that you use a well diluted colour. You can then take out lighter tones by stroking parts of the wash with the clean damp brush.

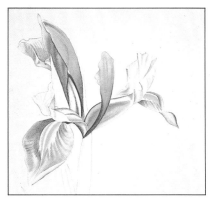

2 Defining the stalk

Mix Winsor Green with Burnt Sienna for the stalk. Paint in the darkest tones. You should take care to keep the lines of the edges as fluent as possible when you do this.

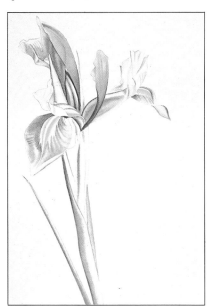

3 Overpainting the petals

Use a wash of Winsor Blue on the petals to create the violet effect of the finished picture. Winsor Blue is a very strong colour, so you will have to use it well diluted, at least to begin with. Your brush should not be too wet — before painting dab the toe of the brush on the saucer's edge to remove excess paint. Work in the same way as for the Permanent Rose underpainting and let each section dry completely before painting over it. Give the two petals immediately above the yellow areas a thin Winsor Blue wash.

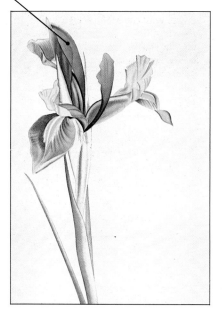

4 Strengthening the flower

Now give leaves, stalk, and petals more definition. Mix Cadmium Yellow Pale with Winsor Blue in a thin wash and paint over the whole leaf and stalk area. You can also make the ridges in the centre of the petals a little stronger at this stage. Use a thin mix of Permanent Rose and Winsor Blue to get this effect.

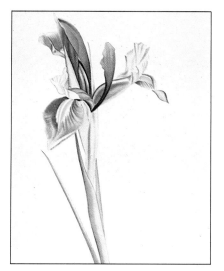

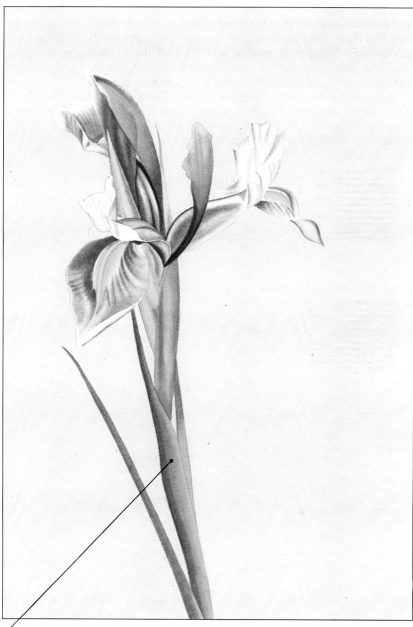

5 Finishing off

Make the leaves and stalk more solid by painting in the dark tones. You can use either a Winsor Green plus Burnt Sienna mix, or a mix of Winsor Green, Burnt Umber, and Winsor Blue. Paint a stripe along the right-hand edge of the top-left leaf with a thin mix of Permanent Rose and Winsor Blue. Finally, give the whole leaf and stalk section another wash of Winsor Green with Burnt Sienna and Yellow Ochre.

APPLES

Medium OILS

THIS PAINTING, A study of three apples, is a contrast to the neat and orderly approach needed for the watercolour painting of the iris (see pp. 114–15), with its careful, well-defined edges and superimposition of colour. It is an example of a more vigorous style of direct painting using oil paint and bristle brushes.

When you begin to paint still lifes, limit yourself to two or three simple objects. The simpler the forms, the easier they are to sketch, and the sooner you will be able to get involved with the painting itself. Composing such a simple still life is not as straightforward as it might seem. You could set up your easel as you might for a landscape – in front of something that already exists, such as a bowl of fruit on the kitchen table where the arrangement of the forms is predetermined for you. Your range of options is limited to the angle from which you choose to paint, and possibly to the lighting conditions. But when you are responsible not only for these choices but also for the initial selection and arrangement of the subject, including the background, then the options are almost infinite. The whole process becomes very conscious. If you wish to make a balanced, harmonious composition for example, your painting's "natural" qualities will be directly proportional to your own skill in arranging your subject. So it is well worth spending as much time as is necessary trying out all kinds of alternative arrangements until you have the most successful composition. Decisions such as choosing the precise number of apples do not just happen. They have to be carefully considered.

You should be prepared to be flexible while you are setting up the still life and not hold on to a fixed idea about it if a better alternative strikes you. Here I had planned to use a plain wooden table as a background until I hit on the more interesting possibility of using the small rug instead. The soft blues, greens, and browns seemed to complement the reds and oranges of the apples. The geometry of the design, with its stepped right angles, seemed to work well with the circular shapes of the fruit.

MATERIALS AND EQUIPMENT

Support
Canvas or board 18 × 24 ins
(46 × 61 cm)

Oil colours

Winsor Red		Oxide of Chromium	
Alizarin Crimson		Burnt Umber	
Winsor Blue		Yellow Ochre	
Cadmium Yellow Pale		Permanent Rose	
Winsor Green		Titanium White	
Burnt Sienna			

Brushes
Two No. 7 and two No. 4 hogs'-hair filberts, No. 4 sable or nylon flat

METHOD

After drawing the basic outlines on a tinted Burnt Sienna ground, the method is to paint the picture directly. There is no subsequent overpainting. The background is painted first and the three apples at the end. Hogs'-hair brushes are used for most of the work, with thick, loosely mixed paint diluted where necessary with turpentine. Vigorous, confident brushstrokes help achieve the bold painting style.

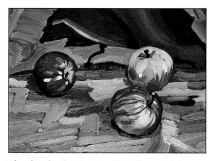

The finished painting. For the guideline sketch on its grid see p. 247.

1 The drawing
Tint the canvas with Burnt Sienna and when it is completely dry carefully draw in the outlines of the fruit and background.

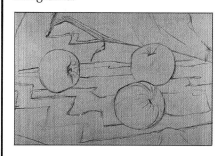

2 The light background areas
Begin with the area of the rug above the apple on the left. The colour is a mixture of Titanium White, Permanent Rose, and Burnt Umber. Mix this loosely on the palette. Do not mix it so that all the colours blend with each other, but stop at a point where you can still see striations of pink and brown in the white. This will make the colour look much more interesting when you paint it on to the canvas. Use a No. 7 hogs'-hair brush for this, filling the area with vigorous brushstrokes. To the right of this patch is a smaller area of similar colour but with a little Cadmium Yellow Pale added to warm it up slightly. At the far right top there is also a small patch of the colour darkened with a little more Burnt Umber (shown in the illustration of Step 3). Paint the area of similar colour at the bottom of the painting, using the No. 7 brush in the same way, with the same loose mix but with Yellow Ochre added.

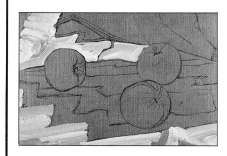

3 The red section

Clean your palette and your brush. Now you can paint the deep red section which comes down into the painting from the top edge. Use the two No. 7 brushes – one for the darker and one for the lighter tones. The colours here are Permanent Rose, Alizarin Crimson, Burnt Umber, Titanium White, and Cadmium Yellow in various combinations. The darkest tones are a mix of Alizarin Crimson and Burnt Umber, while the lightest ones are Permanent Rose plus Titanium White. There are three areas of dark shadow, one above the red apple on the left, one which arches down, pointing to the stalk of the upper apple on the right, and one at the right-hand edge of the shape. Paint these in with broad strokes of a No. 7 brush. Then with the other No. 7 paint in the lightest tones. Use a mix of Permanent Rose plus Titanium White plus Alizarin Crimson for the arc above the top right apple. Next add Cadmium Yellow Pale to it in order to paint in the orange arc in the middle of the shape. After you have done this, fill in the middle range of tones between the light and dark areas.

4 The coloured stripes

Now you can paint the coloured stripes across the foreground and between the apples. Begin with the yellow. Mix together Titanium White, Burnt Umber, and Cadmium Yellow Pale loosely on the palette and paint across the picture with bold strokes of a No. 7 brush. Notice how the colours all work independently as well as creating an overall creamy yellow look. This method applies to all the foreground and background colours. Next paint the light green stripe in the foreground using a loose mix of Titanium White, Oxide of Chromium, Winsor Green, and Yellow Ochre, using a No. 7 brush. Notice the way the brushstrokes relate to the shape of the light green area and how you can see the various colours that go to make up the green within each brushstroke. To the right of the lower right apple there is a fold in the material that catches the light. So at this point, add more Titanium White to your mix. Add a little Winsor Blue and Burnt Umber to your green mix and paint the darker green stripe below the brown stripe that links the top two apples. Now paint the blue shape which links the top left apple with the bottom right one. The colour is a loose mix of Titanium White, Winsor Blue, and Burnt Umber. Use a No. 7 brush. This colour is lighter to the right of the bottom right apple than to its left, so modify your tone here accordingly. For the background, it only remains to paint in the "black" outline around the red shape using the edge of a No. 7 brush and a mix of Winsor Blue, Burnt Umber, and Burnt Sienna, and also the two remaining green and cream stripes below the pink one using the No. 4 pointed flat. Clean your brushes and your palette.

Continued over

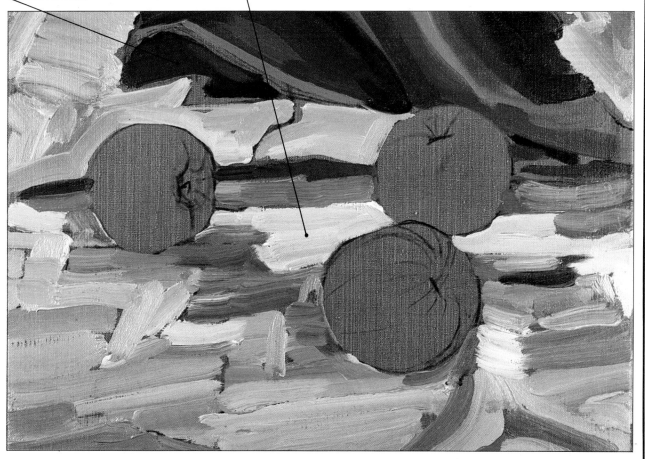

5 Line details
Paint the pink of the striped detailing on the material using a mix of Permanent Rose plus Titanium White with the No. 4 flat. Try to do this with one bold, unfussy brushstroke. Using a No. 7 brush and a mix of Burnt Sienna and Yellow Ochre paint the brown horizontal line which links the two top apples and carries across the whole painting. Clean your palette and all your brushes.

6 The red apple
Now you can begin to paint the red apple on the left. You should use your two No. 4 hogs'-hair brushes, keeping one for the darker red colours and the other for the darker yellow ones. Begin with the very dark red tones around the edge of the apple and at the bottom left. These tones are Alizarin Crimson with a touch of Burnt Umber. Build up towards the lighter tones, working from a mix of Alizarin Crimson plus Permanent Rose with a tiny touch of Titanium White, to a mix of Winsor Red plus Cadmium Yellow plus Titanium White for the warmer orange-red colour. The centre of the apple is a mix of Cadmium Yellow Pale plus Titanium White, with a touch of Winsor Green. Build up the colours, but remember to leave spaces where the white highlights will be. You will be painting these in at the end using a No. 4 hogs'-hair. Because you have left space for them, the white will stay pure. Apply "black" at the centre with the No. 4 flat using a mix of Burnt Umber and Winsor Blue. Clean your brushes and palette.

7 The green apple
Now paint the apple at the top right. The colours here are Winsor Green, Oxide of Chromium, Yellow Ochre, Cadmium Yellow Pale, Winsor Red, and Titanium White. With one of the No. 4 hogs'-hair brushes, paint in the dark tones around the bottom left of the apple using a mix of Oxide of Chromium plus Yellow Ochre. With the other No. 4 paint in the light tones around the top of the apple. Make these tones up of Cadmium Yellow Pale, Titanium White, and a touch of Winsor Green. The illustration (bottom right) shows the apple after these areas have been painted. The next stage is to paint in the intermediate tones including the orange-red area at the bottom right of the apple. This is a mix of Winsor Red plus Cadmium Yellow Pale, with a touch of green added to neutralise it a little. As you did for the first apple, leave space for the two highlights around the centre. At the top is an area of deep shadow from which the stalk emerges. This is also a mix of Oxide of Chromium plus Yellow Ochre with a light mix of Cadmium Yellow Pale plus Titanium White plus Winsor Green immediately above it. Paint the stalk itself with the No. 4 sable flat, using Burnt Umber and Winsor Green.

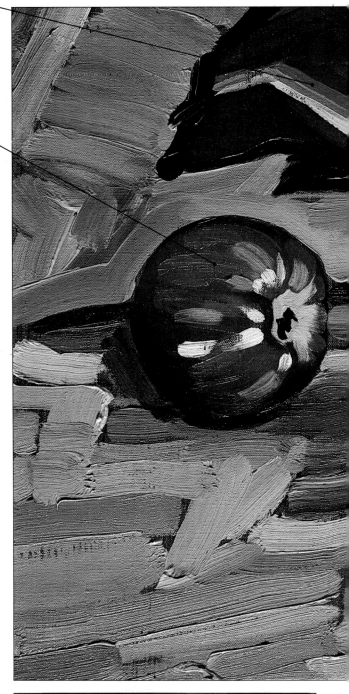

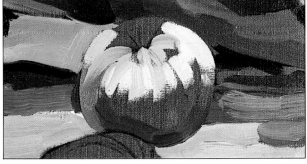

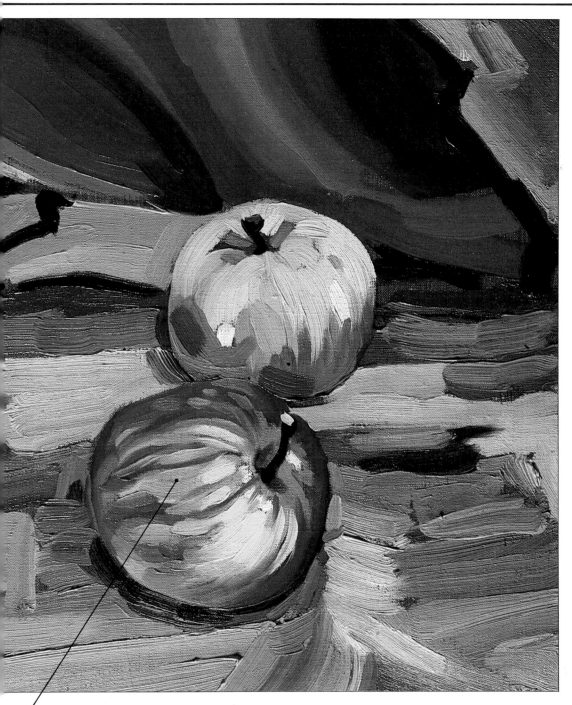

8 The red and yellow apple
Finally paint the apple at the bottom right of the picture. Whereas the red and green apples are painted with the flat end of a No. 4 brush, parts of this apple, where the marking is quite thin, are painted with the edge of it. Keep one hogs'-hair brush for the darker red tones and the other for the lighter yellow ones. Begin with the dark tones around the outside, then paint in the light yellow ones and

subsequently fill in the mid tones. Use various combinations of Alizarin Crimson, Permanent Rose, Winsor Red and Cadmium Yellow Pale for the red-orange colours, and make up the browns from orange mixes with the addition of a little Winsor Blue. Paint the stalk with the No. 4 sable or nylon flat using a mix of Burnt Umber plus Winsor Green and paint a highlight on the end of it. Notice again here how there is a deep shadow around the root of the stalk.

9 The finishing touches
Make any minor adjustments to the painting that you feel are necessary including adding the white highlights to the apples. For my original, I added a little deeper tone around the base of the apples using one of the No. 4 hogs'-hairs. For this type of painting it is better to let your original brushstrokes stand fresh and try not to be tempted to start fussing them up with extra overpainting.

BIRD WHISTLE

Medium WATERCOLOURS

ARTISTS WHO TAKE a watercolour box, a few brushes, and a pad with them when they are on holiday or travelling usually make landscape studies. Indeed, it is very satisfying to work outside in a good climate, responding with fresh eyes to new surroundings. But time restrictions or weather conditions can interrupt this type of work or prevent it altogether. Within the "still-life" category a whole new range of subjects presents itself to the artist. These range from a fresh assortment of natural objects such as stones, shells, fruit, and vegetables, to a variety of interesting man-made objects. Such items make wonderful subjects for quick studies. This picture of a bird whistle is an example. I painted it in Italy. It comes from the southern Italian town of Matera, where such whistles are made in a wide variety of shapes.

MATERIALS AND EQUIPMENT

Support
90 lb rough watercolour paper
14 × 10¼ ins (35.5 × 26 cm)

Watercolour paints

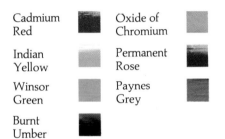

Cadmium Red

Oxide of Chromium

Indian Yellow

Permanent Rose

Winsor Green

Paynes Grey

Burnt Umber

Brushes
Two No. 7 and No. 4 sable rounds

Other items
HB pencil

METHOD

This study shows how you can introduce up to three colours at the same time into one dampened area of the picture. Each part is dampened in turn and colour is introduced into it, beginning with the head, body, and tail, continuing with the wings and legs, and finishing with the whistle itself and the shadow it casts.

For the guideline sketch on its grid see p. 246.

1 The body and head
After drawing the outline of your subject on to your paper carefully paint the whole body shape, excluding the wings, with clean water. Use a No. 7 brush. Mix Indian Yellow and introduce it down the left-hand side of the damp shape with the No. 7. Wash the brush and mix Oxide of Chromium. Run a line of this down from the top of the head along the side of the wing and down to about ¾ in (2 cm) above the end of the tail. Then mix Cadmium Red with the No. 4 brush and paint on the beak and the tip of the tail. Work from the tip of the tail towards the greens, to keep the red pure and clean. Dry the shape thoroughly. Use a hairdrier if possible to speed things up.

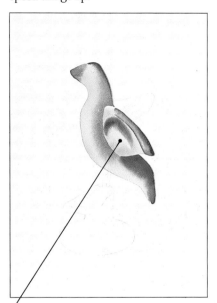

2 The left wing
Paint the shape of this wing with clean water, but do not cover the area where the strip of red will be. Introduce some Indian Yellow with a No. 7 brush and then, with one looping stroke of the No. 7, paint the inverted C shape of Oxide of Chromium that serves as a shadow. When this is dry paint the top edge of the wing with water and introduce Cadmium Red along both thin edges of this shape with the No. 4 brush. Let this dry.

3 The right wing

Dampen the part of the right wing that will be green and paint it with Oxide of Chromium using the No. 4 brush. Dampen the area above it and paint in the red, also with the No. 4. When this is dry paint the stripes with the No. 4, using Oxide of Chromium for the green and Cadmium Red. Dampen the legs and paint them with Indian Yellow and then Oxide of Chromium. Again, use the No. 4. You can also add Oxide of Chromium to the eye at this stage if you want to.

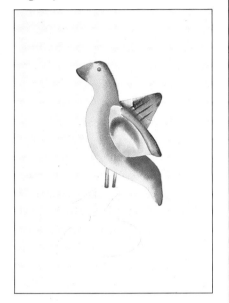

4 The base

After you have dampened this, use a No. 7 brush to paint a thin Winsor Green mix in the middle at the bottom. Then apply Oxide of Chromium in the middle and on the right of the base and along the bottom edge. Use the No. 7, and leave the paper white where the yellow is to go. For this yellow shape take the No. 4 brush and paint the colour firmly with one movement, so that it retains its brilliance. Let this shape dry.

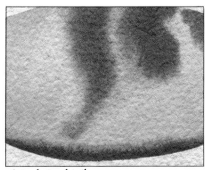

Actual-size detail

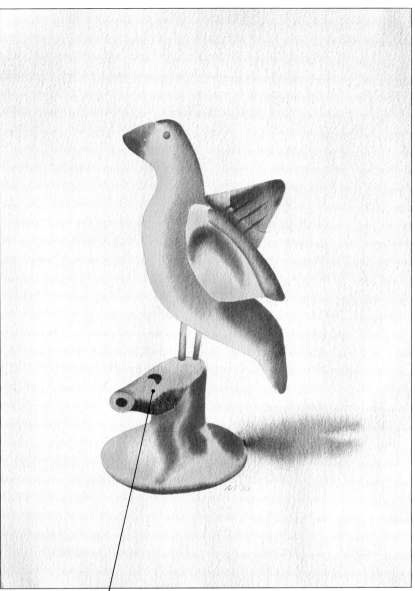

5 The whistle

When you have dampened this part of the image apply the lighter tone using a Burnt Umber and Permanent Rose mix with a No. 7 brush. While this is still damp paint the darker shadow along the bottom. Use the No. 4 and a darker tone of the same mix. Then dampen the area to the right of the whistle and add Paynes Grey with the No. 7 brush to indicate the subtle shadow zone.

ITALIAN GLASS

Medium WATERCOLOURS

THIS WATERCOLOUR still life forms a contrast to the loose, painterly style of the oil painting of the apples (see pp. 116–19). The study aims to reproduce the luminous quality of an arrangement of old glass displayed in the Poldi-Pezzoli museum in Milan. Unlike the apples, the glass is painted as seen, with no rearrangement of the composition.

The glass is lit from behind. This creates a clear, linear composition in which the shapes between the objects become very positive features of the design. The thin horizontal bases and top edges form a grid-like structure of horizontal and vertical lines. The curves that define the contours of the glass operate within this grid and are contained by it. This helps to give the painting its still, quiet appearance and this is reinforced by the controlled style of painting. The colours are very restrained – indeed the painting is almost monochromatic in appearance with only subtle modulations of colour in the very pale cool green of the background, the smoky brown of the glass, the clear pale blue ribbon work in the dish behind the glasses, and the slightly warmer brown of the display shelf.

MATERIALS AND EQUIPMENT

Support
NOT watercolour paper $10\frac{1}{4} \times 14$ ins (26×36 cm)

Watercolour paints

Winsor Red		Winsor Green	
Winsor Blue		Burnt Umber	
Prussian Blue			

Brushes
Two No. 8 or No. 7 and two No. 4 sable rounds, No. 14 squirrel

Other items
B pencil, sponge, sheet of tracing paper (optional)

METHOD

After the shapes of the glasses have been drawn in, the background is given an overall pale green wash. When this is dry, each glass is painted in turn, by overlaying thin washes on the dampened areas being worked. The technique is to paint in the darker details and later to introduce the mid and lighter tones. After each wash, the area should be dried thoroughly before continuing. When the glass is finished, the shelf is painted. Then its colour is incorporated into the glasses' bases.

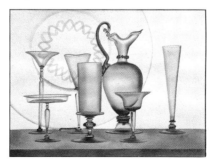

The finished painting. For the guideline sketch on its grid see p. 246.

1 Drawing the outline
None of these glasses is entirely symmetrical, so you will not be faced with the difficulty of matching the two sides of each exactly. Nevertheless, drawing this image accurately will take some time and a certain amount of rubbing out. So it is advisable to draw it on tracing paper before you transfer it to watercolour paper.

2 Applying the wash
Wet the paper with the sponge and mix some Winsor Green in a saucer. This should be very pale indeed. Apply it in an overall wash to the damp surface of the paper using the No. 14 squirrel brush. Then dry the paper thoroughly before continuing.

3 The tall glass on the left
The colour for the glasses is a combination of Burnt Umber and Prussian Blue. Premix three tones of this – if the paint dries up, you can simply add water. Then start on the tall glass. First paint along the line of the lip with water to dampen the paper. Then, using a mid tone and the No. 4 brush, paint along the line. Paint the dark area at the top of the stem in the same way. Then work down the stem, dampening the area to be painted before you introduce the pigment. If it is too dark, you can lift off the pigment with a clean, slightly damp No. 7 brush. Next paint the detail at the top of the stem and work down adding a line of thin paint down each edge with the tip of the No. 4. Make the left-hand edge darker than the right.

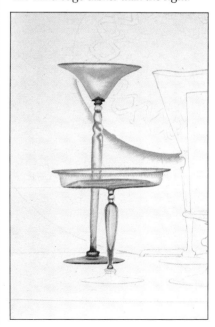

4 The base and bowl

At the base of the stem the tone is much darker than elsewhere, but you should leave a lighter area in the centre of the elliptical bud. Dampen the area of the base as before and run the tip of the No. 4, with a dark tone, along its edge. Then go back to the bowl of the glass and dampen this. With the No. 7 and the light tone paint down both sides and along, but just beneath, the rim. Let the edges of the brushstrokes within the glass area soften freely into the damp paper. Follow the same procedure for the base.

5 The flat-bowled glass

Here, as before, you paint the lip on the rim after dampening the area. Try to reproduce this elegant ellipse as fluently as possible with the No. 4 brush. Notice how the first bubble of glass on top of the stem is highlighted in the middle and has a very dark tone at its base. Beneath it, the next bubble has a curving, horizontal shadow halfway down and two thin, almost vertical lines drawn to the top of the stem proper. Details like this seem insignificant, but their cumulative effect is important, so you should try to reproduce them as accurately as you can. A similar detail on this stem is the V-shaped shadow. Paint this in a mid tone with a No. 4 brush. Add overall washes as for the first glass, but leave the highlights to the left and right of the base of the stem. You should also leave highlights in the middle of the stem of this glass towards the top.

6 The conical glass

Paint the next glass on the right in a similar way, beginning with the lip and the dark detailing and adding overall washes afterwards. Two washes are required. Apply the first after dampening the shapes, running a mid tone along the diagonal edges and allowing it to soften towards the middle. When this is dry, add a lighter-toned overall wash, which you can paint with the No. 7 brush.

7 The cylindrical glass and jug handle

Here begin with the stem. As before, start with the darkest areas, in this case the horizontal shapes. Soften the edges by painting into damp paper or by running the tip of a clean, damp brush along the wet painted edge. Build the tones up slowly and carefully, allowing each section to dry before overpainting. For the glass itself, dampen the whole rectangular area and then paint in thick, mid-tone stripes down the edges with the No. 7 brush. While the paint is still wet use the No. 4 brush to run a darker tone down the left-hand edge and close to the right-hand edge. When this is dry paint in a light overall tone with the No. 7 brush. At this stage you should also paint the jug handle, following the same method as before.

Continued over

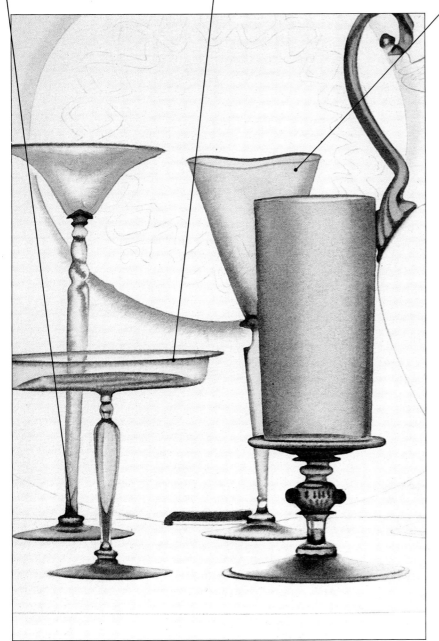

8 **The pattern on the plate**
Next tackle the blue ribbon pattern on the plate. For this use a pale Winsor Blue mix and the No. 4 brush. Paint one zig-zag and let it dry before painting the other. At this stage you can also complete the shadow in the middle of the plate. Do this by introducing a very light-toned brown into the dampened circle.

9 **The jug**
At the top, the detailing is complex, so you should deal with one small area at a time, building up the modelling slowly and carefully. You should also build up the shadow effect methodically – it is impossible to get a realistic effect in one go. Paint the first wash on to the dampened surface with the No. 7 brush.

10 **Building up the shadows**
Next dry the area and paint another wash on to the body of the jug. This time, extend the colour farther into the centre and apply additional darker tones at top and bottom. Dry this again and repeat the process if necessary. Finally paint a thin overall wash with the No. 7.

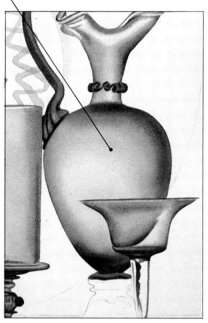

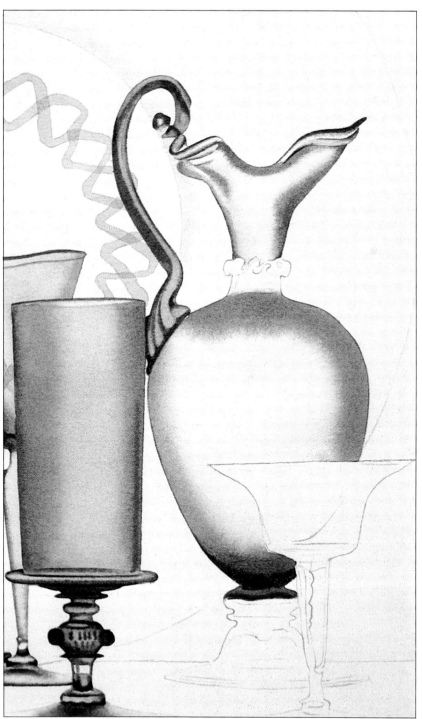

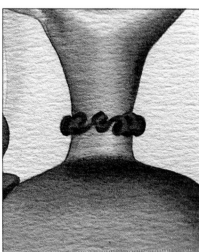

Actual-size detail

11 The display shelf

After you have painted the two remaining glasses (right) following the same method, start on the display shelf. For this use a warmer version of the brown used for the glasses. You make it warmer by adding Winsor Red. Dampen the shelf area (except for the bases of the glasses). Do this a quarter at a time if you find that the area is drying before you can start painting. Use the No. 7 brush, taking particular care of the shapes around the glass bases. Then, with the No. 4, introduce the same colour into the bases themselves. Try to make the bases look as if they belong on the shelf. Paint the front lip of the shelf a deeper tone of the same colour and add the rim round the outside of the plate. Finally make any necessary adjustments.

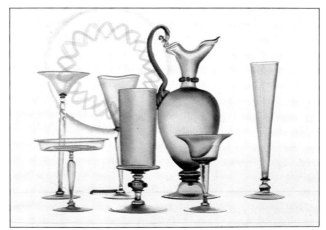

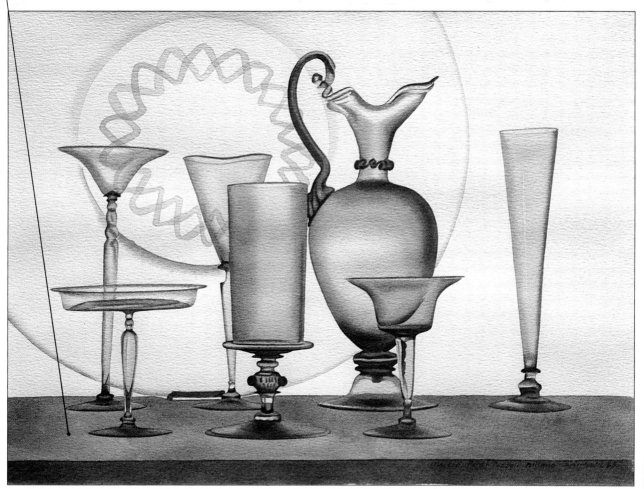

NIGHTLIGHT

Medium OILS

FOR THIS STILL LIFE I have chosen an object which is fairly straightforward in shape. Nevertheless it presents quite a complex exercise in light and shade. The small nightlight has an internal lamp that lights up the mouse family inside their home and makes the facade dark in tone as light spills out over the foreground. But there is another source of light in the painting: a desk lamp that illuminates the object from the top left-hand side, lighting the roof on that side and casting a dark shadow on the right. The colours are warm within the interior of the "house" and cool on the outside. The idea of the painting is to try and recreate the warm and secure atmosphere that helps the child through the night and also, by focusing on this type of image, to express the magical reality that such a world contains for the child.

MATERIALS AND EQUIPMENT

Support
Canvas 18 × 16 ins (46 × 40.5 cm)

Oil colours

Winsor Red		Sap Green	
Winsor Blue		Permanent Rose	
Indian Yellow		Titanium White	
Winsor Green			

Brushes
No. 6, No. 4, and No. 2 sable rounds, No. 7, No. 6, No. 4, No. 2, and No. 1 hogs'-hair filberts

Other items
Painting medium (see p. 10), turpentine

METHOD

This painting is made on a canvas with a neutral mid to light grey tint. The tint is not essential, but if you wish to use it you should be sure that this base colour is dry before starting work. After applying the background colour, the broad areas of tone are painted in. These are left to dry before work is started on the precise details and colours.

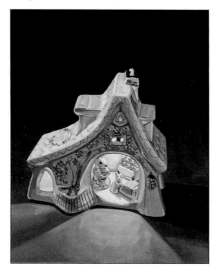

The finished painting. For the guideline sketch on its grid see p. 230.

1 The background

After drawing the outline the first stage is to paint the background. This moves from a dark brown tone above the house to a lighter mid tone behind. Use only turpentine to mix and thin your colours at this stage. Paint in the shadow that extends down from the horizontal on the right-hand side as a very dark tone. The light from the interior in the foreground is a light brown-ochre colour mixed with white. It darkens in tone towards the bottom edge of the painting. Immediately beneath the nightlight paint a thin, dark shadow to indicate where it is held slightly off the background surface. Paint this with the No. 1 hogs'-hair, the rest of the background with the No. 7.

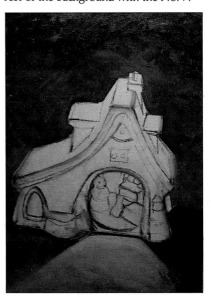

2 The roof

Here it is important to concentrate on tone rather than on colour. Do not deal with any of the detailing at this stage. The sloping roof on the left is a light tone of Titanium White with Permanent Rose and Indian Yellow, with a slightly darker version of this colour at the apex. The other side of the roof is a grey-blue at the top, moving down to a warmer grey midway, and with a deeper version of this colour for the shadow beneath the roof window on the right-hand side.

3 The left-hand attic windows

The roof of the attic window on the left is a pale mix of Titanium White with Winsor Blue and Winsor Green. The side is a dark grey that becomes suddenly paler where the light strikes the corner of the eaves. It turns darker once more, to a mid grey, for the side wall. The edge of this window catches the light, so there is a strip of the lightest tone here.

4 The chimney

At the top of this there is a very dark tone made of Winsor Red, Winsor Blue, and Winsor Green. The side is a dark brown-grey that becomes paler towards the right.

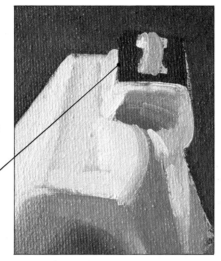

5 The front of the house

Between the light roof and the light interior there is a dark to mid grey tone. The overhang of the roof creates a deep shadow. Use a similar depth of tone over the top of the entrance and for the indentation in the middle. Use a hogs'-hair brush for this and most of the central parts of the house, and the No. 2 round sable for the thin lines. When you paint in these broad areas of tone, apply the different tones separately, painting up to the edge of the adjacent tone and then, after wiping the brush, blending them together along the join. This will produce a completely smooth transition from one tone to the next.

6 The air vents

The indentation above the entrance has two circular air vents which are open with a light behind. Above is another vent, which you should paint in yellow.

7 The interior

Block this in using warmer light-brown tones, variations on a mix of Titanium White, Winsor Red, Sap Green, and Indian Yellow. The whitest areas are the top of the bed and the edge of the table, the ears and nose of the central mouse and the mother mouse's left-hand side. The floor and the top of the wall also reflect light from the concealed lamp. Do not be afraid of the quite dramatic shifts of tone. The darkest areas occur on the mother mouse's body, the front of the central figure, and the side of the bed. Also notice the effect of the light on the arched entrance. The light grey edge tone blends into a much lighter warm brown.

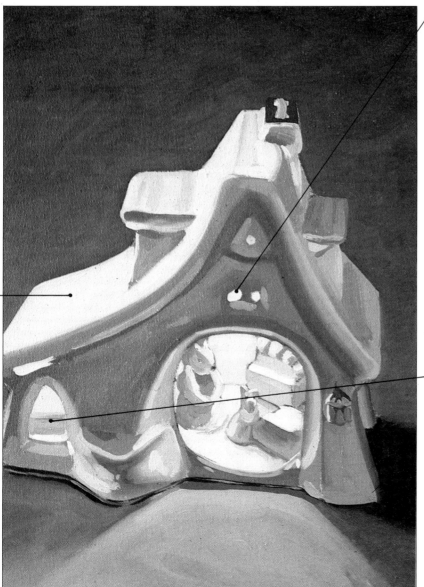

8 The window on the left

Use a fierce orange for this, to express the warmth of the interior. Touch in the places where this light is reflected — the window arch and the roof overhang. You should also paint in the parts that catch the light from outside — the left-hand edge of the house and the bulbous lower portion at the front. Apply the light greenish-grey tone at the bottom of the house.

Continued over

9 Preparing for the details
Let the painting dry before going on to the next stage, which concentrates on colour and detail. But before you start on the details, it is worth intensifying the background colour. This is a dark blue-brown at the top, changing to a deep warm brown and a light warm ochre at the bottom of the painting.

10 The surface of the roof
Indicate the pattern of the tiles with charcoal or a small sable with a thin red-grey mix. Base the colouring on the mix of Permanent Rose, Titanium White, and Winsor Red that you used before, neutralising it a little with a touch of green or blue. The bottom two rows of tiles on the left and right are the only ones that are really clear. Notice how the semicircular edges of the roof tiles are lightest in tone in this area.

11 The attics and chimney
For the flat tops (below) use Winsor Green plus Titanium White and Winsor Blue plus Titanium White. At the apex of the roof paint the top of the chimney (bottom). Use yellow on the facing side and paint four strokes of brown and red to indicate the brickwork. Give the shadow at the top its slightly lilac cast by adding a tiny amount of Winsor Blue to the pink mix.

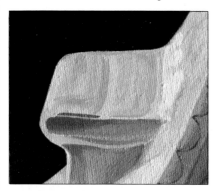

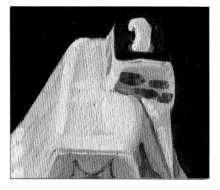

12 The roof overhang
At the front of the house this has a warm yellowish cast. Paint this with a thin ochre mix (Indian Yellow, Winsor Red, and Winsor Blue) over the existing grey. The thin red semicircular decoration is a slightly blue-brown version of Permanent Rose. Apply it with the No. 2 round sable.

13 The decoration
For the decoration on the front of the house, draw in the basic lines of the plant lightly in charcoal and then paint them in using the ochre mix (see Step 12). Paint the dots at the centre of the flowers in the same colour. You can also add the petals around the top air vent. Next add the brown details on the plant stem, the areas of light green foliage, the blue and magenta-red petals, and the darker green leaves. Where the plant joins the bulbous part of the house at the base, apply a mix of Titanium White and Winsor Green for the areas of light greenish blue. Only add the dark grey criss-cross lines, which represent the fence, after you have painted in the warm tones to the left and right.

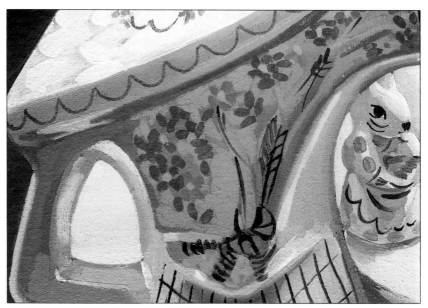

14 The interior
Here warm yellow colours are complemented by blue-violet shadows. Do not add any details before you have painted these colours. When you come to the details (the green food on the plates and in the mother's arms, and the dark outlines that define eyes, noses, mouths, cutlery, and so on) use the No. 2 round sable.

15 The window and arch
Soften the colour in the arched window on the left. Make the colour more of an overall tint. Deal with this window arch and the arch of the opening by enriching the warm ochre where the light is reflected. Above the arch, where light is reflected on to the overhang, diminish the tone of the highlight to make it an orange-yellow.

16 Finishing off
Repaint the lamp on the outside. Replace the yellow-white with an orange that reflects more accurately the colours of the interior. The side of the house, where it is visible, is a deep purple-grey. Repaint the rather neutral tone where light spills into the foreground with a much warmer orange. Make it most intense where it is closest to the entrance. Finally make any adjustments to the painting that you feel are necessary to complete it.

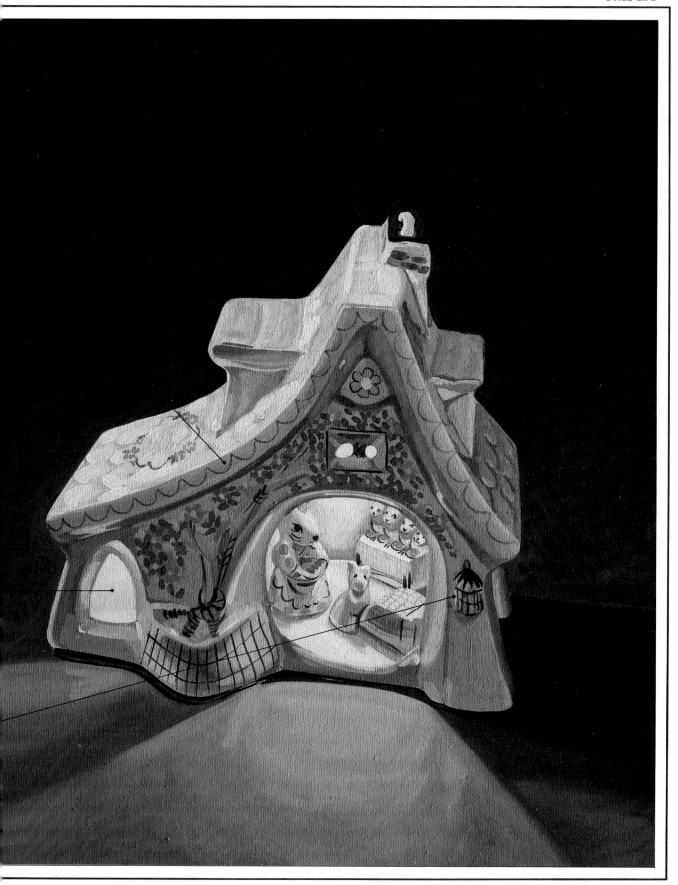

AQUARIUM

Medium ACRYLICS

AN AQUARIUM is a rich source of inspiration for painters. Each tank is a separate, self-contained world of its own, similar in many ways to the world contained within the frame of a painting. It can display a whole range of different atmospheres, appearing highly charged with mystery and teeming with strange life, or having a quiet and lazy clarity. It can contrast with the world we know, or it can seem to reflect it.

In this painting I have explored the richly textured, busy aspect of the aquarium. The orange and red fish dart over the whole surface like single brushstrokes. The overall background colour, a complementary green, helps to enliven the scene and make the fish seem even more dynamic.

I based the composition on several different components rather than on a single aquarium. It is not always possible to paint from a complete image because you may not be able to find exactly what you are thinking of painting. So the answer is to collect the components from several different sources, and combine them convincingly. For my painting the separate elements were: the background, which I painted freely from a printed backdrop for an aquarium; real aquarium plants painted from life; objects (the frog, diver, and sign), also painted from life; the stone arch, which I drew on a visit to an aquarium and then painted from a sketch and from memory; and the fish themselves, which I based on observation and on pictures in books.

MATERIALS AND EQUIPMENT

Support
Heavy watercolour paper A1 size
($23\frac{1}{2} \times 33$ ins/60 $\times$ 84 cm)

Acrylic colours

Cadmium Red   Sap Green

Phthalo Blue   Titanium White

Azo Yellow

Brushes
Two No. 7, No. 6, and No. 1 sable rounds, No. 2 hogs'-hair filbert

Other items
PVA medium, airbrush (optional), stencil film, thin cardboard, scalpel, pencil, chalk, spatula

NOTE
This painting, originally titled "Neon Lights", won a major award in Sainsbury's "Images for Today" competition in 1982.

METHOD
This painting is built up in a series of layers, each of which is sandwiched between coats of tinted PVA glaze. The idea is to separate the fish from objects in the tank and to create an impression of depth. First of all the background and some of the fish are painted, and then the first PVA coat is put on. All the plants, fish and objects are then painted first in white acrylic so that they separate well from the background and can be painted in fresh, bright colours. Next the stone arch, some plants, and a second layer of fish are painted. Then the second coat of PVA is added. After this the detailed objects are tackled – the frog, diver, goldfish, and the large plant. These are painted in considerable detail. The third coat of PVA is put on next and then the sign and a final layer of fish are painted. Lastly, the fourth layer of PVA is the final glaze.

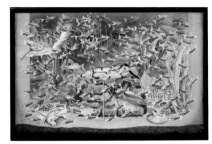

The finished painting. For the guideline sketches on their grids see pp. 232–3.

1 Preparation
Stretch the paper well on your drawing board, making sure the gummed strip is stuck firmly all the way round. Draw the framework of the tank and gravel and then put strips of masking film along each side of the tank. This will allow you to paint freely up to and over the edge and still have a clean edge when you remove the film at the end. Next draw the background roughly in pencil. It does not have to be accurate and you can make up your own if you wish, following the same method.

2 Painting the basic background
Use your two No. 7 round sables for this, painting the colour on with one and softening the edges where necessary with the other. Begin by mixing brown from Sap Green and Cadmium Red. Paint this over the whole of the rectangular background in the dark areas between the plants, the wood, rocks, and pebbles.

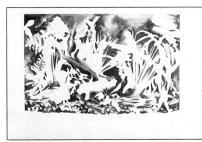

3 The leaves
Now mix Phthalo Blue with Sap Green and paint the straight leaves of the three plants in the centre and to the left and right. Then paint the leaves of the smaller plants around the base of the plant on the left. Use the same colour mix to paint over the brown areas in the dark tones along the top edge of the painting.

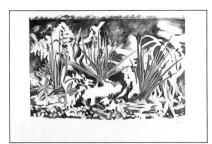

4 The wood and rocks

Mix yellow and orange-brown by adding either Azo Yellow or Cadmium Red to your basic Sap Green and Cadmium Red mix, and apply it in thin washes over the lighter-toned parts of the background — including the wood and rocks. Next paint all the plants which are a lighter green by applying thin washes of a Sap Green plus Azo Yellow mix.

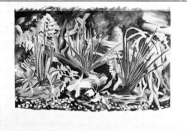

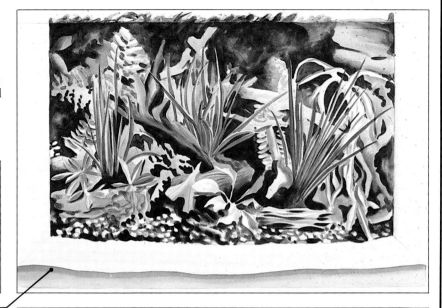

5 The sand and tank sides

By this time you will have sketched in most of the background, so the next stage is to go over it again, deepening the tones and colours where necessary and giving it a more uniform appearance. Then you can also sketch in the sand and the sides of the tank. Do this by dampening each area with clean water before introducing the colour. For the sand, use a mixture of thin Cadmium Red plus Sap Green to make brown and add Azo Yellow. For the sides use Phthalo Blue with a touch of Cadmium Red and Sap Green to take the brightness down a little.

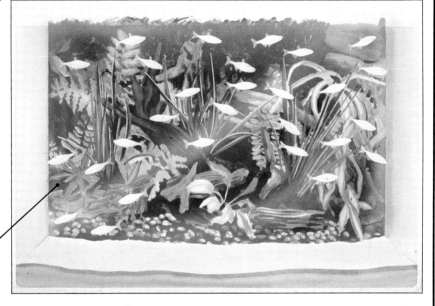

6 Softening the background tone

In order to create the illusion of depth in the tank you should now scrape a film of PVA over the whole painting. Add a tiny amount of Phthalo Blue pigment to the PVA medium. Mix this thoroughly. Although it is opaque when wet, it will dry as a transparent film. Spread it over the surface using a flexible spatula or an old credit card. At this stage, although it is entirely optional, you can use an airbrush to soften the tone at the top of the background and to add two soft white diagonal highlight stripes across the surface. This separates the background from the interior of the tank.

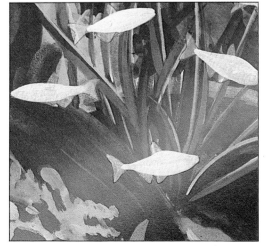

7 Positioning the fish

Next, paint the fish in white acrylic over the background. This constitutes the first of several layers of painting. To do this, cut two basic fish shapes out of thin cardboard and use them as stencils to make pencil outlines on the painting surface. Give the fins and tail only one coat of paint so that they look slightly transparent when dry, and give the bodies two more coats so that they are opaque.

Continued over

8 Painting the fish in colour
When the white paint is dry, paint the fish. For each one begin with the eye and then paint a thin stripe of blue along the body. Follow this with a fatter red stripe, adding a touch of yellow. Soften the red at the front lower end of the body. Just above the blue stripe paint in a slightly thinner purple stripe. Then soften the remaining white areas with a thin fawn and yellow wash.

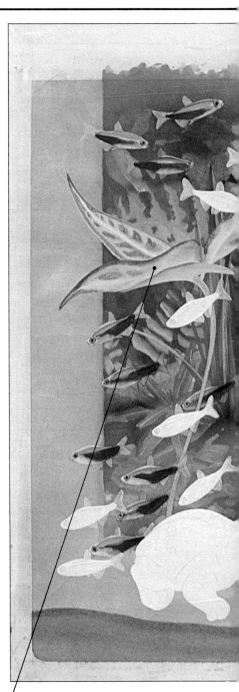

9 Using PVA to create depth
To separate the layers of fish and the objects in the tank, and to create the illusion of depth, scrape a film of PVA over the whole painting after each stage. To do this, add a tiny amount of transparent pigment to the PVA medium and mix thoroughly. The medium is white and opaque when wet but it dries as a clear film. Scrape it over the whole surface to achieve a smooth surface. Tint these layers of PVA with a little Azo Yellow. This will combine with the blue of the previous layer to create the eerie greenish appearance of the light in the tank.

10 Underpainting the arch
Now sketch in an outline of the stone arch. Draw the blocks of stone roughly using chalk. This will adhere to the PVA and you can wipe it off easily afterwards. Then paint the blocks in using two coats of white acrylic. After this is dry, paint the mortar in between in white also. Since this will be darker in tone than the stone, the surface does not have to look so opaque.

11 Painting the arch
When the white is completely dry you can add the colour. Use a dark brown base for the mortar, and a basic fawn mix for the stones (below). Finish off the surface of the stones by stippling darker and lighter colours with your No. 2 hogs'-hair brush. Put a dark shadow under each stone to make the arch look three dimensional.

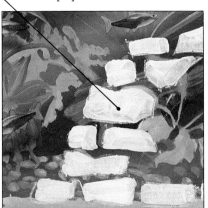

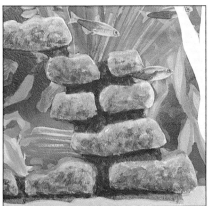

12 The plants and second layer of fish
Now draw the plant outlines on each side of the tank and paint them white. Then put in the second layer of fish in the same way as before. Make your brushstrokes follow the shape of the object they depict. So for the long thin leaves, try to make each leaf form one complete brushstroke.

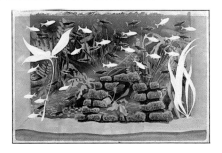

13 The leaves
Paint the leaves in a thin mix of Sap Green and Azo Yellow. The colour will run naturally into the long, smooth brush marks of the white underneath, and this will echo the veins of the plant itself. When you have painted the colours of the arch, the two large plants, and the new batch of fish, you should apply the next coat of yellow-tinted PVA.

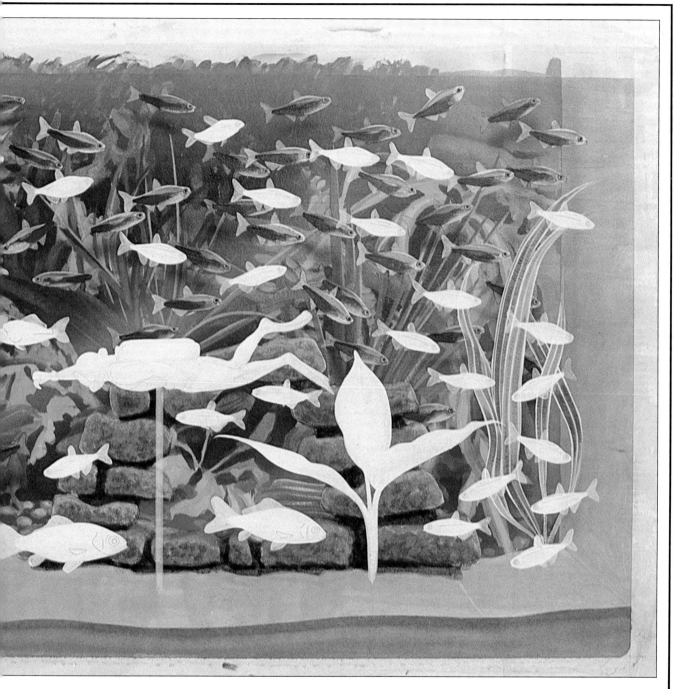

14 **Positioning the items in the tank**
When the last coat of PVA is dry, tackle the next layer. This comprises the frog, diver, the plant in front of the arch, and more fish. I drew the frog and diver from original objects, but if you are planning to put your own objects into the aquarium, draw them on tracing paper until you are satisfied that they are accurate. Then superimpose your drawing on to the painting to check that you have got the scale right. Now trace the outlines on to the painting. If you use a hard pencil with a good point, you will be able to see the indented outline of the shape quite clearly. It will be easy to paint up to this edge with the white paint. Then paint in the shapes in white acrylic. Let this dry and repaint the shapes so that the paint beneath them is entirely obliterated.

Continued over

15 Painting the objects

When the repainted shapes are dry, paint the objects in their correct colours. Tackle each as a complete still life painting in itself. Refer continually to the composition as a whole, so that you do not give any one object too much weight.

17 The frog

Paint the frog in thin, transparent washes of a mix of Cadmium Red plus Sap Green plus Azo Yellow. Use more green and a deeper tone for the colour between the light patches on his back, and for the shadow.

16 The diver

For the diver, use a mix of Azo Yellow plus Cadmium Red plus Titanium White, following closely the lighter tones of his arms, head, back, and legs. The white is added to give the colour opacity and to imitate the matt effect of the plastic. The "black" flippers and belts are a mix of Cadmium Red, Phthalo Blue, and Sap Green. Paint the diver's stand, incorporating his air supply pipe, in a thin white wash. Put in dark shading at each side to emphasise its transparency. Paint the bubbles in a similar way to allow the background colour to come through where they are not highlighted.

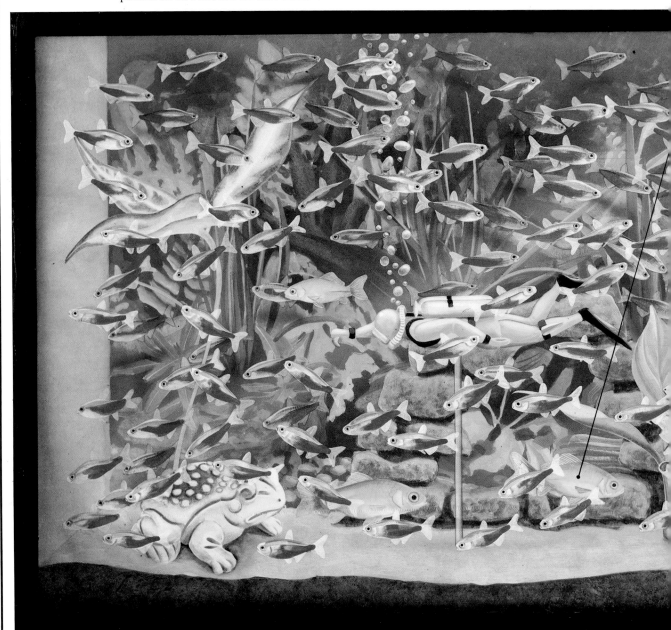

18 The goldfish
Paint in the three goldfish in thin Azo Yellow washes with a touch of Cadmium Red where the tones are deeper. Also paint the remaining red and blue fish in this layer.

19 The plant
Paint the plant behind the sign. In this case the leaves have a little more body. Begin with the areas in shadow that define the darker ridges of the leaves. Use a thin dark green mix (Sap Green plus Phthalo Blue). Then paint each leaf with an overall mix of Sap Green and Azo Yellow.

20 The sign
Paint the sign shape in white acrylic, adding as many coats as are necessary to make the shape opaque. When these are dry, paint the sign in thin transparent washes of colour to imitate the hard shiny glaze of the object itself. The top part of the sign is Phthalo Blue with an additional touch of Cadmium Red and Sap Green. The bottom part of the sign, the stand, is Azo Yellow, also with a very small amount of Cadmium Red and Sap Green added to the mix.

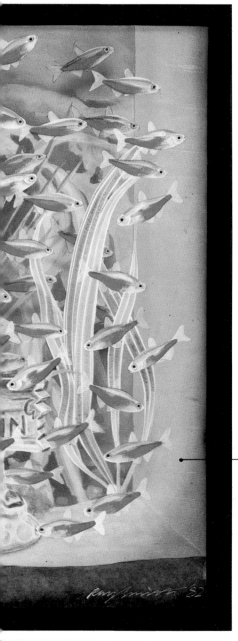

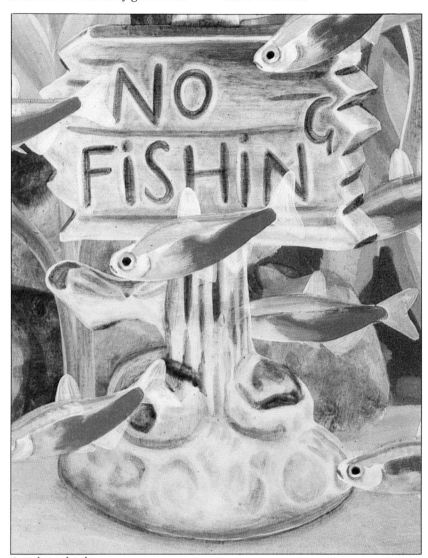

Actual-size detail

21 The last stages
Before you paint the final layer of fish you can airbrush the sides of the tank in a grey-blue tone. The effect of this is to help concentrate the action and light inside the tank – but this is entirely optional. Then trace in the last few fish and paint them as before, and add the final glaze of PVA with just a touch of yellow. Now remove the masking film to reveal the clear shape of the tank.

22 Creating a frame
Such a busy composition clearly needs a darker and bolder frame. So now scrape a thick black layer of PVA paint through the masking film stencil and you will be left with a black frame.

LANDSCAPES

ALL THE PAINTINGS in this section are exterior scenes. As well as the usual rural subjects, the section includes seascapes and various urban landscapes or "townscapes". By incorporating images that go beyond the usual landscape classifications, I hope to show that you can paint any outdoor subject. There is an infinite range of possibilities and you should paint whatever attracts you.

The section explores a series of conventional landscapes, ranging from a formal garden, through rolling countryside, to mountains. The area of townscape is explored in a similar way with the old (Venice) and the modern (New York) given quite different treatments. The first is crisp and realistic, using thin washes of acrylic paint, while the other is more impressionistic, thickly painted in oils. In the seascape category I have painted both a natural and an industrial scene with, on the one hand, the crashing breakers on the Dorset coast and, on the other, a French ship in the docks at Le Havre. Here, although the images are dissimilar, the treatment in oils is almost identical. This demonstrates how, once you have found a technical method of coming to terms with an image, you can apply the same method to almost any subject. If you look at the work of artists who have established a mature style, you can see that the subject is often simply the starting point for a painting that explores its own style as much as the thing it represents.

Within each of the landscape, seascape, and townscape areas I have also introduced a painting with figures. This is to show the particular problems and possibilities that arise when human figures interact with a landscape. In the case of townscape, this is a view of a soccer match, which shows the new kinds of imagery that modern urban landscape affords.

Making these paintings will not turn you instantly into a landscape painter. But it will give you the experience of a wide range of images and techniques that will be invaluable when you tackle subjects of your own choice.

MAKING SIMPLE SKETCHES

You may feel that you want to continue to make paintings based on your favourite paintings, photographs, or prints before working directly from nature. But when you do begin work outside, you do not have to start with a full-scale landscape painting. It is better to begin with small pencil studies, using a pocket-sized sketch book.

When you move from small-scale interior works such as still lifes to subjects like landscapes that actually surround you, it is vital to look in a different way in order to absorb and process all the visual information. Beginners sometimes find it difficult to synthesise this information into the kind of image that can be translated into a drawing or painting. One solution to this problem is to adopt the "window-frame" approach. You can do this

quite literally by looking out of a window in your own home. Consider the distances and relationships between objects according to the rectangle of the window frame. Whether you look out on to an urban backyard or over rich countryside, the approach is the same. You must, of course, stand or sit back far enough from the window to be able to see the whole scene without changing position. Practise making sketches of such views. Concentrate on getting things the right size and putting them in the correct position – do not bother about details. Outside, you can look through a small piece of card with a window-shaped hole in it, held at arm's length.

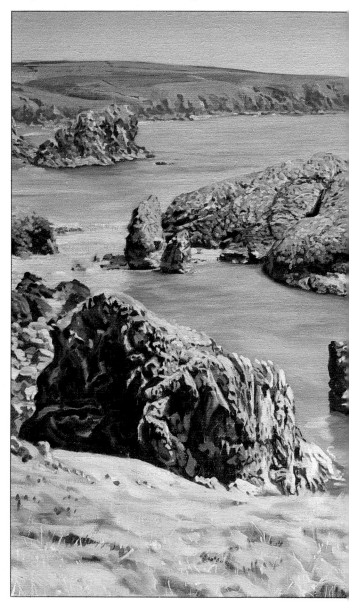

PAINTING OUTDOORS

Once you have got used to sketching in the outlines of a scene in pencil using a small sketchbook, try taking the sketch a little further. Paint in the broad areas of tone and colour in watercolour. A small watercolour box is an excellent travelling companion. It will enable you to build up the confidence to take your painting further, looking in more detail at the various components of a scene you have already described broadly.

If you find that you do not have the time to take the painting as far as you wish, take a reference photograph, so that you can finish the work later at home. An alternative method of getting enough information to work the painting up later is to make a pencil drawing. Do this as accurately as possible, along the lines of the drawings at the end of this book (see pp. 228–48). You can then pencil in letters to indicate the tones and colours of the scene. Most artists develop their own code for this. When you have transferred the outlines to the canvas, you fill in the colours in their appropriate places.

Generally speaking, you can only work outside on an oil painting if the weather is fine and sunny. But if you have a car, you can use it as a portable studio. This can be a comfortable way of extending your range of images. If you do this, watercolour seems the most popular and unfussy medium to use.

When you are working outside, oil paint is, in my opinion, a considerably more practical medium than acrylics. On a hot day, acrylics have an annoying tendency to dry up very rapidly on the palette. In addition, acrylics are not resoluble once they are dry. With oils, the only problem is the rapid evaporation of turpentine. But you can avoid this by using dippers with caps.

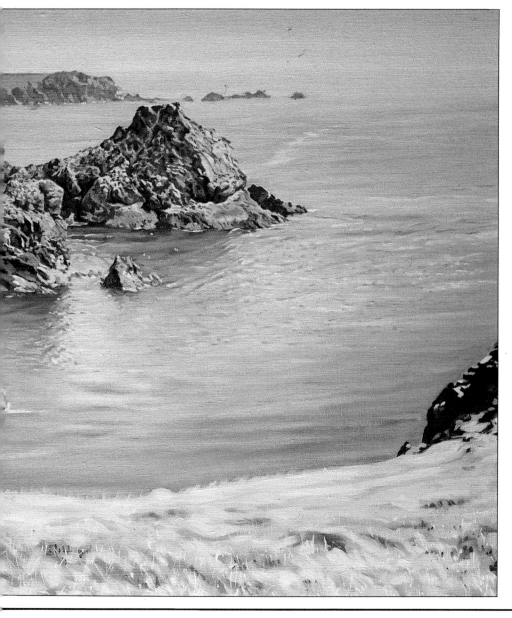

This painting shows a view overlooking Kynance Cove in Cornwall, where the bay sweeps round in a great semi-circle. The rocks in the centre provide a solid focal point. The painting was made on a canvas with a Burnt Sienna ground. For the preliminary work, the shapes of the rocks were sketched in and the darkest and lightest tones indicated. The painting was then made directly by applying small touches of colour over the rocks and headland using flat nylon brushes. Broad horizontal bands of colour for the sea were applied with hogs'-hair filbert brushes. These were also used for the foreground, which is more loosely painted.

Winter Trees

Media WATERCOLOURS or OILS

THESE TWO PAINTINGS have similar subjects. In each case the view is looking up across a bank at a single tree that is strongly lit in the morning sunlight. The paintings illustrate two ways of approaching a similar subject in watercolour and oil paint. For the watercolour, the medium is used transparently with no opaque body colour so that the highlights are revealed by the white paper. In the oil version, the paint is used opaquely so that the highlights appear as ridges of white paint on the surface of the canvas.

If you compare the two versions, you will see that although they are similar, the watercolour is softer and has a more uniform surface. The oil paint seems to push the tree off the surface, physically separating it from its background and giving it a crisper feel. The sharp focus of the oil painting reproduces more accurately the conditions of the clear, bright morning. But the oil is not necessarily the better painting because of this. The watercolour, helped by the diagonal of the bank and the trees in the background, seems to make up in atmosphere what it loses in clarity.

MATERIALS AND EQUIPMENT

Watercolour version
Support
Rough watercolour paper 22½ × 16½ ins (57 × 42 cm)

Watercolour paints

Winsor Blue	Yellow Ochre	
Winsor Green	Burnt Sienna	

Brushes
No. 7, No. 4, and two No. 2 sable rounds, No. 16 round squirrel

Other items
Masking fluid

Oil version
Support
Board or canvas 12 × 16 ins (30.5 × 40.5 cm)

Oil colours

Winsor Red	Cadmium Yellow Pale	
Winsor Blue	Burnt Sienna	
Manganese Blue	Titanium White	

Brushes
No. 4 and No. 2 sable rounds, No. 7 hogs'-hair filbert, No. 0 rigger

Other items
Painting medium (see p. 10)

METHODS

For the watercolour painting the method is first to paint all the highlights of the tree with masking fluid. Then a blue wash is applied over the paper and the shadows are painted. The masking fluid is next removed to reveal the highlights as white, unpainted areas. A similar method of masking is employed for the bank. Finally the details of both bank and tree are painted in.

For the oil version the sky should be painted first and then left to dry. The basic dark and light tones are then picked out and left to dry before the details of trunk, branches, and leaves are added. Then the bank is painted, using the same colours as for the leaves.

For the guideline sketches on their grids see p. 234.

TREE STUDY IN WATERCOLOURS

1 Masking the highlights
First paint all the highlights with masking fluid. Use the No. 4 round sable brush. Wash the brush thoroughly in warm, soapy water immediately after use. Then mix a large quantity of Winsor Blue for the sky and lay a wash over the whole painting, lightening it towards the bottom edge of your paper.

2 The shadows
Use a mix of Winsor Blue and Burnt Sienna to paint the dark shadows on the left-hand sides of the branches and twigs. When you have done this, gently rub off the masking fluid. You can use either your fingers or an eraser. The illustration shows the masking fluid partially removed.

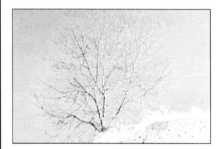

3 The area of the bank
Paint in some highlights with masking fluid where the bracken catches the sunlight. When this is dry, give the bank an overall sandy brown wash. Use a mix of Burnt Sienna and Yellow Ochre, and allow it to dry before you paint the darker patches with the deepest shadows at the back. For these areas use a Winsor Blue plus Burnt Sienna mix. Once they have dried, carefully peel off the film of masking fluid and you will be left with the basis of the bank. Next draw in the distant line of trees with your No. 4 sable. Use a light mix of Winsor Blue and add a touch of Burnt Sienna.

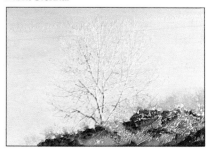

4 Completing the bank
At this stage the bank will look unreal, so you should begin to soften the contrasts between highlights and background and between the sandy colours and the blue-browns. Do this by overlaying thin yellow-brown and blue-brown washes. You can also soften the hard edges created by the masking fluid by stroking them with a damp brush. Then finish off the bank by introducing a little green colour (a mix made up of Winsor Green and Burnt Sienna) into the area at the top right.

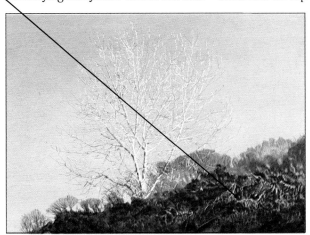

5 The details of the tree
Once you have completed the bank, turn your attention to the tree again. Use a mix of Winsor Blue and Burnt Sienna and carefully work up the modelling of the main trunk and the larger branches.

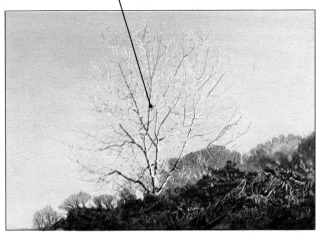

6 Final adjustments
Finish off the outermost twigs and adjust the shape and form of the whole tree by making tonal modifications to individual twigs and branches. If you want the picture to have a warmer effect, you can give it a wash of very pale yellow.

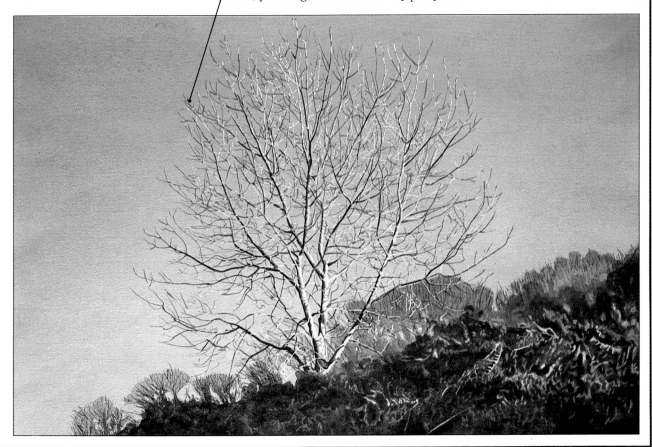

TREE STUDY IN OILS

1 The sky
Start with the sky. Paint it with an opaque Manganese Blue plus Titanium White mix that gets lighter in tone towards the horizon. At the horizon itself add a little Cadmium Yellow Pale. Make the gradation of tones as smooth as possible at this stage, since there is no way of repainting the sky once you have started work on the tree. Then leave the sky to dry out completely. You will find that it is a great deal easier to paint in the minute details of the smaller twigs and branches if you are working on a painting surface that is totally dry.

2 The basic tones
Pick out the highlights on the branches and twigs with Titanium White using the No. 2 round sable. Similarly paint the darkest shadows and silhouetted twigs with a mix of Winsor Blue and Burnt Sienna. Do not blend the tones at this stage: simply leave the tree to dry. Paint the bank in an overall mid to dark tone of the Winsor Blue plus Burnt Sienna mix. Leave this to dry.

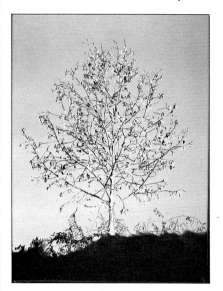

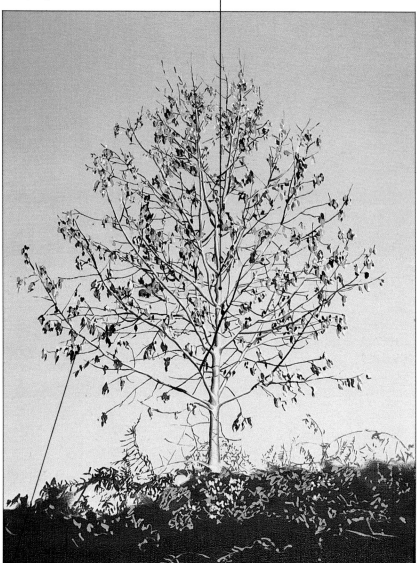

3 Details of the tree
Repaint the central trunk and main branches following the guidelines provided by your underpainting. But this time you should blend the tones as smoothly as you can, to achieve a more finished effect.

4 The leaves
Paint in the last of the autumn leaves, drooping and clustering on the branches. Their darkest tones are a mix of Winsor Blue and Burnt Sienna, with some areas of Burnt Sienna on its own, and a mix of Winsor Red, Cadmium Yellow Pale, and Titanium White for the lightest tones.

5 The bank
Here, as with the rest of the light tones in the painting, it is the fact that the colours are opaque that provides the highlights. Use the same colours as for the leaves, adding touches of colour to suggest the foliage. By using the No. 0 long-haired sable to suggest the stalks and leaves you will be able to get a more active, springy feel to your brushwork.

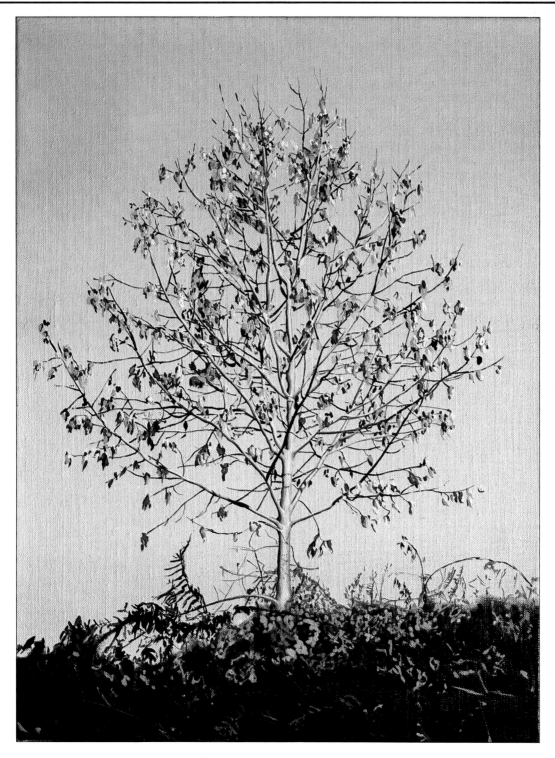

6 The finishing touches
Allow the details of the bank to dry, then apply a thin glaze of Transparent Gold Ochre with a touch of Burnt Sienna to the leaves and the bank. It is a good idea to also apply a thinner tone to the trunk and the main branches of the tree.

OPEN COUNTRY

Medium OILS

IN THE SECTION on black and white techniques, we explored the idea of tonal recession as a series of flat planes of tone that decreased in intensity as they receded towards the horizon (see pp. 30–2). For that simple exercise the edges of the tree line were like a series of flat, cutout shapes which worked only in two dimensions. Indeed, when you look at distant landscapes in mist or fog, or when the atmosphere is hazy, you do lose a great deal of the volume that the shapes normally contain.

In this painting we are concerned not so much with a "diagram" as with the actual experience of such tone differences in a real landscape. Here, the lines of trees and hedges are not geometrically equidistant and parallel, but wander at all angles to the picture plane. The trees are clearly based on three-dimensional objects, even though they are almost silhouette shapes.

Since the most important aspect of the painting is tone, the picture is almost monochromatic. In fact it could have been painted in black and white, but the subtle use of colours (which involves a fair amount of mixing ability) reinforces the particular atmosphere of the image. The cool blue-greens add a sense of detachment that the early evening light seems to generate.

MATERIALS AND EQUIPMENT

Support
Canvas or board 12 × 19 ins
(30.5 × 48 cm)

Oil colours

Winsor Red	Indian Yellow
Winsor Blue	Titanium White

Brushes
No. 7 and No. 1 hogs'-hair filberts, No. 4 and No. 2 sable rounds

Other items
Turpentine, painting medium (see p. 10)

METHOD
The outlines of the image are drawn and the broad tonal areas are blocked in using a thin paint-plus-turpentine mix. The land and tree lines are painted accurately, but details are not painted in at this stage. The method is to work down from the sky, moving from light to dark tones. When the underpainting is dry, the image is repainted using a mix of paint and painting medium and giving the forms more body and dimension.

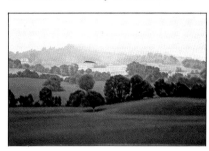

The finished painting. For the guideline sketch on its grid see p. 239.

1 Underpainting the sky
After drawing the outline of the image according to the guideline sketch, start to underpaint the sky. Use turpentine on its own to dilute and mix the paint. Mix a reasonable quantity of Titanium White to a creamy consistency and take the bright edge off it by adding a hint of Winsor Blue with a touch of Indian Yellow and Winsor Red. The amounts of colour you add should be minute. Paint this on with the No. 7 hogs'-hair filbert brush, making broad horizontal strokes. Use the small round sable to paint up to the edge of the tree line, and smooth off any rough brush-strokes with the No. 7.

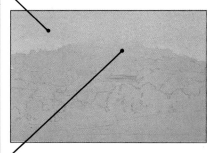

2 The distant land
Paint in the farthest land in a slightly bluer version of the same colour and, at the same time, and using the same colour, paint the patch of land below the hill which catches the evening light. Then sketch in the house on the left, using the same light blue-grey, and paint the facing wall. Use the same colour as the sky for this.

3 The tree line
Next fill in the tone of the tree line on the left at the horizon. Towards the centre the tone lightens with the haze coming over the hill behind it. To get this effect, simply add more white to your colour and blend it in as you go along. You will notice that where the tree line meets the sky the tree edges are slightly softer. You can achieve this effect by running the point of a clean round sable, slightly dampened in turpentine, along the join between the sky and trees. After each stroke, wipe any surplus paint off the brush tip.

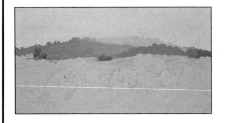

4 Cottage detailing

Now is a good time to sketch some economical detailing on to the cottage. Notice that the trees immediately to the right of the building are darker in tone.

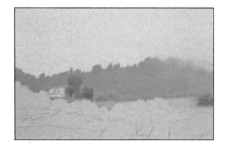

5 Tone areas

Immediately to the right of the darker clump of trees in the centre you will notice three distinct tones. The middle tone blends into the darker one, which stretches to the right across the painting. Soften the edges here so that there is little or no detailing in the broad, elliptical shapes of land.

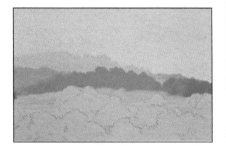

6 Horizontal bands

The best method to adopt is to work down the painting, dealing with horizontal bands of similar tone at the same time. When you come to tackle the tree line that runs from immediately below the cottage across and down into the centre of the painting, make the tone deeper again, and add a little more yellow to the basic blue-grey mix. The modelling on the trees should now begin to be visible — though only broadly. Detail and colour accuracy are not crucial at this stage.

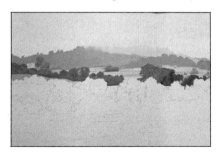

7 Tone shifts

Continue deepening the tones as you move down the painting. Take care to mix the tones as accurately as you can, and be patient. You will notice that something that looks quite "natural" is the result of quite dramatic tone shifts. For example, you may think that the field in the mid-ground looks far too deep in tone. But when you see it in the context of the finished painting, with trees around it, it becomes perfectly acceptable. When you are working with the lighter tones, which have a substantial white base, you will find that adding darker colours can make significant tonal changes. So add the darker colours a little at a time until you have the tone you need. Similarly, when you are working with the darker tones, which have a substantial dark colour base, you will find that adding a very small amount of white will dramatically lighten the tone. So be sparing when you mix your tones. Add only a little dark or light pigment at a time, and mix it in thoroughly.

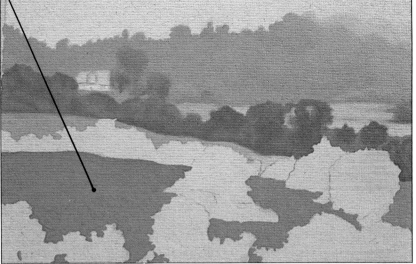

8 The finished underpainting

The difference between the finished underpainting and the final picture is like the difference between a diagram and what it represents. The underpainting is not unattractive — it has a certain antiseptic clarity. But it lacks the resolution and atmosphere of the finished painting, where the dark foreground tones sharpen the focus of the work on to the middle distance. Here the light and atmosphere seem to indicate a world which is visible but inaccessible through the dark barrier of the foreground. This is the atmosphere you should aim for.

Continued over

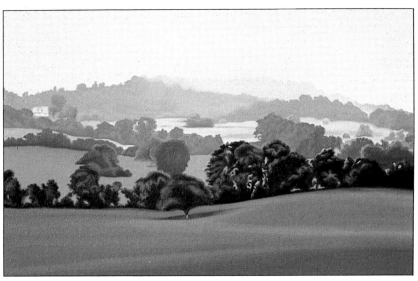

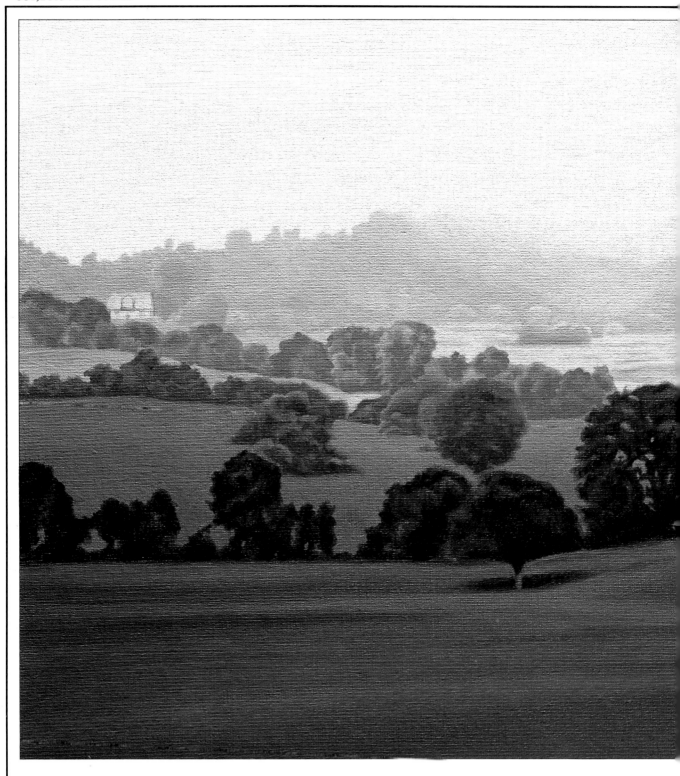

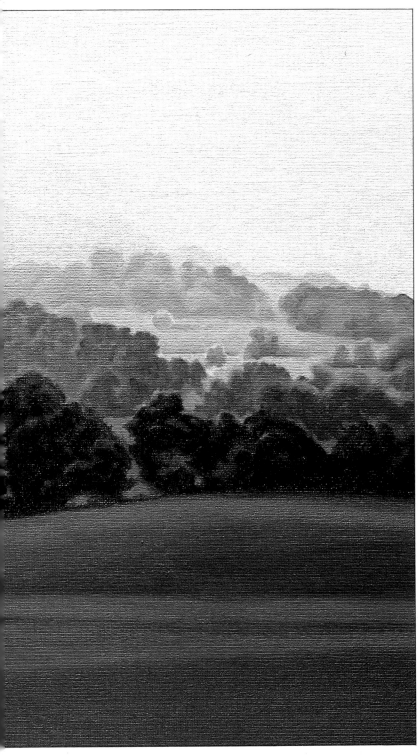

9 Adding body

The method for the top coat is similar to that for the underpainting. You work down from the sky, deepening the tone as you go. But you should now use the painting medium for mixing the pigment to a workable consistency. You can see by looking at the finished painting that it has more body. It holds together as a richer and more satisfying surface than before. Now that the basic features of the landscape are already defined on your canvas, you can begin working them up. You will be able to bring out the more subtle areas of light and shade and use a wider and more flexible range of colours in the blue-grey, green-grey, and red-blue-grey areas.

10 Adding dimension

As you paint, try to give more solidity to areas in the middle distance which were just flat shapes. You can create this effect as much by the brushstrokes themselves and the way you apply the pigment as by the tones and colours you use. As you paint each part of the landscape you should be aware not only of the overall tone of the part but also of the range of tones that go to make it up. Here, for example, there are four basic tonal shifts from the distant tone, which almost blends with the sky, through two stages of tree clumps, to the dark foreground of trees. Give each area discernible tonal variations, to create the impression of form and dimension. As the landscape comes towards you, so the tonal variation within each section should become greater. The nearer the foreground the trees are, the more silhouette-like they should be, though you can add highlights to their outer edges.

11 The single tree

An important feature of this painting is the tree to the left of the centre, near the lower edge. You should make it the active point in the lower half of the picture. Whereas the other trees sit happily on the base line of the hedgerows, this tree seems to spin like a top on its trunk within the area of its shadow. It adds a feeling of vitality to an otherwise placid painting and draws the spectator's attention to the foreground sweep of land.

12 The foreground field

This large, uninterrupted area of field, with its ridges and hollows, gives you the scope to make long, flexible brushstrokes and to do smooth blending. Use the No. 7 hogs'-hair filbert and lay the tones on separately to make up the tonal structure of the land. Then blend the tones with horizontal strokes, wiping the brush off after each stroke, until the transitions are quite smooth.

ITALIAN LANDSCAPE WITH FIGURES

Medium OILS

THIS PAINTING TAKES as its main subject a tiny Italian chapel. The small scale of the building makes it a very attractive subject for a painting. The scene is brightly lit by the afternoon sun, which bleaches the colours on the left-hand side of the chapel and casts deep-toned shadows on the walls at right angles. The season is late spring after a day of rain, which explains the fresh greens in the foliage.

In order to give an idea of the scale of the building I felt it was important to have something of recognisable size to relate to it. Consequently, I have used the figures of the two children in a slightly unconventional composition. This centres around the vertical axis created by the chapel tower. In front of it the tree to the left and the children to the right set up a foreground symmetry that parallels the tree line behind the chapel.

MATERIALS AND EQUIPMENT

Support
Canvas 14 × 18 ins (35.5 × 46 cm)

Oil colours

Winsor Red		Winsor Green	
Winsor Blue		Burnt Sienna	
Cadmium Yellow Pale		Titanium White	

Brushes
No. 6, No. 4, and No. 2 hogs'-hair filberts, No. 4 nylon (or sable) pointed flat, No. 1 nylon round, No. 0 nylon rigger

Other items
Pencil, turpentine, painting medium (see p. 10)

METHOD

After tinting the canvas and drawing in the outline, oil paint is applied directly on to the canvas. The method is to start with the sky and continue with the light tones in the chapel, the darker shadows, and then the line of trees behind the building. Then the middle ground, including the tree in front of the chapel and the children, is sketched in, followed by the foreground grass. The painting is then worked "wet-in-wet" to build the image up to its finished state.

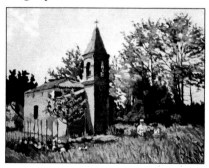

The finished painting. For the guideline sketch on its grid see p. 241.

1 Starting on the sky
After tinting the canvas with Burnt Sienna and drawing the outlines of the image according to the guideline provided, sketch in the sky using Titanium White with a touch of Winsor Blue. Use the No. 6 hogs'-hair, making bold brushstrokes in all directions. When you come to the edge of the tree and the chapel you should use the No. 4 hogs'-hair brush.

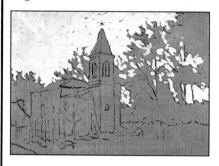

2 The sunlit areas
For these parts of the chapel use pinks, greens and oranges, and paint them with the No. 4 bristle. The lightest cream parts of the building are a mix of Titanium White and Cadmium Yellow Pale, with a touch of Winsor Red and Burnt Sienna. For the pinker areas use more red with the white and less of the other colours. For the yellower area on the left of the tower roof, use more Cadmium Yellow Pale. For the cooler colours below the eaves use the same mix with a touch of Winsor Green. The tinting strength of this is very great — add only a little.

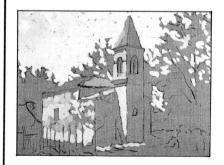

3 The darker tones

The warm browns are a Burnt Sienna and Winsor Red mix. The darker ones have either Winsor Green or Winsor Blue added. The yellow-browns, as in the long triangular shadow on the tower, are Burnt Sienna with Cadmium Yellow Pale and Winsor Blue. The horizontal lines in the tower and roof are Burnt Sienna and Winsor Red with a small amount of Titanium White added.

4 The tree line

You can now start to paint the tree line behind the chapel. On the left the very dark colour is Winsor Green with Burnt Sienna. You should also use this colour for the base of the tree line on the right. Mix all the other greens for the trees from this range: Winsor Green, Burnt Sienna, Cadmium Yellow Pale, and Titanium White. Use a No. 4 hogs'-hair brush.

5 Middle ground greenery

Below the dark green on the left of the painting the grey-green is a mix of Burnt Sienna, Winsor Green, Winsor Red, and Titanium White. The cream patch here is the same mix as for the building. Work along the vegetable plot by the side of the chapel using a similar range of greens. The very light green patches are Cadmium Yellow Pale, Winsor Green, and Titanium White. Use the same colour for the lightest leaf areas in the tree in front of the church. Work with a No. 2 bristle or a No. 4 sable flat here.

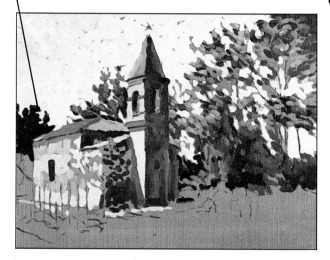

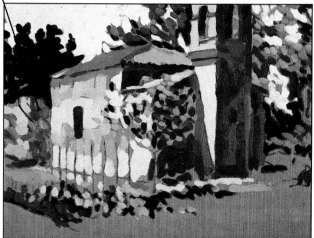

6 Painting the figures

Paint the basic tonal areas that define the children using the No. 4 sable flat. Then paint the arms, which catch the light. Add the darker grey shadows to the shirts, then paint the brown hair, the shadow beneath the hat, and the hair of the boy on the right. Use the greens of the foliage behind to define the shapes of the figures. Notice how the left arm of the left-hand figure is defined entirely by the foliage at this stage. Add the blue of the skirt on the left and the grey shadows below the arm of the boy on the right. Then, using a mix of Winsor Red and Titanium White, paint the tops of the two poppies that the children have stopped for a moment to admire.

Continued over

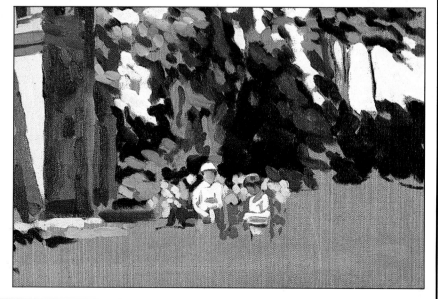

7 Further details

While you are painting details you will inevitably be working a little tighter. So while your hand is steady, you can paint the branches of the trees on the right and those in front of the church. You can also tackle the sticks in the vegetable patch. Use the No. 0 rigger brush and a Burnt Sienna and Winsor Blue mix diluted with turpentine.

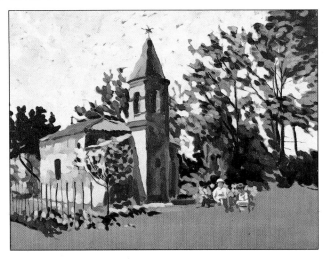

8 Refining the image

Add some touches of colour to the foreground to indicate the grass and you will have the basis of your painting. You can then start working up the image. To integrate the figures with the surrounding details requires a more resolved approach. Pay attention to such areas as the trees behind the chapel, where the scale of the first brushstrokes is rather large. Add a hint of features to the faces of both figures. Use the No. 2 round sable.

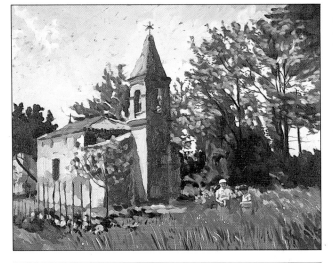

9 Reworking sky and trees

Next rework the sky, giving it more body. Paint over the thin areas where the ground shows through. In particular, give the small white cloud on the top left softer edges. This will make the whole composition more balanced. Then look again at the trees behind the chapel: there are large gaps where the colour of the ground shows through. Rework the foliage with the No. 2 hogs'-hair, reducing its scale and touching in the leaves.

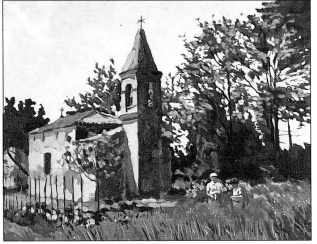

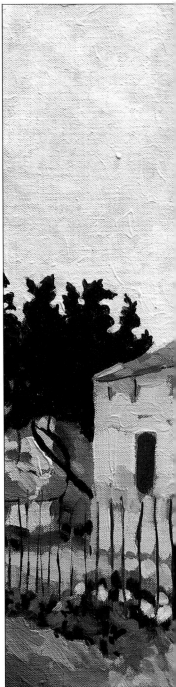

10 Repainting the sky

In the top right-hand corner of the painting branches of a closer tree overhang the composition. At this point I decided to leave these out of the original, so I wiped off this patch of green and repainted the sky there.

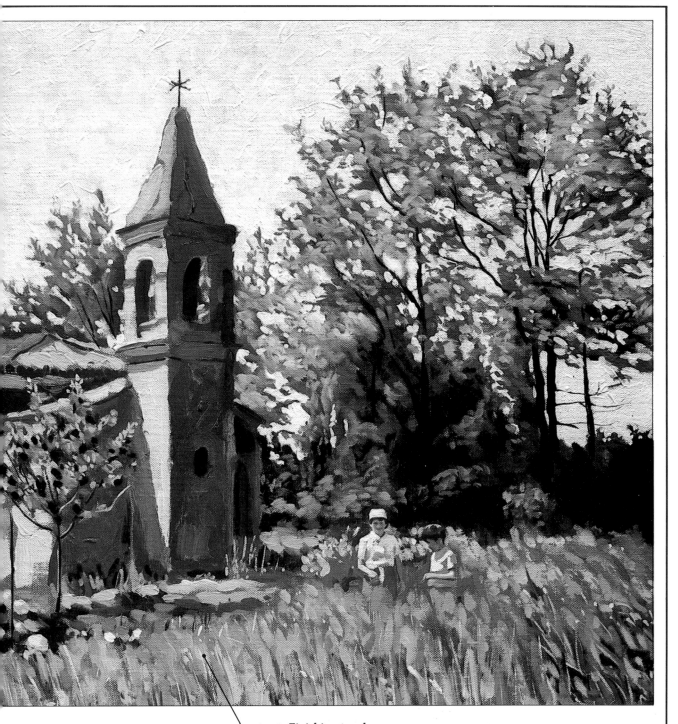

11 Finishing touches

Now turn your attention to the foreground. Paint this in a series of brushstrokes that reflect the direction of the grass. Use a No. 4 hogs'-hair brush and a range of light greens with some of the pink-orange-yellow colours. Break up the foliage on the tree in front of the chapel with smaller touches of light green. Make any changes you think are necessary.

GARDEN SCENE

Medium OILS

THIS PAINTING SHOWS an unusual view in a formal garden. It is an almost theatrical organisation of space – the lower third and two sides are rather like an inverted proscenium arch, and the central section has two symmetrical conifers with the long, thin-trunked pine in between. The steep rise behind the house, which cuts out the sky, is like a painted backdrop, and the whole image is formally enclosed.

This painting passed through two main stages – the rapidly painted first draft, and the more resolved final version. In many ways the first draft is fresher and more spontaneous. It explores the landscape in terms of a patchwork of bright colours on the canvas surface. The final version is more "academic", rather monochromatic, and more closely worked. The process of painting a picture does not always follow a clear path from start to finish – the progress of this particular painting demonstrates how decisions can be made and then reversed or modified when the painting reaches another stage. A particular section may be working well on its own, but it may be necessary to repaint it completely to make the painting work as a whole.

As far as technique is concerned, the first draft requires large, bold strokes, and the overpainting smaller, more careful ones. This reflects the gradual process of refinement from a freer, more colourful approach to a greater accuracy of representation – though it is important not to lose the initial fresh response to the scene. Try to build up a dialogue with your picture, so that you learn something from the decisions you make during your painting. Finally, remember that, with all the overpainting you will be doing, the "fat over lean" approach (see pp. 12–13) must be adopted at each stage.

MATERIALS AND EQUIPMENT

Support
Canvas or board 20 × 16 ins (51 × 40.5 cm)

Oil colours

Winsor Red		Sap Green	
Winsor Blue		Burnt Sienna	
Indian Yellow		Permanent Rose	
Cadmium Yellow Pale		Titanium White	
Winsor Green			

Brushes
No. 7, No. 6, No. 4, and No. 1 hogs'-hair filberts, No. 4, No. 2, and No. 1 hogs'-hair rounds, No. 6 and No. 4 sable rounds, badger blender

Other items
Turpentine, painting medium

METHOD

After tinting the canvas the outlines are drawn in. The first draft can serve as the underpainting or it can be a painting in its own right. The method is to keep style broad and loose, using dabbing brushstrokes. The overpainting is a refinement of the draft: the colours are more realistic, the brushstrokes smaller.

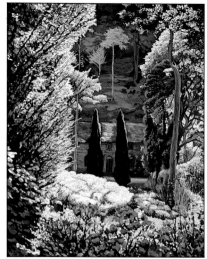

The finished painting. For the guideline sketch on its grid see p. 240.

1 Tinting the canvas
First give the primed canvas a thin overall Burnt Sienna tint. Allow it to dry before you start painting. If you intend to paint the final version immediately, with no overpainting, this warm ground will act as a unifying overall background to the purples, pinks, and greens. Then draw in the outlines according to the guideline sketch.

2 The first draft
I painted this first version in a loose, chunky style which accentuates both the contrast between the light and dark tones, and the difference between the colours.

3 Applying the paint
Dab the paint on to the canvas using the range of hogs'-hair brushes. There is no set procedure, though I recommend moving from light to dark areas. But where there are mid to light tones of pure colour – such as the "blue" foliage on the central thin tree in the background – it makes sense to apply this early so as to avoid contaminating the colour when you are painting it on. Use a mix of Winsor Blue, Winsor Green, and Titanium White for this. If this first draft is to be your final version, try to make each brushstroke as complete and satisfying as you can, so that the cumulative effect is strong and vigorous. If you are blocking tones in as a preparation to overpainting, use thinner mixes of paint and let your work dry before continuing with the overpainting.

4 The background
Paint the very dark-toned background in after the tall central tree, as if to enclose the shape. Use a mix of Winsor Red, Winsor Blue, and Indian Yellow. The adjacent tints of the three primary colours provide a focal point for the painting – the deep pink acts as a central complementary pivot to the surrounding greens, while the "blue" foliage on the spindly stem is like a beacon towards which the eye travels through the foreground frame of trees and shrubs. Although these colours are not accurate depictions of the scene's real hues, they were inspired by the actual colours. If you look at the more accurately coloured finished version, you can still detect the pink and blue in the colours.

5 Working from light to dark

You will find that deviating from accurate colouring is not only a positive approach, but is also necessary. There is very little modelling in this first draft, and you will achieve tonal variation by juxtaposing tones rather than blending them. The surest method is to proceed from light to dark areas, but paint the twigs and branches on the left early on.

6 The pink ground

Paint in the bright pink cast to the ground beneath the tree using a mix of Permanent Rose, Titanium White, and Winsor Red.

7 The house roof

You should next paint the orange-yellow roof of the house in Cadmium Yellow Pale with just a little Winsor Red added.

8 Twigs and branches

Establish the structure of the trees and shrubs. Paint the thin, dark brown twigs rising diagonally from the left and up from the bottom of the canvas. Then paint in the tree trunk on the right in oranges, browns, and ochres. It is a strong and useful vertical in the composition, so paint it early so that the colour stays fresh.

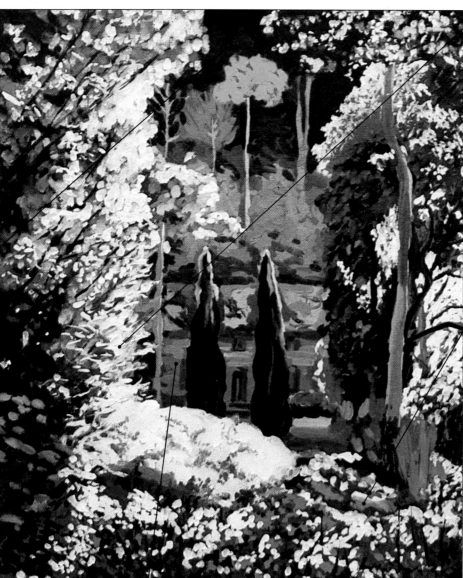

9 The leaves and flowers

Work round the picture anticlockwise from the left. For the leaves in the light use Cadmium Yellow with Titanium White. Add Sap Green for intermediate tones, and Winsor Blue for the slightly darker ones. For the darkest tones use a mix of Winsor Blue, Indian Yellow, and Winsor Red. The light blue colours on the bush are a mix of Winsor Blue, Winsor Green, and Titanium White, while the pink flowers are Permanent Rose plus Titanium White, and the purple ones a mix of Permanent Rose, Titanium White, and Winsor Blue.

10 The dark green tree and fir trees

Working up the right-hand side of the painting, paint the yellow-green foliage beneath the orange tree trunk using a mix of Cadmium Yellow Pale and Winsor Blue. For the dark green tree behind use a mix of Winsor Green, Winsor Blue, Sap Green, and a touch of Winsor Red. For the two symmetrical fir trees use a similar mix with more Winsor Green in it. Add white for the highlights.

11 The house

Paint in the grey tones of the house by adding a mix of Winsor Red, Indian Yellow, and Winsor Blue to Titanium White. Your first draft, which you can, if you wish, treat as a finished work, is complete. *Continued over*

12 The overpainting

If you wish to produce a more resolved version of the painting, you should now start on the overpainting. The finished surface of this version is more resolved. By adjusting colours and adding details you can produce a far more cohesive image. Make sure that your brushstrokes are small and precise throughout the overpainting.

13 The trees and foliage

Make refinements to the trees around the outside of the canvas, and then bring the colours in the central section closer to reality. Increase the density of the foliage from the top to the centre-left by adding light-toned body colour. Apply it with a small round hogs'-hair brush. Paint this over the mid-toned green-yellow. You will find that it has the effect of making the tree's scale look more natural. Treat the top right and foreground foliage in the same way, adding tone and density all the time.

14 The tree trunk

On the right-hand side add details to the tree trunk to give a greater illusion of space behind it. Add orange-brown highlights to the twisting branches and to the area behind the trunk. Repaint the trunk itself in a cooler colour so that the original orange still comes through, but is more ochre-coloured (add semi-opaque grey-yellow paint and light-grey highlights at the edges and on the right to achieve this).

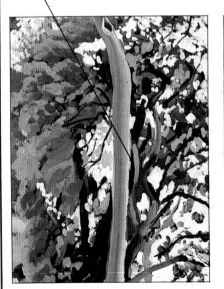

15 The background

Repaint the striking blue of the central tree and the pink of the ground in more neutral colours. Then lighten the very dark tone surrounding the tree to a more mid blue-grey-green. These modifications will pull the tree into the background of the picture and also take the ground on which it stands back into the painting.

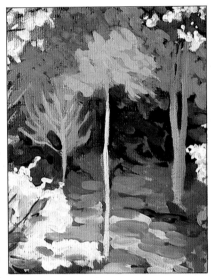

16 The house

Now reconsider the house. Soften the bright orange on the roof to a yellow-cream combination, and bring the two flanking areas to a more credible and uniform colour range. Below this, on the front of the house, modify the effect of the light. You should do this by painting a lighter tone below the middle window and above the arch of the door.

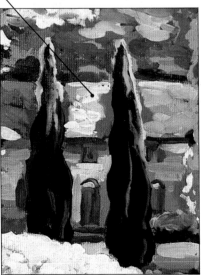

17 Modifying tone contrast

Continue modifying tones and colours so that tonal contrasts become less abrupt. Extend the bank of light tone in the foreground, and make the light serpentine pathway which runs along the bottom and up the right-hand side more conscious. Make the background more uniform in tone and lighten the tone immediately below the central tree and above the two firs.

18 Adding a thin glaze

When the painting is quite dry apply a thin overall glaze of Winsor Blue. This makes the picture much cooler, removing the rather heavy yellow cast. When this is dry overpaint the areas that you want to remain warm.

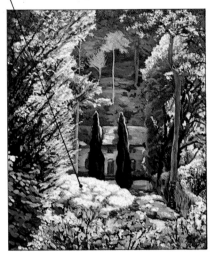

19 Final adjustments

It would be a shame to lose the rich colours of the moss and lichen on the roof, and the warm earth colours beneath the central tree. So you must now do a certain amount of overpainting to reinstate these hues. Adjust tones in general. For example, reduce the tone of the two fir trees so that it is less dramatic and the Winsor Green becomes less harsh. It is important for a painting like this to have uniformity of tone over its whole surface, so if one part is painted more crudely than another, for example, the whole will look awkward. So check that your painting is perfectly balanced in tone and detail throughout.

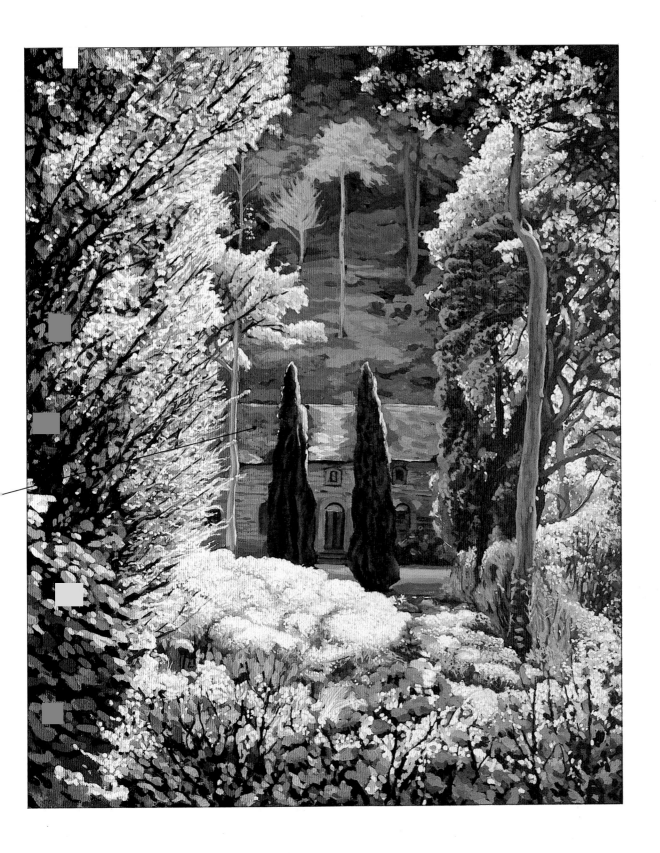

HORSE IN AN ENGLISH LANDSCAPE

Medium OILS

THIS OIL PAINTING is based on sketches, photographs, and the memory of a clear and sunny early morning walk by a river in flat fen country. The sun was still quite low in the east, so that light swept in from the right giving the trees and the side of the horse a crisp focus. This light also gives the painting a full range of tones from the darkest shadows to bright highlights. The horse is placed centrally in the front of the picture with the landscape serving as a framing device, holding and surrounding the shape of the horse with a soft, green field of colour. The painting illustrates an aspect of oil painting that no other medium can match. This is its ability to convey soft-edged relief on a miniature scale. Oil paint has a marvellous flexible quality that enables you to keep moving the paint around until you have the effect you want. This painting is designed to exercise and develop your skill in modelling and control on a small scale. Modelling the features of the horse involves several stages. You first paint in the main tones, then work up the details of the muscles and bone structure, and finally apply a skin-like glaze.

MATERIALS AND EQUIPMENT

Support
Canvas or board 14 × 18 ins
(35.5 × 46 cm)

Oil colours

Winsor Red   Winsor Green

Winsor Blue   Sap Green

Indian Yellow   Titanium White

Cadmium Yellow Pale

Brushes
No. 7 hogs'-hair filbert, No. 7, No. 6, No. 4, and No. 2 sables

Other items
Painting medium (see p. 10), turpentine

METHOD

The outlines are drawn in and the trees are underpainted thinly. Next the tones of the horse are blocked in quite accurately. The method is then to paint the sky using thicker mixes, before over-painting the trees. The next stage is to tackle the details of the horse, building up the ridges and furrows of the body's surface. When this is done, the details of field, sky, trees, and grass are strengthened. Finally the horse is completed by applying an overall yellow-brown glaze.

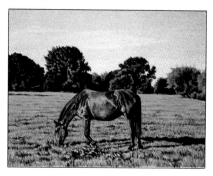

The finished painting. For the guideline sketch on its grid see p. 237.

1 Underpainting the trees
After drawing the outline according to the guideline sketch, you can start the underpainting. Use thin oil colour and turpentine. Sketch in the trees in a grey-green mix and overpaint the darkest areas in a darker green mix. Try to express the shape and form of the trees when you are doing the underpainting, and incorporate most of the main elements of each.

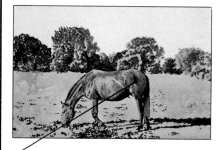

2 Underpainting the horse
Now underpaint the horse, blocking in the tones quite accurately. Start with the darkest tones, using a blue-brown mix for the back of the neck, under the head and chin, the back of the legs, and under the belly. In addition sketch in some of the details round the face, mane, and legs. Indicate the rest of the horse's features with a grey-chestnut-brown. Next block in the patches of dock and dandelion in the field and the horse's shadow. Finally paint a thin green wash over the field.

3 The sky
Mix a reasonable amount of Titanium White with the painting medium to a thick, creamy consistency. Add a little Winsor Blue to some of this. Apply a band of this light blue across the top of the sky using the hogs'-hair brush. Add more white and apply another band of colour. Then wipe your brush and use it to blend the two bands. When you get to an area of cloud, apply pure white with a clean brush and blend its edges. As you get near the trees your mix will be almost white. Paint up to and over the edge of the tree line.

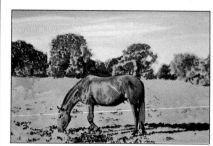

4 Starting to overpaint the trees

For the first stage of overpainting the trees mix a basic colour of Sap Green with a little Winsor Red and Winsor Blue added for all the darker tones. Modify the basic colour a little towards brown (by adding more red), or towards blue, according to the type of tree. To show the three-dimensional quality in the shadows, dilute the mix a little so that it is slightly lighter. As the leaves emerge from the shadows use a lighter mix again, and where they are catching the sun use an even lighter tone with an occasional touch of Indian Yellow. Then return to the dark and mid tones to adjust the overall look of the trees. When you are painting the top edge of the trees the colours may mix with the wet part of the sky. Do not worry about this – you can deal with it when you come to the final stage of painting the trees.

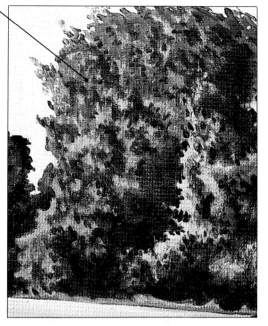

5 Beginning on the details

It is convenient to start detailed work on the horse itself at this stage, since you will be able to rest your hand on the canvas without smudging it. Paint slowly and carefully, taking a small detail at a time. Use the No. 1 and No. 2 sables – you will need one brush to paint with and one, slightly dampened in painting medium, to blend the tones. The colours used are a mix of Winsor Red and Sap Green for the brown, the same mix plus Winsor Blue for the darkest tones, and the same mix diluted or with white for the lighter ones.

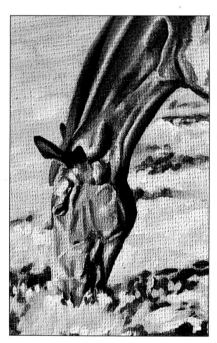

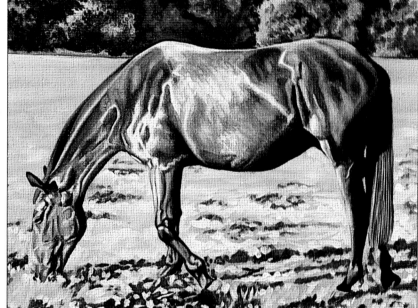

6 Painting the head and body

If you look at the head and body closely you will see that it is an assortment of ridges and furrows that are highly contrasted in the bright morning light. Take one of these at a time, applying the darkest tone to the right, a lighter one in the middle, the brightest tone to the left, and white last of all. Blend them together with soft strokes of a clean sable that you have chiselled between your fingers. You should not put too much paint on to your brush. Think of the head as a small painting in its own right. If you do this you will not be tempted to rush it. At this stage, the surface of the horse will look unfinished: the transparent chestnut washes and the opaque highlights still need to be resolved. The painting needs the later softening glazes to reduce the glaring effect of light and shade, putting a soft skin over the animal whose muscles, veins, and bone structure are revealed in the underpainting.

7 The mane, legs, and tail

Paint these in grey tones, made by adding blue to the basic brown mix. As with the rest of the horse the method is to paint in the darkest areas and make a smooth gradation to the lightest parts.

Continued over

8 The field

Paint in the basic colour of the field, using a mix of Winsor Green, Cadmium Yellow Pale and Titanium White. You should also give the field a little more definition at this stage. Pick out the dark shadows and use white for the highlights in the foreground. This will give some impression of the depth of the field. Now leave the painting to dry for two or three days before you paint the final stages.

9 Softening the sky

If you feel that the sky needs any modification, do it at this stage. In this case, I thought the sky was too blue and decided to soften the colour a little. I also gave the clouds some more body.

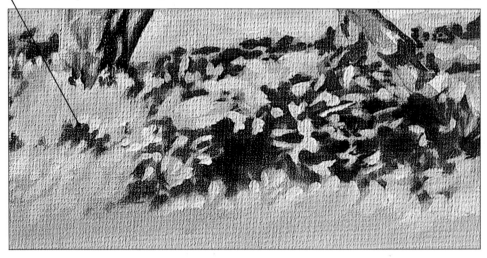

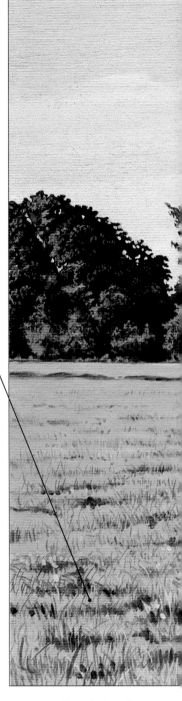

10 Strengthening the trees

The trees need more attention and you should mix a range of greens (blue-greens, yellow-greens, and brown-greens) with white or opaque yellow. Stipple these over the places where the foliage stands out or is highlighted. Use a small sable and dab the paint over these areas. You should also use this method to add some detail in the darkest areas of foliage, though the colour you use here will naturally be deeper in tone. Since most of the trees are about the same distance away try to keep your dots of colour a consistent size. Also try to be sensitive to the shape of the trees, especially the dynamic arch shapes of the two large ones above the head and tail of the horse. They form a refreshing feature in an otherwise still and quiet composition.

11 The grass

Once you have established the broad tones of the field you can make fast, curling touches with the point of the brush that accumulate to give the effect of the grass. Use three or four colours, ranging in tone from dark to light. The blades of grass are large and expressive in the immediate foreground, but as the landscape recedes there is less need for this kind of detail.

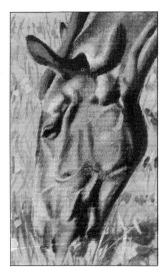

Actual-size detail

12 Completing the horse

Soften the horse's chestnut body with its white highlights by applying an overall yellow-brown glaze. Mix a very small amount of warm brown (Winsor Red

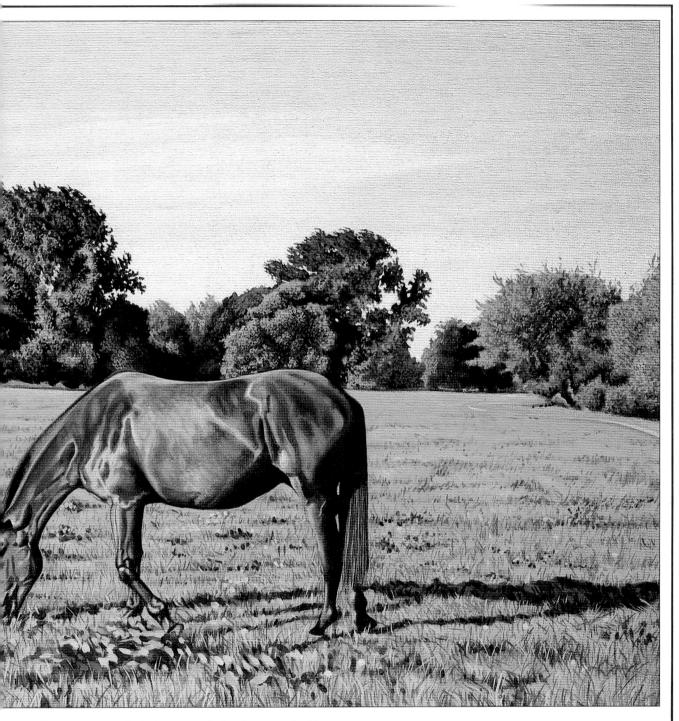

plus Sap Green) and a little Indian Yellow. Add the brown to the yellow and dilute the mix with your painting medium. You should mix enough to cover the whole horse excluding the legs and tail. Apply the glaze with the No. 7 round sable. You can retain the strongest highlights either by wiping off the glaze at the appropriate place or by repainting. If you still find parts of the horse too prominent, simply apply a darker tone.

WELSH MOUNTAINS

Medium ACRYLICS

THIS ACRYLIC PAINTING is an example of a mixed dry brush and wash technique. This method of working provides one way of representing a rugged landscape with rocky outcrops. The first thing to do in such a situation is to try and make sense of the contours of the land. If your painting is to have any solid underlying form, you must rationalise the bumps, ridges, and hollows of the landscape into an overall surface from which the various rocks and ridges can project. The best way to do this is to make outline drawings of the arrangement of land masses. You may have to do a number of sketches before you make one that integrates the components of the scene in a satisfactory composition. You can then work this up to the scale of your painting. You will find it far easier to build up the detail on a canvas that you have already divided up into the smaller components that this method provides.

This landscape with its scattering of rocks and shadows suggests the textural approach of this method of painting. There are no real outstanding features of visual interest, so the overall surface texture becomes the painting's subject. From the point of view of composition, the eye travels into the centre of the painting from the left. It follows a line along an old causeway made as a passage to the slate mines on the other side of the mountain. Towards the centre of the canvas it meets a sweeping curve in the lie of the land, which swings round to the right and then makes a sharp left turn, curving down to join up with the original line. This creates a large ellipse that holds the landscape together and is mirrored in similar smaller shapes.

The colours in the painting are not designed to reproduce faithfully those of the original landscape. The painting explores some of the original colours and leaves out others. So the painting has its own separate colour logic, yet one which is based on visual experience of the scene.

MATERIALS AND EQUIPMENT

Support
Canvas 20 × 28 ins (51 × 71 cm)

Acrylic colours

Quinacridone Red		Phthalo Green	
Phthalo Blue		Burnt Sienna	
Azo Yellow		Titanium White	

Brushes
No. 8 and No. 6 nylon or sable flats, No. 10 and No. 7 hogs'-hair filberts

METHOD

The broad shapes of the landscape are drawn in and the areas painted using thin coloured washes. Then broad detail is painted within each shape using thin but darker-toned versions of the same colours, followed by highlit tones, using thicker white paint. The sky is then painted. The next stage is to repaint the original colour washes in slightly deeper tones. Mid-toned shadows are picked out in colour washes and the depth of tone built up. Thick, light-toned paint is used for all the lighter areas. Thin colour washes are used to pull the painting's surface together.

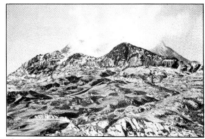

The finished painting. For the guideline sketch on its grid see p. 239.

1 The colour washes

After drawing in the outlines according to the guideline sketch, start to apply thin colour washes with the No. 7 hogs'-hair filbert. First do the sky, using a very pale Phthalo Blue mix. This is really just tinted water that serves to define the clouds which emerge from the mountain tops. These can be left white. The farthest peaks on the line behind the clouds are a pale mix of Phthalo Blue and Burnt Sienna, while those in front of the clouds are the same mix with a little more Burnt Sienna. Paint the land on the left with a Phthalo Blue plus Quinacridone Red mix with a touch of Burnt Sienna to give the violet-brown colour. Immediately below this section and moving up towards the right, paint the land with a mix made from Azo Yellow, Burnt Sienna, and Quinacridone Red with the yellow predominating. Use a lighter version on the right, and on the bottom left intoduce a little Phthalo Green into the mix for the grass.

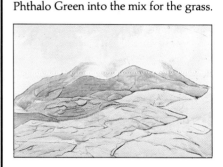

2 The shadow areas

Now mix darker tones of the same colours. Using the No. 6 or No. 8 nylon flat, paint the broad details of the parts of the scene that are in shadow over the whole picture.

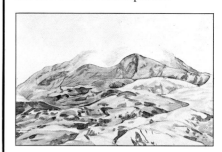

3 The details on the mountains

Using variations on a Phthalo Blue plus Quinacridone Red mix with a touch of Burnt Sienna, work up the detail on the mountain surfaces. Paint this with the No. 6 nylon or sable flat brush. At this stage you should still apply the paint in thin washes.

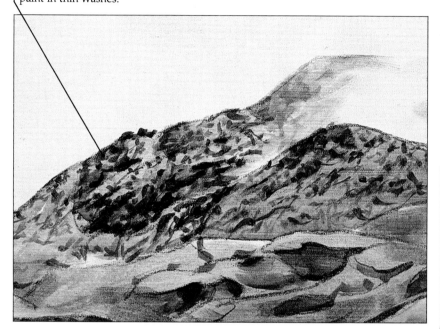

4 Building up the darker tones

Continue the process of building up the darker-toned detail, dealing with small sections at a time. For the most part use the same mix of Phthalo Blue and Quinacridone Red as before. For the orange washes use a mix of Azo Yellow and Quinacridone Red.

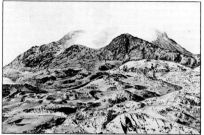

5 Adding body

Do this using the No. 6 flat and a thick Titanium White mix. Paint over the mountains where there are patches of snow and on the areas of rock in sunlight. Continue to add thick white to the areas of lightest tone over the whole painting. This includes all the rocky outcrops and individual rocks.

Continued over

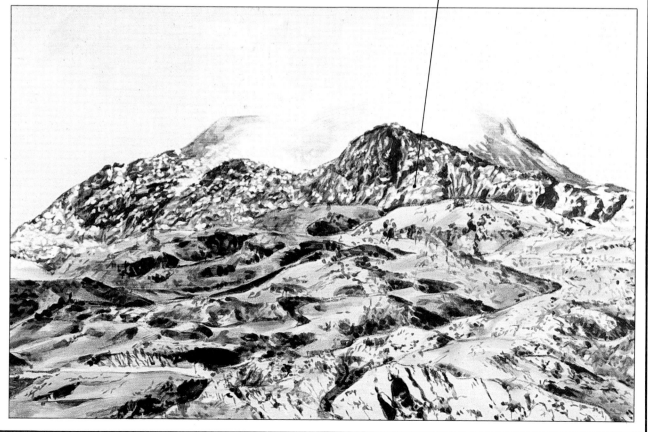

6 Overpainting the sky
Next paint the sky and clouds opaquely using the No. 7 hogs'-hair filbert. For the sky use a mix of Phthalo Blue, Titanium White, and a touch of Quinacridone Red. The clouds are Titanium White with a touch of the last mix. When you are mixing, remember that, if you tint white acrylic with another colour such as blue, the mixture will dry darker than it looks when wet. So do not add too much blue to the white.

7 Painting the coloured glazes
Now overpaint the picture with thin colour washes once more, using colours that are similar to those you used at the beginning, but a little deeper in tone. Paint over each area with these glazes and this will have the effect of giving body to the painting.

8 Creating the "half tone" effect
Pick out the highlights once more with white. Add some texture and form to the smoother areas around the rocks by stroking white paint very lightly over the canvas with the No. 8 flat. If the paint is thick and dry it will only be picked up on the top of the canvas grain and this, in conjunction with the colour beneath, will give a satisfying half tone effect to these areas.

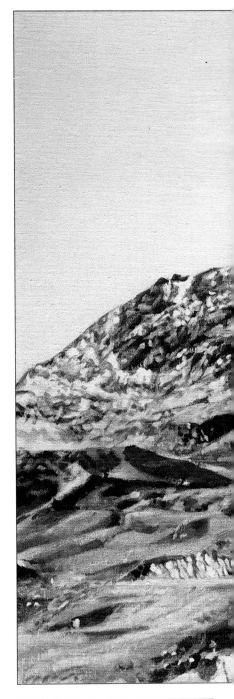

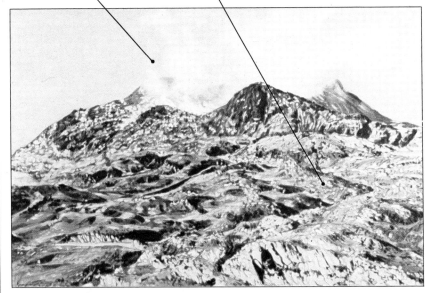

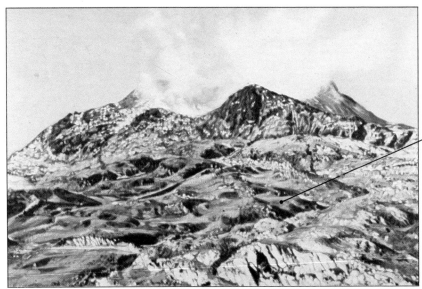

9 Making further glazes
Continue the process of glazing over these areas, modifying the colour of your washes slightly each time and gradually building up the texture of the overall surface. Follow the colours of the original as closely as you can.

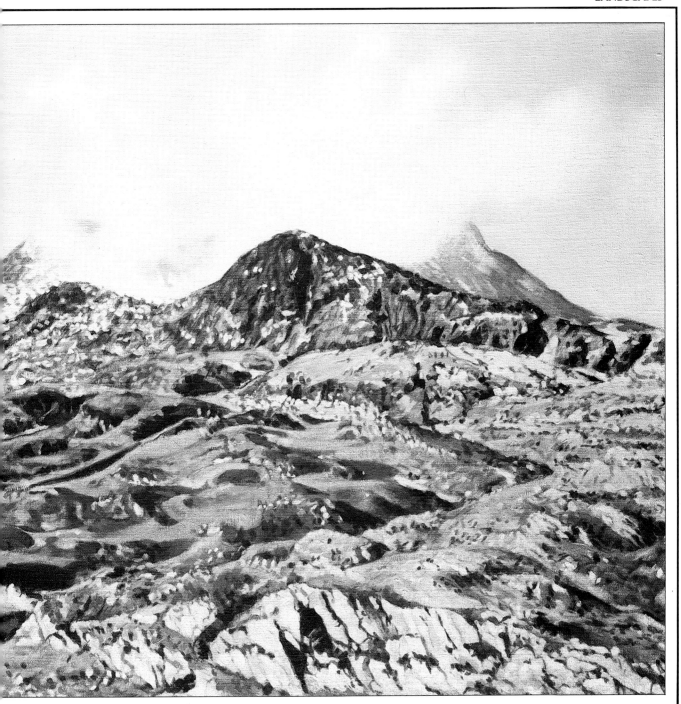

10 **Alternating opaque colour with thin washes**
Go on alternating "dry" opaque colour with thick transparent washes. Over the smoother areas of land mix lighter opaque versions of the colours and apply these by stroking (see Step 8). With this method of painting you can apply quite different colours over each other to good effect. At the bottom left, for example, apply orange-brown and then light green.

11 **Working on small areas**
As you work towards the finished painting you will find that you are concentrating on small areas at a time. To help find your way around, you can draw a grid lightly over the reproduction of the finished painting, so that you can refer to the individual squares as you work.

12 **The final stages**
You may find that you have to repaint the darkest tones if they have been made grey by the overpainting. This may also be necessary with the brightest highlights. Once you are satisfied with the detail over the whole painting, you should apply thin washes to areas that need to be taken back in tone. Finally paint a very thin yellow-brown wash over the whole bottom half of the canvas.

SEASCAPE

Medium OILS

IN THIS PAINTING I have tried to convey what it feels like to walk along a shore with the foam tugging your ankles towards the sea and the waves crashing on to the beach. I have also tried to explore the moment before a storm when the light is still brilliant, before massing clouds blanket the sky and rain starts to fall. Just before the weather breaks you sense an urgency and an expectancy, and the wind begins to whip up the waves while the last of the sun highlights the spray.

As a painter you are faced with a number of alternatives. You may want to express your experience immediately on paper, finding a shorthand notation with brush or pencil that brings together the important elements of the scene. These might be the vertical chaos of the breaking waves, the flat bed of running foam, the solid weighty shapes of land, and the cloud piling up above. Or you may want to focus on just one aspect of the scene and make a small part express the whole. For example, you may want to study the infinite abstractions presented by the turmoil of the waves.

Your approach to a style may be dictated by your choice of medium, or by the tool you use to apply it. Here your choice must be influenced by the subject. You might, for example, find an analogy to the clouds building up by using a painting knife to pull the pigment over a smoothly graduated sky. Or you may be able to echo the movement of the water by making vigorous brushstrokes with a long-haired sable brush, using a flexible wrist action.

Another idea is to paint the scene as realistically as you can, but in a more objective way. If you take a photograph, you can freeze all the action and study it carefully rather than making instinctive, subjective marks while your subject is constantly moving. In this way you can convey more precisely some of the patterns that the waves throw up. Although using photography like this helps to make a painting look authentic and dramatically realistic, an abstract flurry of brushstrokes can often produce the same feeling. You still have to translate the scene into terms that the paint can cope with.

MATERIALS AND EQUIPMENT

Support
Canvas (preferably fine grain)
18 × 24 ins (46 × 61 cm)

Oil colours

Winsor Red	⚫	Indian Yellow ⚪
Winsor Blue	⚫	Titanium White

Brushes
No. 7, No. 4, and No. 1 hogs'-hair filberts, No. 4 and No. 2 hogs'-hair rounds, No. 7 and No. 4 sable rounds, fat squirrel-hair mop or shaving brush

Other items
Painting medium (see p. 10)

METHOD

The main features are first sketched in. Then sky and clouds are painted and blended in, followed by the land on the horizon and to the centre right, and the cliff face. Texture is next added to the rocks, after which the waves are underpainted, the spray stippled, and the foam painted in. Finally a grey glaze is added to the cliffs and sand, and dots of spray are highlighted.

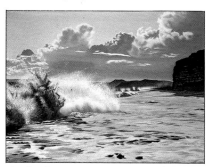

The finished painting. For the guideline sketch on its grid see p. 243.

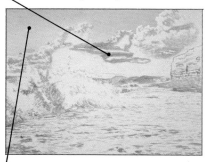

1 Sketching the main features
After drawing the outline sketch, use a thin grey wash to sketch in the main features of the composition. Use a thin oil plus turpentine mix.

2 The sky
Add a very small amount of Indian Yellow to Winsor Red for an orange mix. Mix a reasonable quantity of white and put half of it into the middle of your palette. Tint this with a touch of Winsor Blue and then add a tiny amount of the orange until you have the colour at the top of the painting. Towards the horizon, especially on the left-hand side, the sky becomes lighter and yellower. To get this, mix white with a little yellow and add some of the light blue mix to this. Paint this colour up to and just over the edge of the cloud, and as it meets the light blue above, blend in so that there is a smooth gradation of tone. Paint the edges up to the clouds with your small round sable or hogs'-hair and the rest with the No. 7 hogs'-hair brush.

3 The cloud colours
Mix a basic blue-purple-grey colour. Although the clouds vary in tone, the colour is consistent over the whole area. So mix plenty on one side of your palette and a fair amount of white on the other. By adding white you can lighten the tone as you need to — especially on the left of the cloud mass and along the top.

4 Painting the clouds

Begin by painting the white edges of the clouds on the left. Add the darker tone beneath them and blend the two together using a clean brush. Choose the size and type of brush according to the area you are painting. For example, use a No. 2 sable for the extreme top left-hand side, and a No. 7 filbert for the top right-hand side. It is worth leaving the blending for fifteen minutes or so after painting, when the paint will be a little drier and easier to blend. The joy of oil paint is its flexibility – you can blend all the tones on the canvas itself. Your end result should be far softer than the abrupt two-tone effect that you had at the beginning.

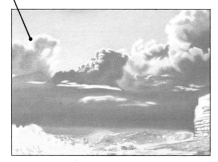

5 The dark cloud area

The flat, grey area below the cloud edges is a perfect backdrop for the white spray that you will be painting at the end. So take the cloud further down than seems necessary – you can paint over it later. Remember also to lighten the tone of the sky and the land mass at the base of the cloud area.

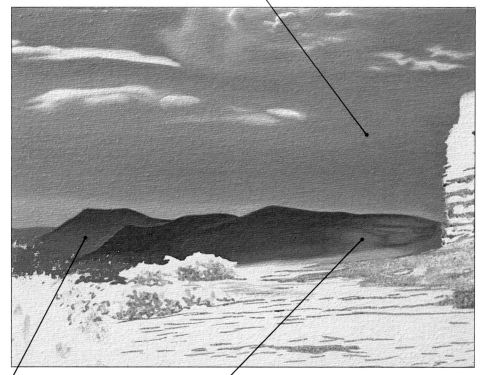

8 The cliff face

Paint the cliff face on the right of the painting initially in two colours – dark brown and yellow ochre. To make the dark brown, mix a little blue with yellow to make green, and add red to this mix. The brown should not be too warm in tone or it will not sit happily with the surrounding land and sea. So put a dash of blue in it and add a touch of white to take the edge off the depth of tone. Once you have painted the two colours in as flat shapes you can merge them and soften their edges carefully with a clean brush.

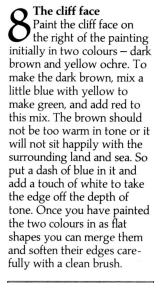

9 The rock texture

To give the rocks texture, use a little of the dark brown mix. By this time it should be slightly stickier than before. Use a round sable with the end chiselled between thumb and forefinger and lightly pull the paint across the rocks.

Continued over

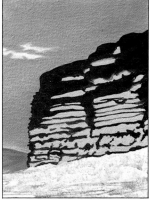

6 The land on the horizon

Begin on the left of this area and work towards the right. Where the land meets the sky it seems darker than it does lower down. So apply two tones of the same colour. The darker one should be above the lighter one. Then blend them in. On the left is a patch of sea below the land. Make sure that the tone here is deep enough.

7 The land to the centre right

For this land, paint right up to the edges of the breaking waves in the distance. To the left and right of these, the land merges more indistinctly with the sea. Notice here that the tone lightens. You achieve this by painting a strip of very light blue-grey and blending it gently with the dark grey of the land.

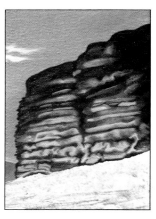

10 The sand below the cliff

The beach below the cliff is the next area to paint. Here the colour is a deepened version of the lighter tones on the cliff. Paint the tide line in a slightly darker tone and put highlights in the pools of trapped water. Also, notice the lighter streaks running down to the water's edge. After you have painted these areas, blend them in so that the overall look is as smooth as possible.

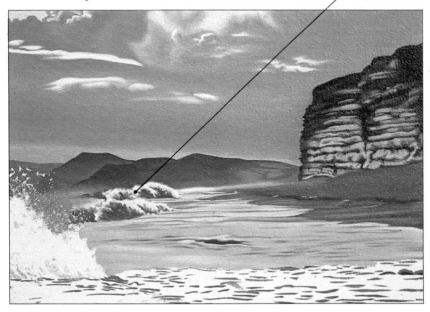

11 The distant waves and sea

Now paint the two sets of breaking waves. Begin with the darkest tone, a deep greenish blue-grey, following it with the mid tones. Finally, add the white cap and blend in all the colours. Be sure to feather out the top edge of the waves so that the effect of the spray is enhanced. At this stage you should also paint the sea, using smooth, horizontal strokes. Alternate the darker and lighter tones and blend them in. You can also blend them slightly with the edge of the sand. As you work down the horizontal area of shallow, foaming water, the best method is to paint in small horizontal shadows in the dark colour and then apply the very light grey-blue-green colours in between and blend them all in. You can add highlights and shadows over this base. For the most distant part of the sea use the small round sable. This will give you a great deal of control. As you move further down the painting and have more ground to cover, change to the No. 1 hogs'-hair filbert for the light colour. This brush will do the blending most effectively.

12 The large central wave

Now underpaint the large crashing wave to the left of the painting's centre. It is very like a cloud, but with a darker, greeny grey tone at its base and some modelling within the shape itself. The wave is at an angle to the shore, as if shrinking back from it. Once you have applied the paint, blend it in using the No. 7 hogs'-hair. Make the brushstrokes go in the same direction as the wave – this will enhance the feel of movement and provide the right background for the stippling later on.

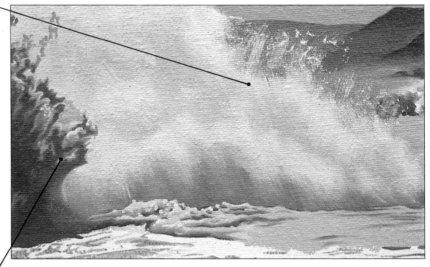

13 The dark wave

Build up the tones of the dark wave to the left of the large central one by dabbing on the dark tones, then adding progressively lighter ones and blending all the tones with a small clean hogs'-hair filbert brush. You will have to wipe it on a rag every time you blend a small section, otherwise you may find that the overall effect is muddy and confused.

14 Stippling the spray

To get the effect of the spray, lightly stipple the white paint on using a very fat squirrel-hair mop. You can use a shaving brush or a large sable if you have one. The essential point is that the brush should be fat, large, and dry. The technique is to mix up Titanium White with the painting medium to make a sticky consistency. Then trowel it flat over the palette with a painting knife. Dab the brush very lightly on the surface of the paint and then dab it lightly on the spray area.

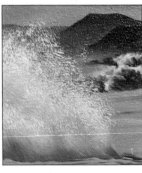

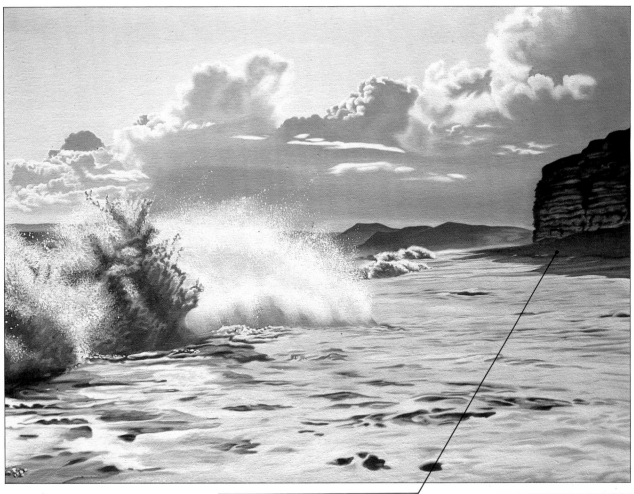

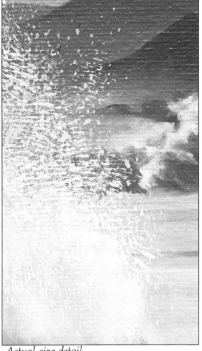

Actual-size detail

15 The sea foam

The foam in the foreground incorporates a whole series of colours: grey-greens, green-blues, blue-mauves, various creams, and white. Use the same technique here as you did for the sea higher up the picture except that the darker areas are larger and more intricate. Notice how the sun catches the foam towards the bottom left of the picture — make it considerably lighter in tone when you blend in. Remember to wipe the blending brush clean after each stroke. And as before, add highlights and deep tones afterwards, as the blending tends to make the colours closer together in tone.

16 Applying the glaze

By now the cliff and shingle areas will be dry enough for you to add a grey glaze. Apply this smoothly with a soft sable brush. Do not overload the brush, or brush the area too heavily, since the paint beneath will begin seeping in. If you are worried by this, do not glaze the area until it is thoroughly dry.

17 The sea spray

Give the sea spray area a little more form by using a thin, semi-transparent white mix, applied in little snake shapes with a pointed round sable. Finally, using a thicker white mix of paint on a pointed sable brush, you should apply the last highlighted dots of spray around the waves.

Beach Scene

Medium ACRYLICS

THIS PAINTING IS an attempt to capture the special atmosphere of one late summer afternoon on a quiet beach. It was the kind of day, with intermittent bright sunshine and heavy rain, which deters a lot of people from going to the beach. So my children Emily and Henry and their cousin Nick are the only figures in this wide sweep of coast and this gives their action a real focus. Because their movements are a direct response to the crashing breakers, foam, and spray, the spectator is brought into close contact with the landscape itself.

A series of photographs taken during the course of the afternoon provided most of the visual reference material for the painting. The children are frozen in positions that reflect their complete absorption in the game with the waves. These positions also have a role to play in the composition of the painting. As a group the children create a central active space above the flat ground of sand and foam. The boy on the left has sand for a background, the girl on the right has water. The central figure, set against both sand and water, has a crucial role, linking land and sea, and boy and girl. Without him, the composition would be flatter, since his scale adds dimension and volume to the scene. He is the pivot on which the composition rests. He is also more self-contained than the other two figures. Whereas there is clearly a mutual enjoyment expressed between the two smaller figures, the larger boy is absorbed with the waves on the far right of the composition. Though the figures are all "frozen" their positions imply a high degree of action in different directions, and this serves to intensify our experience of their setting.

This painting is made by overlaying thin washes of transparent acrylic paint, building up tone and colour quite slowly and carefully. It is, in many respects quite an intricate painting, and it relies very much on a high degree of accuracy in the early stages.

MATERIALS AND EQUIPMENT

Support
Watercolour paper (300 gsm weight) A1 size (23½ × 33 ins/59.4 × 84 cm)

Acrylic colours

Cadmium Red		Phthalo Green	
Phthalo Blue		Sap Green	
Azo Yellow			

Brushes
No. 7, No. 4, and No. 2 sable rounds, No. 12 squirrel round

Other items
HB pencil, masking fluid

METHOD
The method is to paint in the colours accurately using thin washes. When the image is mapped out in this way, the tones and colours are built up in a series of further washes. First the clouds are sketched in with a thin grey wash. The next stage is to paint the sea, starting with the waves and going on to the flat area above them and the foreground foam. Then the sand is blocked in, followed by the cliff and buildings on the right. Finally the clothes and features of the children are sketched in, to give the basis of the whole image. The method is then to build up the painting, using similar colours in further thin washes. Layers are added until the density of tone is satisfactory. This process should be taken slowly and carefully. It is essential to let each separate wash dry completely before starting to apply another one on top.

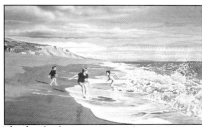

The finished painting. For the guideline sketch on its grid see p. 242.

For the guideline sketch on its grid see p. 242.

1 The outline sketch
After stretching your paper on a drawing board, trace in lightly the outlines according to the guideline sketch provided. Draw in the figures as accurately as possible. For the sand, sea, and sky, such a high degree of accuracy is not so important.

2 Sketching in the clouds
Sketch in the broad details of the clouds with a very thin grey wash. Mix a fair amount of this in a saucer — you do not want to run out half-way across a cloud. Towards the horizon, where the clouds become like loose ribbons across the sky, you should aim for increasing accuracy within the outlines.

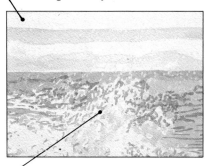

3 The sea
In this painting the white highlights in the foam and the spray of the sea are not painted white. They are represented by the unpainted white surface of the paper. To get this effect, paint in each highlight at the beginning with masking fluid. Dab it on with the point of a sable brush in those areas where the foam and spray are lightest. Let it dry completely before painting over it. If you are worried about painting up to the edge of the figures with the sea and sand colours, you can mask them out too and paint them at the end. But you may prefer to work on the three figures and the landscape at the same time. The sea falls into three main sections: first, the deep-toned area above the breaking waves; second, the waves themselves, where your brushstrokes can reflect the frothy turbulence of the water; and third, the soft foam, which can be reflected in long, smooth brushstrokes. Begin with the second section, using the same grey mix as for the sky. Paint in the splashing water of the breaking waves around the areas you have masked out. Then add a little blue and green to your grey mix and paint the flat area of sea above the waves. Use a slightly bluer version of the original grey wash for the soft foreground foam.

4 The sand

Now sketch in the sand. This also falls into three sections. For the first and lightest, nearest the cliff and above the wave line, use a thin yellow-brown mix. For the second area, immediately beneath the first, use a slightly darker version of the first mix. Work round the figures carefully with a pointed sable. Do not let the colour dry before you pull it to the edge of the dark brown area, otherwise you will have unsightly, harsh lines around the figures.

5 The wet sand area

The third area of sand is the section in the foreground that is both brown and blue. Before you apply the blue and brown washes it is worthwhile dabbing some spots of masking fluid over the wet sand area to represent pebbles. You can remove some before each wash, so each will be a slightly different tone. Paint thin strips of brown with gaps between. Make them almost parallel with the bottom edge of the painting. When this is dry you can add the blue strips of colour in between. The effect of this is to suggest the way the surf pulls back across the sand at speed. Later, when you add brown and blue washes over the whole area, the striped effect will be considerably softer and more subtle. Add some deep-toned touches of colour to suggest the dark pebbles. You should also remember to paint the dark but subtle reflection of the boys on the wet sand, as well as their darker and more hard-edged shadows cast by direct sunlight.

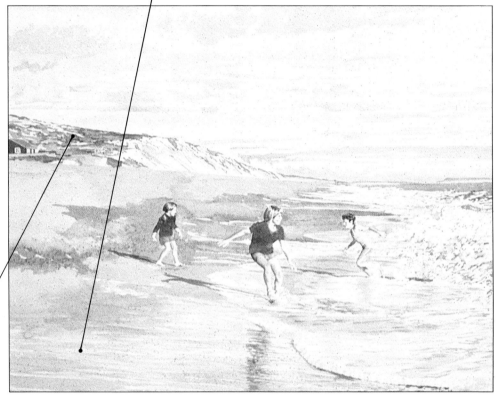

6 The cliff and buildings

Now sketch in this area, including the upturned boats. The grass and bushes on the headland incorporate grey-greens and grey-yellow-browns. The cliff face is a pale yellow-brown at the top and a brown-grey towards the beach. The roof of the hut is a bluer and deeper version of this grey, while the side of the hut facing you is a bottle green and the seaward side a reddish brown.

7 The childrens' clothes

Sketching in the figures is the most intricate aspect of this painting. Start with the clothes. The boy on the left has a jumper the same colour as the central boy's shirt, while his shorts are the basic blue with grey added in the shadow. The central boy's shorts are painted in Phthalo Green, a colour that gives the centre of the composition more vibrancy. The girl's costume is pink with purple shadows.

8 The childrens' features

The colour of the hair is slightly different on each figure. The boy on the left has blue in the basic brown mix, the central figure has yellow and the girl red. As far as the limbs and facial features are concerned, begin with those areas in darkest shadow in a basic brown mix, and remember to feather off the edges as you go along. As you work round the limbs use a tanned flesh colour. Make a basic mix for the central figure, and make it slightly cooler for the little boy, and a little pinker for the girl (right).

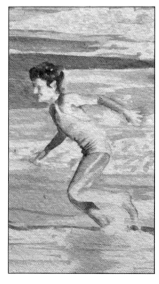

Continued over

9 Building up the composition
By now you will have painted the whole image quite precisely using thin washes of colour. You should now go on building up the painting following the same method. Using similar colours to those already described, add to the tones and colours until you are satisfied with the density of the tone and the atmosphere it is creating. It is important to work carefully in stages — do not try to rush this part of the painting.

10 Building up the sky
Lay a graded blue wash over the sky and pick out the white clouds with a damp sponge. When this is dry, add grey tones to the base of the upper cloud masses and repaint the ribbons of cloud towards the horizon. These too should be deeper in tone. When this is dry you can rub off the masking fluid to reveal the spray standing out against the sky.

11 The distant sea
Next deepen the tones of the flat triangle of sea from the horizon down to the breaking waves. Paint around the areas dotted with masking fluid to create the larger white shapes of the foam. Incorporate deeper tones behind them and this will make them stand out more noticeably.

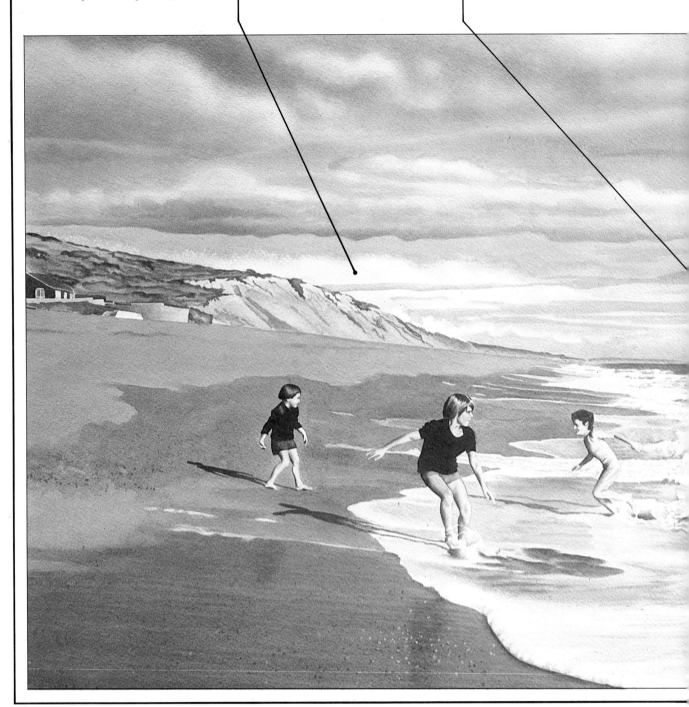

12 The cliff

Now move across to the cliffs and hut on the left. Deepen the tones here according to the colours you used originally. For the darker shadows in the green of the cliff top, add a touch more blue to the original green mix. For the overall green wash here, add a touch more yellow. Paint a thin yellow-brown wash towards the top of the cliff face.

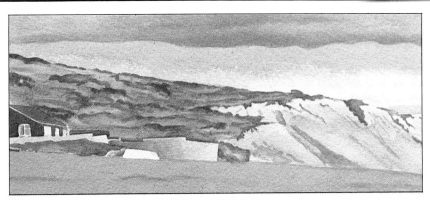

13 The bottom right waves

Define the frilly edges of these waves using deep grey-blue tones. Then work within each section of the waves, bringing it up to its final state.

14 The foreground foam

For the foam, overlay a number of blue-grey washes, softening the edges each time to build up the effect of the original. You should emphasise this by painting a deep tone along its leading edge where it is reflected in the wet sand.

15 Finishing the figures

The final stage is to repaint the figures using precisely the same colours identified before and building them up in thin washes. Do not try to match the dark tones of tee shirt and jumper in one go. Build up to the required tone slowly in stages. Work in a similar way with the skin tones. Work outwards from the edges in shadow, softening the tones as you move round the limbs and allowing each wash to dry before you apply another. All the figures on the beach should stand out quite strongly by the time you have finished. Finally, you should bring the boys' shadows to the right depth of tone and make any further adjustments to the picture that you think are necessary.

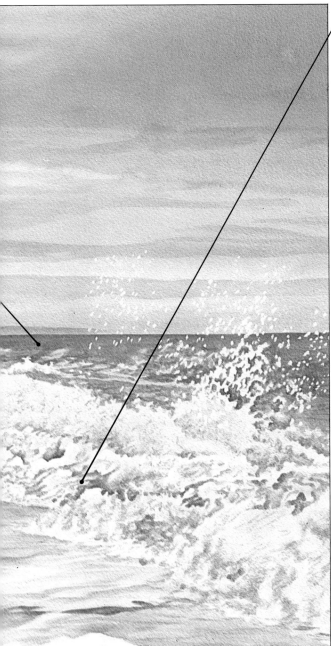

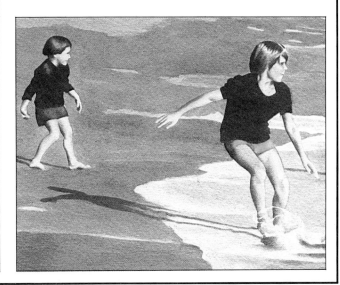

SHIP AT LE HAVRE

Medium OILS

LOOKING AT LARGE SHIPS from a close viewpoint can be highly exhilarating — especially when your usual experience of them is of small shapes moving across the horizon or on a small television screen. In many ways this painting is all about the experience of scale. The ship itself is extremely large — the railway wagons and containers on its deck seem miniature. But you are reminded of the immensity of the ship when you look at the tiny air vents and windows on the bridge. In turn, the vast letters on the ship's side seem to reduce the scale of the ship so that the whole structure looks like a model. The scale seems to shift constantly.

The other aspect of the scene which inspired me to paint it was the brilliant effect produced by early morning light on the ship. The bright, warm white of the ship's superstructure stands out against the deep blue-pink sky, and the dark red and turquoise of the ship's side glowing in the shadows. The abstract simplicity and clarity of these shapes makes a marvellous contrast to the ant-like detail they contain.

It is important to keep your eyes open to the tremendous range of possibilities that surround you, particularly on journeys. Try to make a note of a special experience even if there is no time to sketch or photograph it. In this case, I came back to the ship to draw and photograph it from a number of angles. I also made a charcoal drawing showing the ropes swinging up to the ship from the quay. This emphasized the height and mass of the vessel. I liked this composition, but the glowing red and turquoise colours that I had seen before were not so vivid. So I resolved to try and relive the moment when I initially saw the ship — when I came on deck after an overnight channel crossing. This painting gives you practice in fine, detailed work in oils.

MATERIALS AND EQUIPMENT

Support
Canvas or board 18 × 24 ins
(46 × 61 cm)

Oil colours

Winsor Red   Winsor Green

Winsor Blue   Permanent Rose

Indian Yellow   Titanium White

Sap Green

Brushes
No. 6, No. 4, and No. 1 hogs'-hair filberts, No. 6, No. 4, and No. 2 sables

Other items
Turpentine, painting medium (see p. 10), mahl stick

METHOD
First, the outline is drawn in from the guideline sketch. This is quite a complex procedure in this case, so it must be taken slowly and carefully and maximum accuracy should be aimed for. The entire picture is then underpainted, in as much detail as possible, using thin acrylic or oil in turpentine. If you decide to do the underpainting in acrylic a rigid board should be used rather than a flexible canvas. The next stage is to overpaint the whole picture, making a point of enhancing tone and colour.

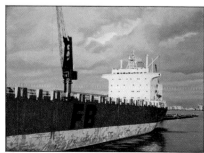

The finished painting. For the guideline sketch on its grid see p. 236.

1 Starting the underpainting
For the underpainting use either thin acrylic (which dries more quickly) or oil diluted in turpentine. In this picture the underpainting is very precise — all the forms are rendered accurately. The reason for this is that when you come to work on the rich top coat of oil paint, you will be able to concentrate on tone and colour rather than on form, which will already be carefully delineated.

2 The crane and gantry
Paint the crane and gantry first using various tones of just one grey colour mix with a No. 2 sable brush. The details will show through the thin washes of blue-grey and pink that you will be using for the sky. The crane is an interesting structure to deal with. Notice how the lines of the rig are silhouetted against the light sky, but against the body of the crane they become light against dark.

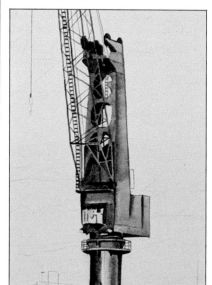

3 The sky

The underpainting for the sky sketches out the detail of the cloud masses. This should be slightly overdramatised at this stage, helping to establish the sky's structure and providing a very useful guide for the painting itself.

4 The main superstructure

Next, using a No. 2 round sable, paint in the ship's superstructure towards the stern. Use a dark, grey-brown mix made from Winsor Red, Sap Green, and Winsor Blue for the windows and parts in deepest shadow. For the structure on top of the bridge where the radar scanners are, use a lighter, warmer brown mix with yellow in it for the shadows. Use the same colour for the rectangular shape behind and to the right of the structure, and a darker brown for the two shapes on top.

5 The superstructure side

The side of the bridge is in shadow and I have used a blue-grey-pink mix. Paint the lifeboat using a dark red-brown mix for the shadows and Winsor Red on its own for the lighter parts. The life-boat cradle extends to the deck below. Here the tones are made darker by a shadow cast by the deck. The colours are colder, too, so use variations on a dark grey mix.

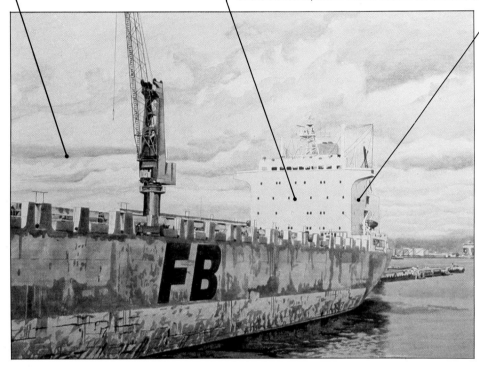

6 The dark reflections

Paint this area in as dark a tone as possible. It will be visible through the oil paint when you come to paint it during the final stages.

7 Details on deck

Immediately below the crane the roof of a warehouse is visible, and below it, machinery and containers. Here, use two tones of grey, two tones of a peppermint green made by mixing Winsor Green, a touch of Winsor Blue and Sap Green, and two tones of brown — one dark, the other a more orange or rusty colour.

8 Horizon details

Next move on to the refinery on the horizon, and the jetty extending from behind the ship's stern. Use similar colours as for the deck details and be as accurate with the tones as possible. If the sea and sky represent a mid tone, then the upper part of the refinery tanks should be considerably lighter because the tanks are picked out by the morning sun. The lower edge, where the land mass joins the water, should be considerably darker. The same applies to the jetty.

9 The upper part of the ship's side

Now begin working on the side of the ship. Use two tones of red here. Make the red slightly brown with a touch of Sap Green, and use a light and a dark tone. The point of making the tones different is to clarify the patterning created by the old and new paint on the ship. When you overpaint this area you will be able to reduce this difference. Now paint the letters "FB" on the ship's side.

10 The lower part of the ship's side

Below the red, the ship's side is essentially blue, green and purple, with rust stains and grey areas. This again represents a mixture of old and new paint on the ship and creates an interesting "abstract" area of texture. Use two colours — Winsor Green with Winsor Blue, and Winsor Blue with Winsor Red. Then paint in the darker stripes running parallel to the water line, bisected at intervals with diagonal lines painted on top.

11 The water

The ship's reflection represents the largest area of very dark tone in the painting. Immediately below the water line use the same colour as the blue-purple stripes on the ship's side. Within this area paint the blue-purple colours of the ship's side which are slightly darker in tone. Below this, use a pink wash where the tones reflected are bright and light.

Continued over

12 The overpainting

By now you should have the whole structure of the painting sketched in, with most of the details recorded accurately. The next stage is to put the "flesh" on, making full use of the richness of pigment that oil paint provides. Your mixture of oil paint and painting medium should have a consistency that is similar to thick double cream for this painting.

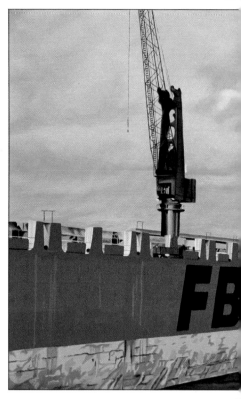

13 The sky

Use hogs'-hair filbert brushes for the sky, switching to a round sable if you are painting up to a detail. Remember that you can easily smooth over any irregular brushstrokes by blending them softly with the chiselled end of a damp sable. You can only glimpse the sky itself through the clouds at the top of the painting, in the middle and to the right. For these areas mix a little Winsor Blue with Titanium White and add a small amount of Indian Yellow. The clouds themselves, which cover most of the sky, are basically blue and pink. For the blue use tonal variations on Winsor Blue plus Titanium White with a touch of Winsor Red and Sap Green to neutralise the blue a little. For the pink, mix Permanent Rose with white, and where it is darker, add a little of the blue cloud mix. When you are painting the sky it is important to remember to make the tones dark enough, particularly towards the horizon. It is this darkness of tone which encloses the bright, sunlit parts of the ship, giving the painting its atmosphere. Another important point about the sky is that it provides a pillowy softness in an otherwise rather angular composition. So keep your brushstrokes free, allowing them to travel the length of the cloud you are defining rather than stopping short at a barrier like the crane and trying to paint carefully round it. If you accidentally obliterate any of your underpainting – for example the delicate lines above the crane and superstructure – you will be able to draw them in again. But remember that you should wait until the painting is dry.

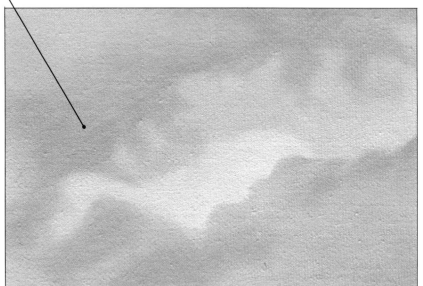

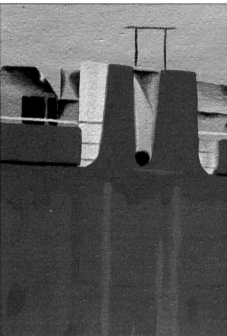

Actual-size detail

14 Supporting your hand

It is better to paint the delicate lines of the crane when the sky is dry. But for a considerable part of the painting it will not be possible for you to rest your hand on the canvas when you are painting details. So use a mahl stick or a long-handled paint brush as a rest.

15 Details on deck

For the warehouse roof and the containers and machinery on deck, follow the same procedure as for the underpainting, mixing up the peppermint green, grey, brown, and orange, and working carefully along the

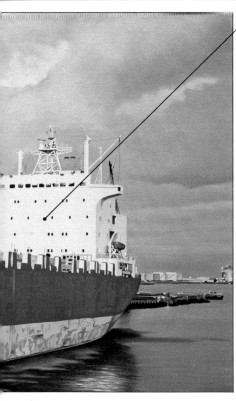

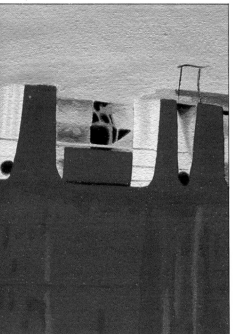

16 The main superstructure

The largest and lightest area of tone in the painting is the flat superstructure of the ship, incorporating the bridge. Within this area are some of the darkest tones — the windows which dot the facade. Paint the windows first. This enables you to surround the dark tone with light paint afterwards and helps to make the windows look as if they are receding into the surface of the painting.

17 The bridge

On the bridge, patches of green in three of the windows, including the two with circular air vents, and yellow plus white in three others give the impression of lit space behind the glass. There is also a light on in one of the windows on the facade. This white facade is, in fact, a warm pink — a mixture of Titanium White, Permanent Rose, and a touch of Indian Yellow. Be careful not to add too much coloured pigment to the white.

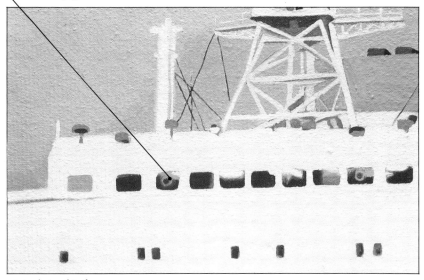

Actual-size detail

18 The superstructure side

This area is in shadow, so you should make slightly darker versions of the same mixture as for the main superstructure by adding a little Winsor Blue. The window edges are a warm ochre colour with a touch of yellow and white where the light spills through. Then paint the lifeboat and its cradle down to the lower deck using a deep, rusty red for the darkest areas through to a Winsor Red plus Permanent Rose, and white mix for the very lightest tones.

Continued over

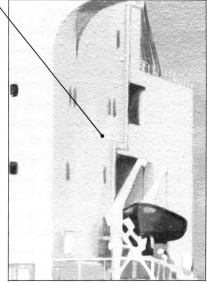

Actual-size detail

decks. At the same time paint the white, rust-stained edges of the deck, which catch the morning sunlight. The orange used here is Indian Yellow mixed with a small touch of Winsor Red and you should blend this mixture smoothly with the white.

19 **Details on the shore**
Work right along to the oil tanks on the horizon since your palette will already contain the green, greys, and light yellow-brown you need here. For the refinery lights paint thin green circles enclosing thick dabs of white paint to provide a sense of illumination. Then mix a similar but slightly darker tone of the blue you used for the sky above the oil tanks and paint the sea immediately below them. Then paint the jetty in the same dark greys and browns you have been using. The lights on the jetty are Indian Yellow with white.

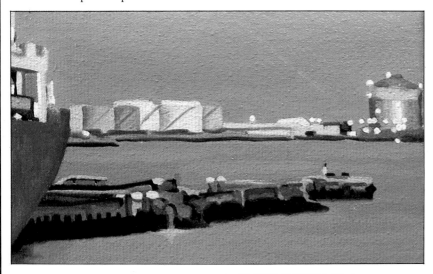

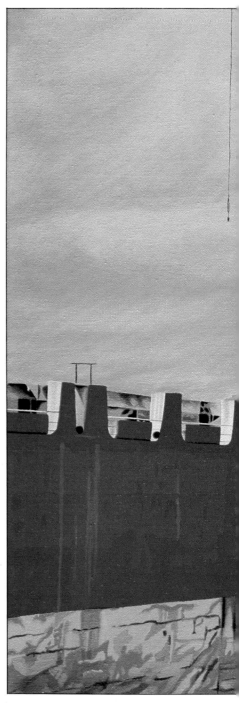

20 **The crane and gantry**
Painting the fine deck and shore details will take some time, so by the time you have finished the sky will probably be touch dry enough for you to paint the crane and gantry. Use Winsor Green with a little Winsor Blue, a touch of Winsor Red, Indian Yellow, and white. Be sure to make the dark tones as deep as they really are and use the mahl stick to steady your hand as you draw in the fine lines of the gantry. Notice how the light reflects off the central portion of the crane stem. Use a warm cream-yellow tinged highlight here.

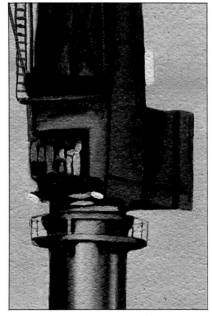

21 **The ship's side**
Paint the red part of the hull in a mix comprising two tones of Winsor Red and Permanent Rose with a touch of Sap Green. There are also streaks of an even lighter tone running vertically towards the sea at intervals. The letters "FB" may look black, but are in fact a mix of Winsor Red, Winsor Blue, and Indian Yellow. The lower hull consists of two main colour combinations. The first is a mix of Winsor Green, Winsor Blue, and Titanium White, while the second is a more purple colour – a mix of Permanent Rose, Winsor Blue, and Titanium White. Paint these two main colours in first, then add the rust stains, the darker horizontal and diagonal stripes, and the odd patches of a more neutral grey-green colour that occur at intervals along the hull.

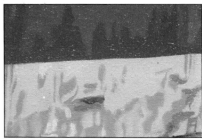

Actual-size detail

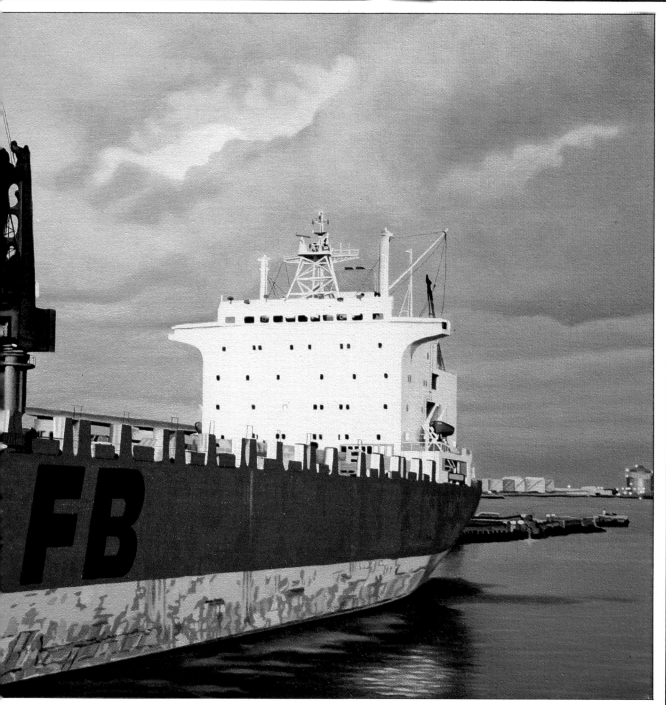

22 The reflections

Where the hull touches the water you find a very deep tone of grey-blue. This is roughly the same colour as the one you used to paint the letters, though with a little more blue and the smallest touch of Titanium White. The other colours reflected in the water are the same as those used for the hull, though with a little extra blue added.

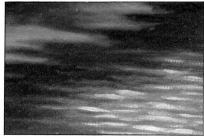

Actual-size detail

23 The finishing touches

Paint the sea down from the jetty to the bottom right-hand edge, incorporating the darker tone from the base of the ship's stern and the smooth horizontal bands of the lighter tone below that to suggest the surface of the water. Finally make any overall adjustments. If there is any detailing you wish to repaint, wait for the painting to dry before you tackle it.

NEW YORK

Medium OILS

EARLIER IN THIS book I mentioned the screen or filter that visual media such as television interpose between the viewer and the real world (see p. 56). Painting provides us with a unique and more personal system of filtration. The way in which the appearance of the world we see is changed when we paint it is determined by the style of the painting and the physical properties of the medium. These have as much effect on the result as our own personal vision of the subject.

But without this vision artists would not produce anything that withstands the test of time and continues to attract our attention and appreciation. As far as the styles of painting and the properties of the medium are concerned, the number of innovative stylistic approaches and the advances in paint technology over the last hundred years present an unparalleled range of options. The possibilities are so great that they may be baffling or intimidating. On the other hand, by demonstrating that no single approach is necessarily any more valid than any other, the range of choices can be stimulating.

When you begin to learn about the practical aspects of painting it is quite natural to want to paint things as closely as possible to how they look – there is a justifiable pride in getting the resemblance right. But there is another important stage in the process of representation. This is the point at which you realise that a single brushstroke can replace a great deal of incidental detail, that a particular colour works much better on the canvas with its neighbour than the actual colour in front of you. You realise that the painting has its own autonomy. This is when the filtering system of painting really works.

This painting, then, is as much an abstract mosaic of colours as it is a representation of the Manhattan skyline. But without that skyline, of course, it could not have been painted. Its structure depends on the geometry of the buildings and its tones on the effect of light on them.

MATERIALS AND EQUIPMENT

Support
Canvas 20 × 30 ins (51 × 76 cm)

Oil colours

Alizarin Crimson   Burnt Sienna

Winsor Blue   Permanent Rose

Cadmium Yellow Pale 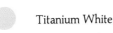   Titanium White

Brushes
No. 8 and three No. 6 hogs'-hair filberts

Other items
Turpentine, painting medium (see p. 10)

METHOD

This is an example of direct painting on a tinted ground. I used oil colour, but you could paint it in the same way using acrylics. Once the ground has been tinted pink and the guidelines drawn in, the painting is made a section at a time, beginning on the left and working round. The light colours are applied first, followed by the darker ones. At the end it may be necessary to give the lightest tones a little more definition. The technique is to mix the colour loosely and dab it on thickly with short single brushstrokes.

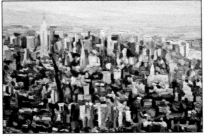

The finished painting. For the guideline sketch on its grid see p. 247.

1 The tint and guideline sketch
Tint the canvas with Permanent Rose and draw in the guidelines. You should try to get the churches and the Empire State building and the angles of the streets in the right places. The resulting shapes will provide a framework within which you can work. Don't be afraid to use bold brushstrokes.

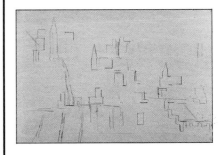

2 Mixing the colours
When you mix the paint, do so straight from the tube – only thin it with turpentine if it is too stiff to work comfortably with the hogs'-hair brushes. Keep the mix quite loose, so that separate colours sometimes show through.

3 The first buildings
Paint these using Titanium White, Cadmium Yellow Pale, and Permanent Rose in various cream and pink combinations. For the majority of the brushstrokes use the flat edge of the brush. You will only need to use the thin edge occasionally to define the side of a building.

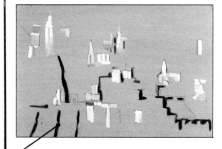

4 The darker lines
Keeping the first brush you used for the pale yellow-pink colours, use another for the light blues and violets, and a third for the darker colours. These are made by mixing Winsor Blue and Alizarin Crimson. Mix these colours thinly and sketch in the three streets at the bottom left, the short horizontal strip above, and the street leading to the Empire State Building. Use the same colour for the dark lines on the right, including the series that looks like a flight of steps.

5 **The area on the left**
Now you can start to paint the left-hand section of the picture. The road and the Empire State Building form the right-hand boundary of this area, while there is a horizontal strip below that acts as its base edge. Make your own approximations to the colours and shapes you see in the original. It may help to cover with white paper the area of the book from which you are not working. This will help you see where you are. Begin with the light cream, yellow, orange, and pink colours as before. Dab your colours on quite freely, but keep roughly to the shapes and positions that are shown in the illustration below.

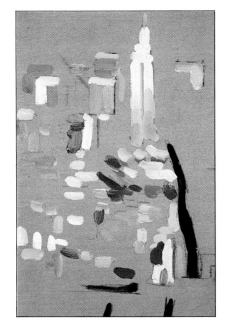

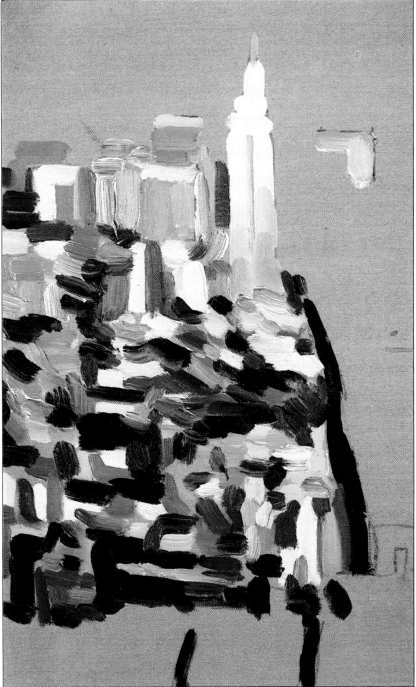

6 **Adding more colours**
Add a little Burnt Sienna to your orange mix and paint in the half dozen warm brown areas. Then change to your second brush and add the light blue patches. These are made by mixing Titanium White and Winsor Blue. After this add the darker blues with the third brush. Finally mix Alizarin Crimson with a touch of Titanium White and Winsor Blue for the darker violet areas. For the darkest patches use a mix of Alizarin Crimson and Winsor Blue.

Continued over

7 The centre left
Paint this part of the picture in the same way. Notice that there is not quite so much deep tone in this area. In addition, the sizes of the patches of colour become a little smaller towards the right. This reflects the diminishing scale of the buildings as they recede.

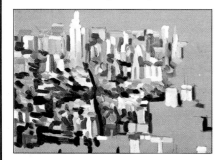

8 The left foreground
In the foreground, especially on the left where there is more shadow, the brushstrokes should be larger and the tones deeper. Keep your brushes clean as you work. You will probably have to wipe your brush after each stroke. If you have painted over part of a highlight, repaint it by trowelling on fresh paint. Keep plenty of fresh colour on your brush and paint with confidence, otherwise you will smear it.

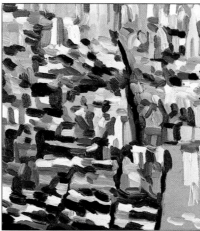

9 Completing the buildings
Continue to paint the city buildings following the same method. Start with the lighter-toned background areas, and complete this part of the painting by adding the darker tones and larger slabs of colour that make up the foreground.

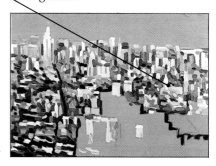

10 The sky
First paint the series of long thick horizontal brushstrokes in yellow, pink, and blue above the buildings. These make the transition from the thick, stubby brushstrokes of the buildings to the smooth sky above. Above this area paint the blues, pinks, and yellows of the sky itself.

11 Final adjustments
Now take a long look at your painting to see if it needs any further alterations. Look at it from a distance with half-closed eyes to give it a new perspective. This is a critical stage – you may be able to pull the whole surface of the picture together by making relatively minor changes.

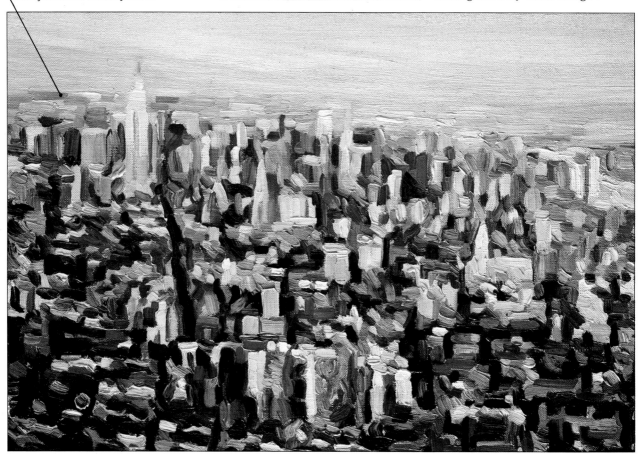

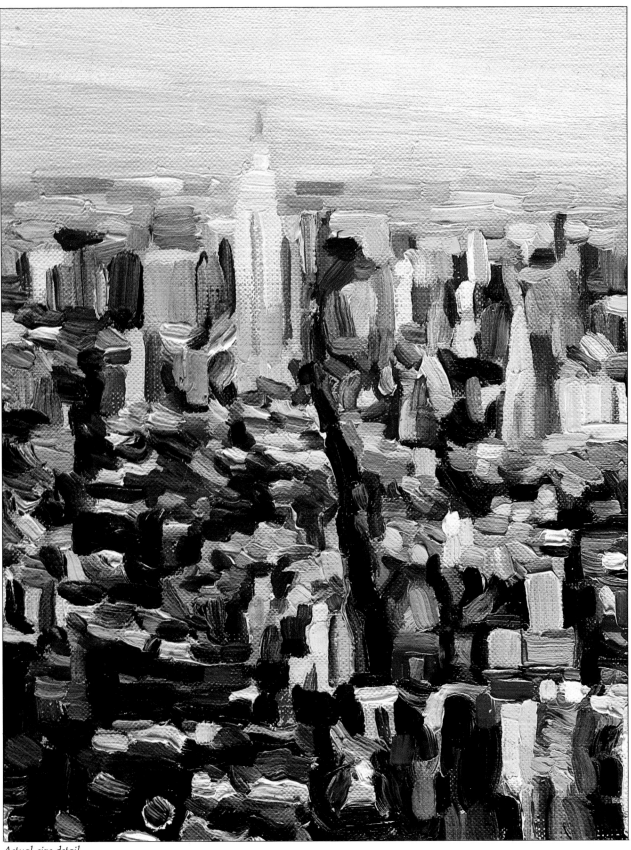

Actual-size detail

VENETIAN CANAL

Medium ACRYLICS

THE CONFIGURATIONS of tall buildings, narrow alleys and canals that characterise Venice are partly responsible for the extraordinary light effects that generations of visitors have noticed. When the sun penetrates a small side-street or canal, its raking sidelight picks out the texture on a wall, the pots of geraniums, or the lines of washing. When the surface of the water is disturbed, it throws back reflections on to the walls. The sun hardly ever washes the whole of a wall — there are always too many buildings in the way. Because of this, there are always deep shadows present that create a mottled camouflage, which breaks up the whole surface into a mosaic of light and shade. So the light is constantly moving and altering the appearance of things. As you walk, you move between shadows and bright sunlight.

In this painting I have tried to explore these special qualities of light. The painting's surface is a pattern of alternating light and dark shapes which would be confusing if it did not have the architectural solidity that the correct use of perspective gives it. The structure of the main building on the left radiates from a vanishing point just outside the right-hand edge of the painting on an eye level which splits the canvas horizontally in a golden section ratio (see p. 86). This vanishing point draws the eye into the painting along the building's facade to a point just above the apex of the triangle formed by the canal. Our gaze is blocked by the solid vertical of the right-hand building just as the lower, distant building turns slightly towards the vanishing point. The sense of wanting to know what is just around the corner is therefore reinforced by the structure of the painting.

MATERIALS AND EQUIPMENT

Support
Canvas 22½ × 14 ins (57 × 35.5 cm)

Acrylic colours

Quinacri-done Red   Phthalo Green

Phthalo Blue   Burnt Sienna

Azo Yellow   Titanium White

Brushes
No. 8, and two No. 4 sable or nylon pointed flats, No. 1 sable or nylon round

METHOD
First the canvas is tinted and the outline sketch transferred from the grid. Then all the lightest tones are painted in. I found it helped to divide the canvas into four and to work on roughly a quarter at a time. Then more details are added fairly loosely, treating the complex shapes and small objects as a mosaic and paying particular attention to colours and their relationships. When the underpainting is completed, the method is to begin overpainting the light areas and to build up gradually richer and richer tones by overpainting the whole canvas in quickly drying layers. Lastly, details are strengthened where necessary.

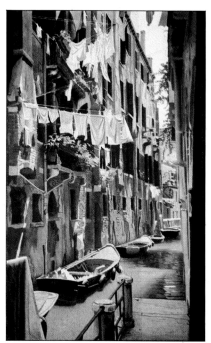

The finished painting. For the guideline sketch on its grid see p. 238.

1 The tint and outline drawing
Give the canvas a toned ground by painting it an overall yellow ochre colour. Make this by mixing Azo Yellow with Titanium White and adding a touch of Burnt Sienna. Draw the outlines of the image using the guideline sketch. Since this is quite a complex image, draw it on tracing paper first, and then transfer it to your canvas.

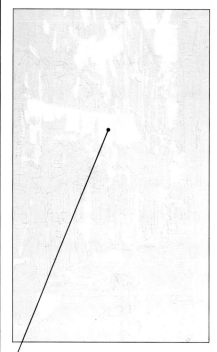

2 The lightest tones
Using a No. 4 nylon flat and a creamy consistency of Titanium White, paint all the areas that are going to be light-toned. Working from the top of the painting, start with the sky, the washing, the window sills, and the boat decks. When these areas are dry paint them again to make sure that they are reasonably opaque.

3 The dark and mid tones
The next stage is to sketch in all the dark and mid tones, working on roughly a quarter of the painting at a time, using thin acrylic paint and a No. 4 brush. You can use a single brown colour, but I preferred to make a variety of mixes from the basic colours used in the painting. If you vary the colours like this, relating them to the finished painting, your work will look more lively.

4 The top left-hand corner

Taking the top left-hand corner first, paint round all the light-toned areas, leaving the ground colour and white unaffected. There is no need to be meticulous about sizes, shapes, or straight edges, and a rather loose approach to handling brush and paint can even contribute to a painting in which there is so much detail. Do not be intimidated by this aspect of the painting. The small sections of window shutter, balcony, and washing line all over the painting mean that you can treat the canvas like a mosaic and work on small pieces at a time. Use a No. 4 brush and relate tone and colour to the areas immediately surrounding the piece you are working on.

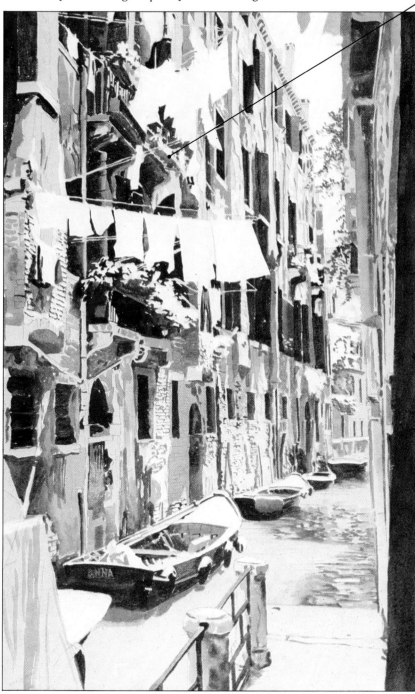

5 The warm browns and greens

For the warm browns use Burnt Sienna with touches of Phthalo Green and Azo Yellow. Where they are cold or black in hue, as in the darkest tones behind the washing, add some Phthalo Blue to the mix. The greens are either a mix of Phthalo Green plus Phthalo Blue for the colder colours, with possibly a little of the dark brown added, or Phthalo Green with Azo Yellow for the warmer ones.

6 The bottom left-hand corner

Moving to the bottom left-hand corner, add touches of either the warm or cool browns to the basic Azo Yellow wash for the walls between the water and the first balconies. Use your No. 8 brush for these broader areas of colour. Begin with the darkest tone — beneath the flowers on the balcony, in the windows, the arched doorway, and the stern of the boat — then add the slightly lighter tones, and so on, to the tone of the ground colour.

7 The top right-hand corner

This section of the underpainting is a little too detailed to allow for much free handling of the paint, though on the extreme right the shadows beneath the eaves form a reasonably large tonal area for the paint to run around in. Now is the time to touch in some of the deeper foliage tones, using the No. 1 round brush and a mix of Phthalo Green and Phthalo Blue with a small touch of Burnt Sienna.

8 The bottom right-hand corner

Indicate the darker areas of the water with a mix of Phthalo Green with a touch of Phthalo Blue. Mix Phthalo Green, Phthalo Blue, and Burnt Sienna for the shadows of the boat hulls. Paint the lighter parts of the stone in your Azo Yellow plus brown mix. For the darker shadows on bollards and railings use a mix of Phthalo Blue, Quinacridone Red, and Burnt Sienna.

9 The finished underpainting

Once you have roughly painted in all the basic tonal areas, you will have an image, which, though bleached in appearance, will nevertheless contain most of the information you need to work the whole painting up to its fully finished state.

Continued over

10 Adding detail to the light areas

The next stage is to add a little more detail to the blank white areas such as the washing and the plants. For the washing adding a few lines in thin grey-pink and grey-blue colours will be sufficient at this stage to indicate the creases in the cloth and give it dimension. For the plants, break up the white areas with touches of a Phthalo Green and Azo Yellow mix. I also added touches of Quinacridone Red for the flowers.

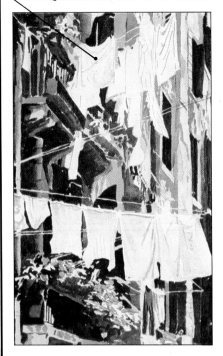

11 Building up rich tones

Compared with the finished underpainting (see Step 9), the finished version is considerably warmer and more mellow. You should aim to create a richer, deeper, and more integrated surface by building up layers of thin, transparent colour. These washes dry rapidly and you can repaint them immediately, so don't aim to get the right colour in one go by mixing your paint too thickly. Try to vary the colours, laying cooler washes over warmer ones in thin veils of paint which combine to give the final colour. Use this technique throughout the painting for small areas as well as larger ones.

12 The walls

As you build up tone and colour you will find it necessary to paint over some of the areas of the wall that you painted white at the beginning. At this stage you should aim to integrate these white areas with the rest of the canvas. For example, the top half of the building that is most distant

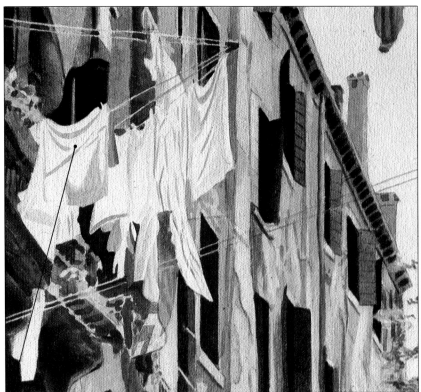

13 The washing

When you have deepened the building's tones and made the surface of your painting more solid, you will need to paint the washing so that it looks more realistic. There should still be a contrast between the lightness of the material and the solidity of the building behind, but you will need to deepen the tones a little and give the folds more dimension. Paint one garment at a time across the washing line, referring to the finished painting as you work. The washing at the top needs less definition because it is further away.

15 The plants

Make sure that the plants below the washing line are well integrated with the balcony and building. Use touches of warm brown between the greens to add shadow and create a link with the colours of the walls. Make any necessary adjustments.

is in sunlight, yet as a solid structure it needs body. So the method is to paint thin ochre and pale blue washes over the whole area, and then repaint the white highlit areas with opaque colour, and repeat the process until the building has sufficient definition. Work over the painting until all its components are integrated into one surface.

14 The water, boats, and jetty

Alternate thin yellow and green washes for the sunlit water, and add a very thin orange-brown wash. Increase the depth of the tone you painted in Step 8 and add a thin orange-brown wash in the middle of the shadow that stretches across the whole canal. The stone colour in the bollards and in the stone of the jetty are made by alternating thin yellow-brown and blue washes. Deepen the tones in the railings with a mix of Phthalo Blue and Burnt Sienna. Deepen the shadows of the boats and add the deck details.

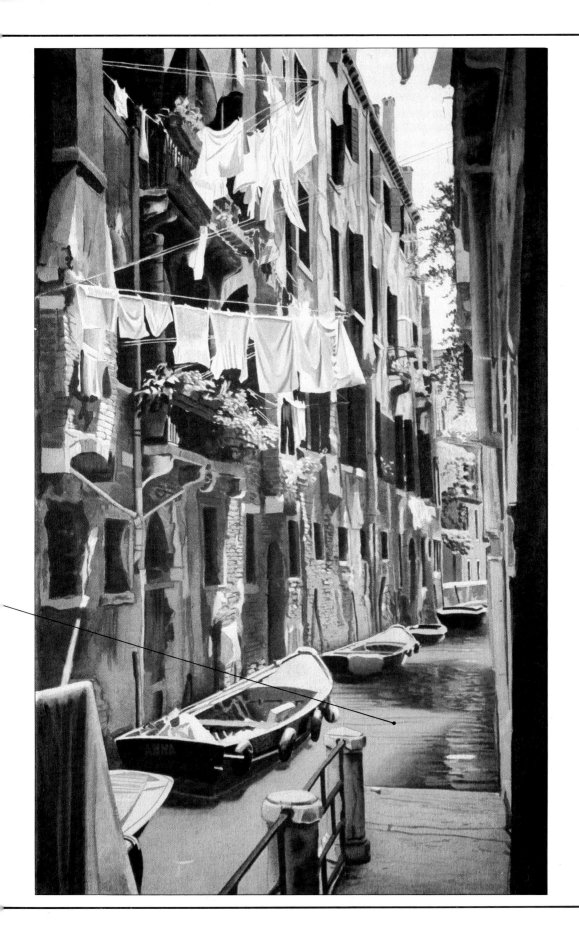

FOOTBALL MATCH

Medium ACRYLICS

THIS PAINTING SHOWS the view from a high block of flats overlooking a football ground. From this vantage point the figures of the players are etched against the flat luminous green rectangle of the pitch. The teams are playing in late afternoon, and strong sunlight directs their shadows across the grass.

At first sight a game of soccer might seem an unusual subject for a painting, but it has marvellous natural visual ingredients. For example, the cool abstract stripes of the rectangular pitch form a perfect foil to the movement of the crowd in the stadium. Here thousands of people stand compacted, swaying in unison to the movement of the game. Similarly the players are each responding to the movement of one small, white ball. Each figure is playing his own individual game and yet is tied to the ball and to his fellows as if by an invisible string. It is this that dictates the painting's structure. It is a natural composition that radiates out in a circular movement from the ball. Although it might seem to be a scattering of tiny figures against a green ground, everything is linked to the ball by the logic of the game.

The ball is about to be passed to the yellow figure who runs to complete the circle of black and white players above the centre circle painted on the turf. These two circles provide a balance to the picture's two main rectangles, the small one of the crowd and the larger one of the pitch. The cut of the grass provides a diagonal for the composition and this is balanced in the opposite direction by the shadows of the players and the ball's projected movement.

MATERIALS AND EQUIPMENT

Support
Watercolour paper (300 gsm weight)
A1 size (23 × 33 ins/59.4 × 84 cm)

Acrylic colours

Cadmium
Red

Cadmium
Yellow Pale

Phthalo
Blue

Sap Green

Brushes
No. 7, two No. 4, and No. 2 sables, No. 14 squirrel

Other items
Masking fluid, gummed strip

METHOD

After drawing the outline sketch, the method is to start with the crowd. The highlight areas are first painted with masking fluid and the colours of the crowd are built up as a series of dots. The masking fluid is then removed and the wall in front of the crowd is painted. The next stage is to underpaint the players, before masking them and applying green washes to the pitch. The masking fluid is removed from the players and they are overpainted.

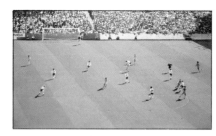

The finished painting. For the guideline sketch on its grid see p. 245.

1 The outline sketch
When you have stretched your paper on a drawing board, draw the outlines of the subject according to the guideline sketch. Use a fairly hard pencil (H or HB, for example) and do not press too hard on the paper – you do not want the outline to be too dark and show through the paint.

2 Masking the crowd
Dab the area of the crowd with spots of masking fluid where the highlights will eventually appear. Use the No. 4 sable brush. You should also mask the goal post. Leave the masking fluid to dry completely – this usually takes several minutes.

3 Building up the crowd colours
You will notice that the crowd consists of a mixture of light and dark patches. Begin with the darker areas, making small dot-like shapes with one of the No. 4 sables. Use a well diluted Phthalo Blue mix with just a touch of red and green to neutralise it a little. Have at hand the other No. 4 brush, dampened with clean water to soften the edges of the blue strokes as you make them. Then mix the blue with more red to make a thin mauve and apply this in the same way over the crowd. Using blue once more, deepen the tones with small dots of colour, continuing to soften the edges with the damp brush. Then paint the red areas in the same way, before returning to the mauve mix and adding more spots of this colour. Do not try to paint the people realistically, just give the impression of them. Once you have built up the crowd to the right depth of tone, mix a very thin grey wash and paint it over the whole area with the No. 14 squirrel brush.

4 Adjustments to the crowd
Once the crowd is dry you can rub off the masking fluid to reveal the white highlights. At this stage you will probably need to make some minor adjustments, adding further spots of colour. Notice that the top of the barrier, separating the crowd from the pitch, is irregular, with people leaning on it and scarves draped over it. Give the impression of this using the same range of colours as for the crowd. For the scarves use thin bands of red wash painted like the rungs of a ladder right up to the top of the surrounding wall.

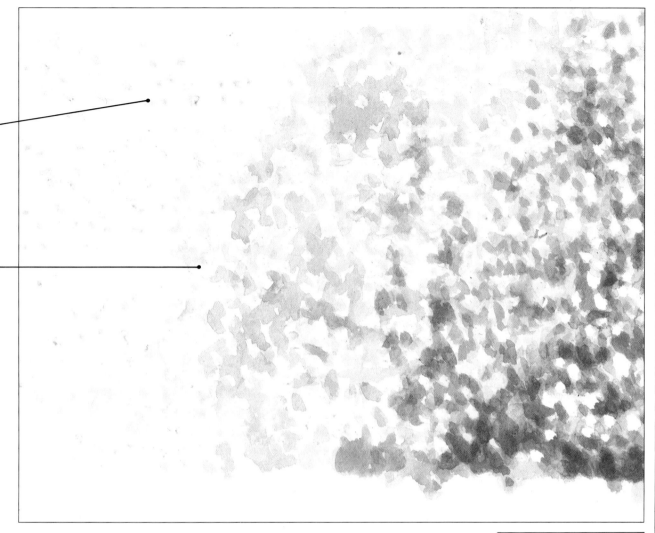

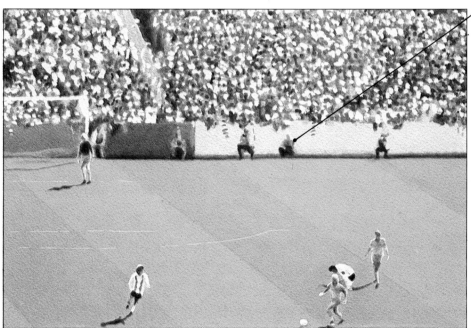

5 The photographers
You need not aim for realism when painting the photographers in front of the wall. You can get a satis- factory effect by painting an approximate shape within the outline. Soften the edges a little as soon as you have painted them. This will have the effect of blurring the focus, making a transition from the crowd, painted in an abstract way, to the players, who are more clearly legible. At this stage you should also paint the wall, which is light grey to the right of the goal and a deep red behind it.

Continued over

6 Underpainting the players

Several colours are necessary for these figures. There are two browns – one warm (a green-red mix with a touch of yellow for the heads, arms, legs, shadows, shorts, and shirts of the yellow team), and the second colder (a green-red mix with a little blue for the hair, the shorts of the opposing side, the boots, and the players' shadows). As well as these, yellow is required for the strip of one team and a pale blue mix for the shadows in the shirts and socks of the other, together with Cadmium Red and Phthalo Blue for the stripes in the shirts. Sketch in the broad details, softening the edges of the patches of colour as you go. When you have done this, cover the figures with masking fluid, working up to and just over the pencil outline. This will allow you to eliminate the pencil marks later. Mask out the lines on the pitch, breaking them up to give a more realistic effect.

Masking fluid, painted carefully up to the pencil outline, covers the players.

Removing the masking fluid shows the colours of the players blocked in.

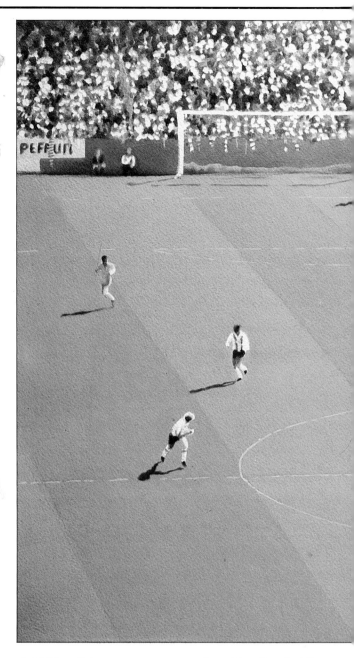

7 The pitch

For the colder of the greens use a mix of Sap Green with a touch of Phthalo Blue. For the warmer use Sap Green with a little Cadmium Yellow Pale. Paint one set of stripes at a time and wait for them to dry (you can use a hairdrier) before painting the next set. To paint them evenly it is best to keep your board at a slight angle and turn it so that the lines are horizontal. Fill your No. 14 brush with colour and apply a line of paint across the top of the strip you are painting. Then paint another line beneath it so that the two merge and blend, and continue adding colour in this way until you get to the bottom of the strip. At this point, to prevent an edge of colour building up, make the

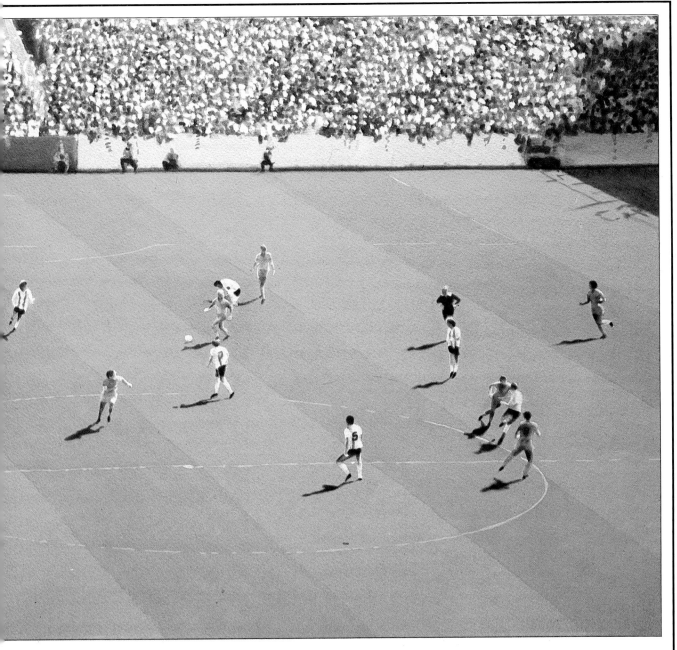

board flat again to keep the colour uniform. You will need to lay down a number of washes to build up the pigment to the required depth, but you should wait until each layer is dry before adding the next. Before the final wash on the grass, remove the masking fluid from the lines. One green wash will soften the harsh, white effect.

8 Overpainting the players

When the final green wash is dry, gently remove the masking fluid from the players and paint them to the required depth of tone. If you think of the grass as an intermediate tone, the figures should cover a whole tonal range from very dark to white. For them to stand out against their background, these tones must be reasonably accurate. The finished figures should look as if you could almost pick them up. Finally paint in the remaining details, such as the shadows of the goalpost and of the stadium to the right of the picture. These shadows are a green-blue mix where they fall over the grass and a grey-blue over the crowd.

BONFIRE NIGHT

Medium ACRYLICS

THIS PAINTING BRINGS together reference material from a variety of sources, including sketches, photographs, and memory, in an attempt to make one unified image in which to express the atmosphere and excitement of a public firework display. The scale of the bonfire is expressed by the size of the spectators, whose silhouettes are etched against the flames. Above them, fireworks explode, fixed at their moment of maximum incandescence.

The composition appears to be straightforward. The line of spectators provides a solid, low horizontal from which the eyes rise along and up the line of the fire first to the firework on the left and then across and up to the larger one on the right. Here the effect of the explosion is to create a three-dimensional space, in which the glowing ends with their trails of smoke reach out towards the spectator. This brings the composition forward off the picture plane so that the eye is left in mid-air, suspended like the firework itself. There is nothing to bring it to earth again. Thus the effect of the composition is to provide an analogy to the idea the painting expresses, of catching and revealing a moment of transient and insubstantial beauty.

If, as in this painting, you are working with a number of separate elements that you want to resolve in one unified composition, you will find that a number of configurations present themselves. Not only do you have to fix on the number of elements and the position of each, but you also have to establish their scale relative to the rest of the picture. Here, I had collected a great deal of imagery but used only the fireworks and bonfire. The best approach is to make sketches of the permutations and choose the best one.

MATERIALS AND EQUIPMENT

Support
Canvas 24 × 18 ins (61 × 46 cm)

Acrylic colours

Quinacri-done Red   Phthalo Green

Phthalo Blue   Ivory Black

Azo Yellow   Titanium White

Brushes
No. 8 and two No. 4 sable (or nylon) pointed flats, No. 11 hogs'-hair filbert

Other items
White water-soluble pencil, masking fluid, airbrush

METHOD
The canvas is first painted a uniform blue-black colour. Then a monochrome underpainting is made of the fire and the smoke trails of the fireworks. The next stage is to cover the figures with masking fluid. The overpainting is done with sable brushes and the colour is softened with an airbrush.

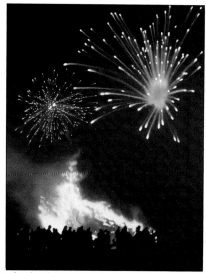

The finished painting. For the guideline sketch on its grid see p. 235.

1 Tinting the canvas
Paint the canvas an overall blue-black colour of absolutely uniform tone. This is not quite as straightforward as it sounds. In order to get sufficient depth of tone, the best method is to apply several coats of thin paint, waiting for each to dry before repainting. You can use a hairdrier on a warm (not hot) setting to speed up the drying process. For each coat of paint, work the final brushstrokes in the opposite direction to those you have used in the previous coat. Use the No. 11 hogs'-hair brush and a mixture of equal parts of Ivory Black and Phthalo Blue. When this is dry, draw the outline. Use a white pencil with a water-soluble lead to show up against the background.

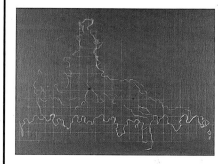

2 Underpainting the fire
Next paint the bonfire and smoke using Titanium White and the small sable brushes. For the lightest tones, use the white reasonably thickly; thin it down for the darker tones. Since acrylic paint dries quickly you can build up the body of the paint by overpainting. Use a clean, damp brush to soften the edges where this is necessary.

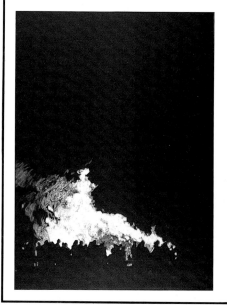

3 The smoke trails
Paint the smoke trails of the firework on the top right using a very thin white mix and one of the sable brushes. You do not have to stick exactly to the lines on the original, as long as the effect of the burst is expressed in your brushstrokes. At the end of each smoke trail, apply a tip of thick white paint. Literally trowel the paint on with the chisel end of your flat brush. Repeat this process for the firework on the left. Here, sprinkle the area of the burst with small dots of thick white paint.

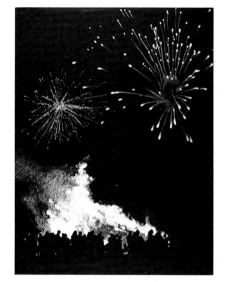

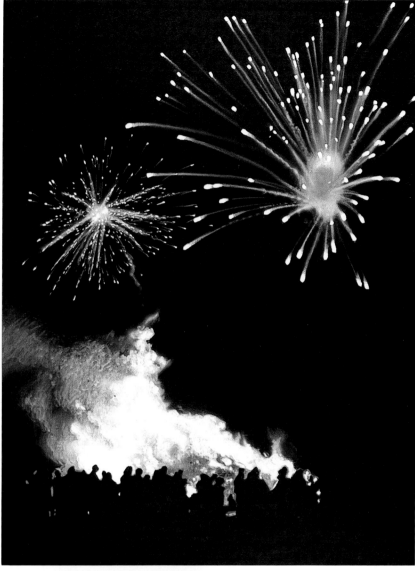

4 Masking the figures
Paint up to the edges of the silhouetted figures with masking fluid and paint down from them about 3 ins (7 cm). This will prevent them being painted with the airbrush.

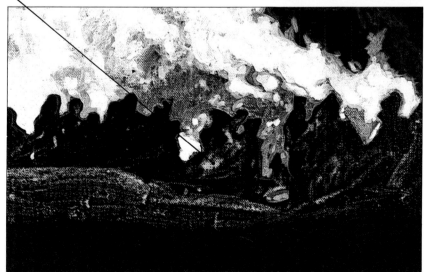

5 Softening the edges
Mix Titanium White to the consistency of thin cream and spray it over the area of the bonfire. Soften all the top edges and spray thinly on the left-hand side to produce the effect of smoke. Spray more paint on the lighter parts than on the darker ones. The idea is to soften the contours of the painting. You should also spray the centre of the firework bursts along the lines of the smoke trails. This will have the effect of softening the trails. (For the photograph of this stage, the masking fluid has been removed to show the effect of the airbrushing. You should leave it on, however, since there will be more airbrushing to do later.) Clean the airbrush thoroughly at this stage.

Continued over

6 Tinting the bonfire

Use the No. 4 nylon or sable brushes to tint the bonfire using various combinations of Quinacridone Red and Azo Yellow. Work with quite thin paint, putting on washes of colour and softening the edges as you go.

Colour the whole of the area of the bonfire using the larger sable brush for the more extensive areas of colour, such as the smoke on the left. This will give you a greater richness and depth than if you had simply sprayed the colour on with the airbrush from the beginning.

8 Removing the masking fluid

When you are satisfied with the look of the fire, leave it to dry and then remove the masking fluid by rubbing it off gently with your fingers. You may find that it has left the area beneath looking slightly darker than it was originally. You can remove this effect by simply painting over the whole bottom area with clean water using a large flat hogs'-hair brush. When the area has dried, the dark tone will be uniform once more. If any of the white lines of your grid still show on the dark surface, you can remove them by rubbing gently with a clean, damp cloth.

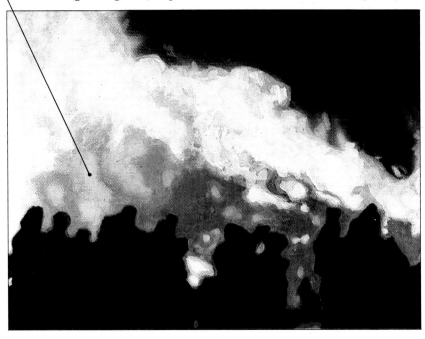

7 The orange colours

Now you can use the airbrush again, spraying a thin Azo Yellow where appropriate. Follow this with a mix of Azo Yellow and Quinacridone Red round the edge and in the centre.

You can use a deeper orange-red for the smoke on the left. At this point you may have lost some of the intensity of the whitest parts of the fire. You can repaint these, using both the sable and the airbrush, to the correct intensity.

9 Painting the fireworks

For the firework on the left spray a straight, thin Quinacridone Red mix over the star shape, and for the one on the right spray a thin Azo Yellow mix over the smoke trails. Next you should paint over the bright white highlights again. For the firework on the right I sprayed over the yellow with white to give it a more creamy colour. Next spray the smoke trails on the right with a pure Phthalo Blue wash. This stays pure blue in parts and looks greenish where the yellow underneath is more evident. Again you should repaint the white tips and then use one of the sable brushes to give the stems of the smoke trails thin glazes of various green-blue combinations. For the bright green trails, mix Phthalo Green with Azo Yellow. For others, use Phthalo Green on its own or pure Phthalo Blue. The effect of this is to give the burst a range of colours that is visually satisfying and that looks much more interesting than if it had all been painted in the same colour.

10 Finishing off the fireworks

Where the colours come to the white tips of the smoke trails soften them in tone with a clean, damp brush. Glaze over the white sparkles of the firework on the left with Azo Yellow. Then dot the central core with Titanium White. Finally make any overall adjustments to the painting that you feel are necessary.

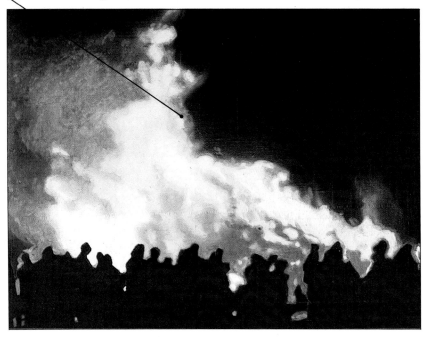

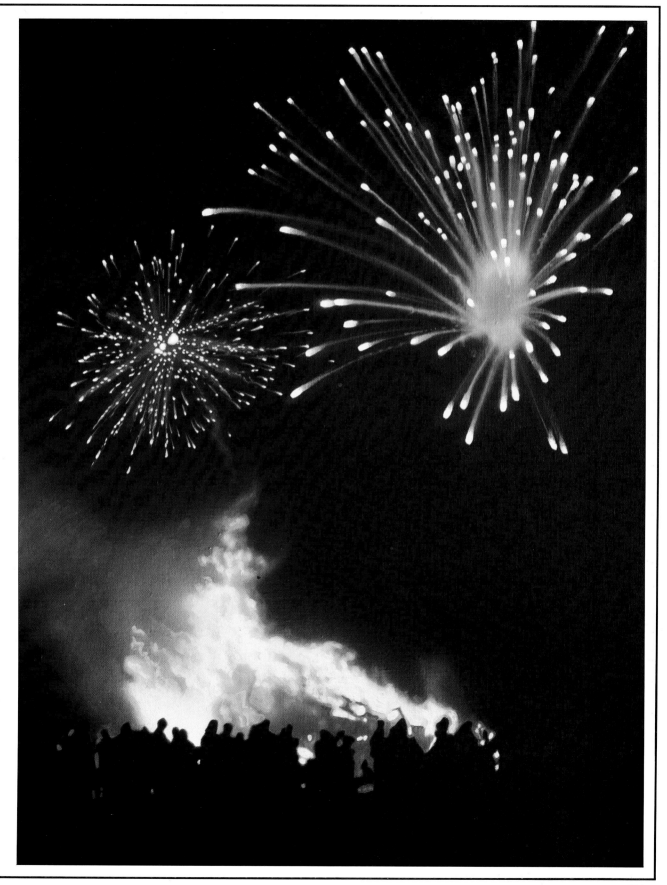

PORTRAITS

MAKING IMAGES OF ourselves is basic to our lives. From an early age, children draw portraits. Usually they first draw their parents — especially their mother. They also draw brothers, sisters, and pets. Later comes a wide range of witches, fairies, and monsters that seem to inhabit a world as tangible for the child as the world of the family. Portraiture is also important for most adults, even if this is expressed only in family snapshots.

For children, resemblance seems unimportant. Their portraits are more diagrammatic than realistic. For adults, getting an exact resemblance assumes a far greater importance, although, in my opinion, they could learn a lot from children in this respect.

Given the interest and curiosity that images of ourselves always provoke, it is not surprising that portraiture can provide a special thrill for the artist. The task of reconstructing a subject's features is in itself an exacting one. A simple touch of the brush can transform the portrait. But there is also the challenge of recreating the spirit of the sitter, a task which is controlled by the artist's personality and capability, and by the limited tools we use for painting and drawing. In addition, the portrait has to work in its own terms, purely as a painted image, if it is to succeed at all. In fact, most artists discover that the only way to come to terms with the living reality of a subject is by regarding the painting as having its own life, parallel to but quite separate from the life of the sitter.

BEGINNING PORTRAITURE

Approaches to portraiture are many and varied, but perhaps the best way to begin is by making simple, small-scale pencil sketches. People asleep in trains and in committee rooms make good subjects. Try to sum up in a few lines the essential characteristics of your subject — those

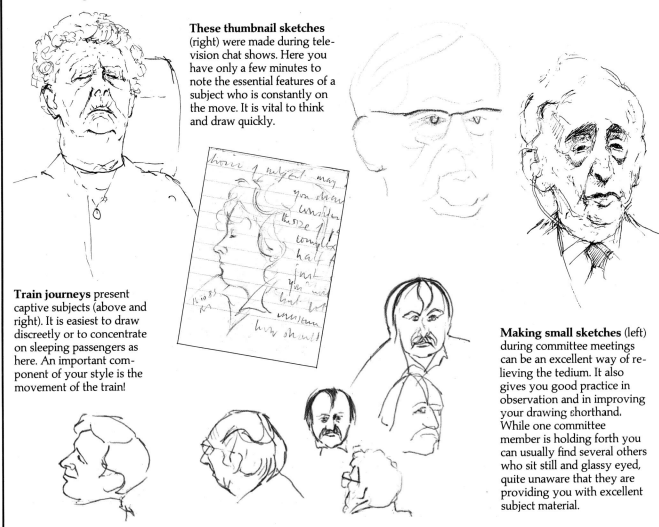

These thumbnail sketches (right) were made during television chat shows. Here you have only a few minutes to note the essential features of a subject who is constantly on the move. It is vital to think and draw quickly.

Train journeys present captive subjects (above and right). It is easiest to draw discreetly or to concentrate on sleeping passengers as here. An important component of your style is the movement of the train!

Making small sketches (left) during committee meetings can be an excellent way of relieving the tedium. It also gives you good practice in observation and in improving your drawing shorthand. While one committee member is holding forth you can usually find several others who sit still and glassy eyed, quite unaware that they are providing you with excellent subject material.

things that strike *you* as being important. Your sketches may be no more than caricatures, but they will give you good practice in observation.

Next, take a long, hard look at one particular face and try to make a much more realistic image. The best sitter for this is yourself. You can take as many liberties with your own features as you like and make mistakes without fear of doing injustice to your sitter. Once you get used to having a real face in front of you, start to make portraits of your family and friends. A good way to begin is with profile drawings, since with full-face or three-quarter views it can be more difficult to pin down the features. Work with the same sitter for a number of drawings. This will enable you to relax into the work and build up confidence. Do not confine yourself to pencil drawings. Try making a portrait with a pen – you will have to think hard about each stroke since every mark you make will tell in the finished drawing. This is equally true when you work with a brush.

When you want to start making a painted portrait, you should do a drawing of your subject on paper the same size as your canvas. When you are happy with the positioning of the features, trace them on to the canvas. This will give you a framework on which to base your painting, while you get used to the idea of mixing flesh tones and matching shadows. Later on you may have the confidence to start with the brushes themselves.

Tackling the four portraits described in the following pages will give you experience of four different ways of working with acrylics and oil colors. The first example shows the face being built up with thin transparent washes of acrylic. The second uses a thin underpainting with a thicker overpainting in opaque oil color. The third is an example of direct oil painting on a colored ground. The fourth is more complex, showing careful modeling in a white underpainting over a Terre Verte ground. This is colored by glazing with transparent or semi-transparent oil color. Once you have tried these techniques you will be able to apply them to your own subjects.

PAINTING GROUP PORTRAITS

In this section I have concentrated on heads because they are clearly the most important aspect of portraiture. But you should not underestimate the role of everything that

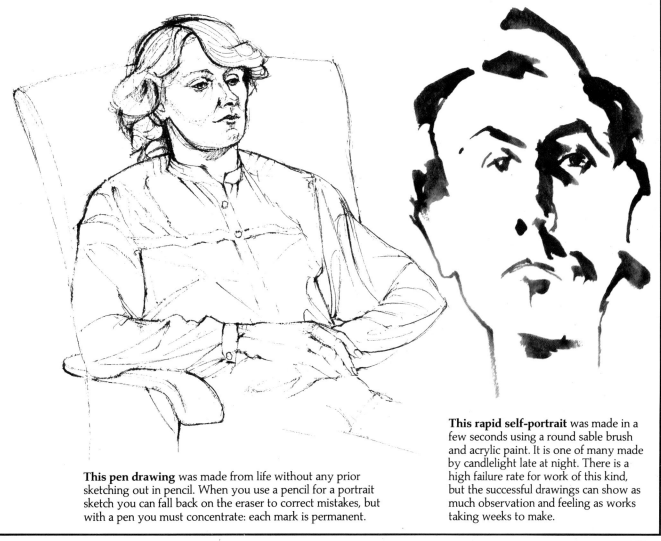

This pen drawing was made from life without any prior sketching out in pencil. When you use a pencil for a portrait sketch you can fall back on the eraser to correct mistakes, but with a pen you must concentrate: each mark is permanent.

This rapid self-portrait was made in a few seconds using a round sable brush and acrylic paint. It is one of many made by candlelight late at night. There is a high failure rate for work of this kind, but the successful drawings can show as much observation and feeling as works taking weeks to make.

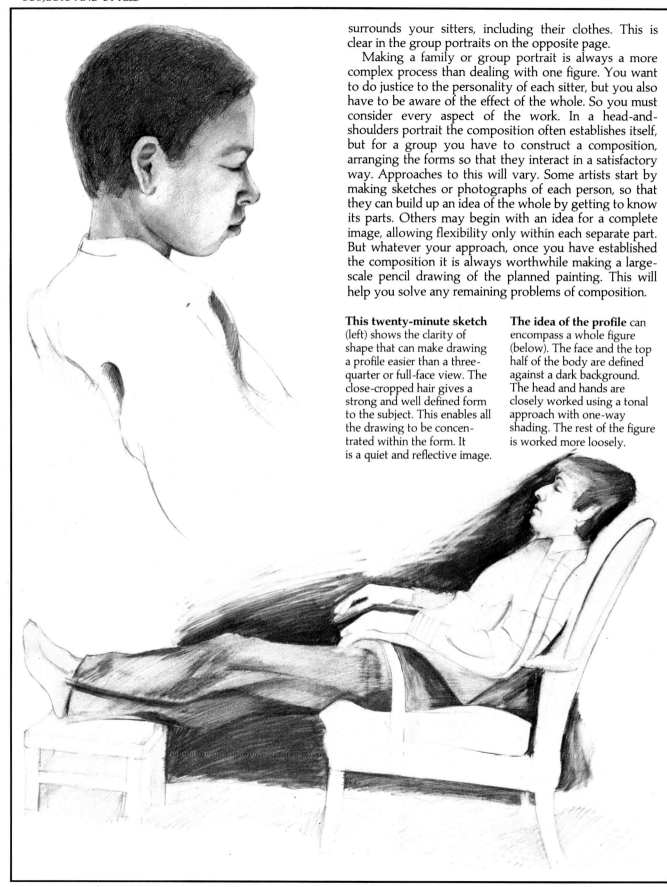

surrounds your sitters, including their clothes. This is clear in the group portraits on the opposite page.

Making a family or group portrait is always a more complex process than dealing with one figure. You want to do justice to the personality of each sitter, but you also have to be aware of the effect of the whole. So you must consider every aspect of the work. In a head-and-shoulders portrait the composition often establishes itself, but for a group you have to construct a composition, arranging the forms so that they interact in a satisfactory way. Approaches to this will vary. Some artists start by making sketches or photographs of each person, so that they can build up an idea of the whole by getting to know its parts. Others may begin with an idea for a complete image, allowing flexibility only within each separate part. But whatever your approach, once you have established the composition it is always worthwhile making a large-scale pencil drawing of the planned painting. This will help you solve any remaining problems of composition.

This twenty-minute sketch (left) shows the clarity of shape that can make drawing a profile easier than a three-quarter or full-face view. The close-cropped hair gives a strong and well defined form to the subject. This enables all the drawing to be concentrated within the form. It is a quiet and reflective image.

The idea of the profile can encompass a whole figure (below). The face and the top half of the body are defined against a dark background. The head and hands are closely worked using a tonal approach with one-way shading. The rest of the figure is worked more loosely.

TWO GROUP PORTRAITS

These commissioned family portraits show two different solutions to the problems posed by painting a group of people. In the first all ten figures are posed frontally in a mosaic of interlocking shapes on a single flat plane parallel to the picture plane. Within this solid shape, which binds the family together, there are subtleties of composition that establish particular relationships and bonds within the group. The composition came about as a result of working with the family, not from a preconceived idea. The painting was based initially on photographs and then worked from life. For the second painting, the basic idea resulted from a solo visit to the landscape. It created a space that was just waiting to be articulated by standing figures. The arrangement came about naturally when everyone had got used to the situation.

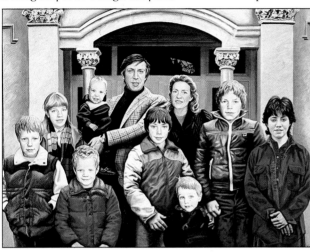

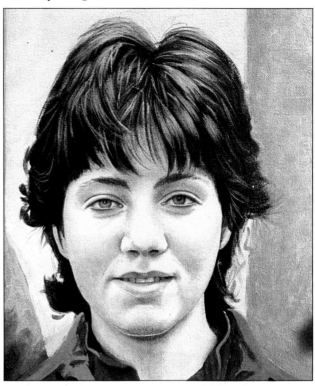

The heads (above and right) create a strong circular pattern around the center axis of the dark-haired boy. This makes an intimate space that holds the family together. This is enhanced by the closeness of the figures and the way they touch and hold each other. The parents, for instance, lean slightly toward each other, touching at a point just behind the dark-haired boy, who lightly holds his younger brother. This restrained intimacy balances the formality of the composition.

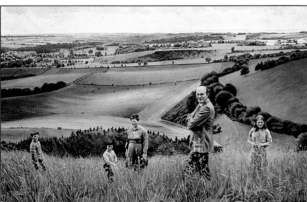

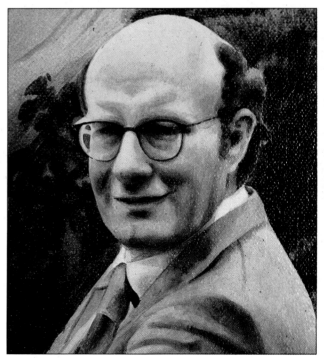

This painting (above) is in one sense very stylized, with each stationary figure occupying a quite separate space. It is almost as if they were in some form of theater, with the landscape as a painted backdrop. But the landscape also creates a real sense of space behind the figures. In addition, the painting sets out to capture a warmer human feeling. The eyes of the father (right) and his older children engage actively with the spectator, while those of his wife, who is closest to their smallest child, look down at him with an amused affection.

Henry With A Baby Rabbit

Medium ACRYLICS

ONE OF THE main problems in painting young children from life is keeping them still. In fact, up to the age of about nine or ten, it is well-nigh impossible unless, of course, you draw or paint them when they are asleep – a separate and rewarding activity in itself.

Photographs of children, on the other hand, never seem quite to reflect the softness of their skin, their clear eyes, or the personal bond between the child and its parent. The answer, it seems to me, is to base all the preliminary work for a painting on a favorite photograph, retaining and enhancing those aspects of the photograph that do seem to express the character of the child and leaving out the parts which do not. If the preliminary work is painted softly, the final stages can be made from life, when such details as the color of the flesh tones, the eyes, and the hair can be accurately recorded. If this accuracy is desirable, then the amount of time and care spent on a portrait of a child is almost inevitably reflected in the finished work. Certainly the desire to be faithful to the original very often inspires the artist to new heights of subtlety and sensitivity in the handling of the paint. In no other area of painting can a misjudged tone or color appear so distorted or exaggerated. A feature has only to be marginally out of place for the child to become quite unrecognizable.

For this particular portrait, the essential element of the image seems to me to be the intimacy expressed by the touch of the cheek on the fur of the rabbit and by the expression in Henry's eyes. Moreover, all this is concentrated within an oval composition created by the crook of the arm and the fringe of dark hair. The arm and the hair seem to add to the intimate and tender atmosphere, and the quality of the light – with half the face and half the rabbit in shadow – reinforces this.

MATERIALS AND EQUIPMENT

Support
Watercolor paper, 300 gsm weight, $23\frac{1}{2} \times 16\frac{1}{2}$ ins (60 × 42 cm)

Acrylic colors

Cadmium Red		Azo Yellow	
Phthalo Blue		Sap Green	

Brushes
No. 8, No. 4, and No. 2 sable rounds

METHOD

The technique used for this painting is that of glazing. This means building up the tones by overlaying many thin washes of transparent acrylic paint. It is essential to work slowly and carefully, building the tones gradually and allowing each wash to dry before overlaying the next one. It is also important not to let any edges of color dry on the face itself without "feathering" them off with a damp, clean brush. If this is not done, a harsh edge will ruin the essential softness of the features.

For the guideline sketch on its grid see p. 231.

1 Painting the darkest tones in the hair
Make a thin mix of Cadmium Red and Sap Green with a little Phthalo Blue. Begin by painting the darkest shadows in the hair. Let your brush follow the lines of the hair and try to make each stroke as fluent as possible. Before each brushstroke can dry soften the edges immediately with a damp, clean brush.

2 Defining the features
Using the same color and an identical technique, paint in all the features with a similar dark tone. These are the eyelashes, the outer edge of the iris (be sure to soften the edge of this; there must be *no* sharp edges here) and the eye, the nostrils, and the parts of the rabbit in deepest shadow.

3 Building up tone and color in the hair
Reduce the amount of blue in your soft brown mix, and go back to the hair again. Repeat the same fluent strokes, but this time make them slightly wider than the first. Soften the edges immediately as you did before. By changing the mix slightly each time – adding a touch of Azo Yellow for one wash or more Phthalo Blue for another – you will gradually build up the depth of tone and add to the subtlety of the effect.

4 Adding color to the eyes
Turn again to the eyes, the most expressive feature of the image. Start with the part of the iris closest to the pupil and to the highlights. It is a yellow-brown mix. The amount of paint you need for it is so small that it is worth experimenting carefully to get the color exactly right. Now move out from the pupil and use a more neutral brown. Finally, paint in the outside ring of the iris with a blue-green-gray mix made from Phthalo Blue with a touch of Sap Green and even less Cadmium Red. As before, it is very important that after every stroke of the brush you should soften the edges slightly. It is possible, though admittedly rather difficult, to train yourself to work with your "paint" brush in one hand and your clean, damp "softening" brush in the other.

Continued over

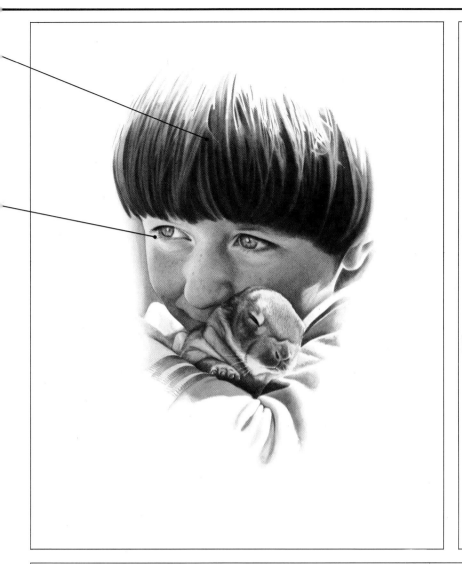

SOFTENING THE EDGES

Making the edges of the colors soft is very important in this painting. The three examples below show the different softening effects you can achieve and how they change the appearance of a fluent, hard-edged brushstroke. Before the paint dries, take a clean, damp brush and "feather" it along the edge. This will give you the soft, delicate appearance that you are aiming for in this portrait.

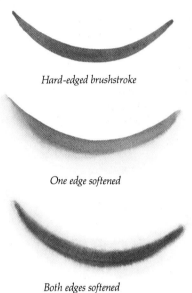

Hard-edged brushstroke

One edge softened

Both edges softened

THE EYE DETAILS

The eyes are built up in stages, as shown in these details, which are reproduced to their actual size in the finished painting. First the structure of each eye is sketched in, to give an indication of where to place the colors. The lashes are also added at this stage. Then you start to add color, applying a very small area of yellow-brown near the pupils' centers, a neutral brown farther out, and a blue-green-gray mix around each iris.

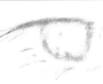

The structure of the eyes

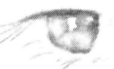

Starting to add color to the eyes

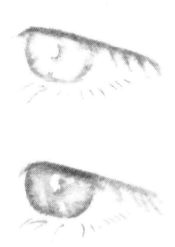

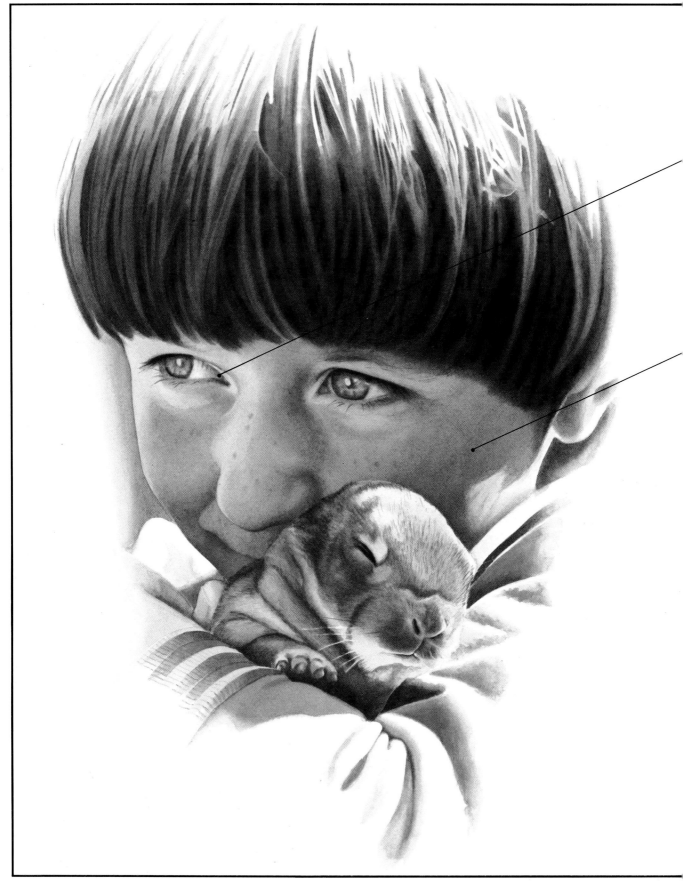

5 Working tone and detail into the eyes

Paint in the corners of the eyes with a thin brown mix of Cadmium Red and Sap Green. When it has dried, repeat the procedure with a thin mix of Cadmium Red plus a touch of Phthalo Blue. Build up the shadow beneath the eyelashes, and see that it falls over the whites of the eyes as much as it does over the iris — especially in the top third of the eyeball. You will see from the finished painting that the "whites" of the eyes are considerably darker than the white paper. Now make a gray mix Cadmium Red, Phthalo Blue, and Sap Green, and with a sharp pointed brush paint in the eyelashes. Since the painting is made up entirely from transparent glazes, the lashes will continue to show through the larger washes that build up the face itself. Toward the end of the painting you can easily re-paint the lashes to give them more definition.

PAINTING THE EYES

The details of the eyes are shown here actual size. You start by painting the eye corners, then tackle the shadows under the eyelashes, paying particular attention to the way they fall on the eye whites.

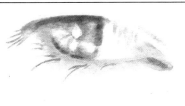
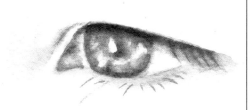

6 Modeling the shadows

Turn next to those parts of the face that are in deepest shadow. These are the right-hand side of the face, the right-hand side of the nose, the upper lip, and the chin. Begin modeling these features with very thin brown washes of color, using the larger brush and carefully softening out the edges. It does not matter how many glazes you lay on top of each other, provided the layer beneath is dry. This means that you can afford to make your first wash weaker in tone than the colors will end up. You will feel the face building up form with each new layer of color, and you will gradually get the feel of the geography of the features.

7 The choice of color

In color terms, the darker tones on the face comprise washes of gray, light brown and pink (with a touch of blue). An overall color can be made from a thin mix of Azo Yellow with a touch of Cadmium Red and a very small amount of Sap Green to neutralize it a little. In each case, the quantities of pigment are tiny.

8 Painting the rabbit

Use an identical procedure for building up tone in the figure of the rabbit. Use cooler colors than those on the boy's face, especially when you come to the side of the rabbit in shadow. Notice here how thin strokes of the No. 2 sable give an indication of the direction of the rabbit's fur and thereby define its shape.

9 The rabbit's mouth and nostrils

Use a pink wash around the animal's mouth and nostrils and the edge of the fur on the side of its head in order to point up the sensitivity of its features and emphasize its immaturity.

10 Henry's arm

Use Phthalo Blue on its own for the sleeve of the boy's sweatshirt, and add some gray to bring out the creases in deepest shadow. The blue of the arm serves to cool the face's warmth and expand the color range.

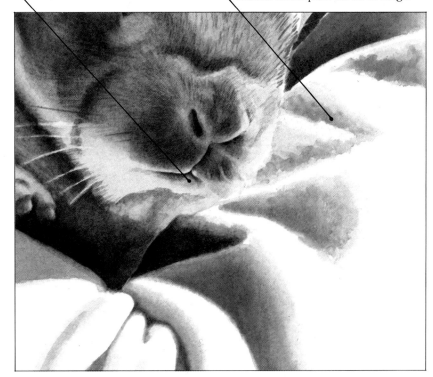

11 Making overall adjustments

Once you have painted in the detailing on the features and most of the modeling, you can begin to adjust the overall look of the picture with washes which cover much larger areas. The hair, for instance, can be treated as a whole shape in which the detailing will show through any final washes. Where the ends of the bangs join the face above the eyebrows, chisel your sable and gently stroke the ends in.

MARIANNA

Medium OILS

THE STRUCTURE of this portrait of a little girl makes a straightforward composition – the strong green shape of the parka fills the canvas, enclosing her absorbed face. But it is the mood of the picture that is important here. In the portrait of Henry holding a baby rabbit (see pp. 196–9), I focused on the boy's evident delight in the animal, and in that sense it is a painting in which everything is revealed. Here, there is more mystery, for we can only speculate about what is passing through the girl's mind. Her eyes are fixed on something out of the canvas frame, yet there is an abstraction in her gaze, as if she is spellbound in a world of her own. Consequently, there is a complete lack of self-consciousness about her expression.

To make this crucial aspect of the portrait into the main point of the painting, I left the background empty. There is nothing there to give us any clue about what is happening. The flat background is a relief from the extensive modeling of the face and hood, and the contrast in color between the hood and the face reflects a contrast in materials – the hard, shiny plastic of the hood reinforces the face's soft warmth. The hood also acts as a light shield which casts the top half and left-hand edge of the face into shadow, softening the contours and details of the face. This provides a physical parallel with the idea of self-absorption which this portrait generates.

This painting is essentially about accurate modeling on a reasonably large scale. The figure painted to this scale would actually be larger than life size. So it is important to be as accurate as possible in the mixing and application of tone. As your painting progresses, you will see how painting adjacent areas or adjusting one part often necessitates the reappraisal of another.

MATERIALS AND EQUIPMENT

Support
Canvas 20 × 16 ins (51 × 40.5 cm)

Oil colors

Winsor Red   Burnt Sienna

Winsor Blue   Permanent Rose

Cadmium Yellow Pale   Titanium White

Winsor Green

Brushes
No. 7, No. 6, No. 4, No. 3, and No. 1 hogs'-hair filberts, No. 4 sable round

Other items
Turpentine, painting medium (see p. 10)

METHOD
The canvas is first given a pink tint (or "imprimatura"). This is allowed to dry before the face is drawn in charcoal or pencil. The method is then to underpaint the whole of the face thinly, beginning by blocking in the light tones roughly and working through the mid tones to the darkest tones. All the features should be defined by this stage. Then the broad tonal areas of the parka and hood are blocked in, after which these areas are worked up to an almost finished state by blending and refining. Finally the tones of the face are reassessed and readjusted, to bring the image to its finished state. This process consists of softening and rounding the tones of the face.

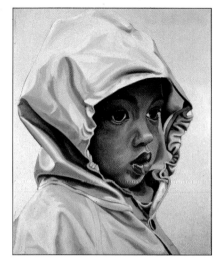

The finished painting. For the guideline sketch on its grid see p. 228.

1 The light face tones
Using a mixture of Titanium White, Cadmium Yellow Pale, and Winsor Red, and a No. 6 hogs'-hair brush, start by blocking in the mid to lightest tones of the face. Leave the highlights untouched. When you mix, remember to begin with white and add only tiny amounts of colored pigment to begin with. Apply the paint using short dabbing brushstrokes, moving up and down in tone according to the contours of the face. As you work, try to be aware of how the light defines these contours. Your modeling at this stage is basic and should comprise a series of flat planes of tone corresponding to single brushstrokes.

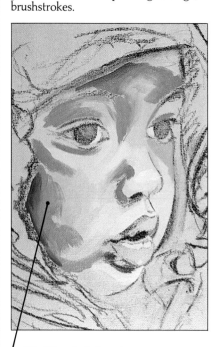

2 The dark face tones
When you move on to the dark tones, try not to be too tentative. There is a wide range of tones in the face, and your painting will have a flat quality if your range of tones is too timid. Don't worry about blending the tones at this stage. Try to keep your colors as pure and separate as possible. If you put a light tone on your painting and it is wrong, it is easier to darken it slightly later than it is to lighten it.

3 The eyes
As you move toward the eyes and eyebrows, define the eyebrow, the line above the upper eyelashes, the iris, the pupil, and the lower eyelashes with a mix made of Burnt Sienna and Winsor Blue, using your No. 1 hogs'-hair. Do this *before* painting in the surrounding tones so that you can keep the features in the right places and create a structure for the eyes themselves. As you paint the upper eyelid, for example, you will probably paint over the dark lines above and below. This does not matter because you will be able to retrieve the line and tone later. If those dark lines were not there they would be difficult to paint in accurately and with enough intensity over the lighter ones.

4 The darkest face tones
Paint in the very dark tones on the face, where shadow is deepest. Use Burnt Sienna as your basic color, with touches of Winsor Blue, Winsor Green, and Titanium White.

5 The green reflections
Where the light filters through the green hood on the right-hand edge of the forehead there is a green cast to the skin color. Mix Winsor Green with Titanium White, but incorporate a little of the light brown of the flesh tones. Paint in similar green casts under the rim of the lower lip and the chin.

6 The lips
For the lips, use Winsor Red, Permanent Rose, Titanium White, and Burnt Sienna. Aim for tonal accuracy here. Look at the structure of the lips. Notice how the upper lip is in quite deep shadow with just the center part protruding a little. It is consequently lighter in tone. Immediately above it, the line of top lip and upper lip catches the light. This is similar in tone to the light that reflects off the top of the nose and only slightly darker than the highlight which runs across the lower lip two-thirds of the way up. Block in all these tones using your No. 1 hogs'-hair. The light pink color on the lower lip is Titanium White with Permanent Rose and a touch of Winsor Red. Below the lower lip is a dark shadow and immediately below that a much lighter tone on the lower part of the chin. Try to express this tonal contrast boldly. Move away from your painting frequently to look at it from a distance. Look at it through half-closed eyes to see if the image is holding together.

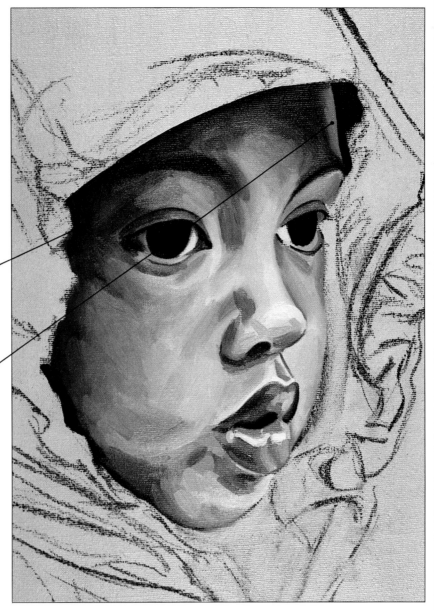

7 Colors and brushes for the parka
When you have painted in the face tones, start on the parka. As you did for the face, begin with the lightest tones and work toward the darkest ones. The color to use here is a basic green, made by mixing Winsor Green and Cadmium Yellow Pale. Lighten it with Titanium White and use Winsor Blue and a touch of Winsor Red to darken more neutral tones. Try working with three separate No. 6 hogs'-hair filbert brushes — one for light tones, one for mid tones, and one for dark tones.
Continued over

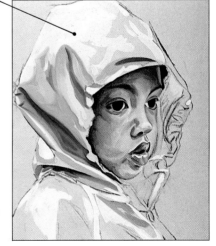

8 Painting the parka

Before you begin painting the parka and hood, look at the finished version carefully to see where the main areas of tone are. Begin at the top and work down to the left. Leave the gathered edging on either side of the face until last. There is a good deal of painting to do in this section, with a wide range of colors, and it will take you some time to block in. Blend the tones where necessary using the same brushes but wiping them off first. The "thin" end of the brush is particularly useful for this. Modify or change any tones until you feel that you have got them right. Artists have always enjoyed painting drapery, and this modern, plastic version will provide relief from the accurate work on the face.

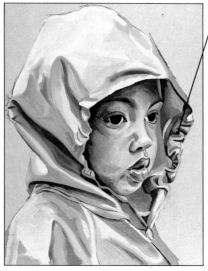

9 The hood edges

The edges of the hood are more intricate than the folds in the hood itself, but the procedure is exactly the same. You must simply use smaller brushes. Use your No. 1 hogs'-hair, and if necessary, your No. 4 round sable.

10 Assessing the face tones

Once you have painted the hood to your satisfaction, go back to the face. In my painting I decided to paint in a darkened background at this point to help me decide how to achieve greater tonal accuracy in the hood and face. I later wiped it off and repainted it very pale blue, as in the finished version.

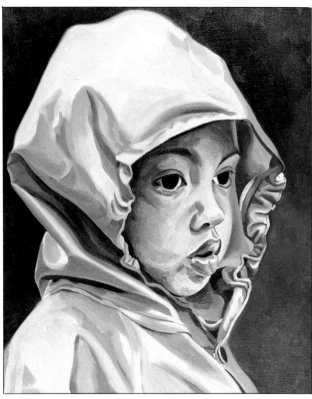

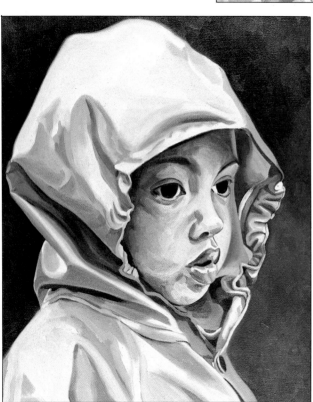

11 Adjusting the face tones

With the dark background I could see where I needed to adjust tones on the face. Immediately I could see that the shadow cast by the hood on the top part of the face and on the left-hand side was not deep enough. So I darkened the tones over most of the face. For the top and left I made up deeper tones using a mix of Burnt Sienna, Cadmium Yellow Pale, Winsor Red, and Titanium White. For the very deepest shadows at the edge of the hood I added a touch of Winsor Blue or Winsor Green to this mix. Where the face emerges into the light I used richer and warmer reds, oranges, and browns. These seemed to reflect the skin color in this light.

12 Repainting the face

Repainting involves the blending and refining of the more vigorous brushstrokes. This will give a much more accurate sense of the smooth contours of the features. It will also help you to see inconsistencies in tone more clearly — particularly where there is too much contrast between two adjacent tones. The shadow running down toward the nose from the left eyebrow, and the shadow on the left nostril are two examples of this.

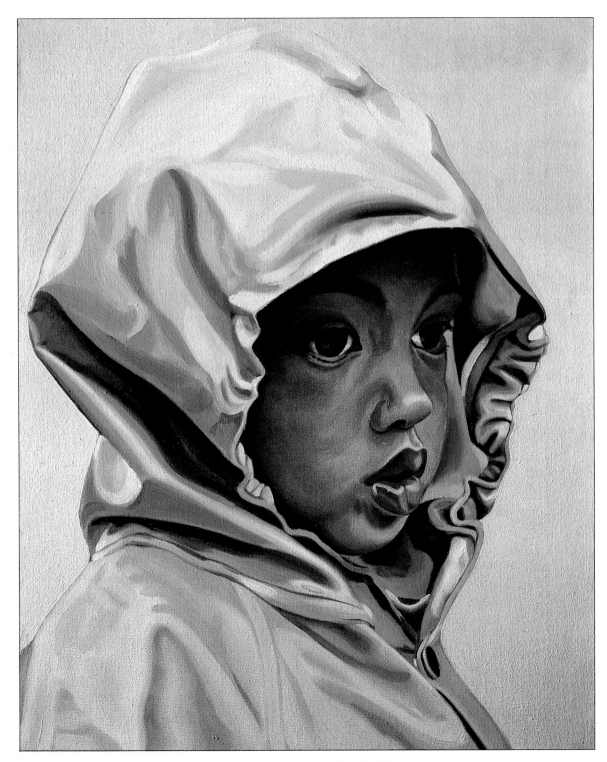

13 Softening and rounding the features

When you blend the tones — by stroking the paint surface with a wiped-off hogs'-hair brush — you will notice a certain sharp angularity in the way you applied the tones. This needs to be softened and rounded. Give this treatment to all the features, including the eyes, nose, and mouth.

They should all have equal attention. In any portrait you should give consistent treatment to all areas of the picture. All portraits need not be brought to the same level of refinement, but you should aim for a uniformity of technique within each painting. Finally, I repainted the background using a mix of Winsor Blue and Titanium White.

THERESA

Medium OILS

WHEN YOU PAINT someone you know well, it is often difficult to be objective. You have built up a complex set of impressions of them and these can have the effect of blurring your visual focus. When you paint the portrait of a stranger you have at least had the opportunity of having a really objective look at their features in the first few minutes of meeting. This initial impression can provide a strong guiding impulse for your work. But with friends or relatives, the desire to do justice to your subject can give rise to an anxiety that evaporates confidence and results in a less effective painting.

The first study (below right) that I made of Theresa — whom I have known for many years — demonstrates this lack of confidence. The objects on the dressing table are painted in a direct and relaxed way, but the face has been reworked several times and is tighter and more cramped in style. The painting has no overall unity. In such circumstances a measure of detachment is called for to enable you at least to see your painting objectively. Here, the finished painting shows a much more relaxed overall approach and a direct style. It is made by laying premixed colors directly onto a tinted canvas. The Permanent Rose 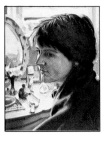 tint acts as a unifying background color that shows through the gaps between the touches of paint. The effect of gradation of tones is achieved by putting close together tones that are similar but separate. These work together to indicate the transitions of light and shade. The finished picture, although incorporating a wide range of colors, gives a gentle effect.

MATERIALS AND EQUIPMENT

Support
Canvas 24 × 18 ins (61 × 46 cm)

Oil colors

Winsor Red		Transparent Gold Ochre	
Winsor Blue		Burnt Sienna	
Manganese Blue		Permanent Rose	
Cadmium Yellow Pale		Titanium White	
Winsor Green			

Brushes
Two No. 4 and one No. 1 sable (or nylon) pointed flats, No. 6, two No. 4, and one No. 2 hogs'-hair filberts

Other items
HB pencil, turpentine, painting medium (see p. 10)

METHOD
The method is to work methodically around the center section of the portrait, moving gradually toward the edge. A small section of the picture is worked on at a time and there is little or no overpainting. The picture involves careful mixing of colors.

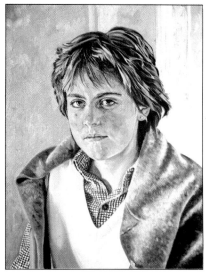

The finished painting. For the guideline sketch on its grid see p. 229.

1 The tint and outline sketch
First tint the canvas by diluting Permanent Rose thinly with turpentine, brushing it on with the No. 11 hogs'-hair and wiping it off with a clean cotton rag. Then draw in the features as accurately as you can according to the guideline sketch.

2 The eye on the right
Start in the corner, using the No. 1 round sable and a mix of Burnt Sienna, Permanent Rose, and Titanium White. Make the mix lighter and pinker in the middle and at the edges. Around the line of the top eyelid use a mix of Burnt Sienna, Winsor Blue, and Titanium White with, just above it, a line of Winsor Green plus Titanium White and, just below it, on the left of the iris, a mix of Manganese Blue plus Titanium White.

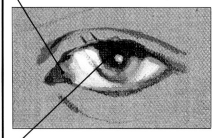

3 The iris
This is Burnt Sienna at the top. Over the pupil, where the eye catches more light, it is a mix of Cadmium Yellow Pale, Transparent Gold Ochre, and Titanium White. The pupil itself is a Burnt Sienna, Winsor Blue, Titanium White mix. For the deepest tone beneath the eyelid add a little of this to a Manganese Blue plus Titanium White mix. Use very small amounts of these colors. The highlight of the pupil is Titanium White.

4 The whites of the eye
Paint these with the No. 4 pointed flat. They are darker on the right, where you use a Transparent Gold Ochre and Titanium White mix. On the left use white on its own up to the edge of the iris, but darken it slightly near the corner where you began. For this use a mix of Winsor Red, Transparent Gold Ochre, and Cadmium Yellow Pale.

5 The eye on the left
The other eye incorporates an almost identical range of colors. Around the edges use the No. 1 sable and in the middle the No. 4 flat.

6 Around the eye on the right
For the area around this eye use the two No. 4 flats – one for the lighter colors, the other for the darker ones. On the left, where it is in shadow, the eyelid incorporates a similar red-brown color to that in the corner of the eye. Lighten it to a mix of Titanium White, Transparent Gold Ochre, and Winsor Green in the center and darken it with the addition of more Transparent Gold Ochre and some Winsor Green toward the right. Where the two eyelids meet at the right-hand corner of the eye use a mix of Transparent Gold Ochre, Winsor Green, and Titanium White. Below it there is a similar but lighter mix where the lower eyelid moves around to the left. For the eyelashes use a Winsor Blue and Burnt Sienna mix. The mix for the lower lashes is a lighter and browner version of that for the upper ones. Below the line of the lower lashes use tones of the Transparent Gold Ochre, Titanium White, and Winsor Green mix.

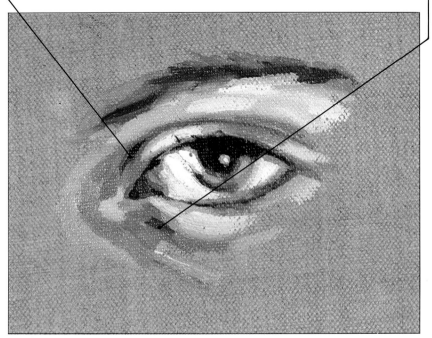

7 The shadow colors
As the lower eyelid moves toward the left of the eye it incorporates the same red-brown colors used for the upper one. Notice how the reddish lower eyelid is complemented by the green below it. In a similar way, just above the reddish shadow on the upper eyelid, there is a complementary area of green. Above the central, blue-green section of the upper eyelid, an orange area (Cadmium Yellow Pale plus Winsor Red) plays a similar complementary role. Throughout the shadow areas complementaries are used like this, though not in a precisely organized or mathematical way.

8 The eyebrow
Above the upper eyelid add a touch of Winsor Green to the Transparent Gold Ochre plus Titanium White mix, to cool it down a little. Then paint the eyebrow itself. This is a three-layered sandwich. On the bottom layer from left to right, use a touch of Burnt Sienna, a Manganese Blue plus Titanium White mix, and a mix of Winsor Green, Transparent Gold Ochre, and Titanium White. For the middle layer apply a greener version of the last mix, then a mix of Burnt Sienna, Winsor Blue, and Titanium White, and at the end a little orange dulled by a touch of the previous mix. The top layer has the same orange a little less dull, followed by Burnt Sienna with a touch of Titanium White and Transparent Gold Ochre.

9 Around the eye on the left
The colors around the eye on the left are similar to those on the right, except that they are rather more bleached out by the sunlight. The flesh tones are variations on a basic Titanium White with a touch of either Cadmium Yellow Pale or Transparent Gold Ochre and a very small amount of Winsor Red.

Continued over

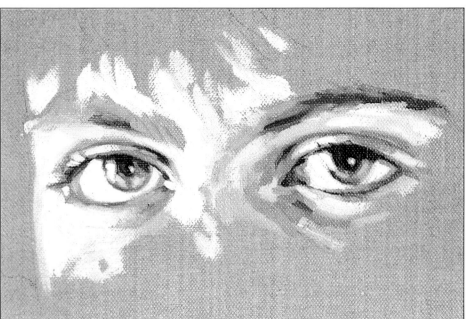

10 The nose

Notice how the nose has four main vertical tonal areas. The light tone on the left is white with just a touch of Cadmium Yellow Pale. You make the second tone pinker by adding a little Transparent Gold Ochre and Winsor Red. The third band has more Transparent Gold Ochre and less red, with a touch of Winsor Green, while the fourth has the same combination of greens and oranges as the area above the eyelid (see Step 7). Next paint the highlight that runs from the tip of the nose down to the upper lips. You can use this as a framework for painting the colors around it.

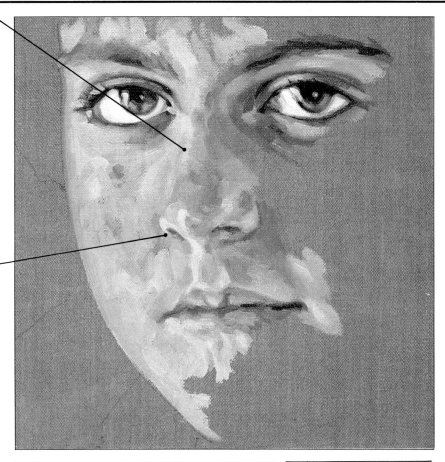

11 Details of the nose

Next paint the nostrils, taking care not to make their tones too dark. On the left use a mix of Burnt Sienna, Titanium White, and Winsor Green. To the right put a dab of pink (Titanium White plus Winsor Red) dulled a little with the previous mix. For the right-hand nostril use a slightly darker pink at each side with a dulled orange (Cadmium Yellow Pale and Winsor Red) between. Where it is deepest in tone use a darker version of the mix used for the nostril on the left. Above this is a touch of Titanium White plus Winsor Green, below it more pink.

12 The lips

Begin with the darkest shadows on the right and left. These use similar colors to those described for the nostrils. In the center section, paint the shadow on the upper lip with a pink made from Titanium White and Winsor Red. This is not a simple slab of color, but moves with the contours of the lower lip. On the right, above the brown-red shadow, incorporate a thin strip of Winsor Green plus Titanium White. Then define the highlight on the center part of the upper lip with a lighter flesh color. There is little tonal or color difference between the center part of the lower lip on the left and the left side of the chin, so be careful not to define the outer edges of the lips too clearly. On the right-hand side of the lower lip, the shadow includes a dull orange and a greenish brown.

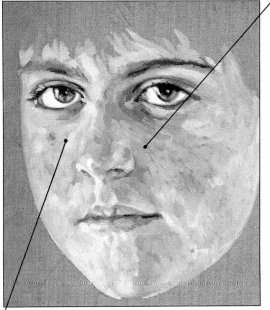

13 Left-hand side of the face

Use the No. 4 hogs'-hair with variations on the basic flesh tone. The left-hand side of the nose leads to a lighter, yellower color than the orange-pink of the cheek. Where the cheek curves in at the nostril use a duller pink.

14 Right-hand side of the face

You can now paint this section up to the line of the chin using the No. 4 hogs'-hair brushes. Extend the use of the green and orange shadow colors you painted around the right eye. Take these colors down the left-hand side of the cheek, under the right nostril and below the right-hand side of the lower lip. This creates a uniformity in shadows, so that it does not look as if the girl has actually painted her face green. Keep the area broken up in a series of dabs of different tones and colors, continuing this technique to the right of the nostril where the greens and oranges give way to the dull pink of the cheek. Paint the neck at this stage in similar colors. For the shadow of the collar use deep reds, oranges, and browns, with a small amount of green.

15 The hair
You should begin painting the hair on the left-hand side, working gradually around to the right. The colors used are similar to those you have used for the face. The darkest tones are Burnt Sienna plus Winsor Blue with a touch of Titanium White. In addition, some of the deepest tones incorporate touches of Winsor Green. The slightly lighter browns are Burnt Sienna with a little Titanium White or Transparent Gold Ochre. There are also comparable tones of Manganese Blue with Titanium White, Winsor Green with Titanium White, and Cadmium Yellow Pale with Winsor Red. For the highlights, use a lighter range of the same colors, adding Transparent Gold Ochre with Titanium White or Cadmium Yellow Pale with Titanium White. Build up the hair with the No. 4 hogs'-hair brushes and the No. 4 flat for a thinner line.

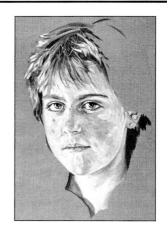

16 The background
As a relief from the detailed work on the hair, next paint the background. You will need three colors: Titanium White, Transparent Gold Ochre, and Winsor Blue. On the left there is more Transparent Gold Ochre around the head and an increasing amount of Winsor Blue toward the edges. On the right-hand side there is almost no Transparent Gold Ochre where the background is lightest and more Winsor Blue at the top right-hand corner. Do not use too much color here — it is a pale background. Do not cover all the pink in the background — the broken effect suits the painting.

17 The check shirt
This incorporates the pink of the background. First pencil in the check pattern to give a grid that follows the contours of the cloth. Then with a No. 4 flat dab on Titanium White, with varying amounts of Transparent Gold Ochre, in the squares on the grid. Next paint the vertical lines in light brown tones and the horizontal lines in pink, covering your pencil lines.

18 The sweaters
Paint the cream short-sleeved sweater with the No. 6 hogs'-hair using Titanium White with a touch of Transparent Gold Ochre. Include a little Winsor Blue in the shadows. Then paint the sweater draped over the girl's shoulders with the No. 4 hogs'-hair. The colors you require are Winsor Blue, Manganese Blue, Burnt Sienna, and Titanium White. Use short, dabbing brushstrokes in all directions to suggest the fluffy woollen texture. Finally make any necessary adjustments.

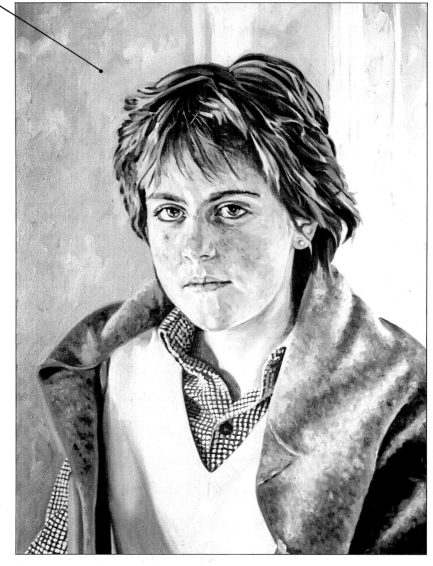

GLEN

Medium OILS

IN CONTRAST TO the direct technique employed in the previous portrait (see pp. 204–7), this example demonstrates a more systematic approach. The head and hands are modeled with Underpainting White on a traditional Terre Verte ground, and then glazed using thin transparent or semi-transparent colors. The result is a highly modeled portrait in which the green of the ground and the warm reddish glazes complement each other, producing a strong, resonant image. The technique, which has been used for centuries, takes various forms, and each artist adapts it to his or her own needs. In the past artists often painted over a tempera underpainting which had the advantage of drying immediately and enabling them to work over it at once with oil glazes. This so-called "mixed" technique is best employed on rigid panels. Acrylic paint, since it dries quickly, is useful for this kind of work, but the "fat over lean" rule must be observed.

In this portrait, the overall composition is unconventional, with the head, shirt front, and the hand and cuff almost disembodied in a blue-black void. The leather sofa, with its glinting brass studs, and the highlights in the tiles behind, are situated in a corner of a recording studio. This is the kind of place where it is usually impossible to tell whether it is night or day.

The frame is also an important component of the painting. I chose a sealed plain wood molding, whose width seemed appropriate to contain the image. I tried various colors out on offcuts until I arrived at a combination of Winsor Blue and Burnt Sienna. When painted on with a brush and wiped with a clean cotton rag, this produced just the right greenish color. It has a positive effect on the painting and shows the importance of getting the frame right.

MATERIALS AND EQUIPMENT

Support
Canvas 29 × 40 ins (74 × 102 cm)

Oil colors

Winsor Red		Terre Verte	
Winsor Blue		Burnt Sienna	
Cadmium Yellow Pale		Permanent Rose	
Winsor Green		Underpainting and Titanium White	

Brushes
No. 10, No. 6, No. 4, and No. 2 hogs'-hair filberts, No. 5 and No. 4 nylon flats, No. 0 round, fan blender, badger blender

Other items
Turpentine

METHOD
First the outlines are drawn in and the shapes of the head and hand are painted in Terre Verte. While this is drying the dark areas are painted. Next the details of the shirt and necktie are drawn and then painted. When the Terre Verte is dry the underpainting of the head and hand is begun, using a soft brush and flat dry brushwork. When this is completely dry the overpainting is done. This is a process of building up thin glazes of transparent color.

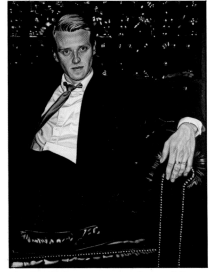

The finished painting. For the guideline sketch on its grid see p. 248.

For the guideline sketch on its grid see p. 248.

1 The outline
Sketch in the broad outlines according to the guidelines provided. Pay particular attention to the shapes of the head and hand.

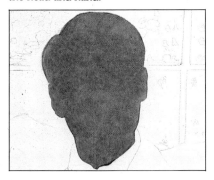

2 The head and hand shapes
Paint in the shapes of the head and hand using Terre Verte and a little turpentine. Use your No. 6 hogs'-hair brush. Smooth out any brushstrokes with a fan blender brush. You should aim for a smooth, flat overall tone.

3 The dark areas
Mix enough Winsor Blue and Burnt Sienna with turpentine to cover the dark areas. Begin with the background around the head. Then paint the tiles with the No. 6 hogs'-hair filbert and leave gaps where the lighter tones and highlights will go. Continue with the suit and sofa leaving white showing for the shirt, the highlights on the leather and the brass studs. Use the No. 4 flat to paint around the intricate details and the No. 10 hogs'-hair filbert for the large expanses.

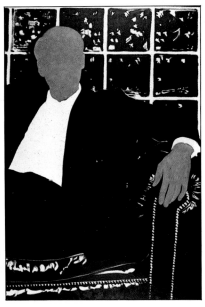

4 Working up the background

Continue working up the background tiles while the Terre Verte is drying. Use the No. 6 or No. 4 hogs'-hair filbert with a mix of Winsor Blue, Burnt Sienna, and Titanium White. Use more or less blue or white according to the colour and tone you need. I introduced a little Winsor Green into the mix here and there. None of the shapes or colours has to be particularly accurate, but do leave spaces for the highlights.

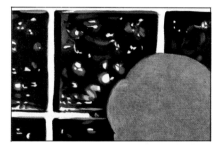

6 The sofa

Turn to the sofa and use a similar mix for the colours around the highlights as for the tiles – Winsor Blue, Burnt Sienna, and Titanium White. Use the No. 4 and No. 6 hogs'-hair filberts or the No. 4 nylon flat for the thinner areas. Blend the colours into the surrounding dark tone with one of the bristle brushes, and add the lightest tones at the end with single strokes of a well-filled brush.

5 The tiles

Use the No. 2 hogs'-hair filbert to add the white highlights to the tiles. Mix a deep ochre of Burnt Sienna, Cadmium Yellow Pale, Winsor Blue, and Titanium White for the cement around the tiles and apply this with the No. 6 hogs'-hair filbert. Soften the edges where this joins the dark blue of the tiles by using the edge of the wiped-off No. 4 hogs'-hair.

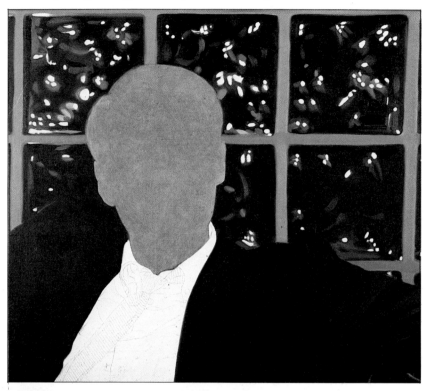

7 The brass studs

Adjacent to the brass studs paint a dab of orange-brown (a mix of Cadmium Yellow Pale, Burnt Sienna, and Winsor Red), using the No. 2 hogs'-hair filbert. Then paint a thin yellow band of Cadmium Yellow Pale using the No. 0 round. Follow this with a dab of Titanium White in the middle of each stud using the No. 2 hogs'-hair filbert. Wipe the brush off after each dab to keep the colour pure. Soften the edges of the orange dabs you painted first of all, and add a dab of Burnt Sienna with the No. 4 hogs'-hair filbert to link in with the Winsor Blue-Burnt Sienna background. Then tidy up each shape with the same colour mix.

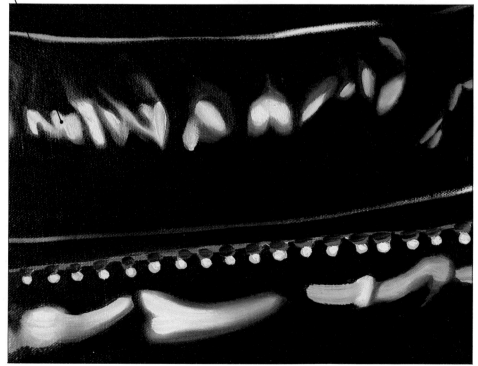

Continued over

8 The shirt

Draw the details of the shirt in pencil and begin painting it. Use the No. 4 hogs'-hair filbert with Titanium White for highlights. Paint these in first to keep them pure, and then work on shadows using various combinations of small amounts of Permanent Rose, Winsor Blue, and Burnt Sienna, with Titanium White. Paint in the tones adjacent to each other, then wipe off the brush and blend them together. Work on a small section at a time, moving down the left-hand side of the shirt and across and down the right-hand side. About one-third of the way down the shirt introduce a little Cadmium Yellow Pale into your shadow mix. This, in conjunction with the Burnt Sienna and Permanent Rose, will help to indicate body colour beneath the shirt.

9 The tie

Work on the tie before you paint the right-hand side of the shirt. Its colour is based on a mix of Permanent Rose, Burnt Sienna, and Titanium White, with a touch of Cadmium Yellow Pale where it looks orangey. Begin with the dark tones, followed by the mid tones, and finally add the lightest ones.

10 Finishing the shirt

When you paint the right-hand side of the shirt, notice that the tones appear a little lighter than on the left. Then paint the cuff. Notice how shadows here are cooler (bluer) than on the shirt front.

11 Repainting the darkest tones

You should now repaint the darkest tones of the suit and sofa in the same Winsor Blue-Burnt Sienna mix that you used before.

12 Underpainting the head

Trace the position of the eyes, nose, and mouth lightly on to the Terre Verte ground, positioning them as accurately as possible. Begin the underpainting using Underpainting White and turpentine, and the nylon flat. Use the brush flat and the paint dry, building up the tone very slowly and carefully. Begin with those areas that are highlit, such as the central part of the forehead, and work outwards, stroking the paint lightly over the canvas to achieve half-tone effects. It is essential to work methodically, moving around the face a section at a time, and gradually building bridges between the various sections. Initially, as the face emerges, the tonal contrasts will be too heavily accentuated, but the more you work the more subtle the transitions will become. For the hand you should use a similar technique, starting with the highlit areas and building up the half tones by lightly stroking on the paint.

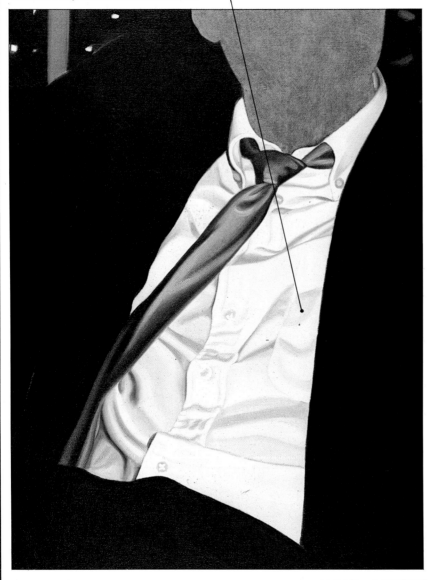

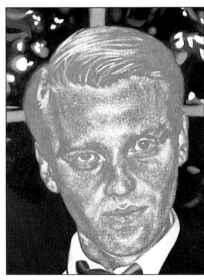

13 The tile cement

At this stage paint a glaze of Winsor Blue and Burnt Sienna over the ochre of the cement. This will have the effect of taking it back from the figure a little and will help the rather camouflaged look of the background.

14 Reworking the head and hand

Rework the head and hand with the thinner white mix so that even the darkest tones are lightly "dusted" by underpainting. Look at your work carefully to ensure that highlit areas are not too protruberant or that the dark ones are not too dark. Broadly speaking, the underpainting should present an accurate but slightly mellow tonal version of the subject in which there are no overly dramatic tonal shifts. It is easy enough to adjust too dark a tone simply by applying more white, but it is not so easy to adjust too bright a tone. I find that scraping very gently with the edge of a painting knife will take the underpainting right back to the original Terre Verte ground if necessary.

15 The overpainting

Mix your colours with the painting medium, and for any subsequent layers add a drop more oil to the medium. Use reds, oranges, and yellow-browns mixed from Cadmium Yellow Pale, Burnt Sienna, and Winsor Red, with an occasional touch of Winsor Blue or Winsor Green for the darker brown colours that occur at the outer edges of the head.

16 The warm glaze

Begin with an overall warm glaze for the head and hand, but not the hair, using a thin mix of the three colours (see Step 15). Apply this with the No. 7 hogs'-hair brush and use a badger blender to take off excess colour and create a thin overall glaze. For the hair use a basic Cadmium Yellow Pale mix with a touch of Burnt Sienna and Winsor Green.

Continued over

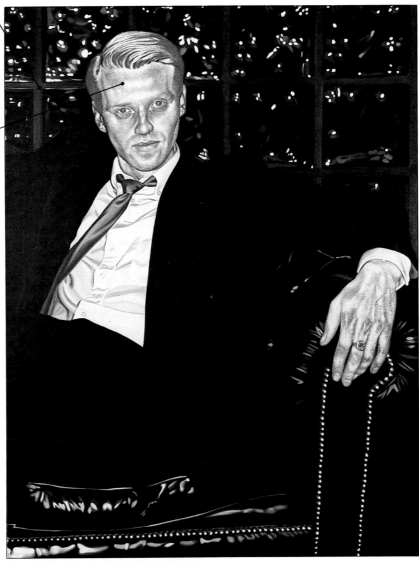

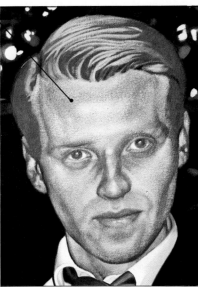

17 **Overpainting the hand**
Turn to the hand, working in the shadow areas to begin with. Apply small amounts of colour to particular areas with the No. 5 flat and work it on with the No. 2 or No. 4 hogs'-hair filbert. Then fill in the areas between the darker tones, working the colours out to a suitable boundary — an edge or an area of darker tone. As you work over the surface in small steps try to keep the overall shape and balance of the colours in mind. Then apply a thin warm overall glaze of Burnt Sienna and Cadmium Yellow Pale, stroking the colour on gently with the No. 5 flat, working down the hand. Next, dip the No. 4 or No. 2 hogs'-hair into turpentine, wipe it off and then pick out any highlights which have been submerged under the last glaze. You can paint the rings at this stage. The ring on the middle finger (shown on the underpainting) has grooved facets that reflect the light. The one on the ring finger is plain. For both, the dark tones are Burnt Sienna, the mid tones Cadmium Yellow Pale with Burnt Sienna and Winsor Red, the lighter tones Cadmium Yellow Pale, while the highlights on both the rings are Titanium White.

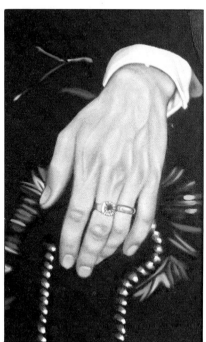

18 **Overpainting the head**
Next turn to the head and work in the same way, dealing with a section at a time. For the hair, use Burnt Sienna with a touch of Winsor Blue for the dark areas. Apply it with the No. 5 flat and soften it if necessary with the No. 2 hogs'-hair. Then work on the forehead, the left side of the face and ear in a similar way as for the hand, and gradually move across to the eyes, nose, and mouth. You will find that the glazes make the head look more three-dimensional, as well as adding colour. But it is the success of the underpainting which determines that of the whole image.

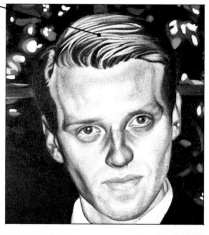

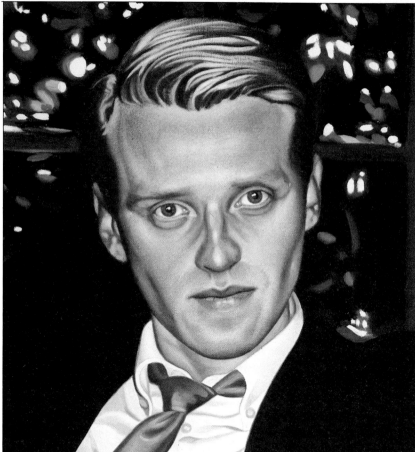

19 **Lightening and darkening**
Once you have worked up and reworked your glazes to the point where the face is balanced, you may want to lighten or darken particular areas. If, for instance, the tones of the underpainting have been a little too dark in places, then it is perfectly in order to rework these areas using opaque colour, and reglaze them afterwards.

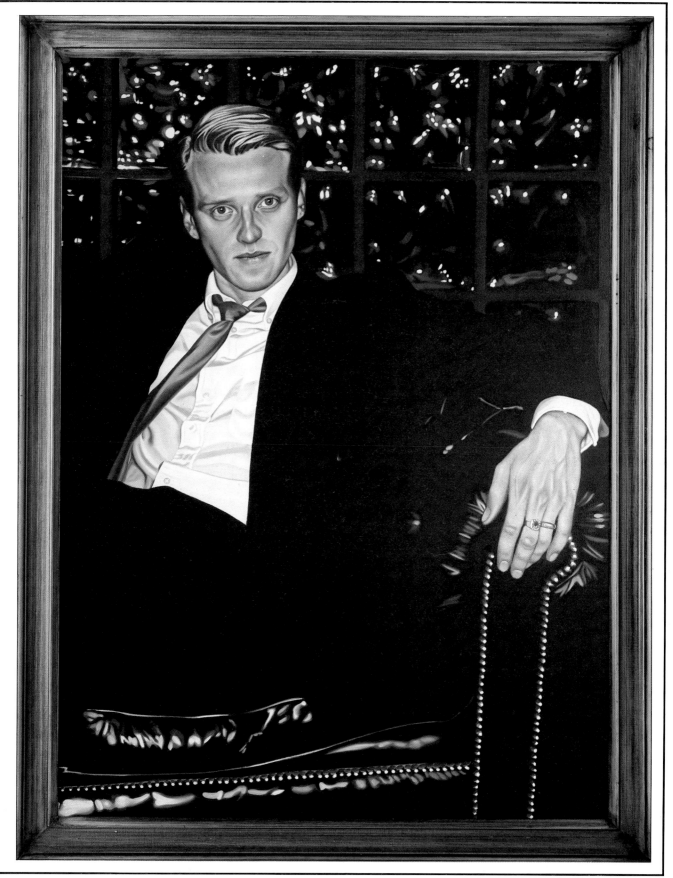

NUDES

DRAWING THE human figure is a testing and rewarding activity in itself. It is also a very good way of practising your drawing skills. The human body is such a complex and elastic arrangement of forms that with every new pose the relationships between all the parts change completely, presenting the artist with an entirely new subject. To be able to express this complexity in a way that reflects the harmony and beauty of the human form is a skill that even the most talented artist should practise.

Most artists begin drawing the nude figure when they attend life-drawing classes at art school. For those who are not full-time students, there are many evening classes that form part of adult education programmes. If you have never worked from the nude before this is probably the best way to begin. Of all art school classes, life-drawing sessions are the quietest and most concentrated. The presence of a live model creates a unique focus for all your drawing and painting skills. Such classes provide a useful preparation for further work on your own, since, apart from the obvious practical benefits, they reveal something of the special relationship between artist and model.

The first thing to strike most artists is that the action of drawing creates a sense of separateness from the figure. Making an accurate representation of a figure is such an intensive, almost scientific, activity that the drawing itself can become more real to you than anything else. This sense of detachment may well be similar to that experienced by a surgeon, and is possibly equally necessary. But for the artist the commitment to the image is a measure of his or her commitment to the subject.

The more life classes you attend, the more you realise how important the model is. If you put a large number of people in identical poses, you would find that very few of them had that special degree of commitment and sympathy that can make an ordinary pose special – a quality which is so helpful to the artist. Really good models manage to endow each pose with real presence and thus give the artist something very positive to respond to. Very often it is the models who are less obviously attractive who manage to convey a real sense of beauty and poise. It is not particularly easy to find gifted models, and artists very often work with the same model over a considerable period of time, building up a high degree of mutual respect and professional understanding.

From the practical point of view, if you are working in your own studio, turn the heating up before you start so that the model is warm and comfortable. Provide suitable changing facilities, or at least a portable screen with a chair behind it. Close the curtains on any windows that could give a view into the studio and make sure you are not disturbed. Decide beforehand on the nature of the pose and prepare items such as cushions and drapes. But be prepared to modify your ideas in conjunction with your

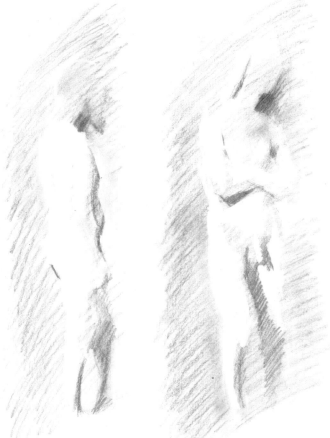

Using an eraser
An interesting technique, especially for short poses, is to work with an eraser. Prepare your paper in advance by shading it with a mid to dark tone. Use a soft pencil such as a 6B. Then work into the tone with a sharp wedge of eraser, taking out high- lights and defining the shape of your model. You will not be concerned with recording detail but with creating a sense of form. Drawings of this type can be very atmospheric. They are best when the model is brightly side-lit. You can add definition by shading in the darkest tones.

model. If you can use natural light, make sure the model is not in direct sunlight, since the sun will move round and change the appearance of your subject. It will also create harsh shadows. A constant diffused light is best, unless you have a dramatic effect in mind. You can create your own controlled effects with artificial light.

Posing motionless for any length of time is particularly arduous. All artists should, at some time, put themselves in the model's situation, in order to experience the rigours of the job at first hand. Frequent rests are necessary, their exact frequency depending on the pose. To help the model get back in position, you can draw chalk guidelines.

STARTING TO DRAW THE NUDE

When beginning to do life drawing you may at first feel a little intimidated by the situation. But you will soon get

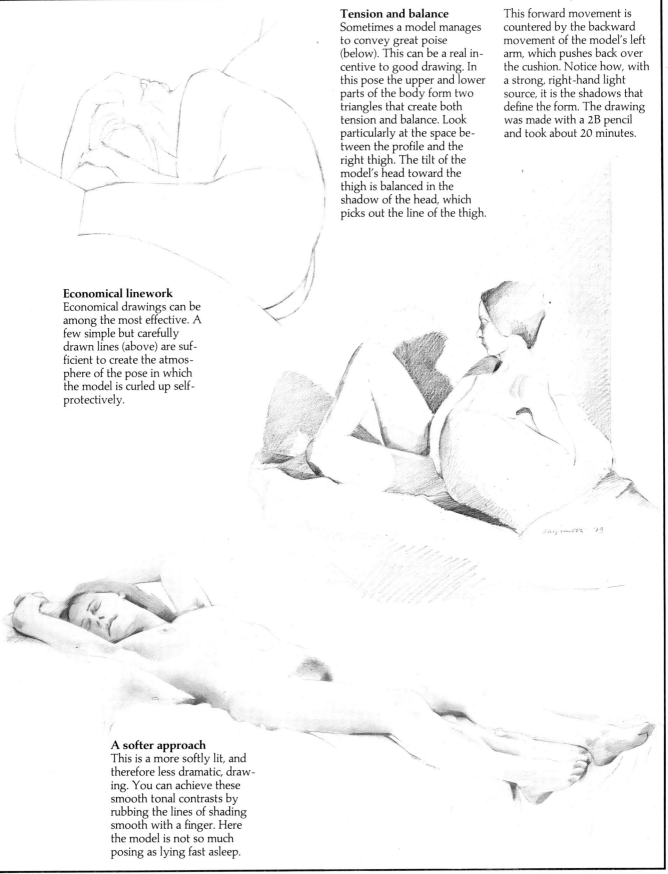

Tension and balance
Sometimes a model manages to convey great poise (below). This can be a real incentive to good drawing. In this pose the upper and lower parts of the body form two triangles that create both tension and balance. Look particularly at the space between the profile and the right thigh. The tilt of the model's head toward the thigh is balanced in the shadow of the head, which picks out the line of the thigh.

This forward movement is countered by the backward movement of the model's left arm, which pushes back over the cushion. Notice how, with a strong, right-hand light source, it is the shadows that define the form. The drawing was made with a 2B pencil and took about 20 minutes.

Economical linework
Economical drawings can be among the most effective. A few simple but carefully drawn lines (above) are sufficient to create the atmosphere of the pose in which the model is curled up self-protectively.

A softer approach
This is a more softly lit, and therefore less dramatic, drawing. You can achieve these smooth tonal contrasts by rubbing the lines of shading smooth with a finger. Here the model is not so much posing as lying fast asleep.

215

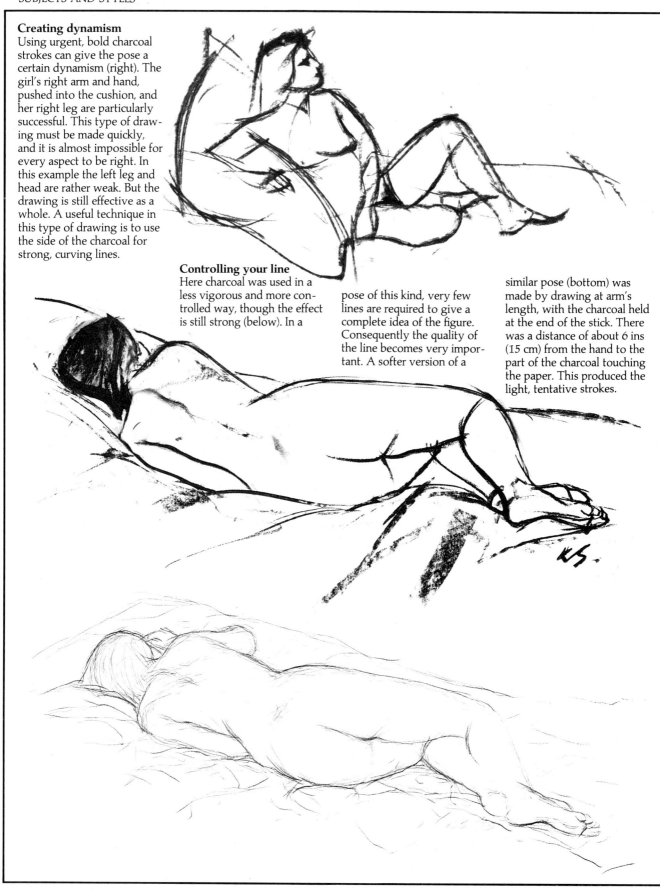

Creating dynamism
Using urgent, bold charcoal strokes can give the pose a certain dynamism (right). The girl's right arm and hand, pushed into the cushion, and her right leg are particularly successful. This type of drawing must be made quickly, and it is almost impossible for every aspect to be right. In this example the left leg and head are rather weak. But the drawing is still effective as a whole. A useful technique in this type of drawing is to use the side of the charcoal for strong, curving lines.

Controlling your line
Here charcoal was used in a less vigorous and more controlled way, though the effect is still strong (below). In a pose of this kind, very few lines are required to give a complete idea of the figure. Consequently the quality of the line becomes very important. A softer version of a similar pose (bottom) was made by drawing at arm's length, with the charcoal held at the end of the stick. There was a distance of about 6 ins (15 cm) from the hand to the part of the charcoal touching the paper. This produced the light, tentative strokes.

used to the conventions. If you do feel uncertain, try approaching the subject as you would a drawing of an inanimate still life. Your style and approach need not suddenly have to change radically simply because you are drawing from a live model.

One of the main problems for people who are new to life drawing is accommodating the whole figure comfortably within a sheet of drawing paper. You may find the legs cut off at the bottom of the paper or, worse still, that there is only room for half a head at the top. The reason for this is that you have not started out by considering the figure as a whole. To do this, look at the model through half-closed eyes or blur your focus a little. This will eliminate the details and give you a sense of the whole figure. You can relate this to your drawing paper and sketch it in very roughly. Another method is to hold at arm's length a rectangle of card with a hole in it to the scale of your drawing paper. This will show you how the shape of the model fits into your paper. Other methods of getting the overall sense of the pose include hanging a muslin or tinted polythene drape in front of the model so that your view of all but the larger shapes is obscured, or lighting the model as a silhouette so that you can fit a complete "cut-out" shape on to your paper. But whichever method you adopt, the essential thing is to start with the whole shape, not with a detail such as an eye.

Another problem is that beginners often accumulate portfolios of unfinished drawings. It is not going to be helpful to your understanding of the whole figure if you have a series of detailed head-and-shoulders portraits that dissolve into a series of vague lines to indicate the rest of the body. This difficulty is easily resolved if you know how much time you have for a particular pose. There is no point in trying to make a six-hour drawing in two. So adapt your style and techniques so that you can draw the whole image in the time available.

When you start a new drawing, the preparatory stages are among the most important. Make an overall assessment of the structure of the pose. This should establish where the weight of the body is supported, which muscles are tense and which relaxed, and which are the major lines and angles of the pose. If you keep these things in mind as you work, your drawing will reflect your appreciation of the basic forms and will be stronger as a result.

There are several ways of practising accuracy in your drawings. You can set the model against a screen with a grid of squares on it. By drawing a similar grid on your paper you can ensure accuracy of the subject's shape by working from square to square. A less mechanical way of doing this is to relate parts of the figure to background horizontals, verticals, or other shapes. Test the angles and distances on your drawing with those of the subject by using a pencil held at arm's length.

Vary the type and length of the poses and alter your technique to suit them. Often a two-minute brush sketch has more life and accuracy than a detailed academic pencil drawing that you have laboured over for hours. Remember that ultimately the drawing alone is the thing that succeeds or fails. It does so on its own terms and not by being compared with a live model.

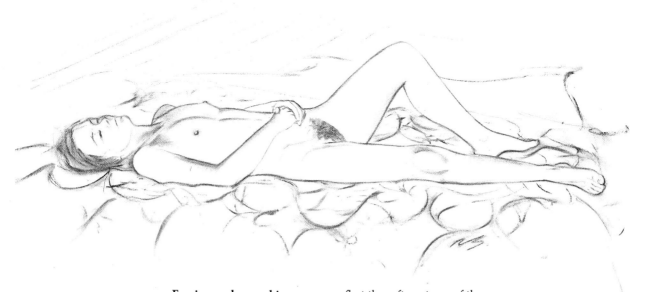

Erasing and reworking
This relaxed pose was drawn with the charcoal used quite precisely. To get this effect you can rub out and rework the charcoal lines until they reflect the soft contours of the pose. Work the lines with the tip of your finger to indicate tones. This will allow you to soften tonal depth in the contours themselves.

NUDE I

Media WATERCOLOURS, OILS, or COLOURED PENCILS

FOR THIS PAINTING I asked the model to lie on her stomach as comfortably as possible on a bank of floor cushions. The idea was that her figure would sink into the cushions so that their curves would reflect those of her body. This soft contact between body and cushions is an important element in the painting. It is particularly evident in the space between the left arm and the head, and where the left hand tucks in between the cushions.

The painting is composed rather like a national flag. It comprises a large central diagonal stripe (the figure and cushions) with a blue wedge above and a striped green and cream wedge below. The striped rugs on the floor lead the eye up to the figure and form a diagonal opposite to the one created by the angle of the figure. They create an open space in front of the model. I did not want to extend the space behind the figure, so I left the background a neutral mid tone to stop the eye travelling beyond her.

The colours for the watercolour version were as seen, but for the later oil painting, I modified them a little, replacing the two green cushions with pink and blue ones, and cooling down the green stripes of the rug. To light the figure, I used directional indoor lighting from a source behind the top left-hand corner of the painting.

When you wish to make a highly worked painting of this kind it is worth doing some short, preliminary sketches. These enable you to get a real idea of the pose and help indicate how you might approach the painting. I did a preliminary sketch in coloured pencils for this painting (see p. 221). You can then make a more accurate drawing of the figure, which you can transfer to your paper or canvas. You can do this drawing directly on your painting surface, but with a linear subject like this it is best to do it separately.

MATERIALS AND EQUIPMENT

Watercolour version
Support
200 lb rough rag paper 20 × 30 ins (51 × 76 cm)

Watercolour paints

Winsor Red		Winsor Green
Winsor Blue		Burnt Sienna
Cadmium Yellow Pale		Permanent Rose
Burnt Umber		

Brushes
No. 7 and two No. 5 sable rounds, No. 16 squirrel round

Oil version
Support
Canvas 20 × 30 ins (51 × 76 cm)

Oil colours

Winsor Red		Winsor Blue
Cadmium Yellow Pale		Permanent Rose
Winsor Green		Titanium White
Burnt Sienna		

Brushes
No. 7, No. 4, and No. 2 hogs'-hair filberts, No. 4 sable (or nylon) pointed flat

Other items
Turpentine, painting medium (see p. 10)

METHOD
For the watercolour, the outlines are pencilled in and light colour washes used for background, foreground, and cushions. Then the figure's shadows are lightly painted in and its tone and colour built up with thin washes. The painting is brought up to the right tone and finished with thin washes.

For the guideline sketch on its grid see p. 244.

1 The outline sketch
First stretch your watercolour paper. When it is dry, draw the outlines of the figure according to the guideline sketch. You should pencil in these outlines as accurately as you can.

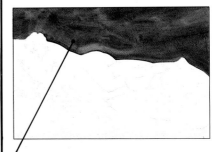

2 Painting the background
When I made the original painting I chose a background that was rather too dark. So paint the background in a lighter tone than you see in the illustration, using a mix of Winsor Blue and Burnt Sienna. Apply it either with a 1 inch (2.5 cm) flat brush or with a No. 16 round squirrel. To do this, turn the painting upside-down on a slight slope and apply clean water up to the edge of the figure and cushion. Then dampen the whole area beneath and introduce your colour on to the damp paper. Since the area of the figure and cushion is dry the paint will not run into it. You can vary the tone and colour of the background a little by changing the depth and combination of your mix.

3 The large red cushion and the green stripes
Paint the large central red cushion by dampening the whole area to be painted, taking care to follow the edges accurately. Then introduce colour (a mix of Winsor Red and Permanent Rose) as in the illustration. Let the paint flow off the toe of the No. 7 brush around the perimeter of the shape. The tone will be lighter in the middle of the cushion. Next make a thin mix of Winsor Green and Cadmium Yellow Pale and paint the green stripes using a No. 5 brush.

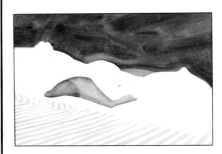

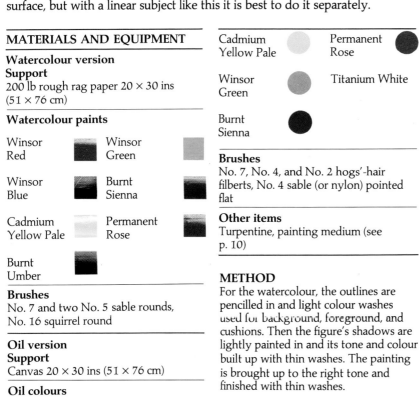

4 The other cushions

Use the same green mix that you used for the stripes and paint the two green cushions. Work in the same way that you did for the red cushion but, for the shadows on the right, darken your mix with a touch of Burnt Sienna. Paint with a No. 5 sable and soften the shadow edges with a clean damp sable as you go. The same applies to the shadows on the pink cushion beneath the girl's head, which you should paint in Permanent Rose at this stage. For the two blue cushions use a Winsor Blue wash with a little Burnt Sienna.

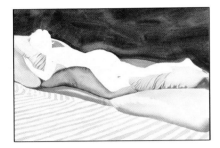

5 Starting work on the figure

Mix Burnt Sienna with a little Winsor Red and Cadmium Yellow Pale to paint in lightly the areas that show the darkest tones in the finished painting. Do the body before the head — it will give you a little practice in the careful manipulation of tone. Use the two No. 5 brushes, one clean, to dampen an area slightly larger than the one to be painted, and the other to apply the paint itself. Once you have painted on the colour, use the clean brush to remove any colour that has gone where it shouldn't, and to soften the edges further. This painting depends on the slow build-up of small areas of tone and its success rests on the accuracy of these layers. Paint in the "white" stripes of the rug. Use a thin mix of Cadmium Yellow Pale and Burnt Sienna. Then add a thin Winsor Blue wash over the green stripes.

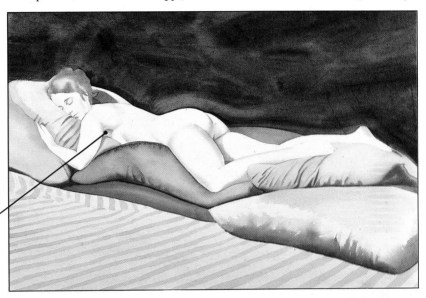

6 Painting the shadows

Begin with the curving shadow above the breast and under the arm. When this is dry, extend the shadow further up in a crescent shape towards the shoulder and back. Then paint the two shadows at right-angles by the elbow and the one at the wrist. The next area to be painted is the soft shadow over the shoulder blade and that below the breast. None of these shadows should have a hard edge. Then indicate the line of the pelvis, followed by the bottom and upper legs. The shadows around the buttocks are very complex. You should copy what you see in the illustration and paint only a small area at a time. Finish the preliminary shadow work by painting shadows on each side of the left leg and on the sole of the right heel.

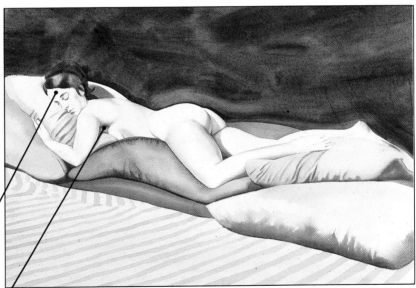

7 The head

Use the same colour to define the facial features and to paint an overall tone for the hair. When this is dry, add Burnt Umber to your mix and overpaint a wash on the hair. Leave a gap for the highlights. You should also use this colour for the eyebrow and to indicate the eyelashes and nostrils.

8 Extending the shadow areas

Now begin to build up tone and colour on the body. Extend the shadows you have just painted, varying the wash by adding a touch more red and yellow. Keep the washes thin and soften any hard edges as you did before with a clean, damp brush.

Continued over

9 Repainting the cushions
At the moment the colours of the cushions are too bright and thin. Repaint each in turn using the same technique as you did before, but incorporating Burnt Umber in your washes. The deep shadows between the cushions are a deeper mix of Burnt Umber with the colour of the cushion. Build up the tones in a series of washes, allowing each to dry before you attempt to overpaint it. Although they are soft, the cushions should look solid enough to support the model. At this stage you should also add colour to the spaces between the green stripes. Use a thin wash made from Cadmium Yellow Pale and Burnt Umber and this will give the rug some body. When this is dry subdue the green stripes a little, using a thin wash of Winsor Blue and Burnt Umber.

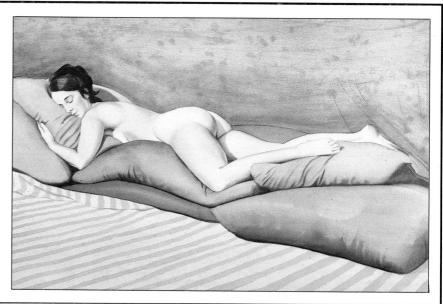

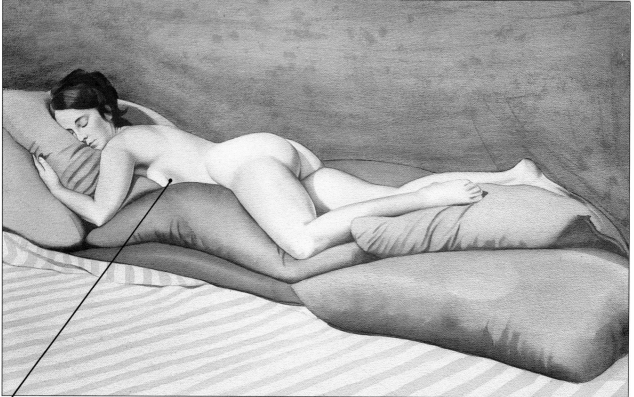

10 Adjusting the flesh tones
The figure will look rather pale against the light background, so you should continue to build up tone and colour. The process of adjusting tone and colour is one of fine tuning, and adding tone to one area means you will have to balance it in another. Notice that the model's bottom and breast are slightly pinker than the rest of her body. Your washes, as you build them up, should now extend beyond the areas of obvious shadow and cover a whole limb rather than just part of it. Keep the washes very thin, with only a hint of colour. Where you need to take out highlights, you can do so with a clean, damp brush while the paint is still wet.

11 The final washes
To finish off the painting, you should apply overall washes to the figure and background. Add a very pale flesh tint to the body. Use a mix of Burnt Sienna, Cadmium Yellow Pale, and Winsor Red. For the background, use a thin warm brown wash made of Burnt Sienna plus Burnt Umber.

OIL VERSION

To paint an oil version of this image, first tint the canvas with Burnt Sienna, allow it to dry and draw in the outlines. Use your No. 7 hogs'-hair to block in the main features of the painting. Start with the background and blue cushions, using a thin mix of Winsor Blue and turpentine. Add Titanium White for the lighter tones, but keep the mix thin. Paint the red and pink cushions in the same way, using Winsor Red, Permanent Rose, and Titanium White. Then paint the green stripes on the rug using a mix of Winsor Green, Cadmium Yellow Pale, and Titanium White. Block in the light tones of the figure with a mix of Titanium White and turpentine. Use a Winsor Blue plus Burnt Sienna mix for the darkest tones. By this stage the whole painting should be blocked in, with enough information for you to begin to paint the second, more finished, stage of your work.

From now on, use painting medium to mix your paint. Paint the background with a mix of Winsor Blue, Burnt Sienna, and Titanium White, dabbing on the paint with the No. 7 brush. Vary the direction of the brushstrokes and make the blue deeper towards the top of the painting. Paint the pink cushions loosely

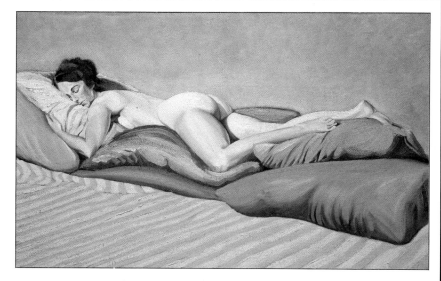

and thickly. Use both the No. 4 and the No. 7 hogs'-hairs and mixtures of Winsor Red, Permanent Rose, Burnt Sienna, and Titanium White. Try to make your brushstrokes as bold as possible, while retaining the tone and dimensional quality of the cushions. Tackle the figure in a similar way with combinations of Titanium White, Cadmium Yellow Pale, Winsor Red, Burnt Sienna, and, occasionally, Winsor Green. Indicate the features with the No. 4 flat. For the hair

use Burnt Sienna, Winsor Blue, Winsor Red, and Cadmium Yellow Pale. Next bring all the blue cushions to the same level of finish as the others. Then paint the rug with a cooler peppermint colour for the green stripes (Winsor Green, Winsor Blue, and Titanium White) and cream (Titanium White, Cadmium Yellow Pale, and Burnt Sienna) for the colour between. Finally make any adjustments to the figure that you think are necessary to complete it.

COLOURED PENCIL VERSION

Coloured pencils are particularly effective for creating soft forms and colours and for giving a drawing a gentle appearance. Such a treatment is appro-

priate in this kind of image. This drawing was the first version I made of this pose. If you want to make a version of the drawing, start by using a pink pencil to sketch in the outlines of the figure and to indicate areas of light and shade.

Then accentuate the darker tones with a dark brown pencil. Use a yellow ochre pencil to give the figure a little more body, shading loosely on a diagonal. Finally indicate the cushions' colours with pink, green, red, and blue pencils.

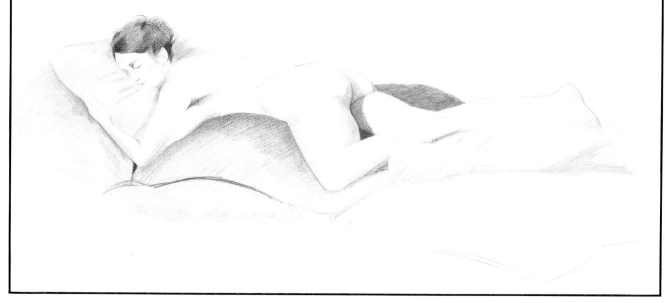

NUDE II

Medium OILS

THIS SMALL-SCALE oil study shows the result of two three-hour sessions with the model. These sessions also produced half a dozen preliminary drawings. For the oil study I used contrasting colours, juxtaposing warm shadows (painted pink, orange, and brown) with cooler (green and blue) areas.

Images from the history of art can provide you with many ideas for poses. In this case we used a pose similar to the one used by Gauguin in his painting "Nevermore" (see p. 227). You will find that each model will have her own natural way of making a similar pose. You should not try to force your model into an identical posture, or the result will look very unnatural. Try one or two similar poses and make charcoal drawings of each on paper. From these you will get a good idea of which one is going to look best.

Once you have established the pose in this way you will have to draw it again on the canvas. It can sometimes be difficult to reproduce the flowing lines of your original drawing, but if you use charcoal on the canvas you can model and modify your lines by using a clean, dry No. 10 hogs'-hair brush.

MATERIALS AND EQUIPMENT

Support
Canvas 20 × 30 ins (51 × 76 cm)

Oil colours

Winsor Red		Burnt Sienna	
Winsor Blue		Permanent Rose	
Cadmium Yellow Pale		Titanium White	
Winsor Green			

Brushes
No. 10, No. 7, No. 5, and No. 4 hogs'-hair filberts, No. 4 nylon (or sable) flat

Other items
Charcoal, turpentine

METHOD

After tinting the canvas and drawing the outline, the darkest and lightest areas of tone are indicated. Next the shadows are painted, followed by the middle tones, leaving out the fine details. Then the background is painted, beginning with the dark blue around the edge of the ship and adding the green and orange touches. The next stage is to work up the details on the head, hands, and feet, and to make adjustments to the figure. After this the background is reworked and the bed and floor painted. Finally, the brown area in the top left-hand corner is added.

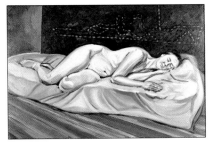

The finished painting. For the guideline sketch on its grid see p. 244.

1 Outlining the figure
First give the canvas a Burnt Sienna tint and draw in the outlines according to the guideline sketch provided. Then take your No. 5 hogs'-hair filbert and, with a mix of Winsor Blue and Burnt Sienna thinned with turpentine, outline the contours of the figure where there are areas of dark tone.

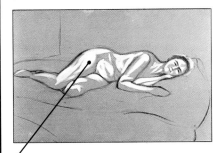

2 The light tones
Mix a very pale flesh colour using Titanium White with a touch of Cadmium Yellow Pale and Winsor Red. With this colour paint in the light tones over the whole body. Use the No. 7 hogs'-hair brush.

3 The shadow areas
Mix Winsor Green with Titanium White and use the No. 5 hogs'-hair brush to paint the cool shadows around the thigh, stomach, arms, and neck. Then paint the warmer shadows adjacent to these areas. Use the same size brush with varying mixes of the following range of colours: Permanent Rose, Winsor Red, Cadmium Yellow Pale, Burnt Sienna, and Titanium White.

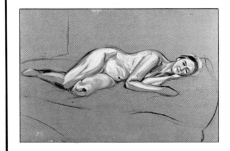

4 Starting to paint the background

Paint the blue shape of the ship with the No. 5 hogs'-hair. Use a mix of Winsor Blue and Burnt Sienna with a touch of Titanium White. Leave the outline unpainted. Then dot along the outline with the No. 4 flat and the same colour mixture. Next use the same brush to paint in first the orange dots (Cadmium Yellow Pale plus Winsor Red) and then the green (Winsor Green plus Cadmium Yellow Pale). Wipe your brush if the green or orange begins to discolour. Blend the top edge of the figure by running the clean No. 5 hogs'-hair along the edge of the join.

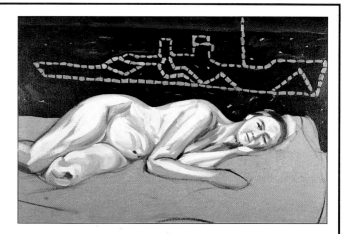

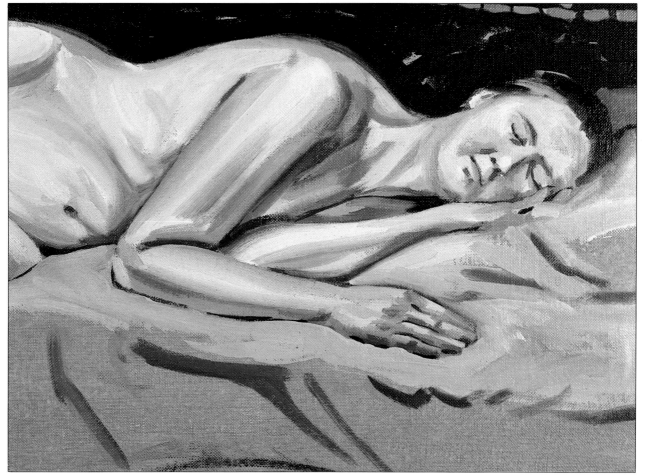

5 Painting the head

For the details on the face use the No. 4 flat. The areas in shadow on the side nearest the bed are Winsor Green and Titanium White, subdued a little with a touch of Winsor Blue and Burnt Sienna. On the other side, apart from a touch of green in the eyebrow, the shadows are brown and red, colours which are picked up in the cheek resting on the hand. The forehead flesh colours have a yellow cast in the lighter areas, a dull orange-red in the middle, and a dull green towards the shadows. The hair is Winsor Blue plus Burnt Sienna, and the transition from the hair to the flesh tones is Burnt Sienna on its own followed by a deep ochre (Titanium White and Burnt Sienna with Cadmium Yellow Pale and a touch of Winsor Blue). For the bed use a mix of Winsor Blue and Titanium White, with a touch of Burnt Sienna.

6 The hands

The hand resting on the bed follows a similar pattern of shading. The line between the fingers is a mix of Winsor Green and Titanium White, while the adjacent colours are brown and dull pink. The underlying colour is a dull yellow-orange and the lightest tones are a pink flesh colour. The fingers supporting the head are a dull pink.

Continued over

7 The rest of the figure

Part of the neck is highlit, with a Z-shape of flesh colour and light orange and green areas. The lower shadow is Burnt Sienna plus Permanent Rose. For the chest shadows use deep dull reds and oranges. The arm supporting the head has green and dull red shadows; the other arm goes through yellow-orange, pale flesh colour, red, and green, to red. Warm yellow-oranges and cool greens define the stomach.

8 The legs and feet

Paint the thighs using pink flesh colours with one green shadow on the lower edge of each. Use a dark mix of Burnt Sienna and Permanent Rose for the lower part of the foot resting on the calf. Moving up, this foot has an orange-pink area, a strip of pale flesh colour, and a dull pink at the top. The other foot is light pink at the top, followed by orange, brown, green, a flesh colour, dull pink, and green at its lowest edge.

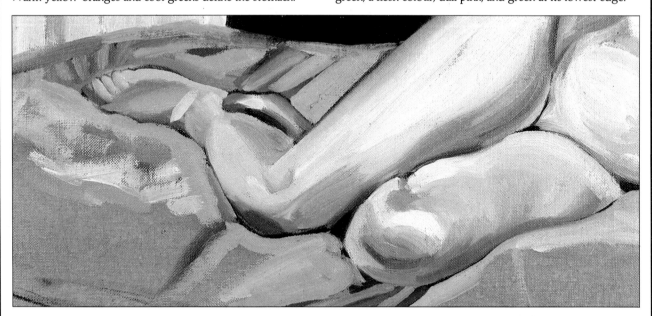

9 The background and bed

Blend the orange and green a little more into the background and subdue the colour a little by stroking over each small section with a clean No. 5 hogs'-hair. Wipe the brush after each stroke. Mix a lighter mix of Titanium White, Burnt Sienna, and Winsor Blue and dab this over the surface with the No. 5 brush. Paint the folds of drapery on the bed using a mix of Permanent Rose, Titanium White, and Winsor Blue for the violet areas. For the dark blue areas use a mix made from Winsor Blue, Titanium White, and a touch of Burnt Sienna. For the greener colours mix Winsor Green, Titanium White, and a touch of Winsor Blue. Use lighter tones of the same colours and the No. 7 brush for the rest of the bed.

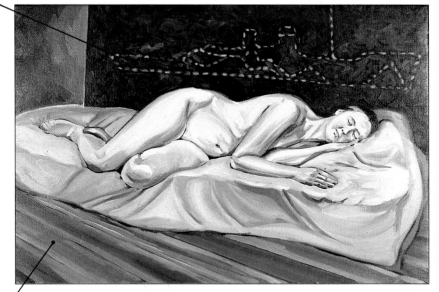

10 The finishing touches

Loosely mix Burnt Sienna, Winsor Red, and Cadmium Yellow Pale and apply this colour to the floorboards using long strokes of the No. 10 hogs'-hair. Vary the tones of each board to get the effect shown in the illustration. Some of the boards have a light grey edge. Mix this colour by adding Winsor Blue, Burnt Sienna, and Titanium White to the colour you have just used. Finally, paint the top left-hand corner of the canvas a cool brown. Use a mix of Burnt Sienna and Titanium White with a touch of Winsor Blue. The tone should lighten towards the edge of the ship. The effect of this will be to indicate space behind the ship panel. When you have done this, make any adjustments you think are necessary.

APPENDICES

DRAWING UP AN IMAGE

IN ORDER TO paint the pictures in this book you will have to transfer the outlines of each image on to your canvas or paper. Learning this technique is useful in other ways, too, since the accurate transfer of an image from a source is an important part of most painters' work.

THE GRID METHOD

When you want to increase the size of your original, as with the paintings in this book, the oldest and best method is to use a grid of squares. You draw or superimpose the grid over the original and draw a similar, but larger-scale, grid with the same number of squares on your canvas. Then you draw the outlines of the original, square by square, on to the canvas. In this book, each painting is accompanied by an outline sketch on a grid, so all you have to do is to draw a grid on your canvas and copy the outlines.

If you are scaling up an original that you do not mind marking, you can draw your grid directly on to the original. This can be a useful technique when copying items such as postcards. But in the case of a careful preliminary drawing or a unique photograph, you will not want to mark the surface. The answer is to draw the grid on to a sheet of clear acetate or perspex. A thin black indelible felt-tip pen or a drawing pen is best for this. You can then place this over the original.

The most important aspect of this method of transferring an image is that the size of the squares should be appropriate to the image. The more detail there is to transcribe, the smaller the squares will have to be for you to be able to do it accurately. You may find it useful to prepare several grids of different dimensions that you can call upon when required. You will often find that one part of a picture will need smaller squares than the rest. For example, a portrait of a figure in front of plain curtains will require smaller squares for the face than for the background. You can bisect the relevant squares on your original grid and do the same on your canvas to overcome this problem. You may also find it useful to bisect the squares on an original perspex or acetate grid in a different colour. This will give you a smaller grid that you can call into play when necessary. It is also helpful to number and letter your grids as for map references. This will help you to locate quickly the part of the picture you are working on.

The best method to use when drawing up with a grid is to mark on the edge of each square the points at which lines cross it. Then you join up the dots according to the original square. If a straight line passes through the square, it is simple to join the dots with a ruler. When the line is curved, you should match it as closely as possible with the original. As you follow this method through a number of adjacent squares, the lines of your original will begin to emerge. At this point you can adjust the flow of each main contour by altering your line with pencil and eraser or charcoal and brush.

Transcribing a "linear" work, such as the Gauguin painting copied here is a more straightforward process than transferring a purely tonal image where edges are less well defined and shapes are difficult to follow. One method of dealing with tonal areas is to shade them in lightly with the side of the pencil or charcoal rather than trying to define their outlines. But it can be useful to plot areas of tone like the contours on a map. It is even worth marking the depth of a tonal area you have outlined. You can use letters such as "D" for dark, "M" for mid tone, and "L" for light. "D–M" would represent a dark to mid tone using this system. This may sound a rather mechanical way of working, but it is easy to get lost in a maze of irregular shapes if you do not do this. One way of practising transcribing areas of tone is to make tracings from large photographs or magazine illustrations of simple objects. Images such as these allow you to see and mark out the shapes of particular areas of tone.

TRACING

With an original image that is the same size as your intended painting, the easiest method is to trace it. Use good quality tracing paper or, better still, translucent drafting film with a matt surface. This is more expensive than tracing paper, but pencil takes to it and transfers from it so well that it is worth the extra cost. With tracing paper use a soft pencil, with drafting film a harder one. To transfer the image the right way round, you will have to trace it twice, once on each side of the paper or film. It is easier to trace on to a board than it is on to the springy surface of a stretched canvas. One solution if you are working with a prepared canvas that you are stretching yourself is to trace the image before stretching. You can then lay the canvas flat on your drawing board or table. A convenient way of attaching tracing paper or film to stretched canvas is to cut holes at points in the tracing paper where no lines appear and put drafting tape over these. Rub the tape well into the canvas with your thumb-nail. This will hold it much more firmly than the usual four pieces of adhesive tape, attached one at each corner.

If you are tracing from a sketch or photograph on relatively thin paper you can avoid having to draw the outline twice. Tape the original face down on to a window pane, facing the light. When you trace it, it will already be back-to-front. The method is a crude but satisfactory substitute for the piece of equipment known as a light box.

When tracing from an original with a fragile surface, such as charcoal or pastel, it is worth protecting it. Place a sheet of glass or acetate over it before you superimpose the tracing paper.

MECHANICAL METHODS

There are several types of projector that can help you when transcribing an image. Projectors called epidiascopes or episcopes are specially designed to project the original flat artwork. You place this under a glass and project the

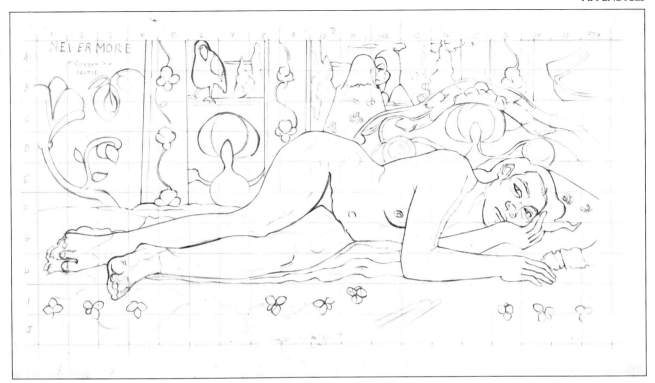

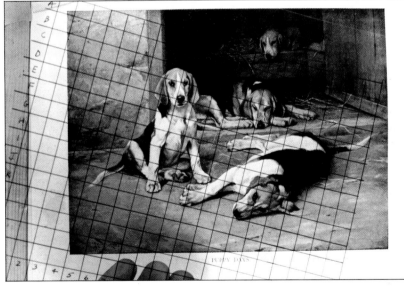

An acetate grid can quickly be placed over any image that you want to copy (right). It is especially useful because you do not damage the original. In addition, once you have drawn an acetate grid you can reuse it indefinitely for any images that demand its particular size of squares. The tracing of Gauguin's painting "Nevermore" (above) shows an image drawn up using the grid method.

image directly on to the canvas. Epidiascopes have two main disadvantages. The cheapest models do not have very good illumination, and even the better quality designs must be used in a darkened room. In addition, there is a limit to the size of the original you can project. Even a medium-sized drawing has to be projected a quarter at a time.

An ordinary slide projector is much more versatile. If you have a camera and projector, you can take a slide of the original drawing or of the scene you wish to paint and project it on to the canvas at the appropriate size. This allows you to speed up the time-consuming task of drawing up, giving you more time for the painting itself. It is also very accurate.

Any slide projector will do, but one with an internal fan to keep the machine and slide cool during projection is best. A zoom lens, with its variable focal length, is also useful. This enables you to get the image size you require without altering the distance between canvas and projector. The most important thing is to ensure that both canvas and projector are stable. If there is any movement while you are drawing you will find it difficult to get the image back to precisely the same place. Slide projectors give much stronger illumination than epidiascopes — by drawing the curtains you will get a clear image but you will also have enough light to work in. You will find that you have to work at one side of the image, so that you do not obscure the projector's light with your body.

227

GUIDELINE SKETCHES

MARIANNA See p. 200.

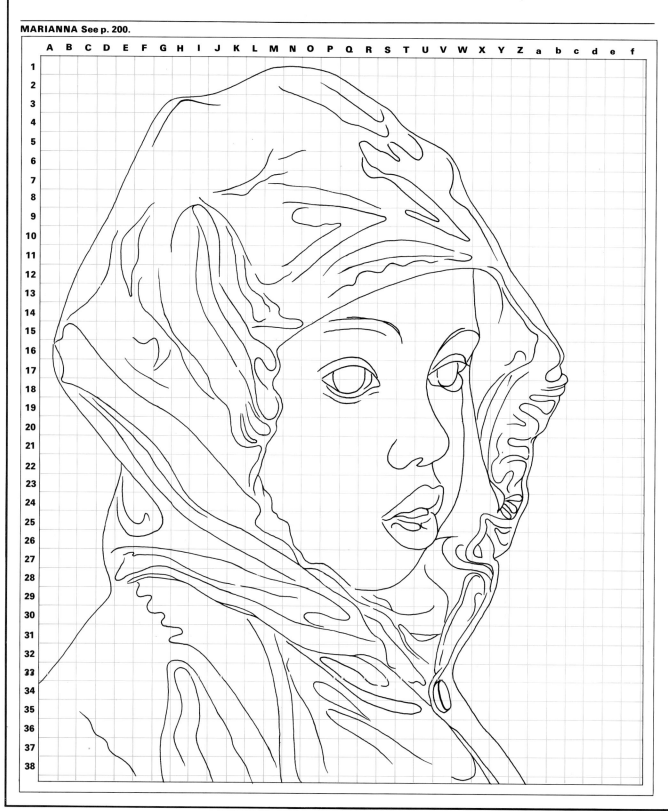

THERESA See p. 204.

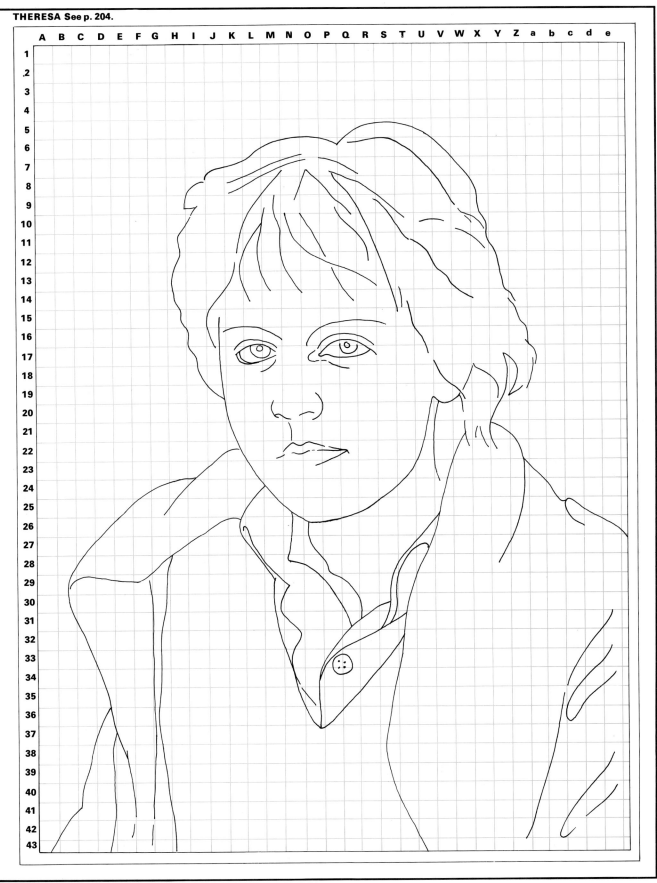

NIGHTLIGHT See p. 126.

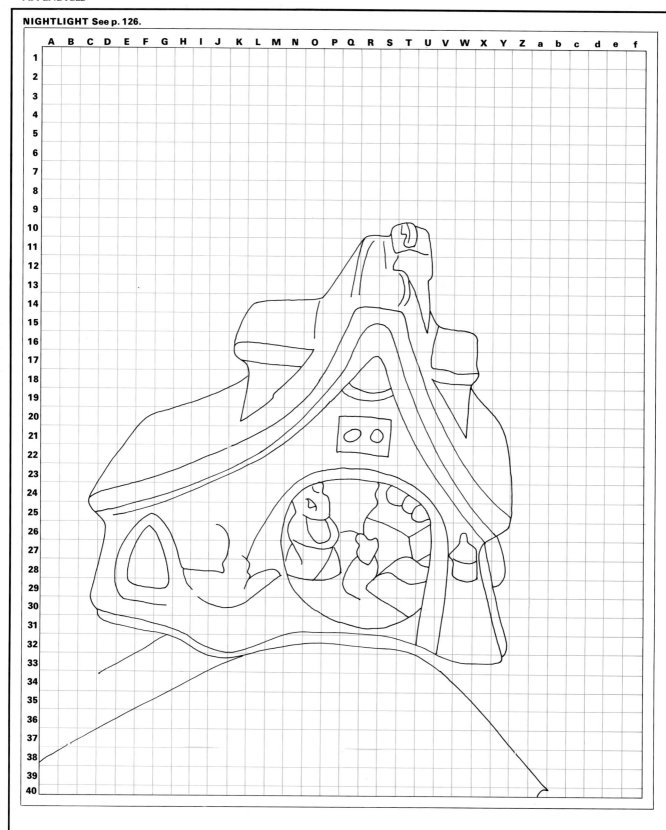

HENRY WITH A BABY RABBIT See p. 196.

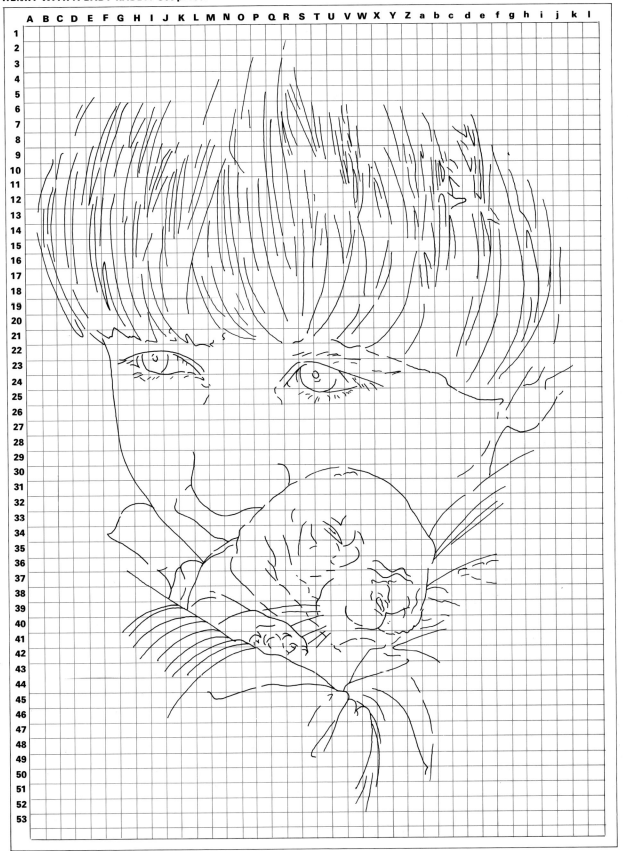

AQUARIUM See p. 130.

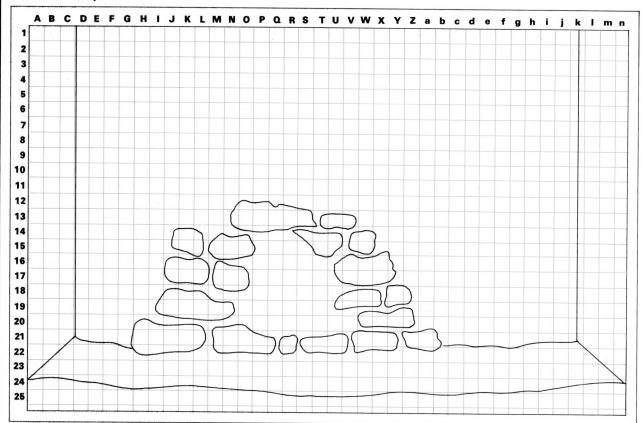

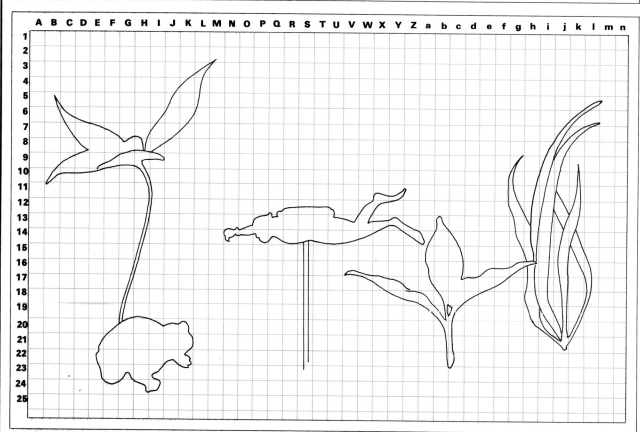

NOTE
This painting is built up in a number of layers, so it would be impossible to give all the information you need to draw it up on a single guideline sketch. Seven guideline sketches are therefore included, showing the arch and plants (opposite) and the principal objects in the tank. There is also a sketch for one small fish (below).

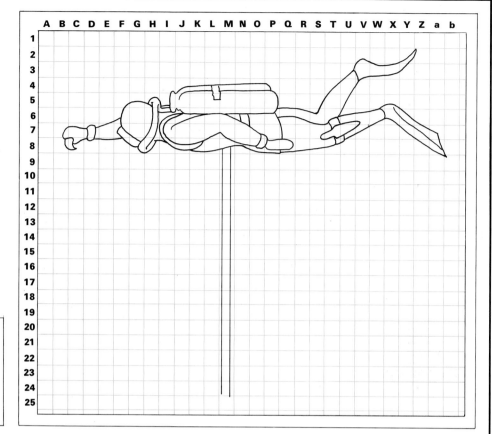

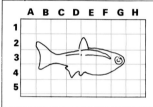

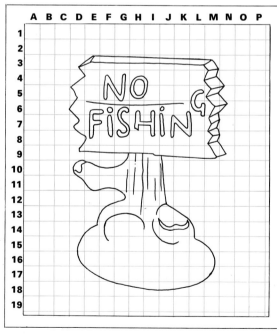

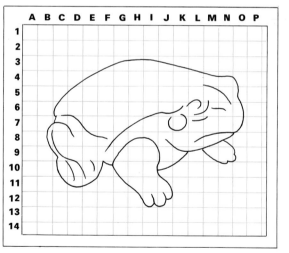

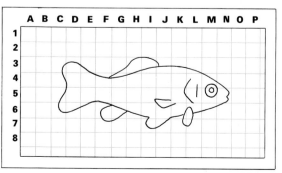

WINTER TREES See p. 140.

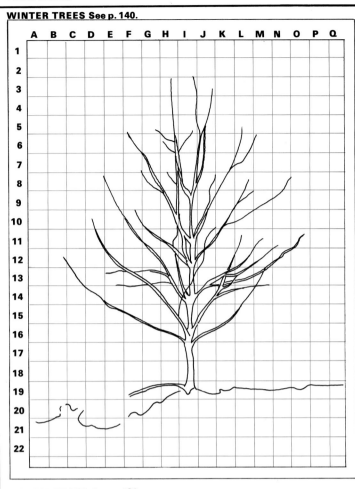

IRIS See p. 114.

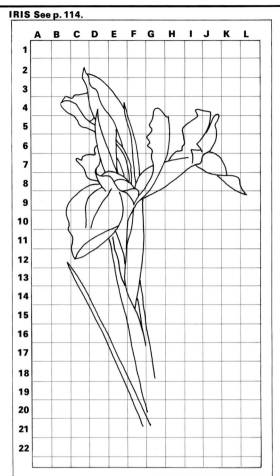

WINTER TREES See p. 138.

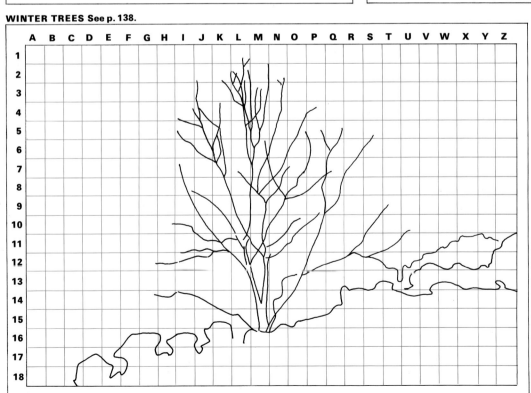

BONFIRE NIGHT See p. 188.

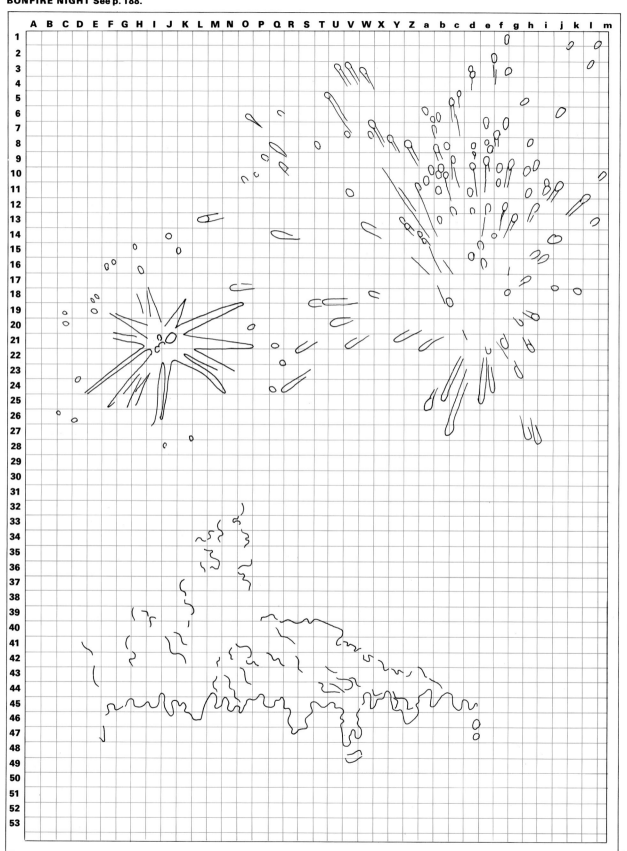

SHIP AT LE HAVRE See p. 170.

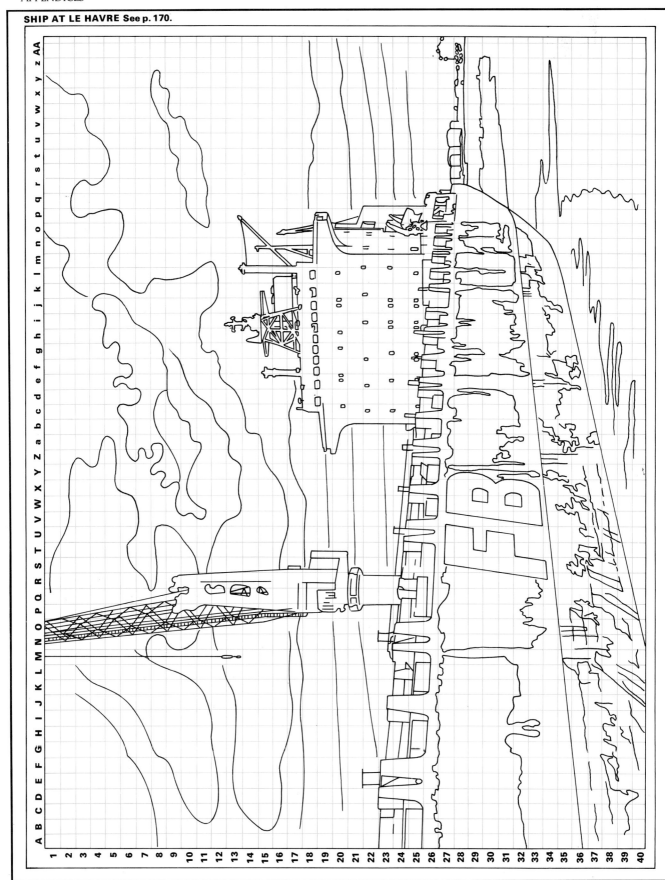

HORSE IN AN ENGLISH LANDSCAPE See p. 154.

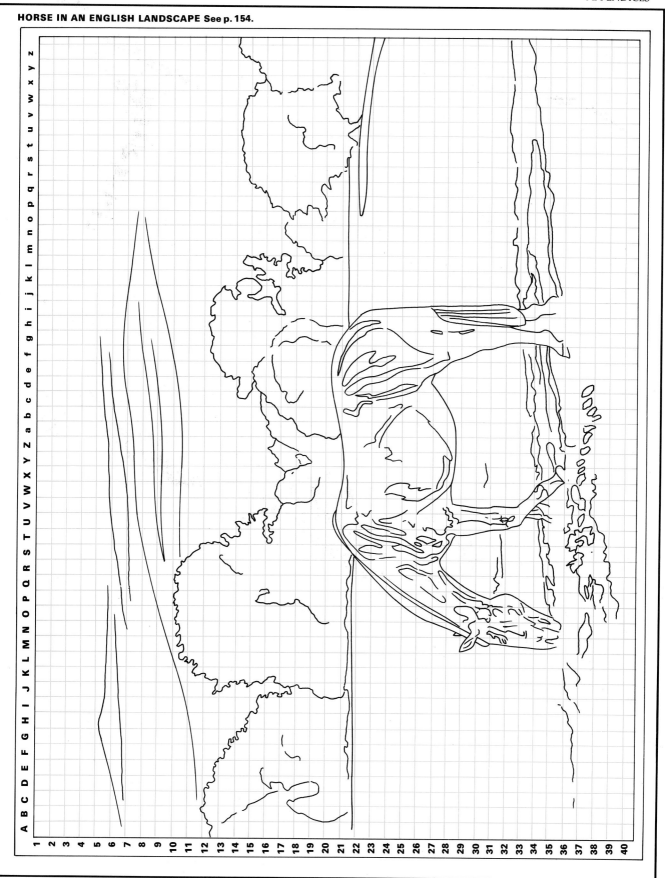

VENETIAN CANAL See p. 180.

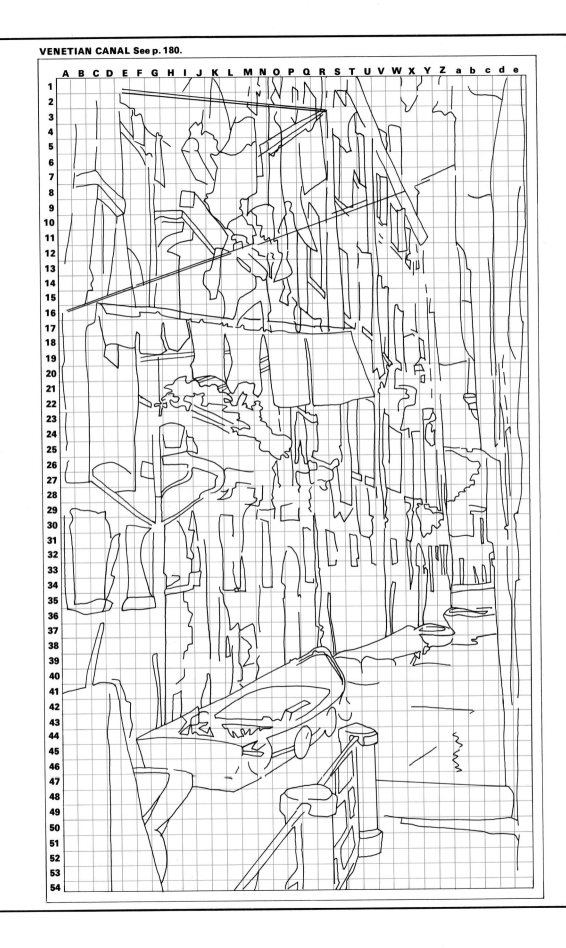

OPEN COUNTRY See p. 142.

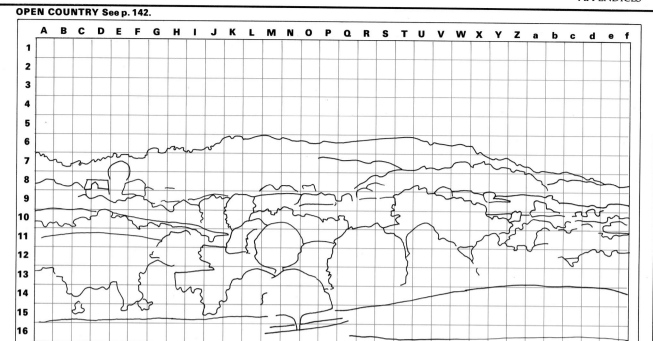

WELSH MOUNTAINS See p. 158.

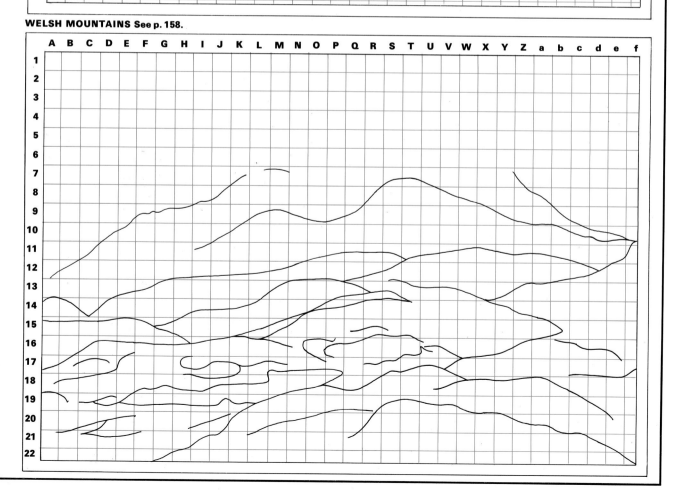

GARDEN SCENE See p. 150.

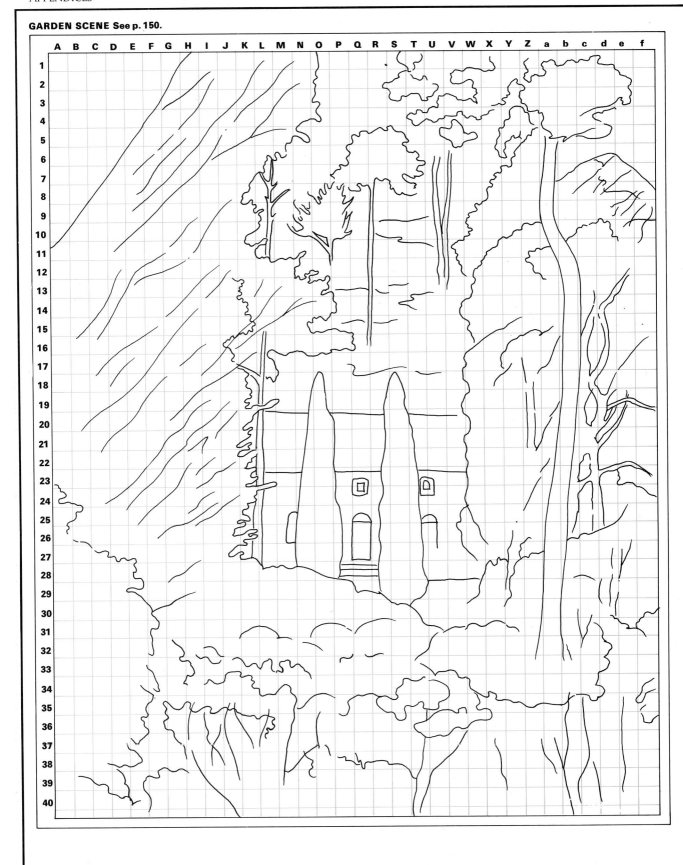

ITALIAN LANDSCAPE WITH FIGURES See p. 146.

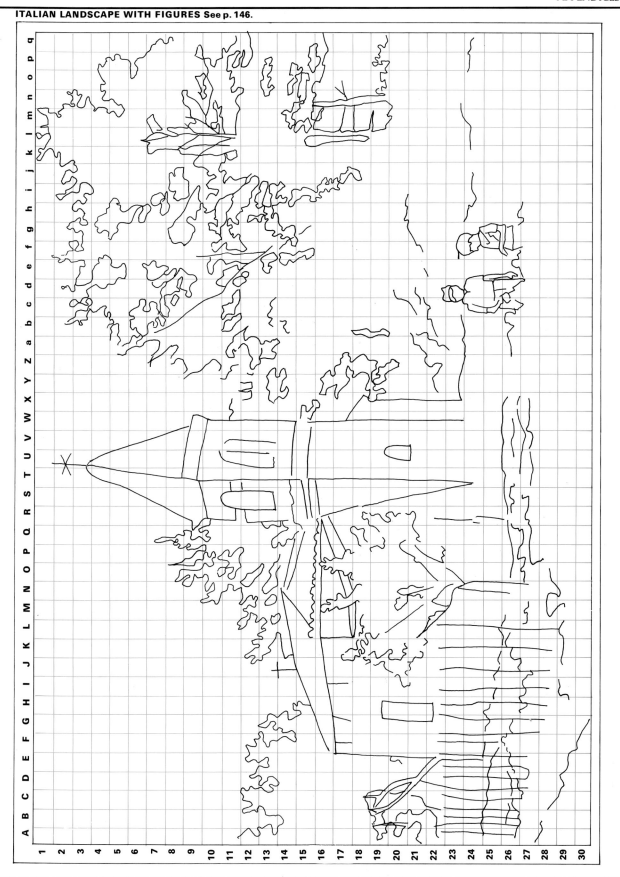

BEACH SCENE See p. 166.

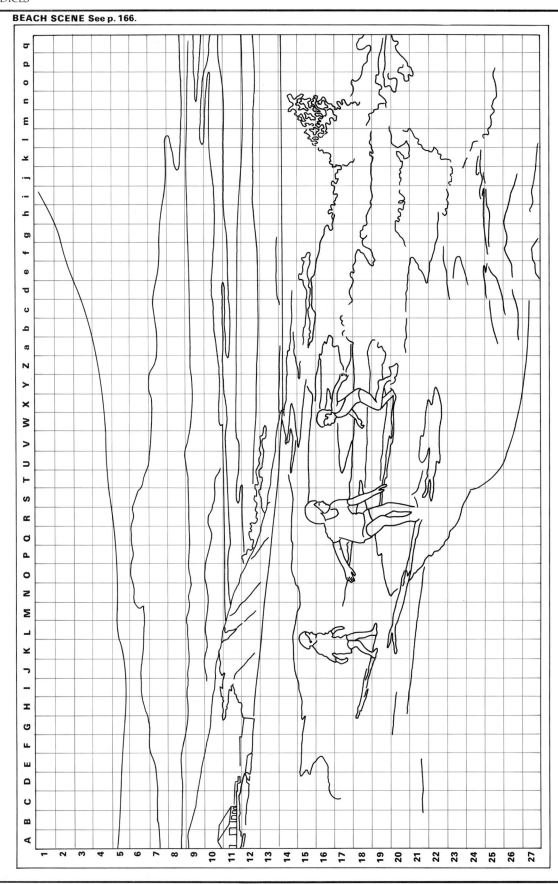

SEASCAPE See p. 162.

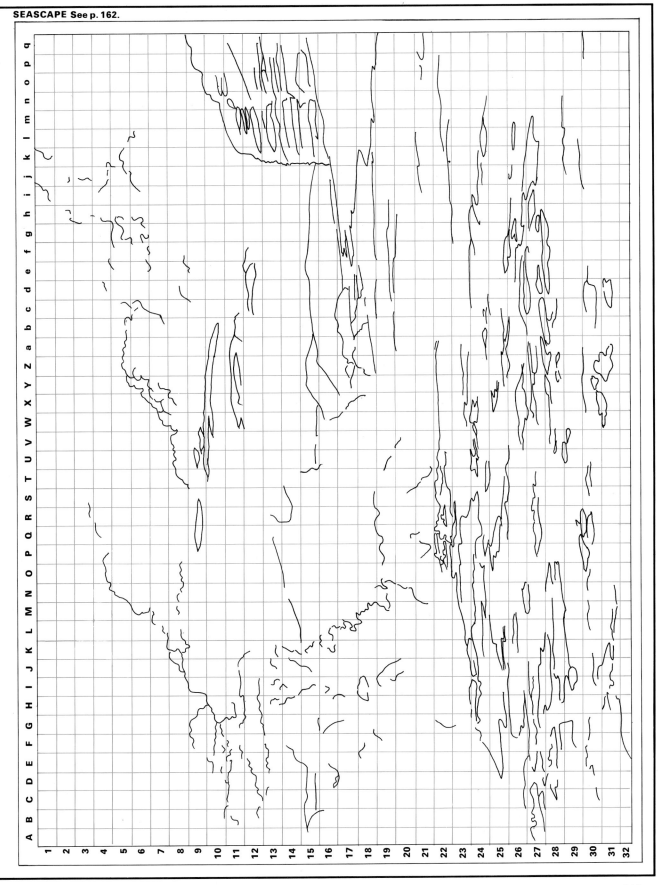

NUDE I See p. 218.

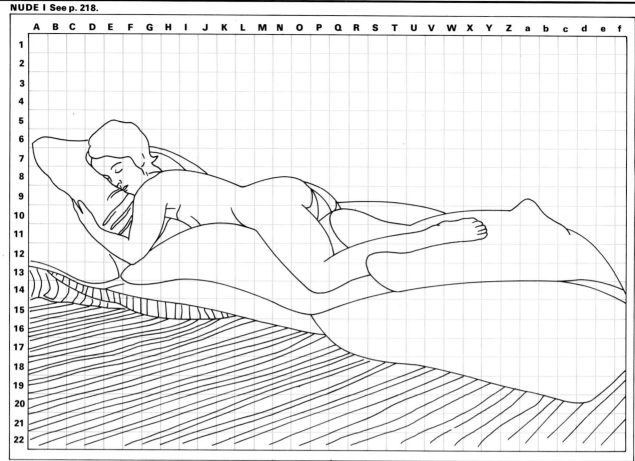

NUDE II See p. 222.

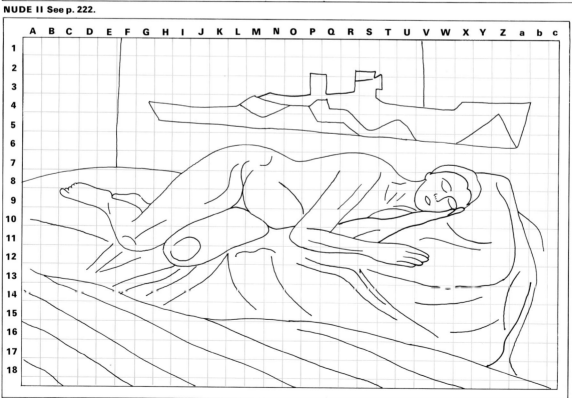

SOCCER MATCH See p. 184.

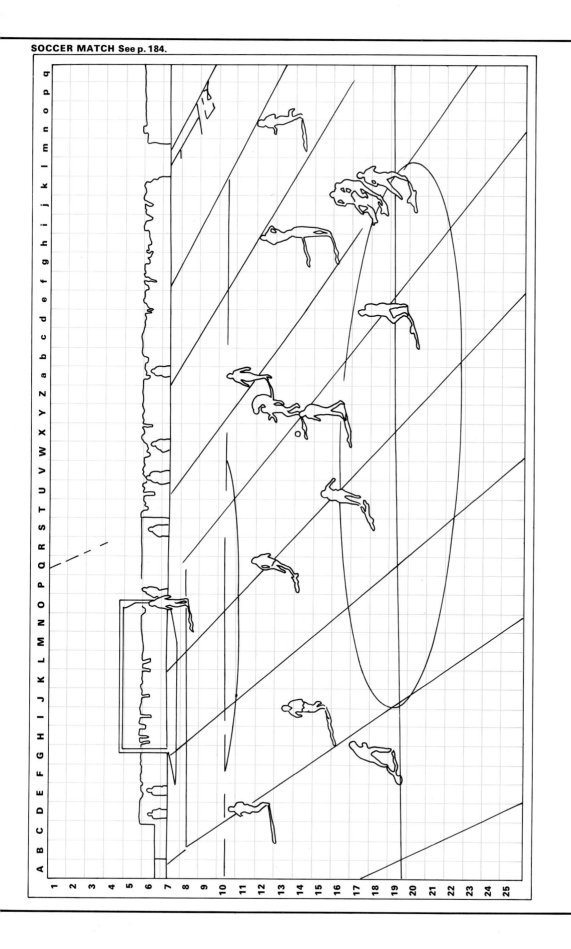

BIRD WHISTLE See p. 120.

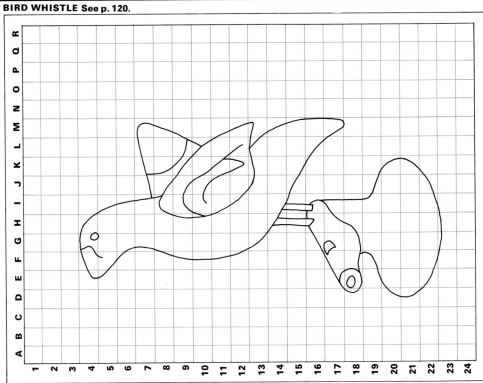

ITALIAN GLASS. See p. 122.

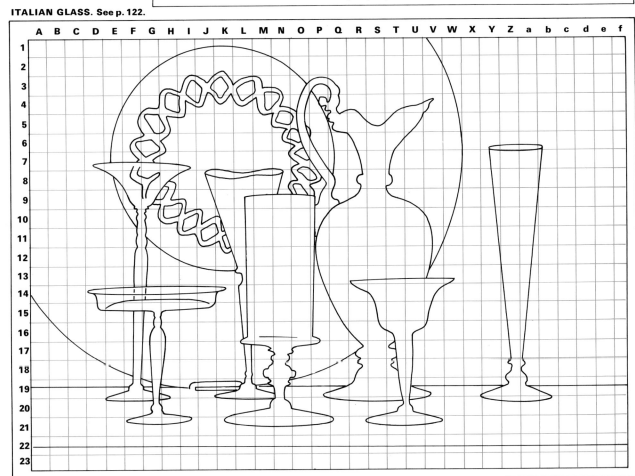

APPLES See p. 116.

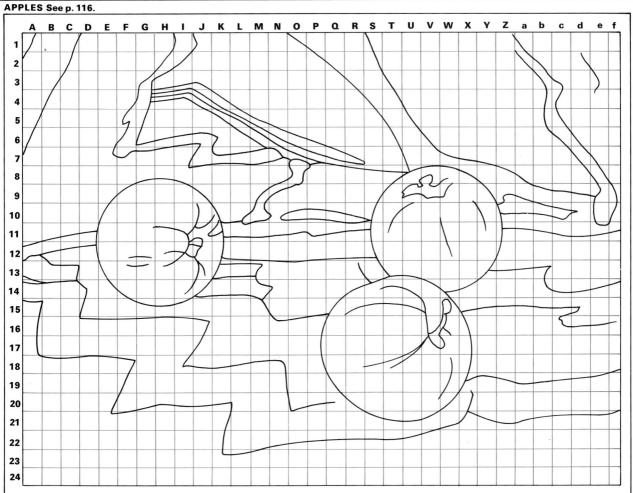

NEW YORK See p. 176.

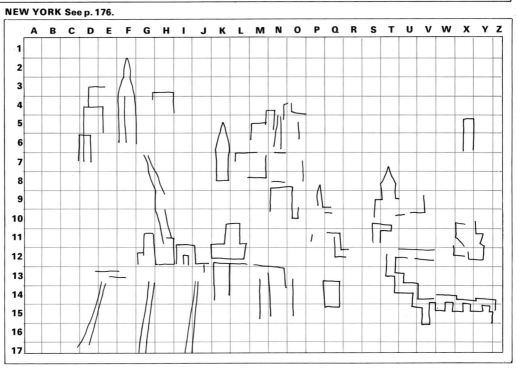

GLEN See p. 208.

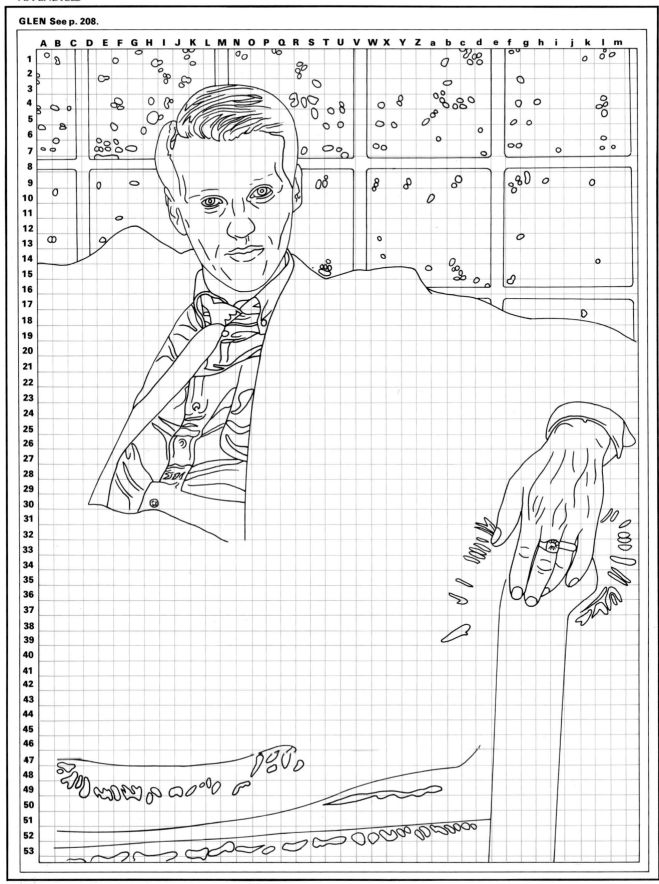

FRAMING

PUTTING A SIMPLE molded frame around an oil or acrylic painting is quite straightforward. A frame will enhance the appearance of your painting and will give it some protection. But you do need a basic set of tools. The most specialized is a miter block or miter cutter to enable you to cut precise 45 degree angles, to make your frame square up accurately. The cheapest miter blocks are wooden. They have grooves to guide your saw blade at the correct angle. Unfortunately, these grooves tend to become inaccurate with use, so if you want to do a lot of framing you should choose better quality equipment. You can buy metal miter boxes, which allow you to cut two sections of molding at once: this ensures perfect corner joining. These boxes are best suited to thinner types of molding. Heavier duty miter cutters with attached saws are also available, but they tend to be considerably more expensive.

You will also need a tenon saw and a pair of corner clamps. These hold your pieces of molding at precisely 90 degrees while you are gluing and nailing them. They are particularly useful to keep your molding flat while it is being assembled. Another method of holding pieces of molding together is to grip them in a vise. Finally you will require a hammer, nails, a nail punch, woodworking adhesive, and sandpaper.

CHOOSING THE MOLDING

Local suppliers may often have only a limited selection of moldings, containing nothing that seems right for your painting. Even with a larger range it is often very difficult to choose. In my opinion, the frame is so much a part of the painting itself that in such a situation you should buy a plain or sealed wood molding and paint or stain it yourself. You can then use colors that complement or relate to those of the painting. The frame becomes a much more personal element and this makes the painting and frame come together as a satisfying complete object. There are, of course, some very beautiful (and costly) traditional moldings that can make a good painting look even better. But it is important to remember that your options are unlimited and that the imagination you bring to your painting can be equally well expressed in the nature of your frame.

Measure up your painting and buy a little more molding than you think you will need. Molding commonly comes in 8 foot or 10 foot lengths so, if you do not buy it cut to length, make sure you buy enough to cut out all four sides, with a little over. You will find that you come to use some moldings more than others, and it may be worth buying 100 foot batches from wholesale counters.

Measure the canvas along the edges rather than across the middle where it is invariably less wide. Make the first 45 degree cut at the end of the molding and measure the length you require from the inside edge of the rebate. When you have cut the four sides join two at a time. Apply a small amount of glue to the two sawn edges and position the wood in the corner clamps. If necessary use felt or hardboard to protect the metal from the molding. Push the two sides slowly together and tighten the clamps. Wipe off any excess glue. Then pin the molding from each side using a small hammer and panel pins. Finally use a nail punch and hammer the heads of the pins into the timber. Leave the two halves of the frame in the clamps for the glue to set. Put the two halves together by gluing, clamping, and pinning the two remaining corners of the frame.

When the frame is made you can fill the nail punch holes. Use a white powder filler mixed with PVA, or a plastic wood filler. When this is dry, sand the wood down and retouch the areas you have filled. If you are not using a prepared frame, now is the time to paint or stain it.

Place the painting in the frame and secure it with cork slices. You can glue these in if you wish. Then nail panel pins into the back of the frame adjacent to the edge of the canvas. When they are secure, bend them back over the painting to hold it firmly in the frame. Finally insert two screw-eyes into the back of the frame about two-thirds of the way up and attach picture wire to them.

FRAMING DRAWINGS AND PAINTINGS ON PAPER

With originals on paper you make the frame in the same way as for a painting on canvas. But you put into the frame a sandwich that comprises front glass, mount or mat, drawing, backing board, and hardboard. The mount prevents the drawing coming into contact with the glass. But it also gives the work some space, separating it from the solidity of the frame. This allows the drawing to be seen in a more focused and concentrated way. This is as important for a quiet, subtle work as it is for a bright and busy one. For this reason the most successful mounts are generally quite neutral and unobtrusive, with a range of ivory and gray tints predominating, often with a slight cool or warm cast appropriate to the colors of the image. To preserve your work for as long as possible (assuming you have used permanent rag paper for the picture itself) use museum board for the mount and the backing card. This material is acid-free and made from pure rag. It is costly, but is the only sure way of protecting your work from contamination.

Cutting a mount with a bevel edge requires some practice. Use a heavy metal ruler and a sharp knife (the Stanley type is best). Or you can buy a mount cutter designed for this purpose. The latter practically guarantees a good result every time, so if you plan to mount and frame most of your work it is a good investment. Do all your marking and cutting on the reverse side of the card.

To attach the artwork to the mount many people use drafting or masking tape. But plain flour and water paste, applied only to the top edge of the work, is adequate. To position the mount correctly, place the image the right way up, with one strip of tape already attached (or the top edge pasted). Then carefully lower the mount on to the image. It is far less easy to position the work correctly when you are looking at it from the back.

When the glass and backing cardboard and hardboard

are cut to size, you can assemble the frame. The glass should be spotlessly clean, especially on the inside. Use a commercial glass cleaner or methylated spirits and polish it well. It is best to put the glass on a towel or a sheet of baize while you are doing this. Then place the frame next to the glass, lift the glass carefully by the edges and put it into the frame. Look for any dust on the surface and flick it off. I use a large round soft dry squirrel-hair brush to remove specks of dust. Then put in the mount, followed by the backing card and the hardboard. Picture framers usually use special flat diamond staples to secure the hardboard backing, but small panel pins, tacked all the way around the back of the frame, are perfectly adequate. When the backing is secure, you should seal the work by attaching gummed paper strip all the way around the back of the completed frame.

To frame an original on paper, you should make a sandwich containing these items: the frame itself, the glass, the cardboard mount, the original painting or drawing, the backing board, and the sheet of hardboard that makes up the back of the frame.

MAKING A FRAME

1 Cut the bevelled inner edge of the mount with a mount cutter. Use a steel rule to get an accurate straight edge.

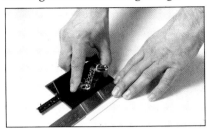

2 With a strip of masking tape along the edge of the painting, lower the mount down into the correct position.

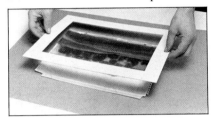

3 To cut the corners of the frame use either a special miter cutter (below left) or a simple miter box (below right).

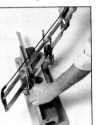 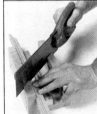

4 Spread glue thinly over the cut surfaces of the molding before you pin them together.

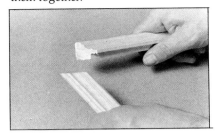

5 Holding the pieces together by means of a corner clamp, pin them securely together.

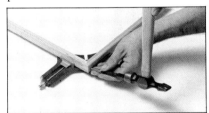

6 While the corner is still clamped, drive the pins into the wood using a nail punch.

7 Insert glass, mount, painting, backing, and hardboard into the frame and drive pins in to secure the hardboard.

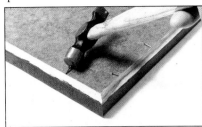

8 Seal the back of the frame using gummed paper strip all the way around the edges.

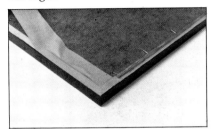

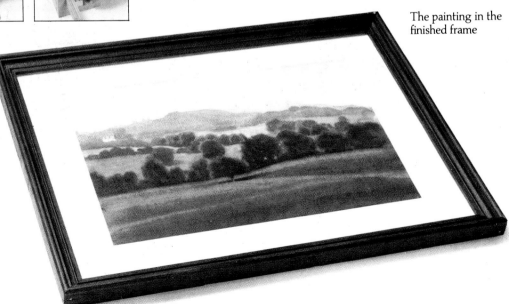

The painting in the finished frame

NOTES ON TECHNIQUES

Alla prima painting (or "direct painting") is a technique in which the first layer of paint on the canvas is also usually the last. The ground may be white, or colored with an imprimatura or toned ground. There is a purity of approach about this technique which makes it very appealing since the paint is not being disguised in any way. It can show great freedom and fluency of execution, but it is a difficult style to master and one that artists usually arrive at after using more controlled techniques. See "Ballroom dancers", pp. 56–9 and "Apples", pp. 116–19.

Blending, the fusion of tones to create gradations from light to dark, is a fundamental technique of drawing and painting. Oil paint lends itself well to blending since it stays workable on the canvas for some time. You can lay in adjacent areas of tone and then blend them with a dry or wiped-off brush (see "Trees in silhouette", pp. 20–1). You can use blending to soften the edge where two tones abut by stroking along the edge with a damp soft-haired brush chiselled between finger and thumb (see "Windmill", p. 41). With oil paint, glazes can be blended by dabbing with a dry badger blender brush or a shaving brush. You can make very soft transitions by dusting the wet surface with a fan blender brush. See "Rose", pp. 68–70 and "Glen", pp. 208–13.

Tones and colors can also be blended optically by placing adjacent touches of the two tones to be blended, so that the eye makes a soft transition from one to the other. See "Theresa", pp. 204–7.

Another method should be used for blending with thin acrylic paint. You soften the edge of a color immediately after painting it by running a damp brush along it. When this color is dry, a second color can be laid adjacent to it and softened in the same way at the join (see "Henry with a baby rabbit", pp. 196–9). There is a similar technique for blending with watercolors. The method is to dampen the area before painting, so that the paint dilutes and is softened when it touches the damp paper. See "Sunsets", pp. 54–5.

In drawing, tones are "blended" with each other by shading. Tonal gradation can be achieved by the effect of the shading on the drawing surface or by manipulating tone using fingers or an eraser.

Body color is, strictly speaking, watercolor paint with white added to make it opaque. More generally, the term refers to any painting technique that makes use of opaque rather than transparent color.

Broken color is color that has been dulled by mixing with another color, or affected optically by the juxtaposition of small touches of another color.

Chiaroscuro in a painting exploits the tonal contrasts between light and shade. It comes into its own in "low-key" painting or where a scene is lit dramatically from a single light source. See the painting of the eagle lectern, p. 77.

Cross-hatching is a technique of shading that produces tonal effects by superimposing rows of thin parallel lines at right-angles. See the portrait of a mother and baby, p. 79.

Direct painting See Alla prima painting.

Dry brush technique is a method in which paint of a dry or quite stiff consistency is stroked across areas of the canvas. The paint is picked up by the "tooth" or roughness of the canvas or by the texture of the paint already on it. This produces a broken effect. See "Welsh mountain", pp. 158–61.

Fat over lean is a rule that applies when you are painting in a number of superimposed layers of oil paint. It directs each layer of paint to have a drop more oil in the medium than the one beneath had. This means that each dried film of paint will be slightly more flexible than the one beneath. It will ensure that the paint film as a whole is permanent and adheres to the ground. See "Marianna", pp. 200–3.

Glazing is a technique for laying films of transparent color over a dried underpainting. The transparent paint is mixed with the painting or glazing medium to a purée-like consistency. It is then painted on to the area to be glazed and worked to a smooth, thin, uniform layer by dabbing with a badger blender or shaving brush. You can also use a wad of cotton in the form of a cotton pad for larger areas. For very small areas you can work the glaze with any small, soft-hair brush. You can superimpose a number of glazes

to achieve particular color effects, but you must add a drop more oil to the glazing medium with each subsequent layer. For glazing with oil paint see "Rose", pp. 68–70 and "Glen", pp. 208–13. For a similar technique in acrylics see "Firework display", pp. 188–91.

Gradation See Blending.

Grisaille is a method of monochromatic painting, or painting in different tones of a single color – usually gray. This is often used as an underpainting so as to get the forms and tones accurate before color is applied either opaquely or by glazing with transparent colors. If grisaille is used as the underpainting, it is customary to paint in tones that are more subdued than they will be in the finished painting. All the paintings in the "Black and White Techniques" section (pp. 19–50) give practice in the techniques of grisaille. See also "Rose", pp. 68–70 and "Glen", pp. 208–13.

High-key painting uses mainly bright, light-toned colors. See "Beach scene", pp. 166–9 and "Soccer match", pp. 184–7.

Impasto refers to painting done with thick paint. This is usually applied with a painting knife (see the painting of the eagle lectern, p. 77) or with a bristle brush (see "Ballroom dancers", pp. 56–9 and "New York", pp. 176–9). The paint is heaped up in ridges to create a heavily textured surface. In oil painting, an excessive use of impasto is said to threaten the durability of the paint film. With acrylics, impasto is likely to be more permanent.

Imprimatura (or "veil") is a very thin, uniform, transparent stain of color laid over the white ground before beginning the painting. The reflective qualities of the ground are hardly affected by the color. It provides a useful unifying background color and makes it easier to move between light and dark tones when painting. Today, artists usually apply an imprimatura by painting on the chosen color in a well diluted mix of oil and turpentine. Most of this is then wiped off using a clean cotton rag. The result is a uniformly stained canvas that dries very quickly and does not affect the adherence of subsequent films of paint.

Low-key painting is characterized by the use of dark and somber tones. It is the opposite of high-key painting. See the painting of the eagle lectern, p. 77 and "Nightlight", pp. 126–9.

Masking (or "masking out") is a technique generally used with watercolors or acrylics. It involves covering areas of the paper to prevent the paint from running into them. The most common method of masking is with rubber masking fluid. This is painted over the areas of the paper that you wish to leave free of paint. The solution is allowed to dry and the next color is overpainted or sprayed on. When this is dry the masking fluid is rubbed off with an eraser or with the fingers, leaving the protected area as it was before. See "Trees in silhouette", pp. 22–3, "Windmill", p. 41, "Beach scene", pp. 166–9, and "Firework display", pp. 188–91. Other methods of masking involve the use of masking film, masking tape, or cardboard stencils.

Monochrome painting See Grisaille.

Opaque painting See Transparent painting.

Optical mixing involves placing small dots of color near each other so that they are "mixed" by the eye of the observer. Two dots of red and yellow will appear as orange. In this book, techniques of optical mixing are used in those paintings which juxtapose small touches of separate colors to indicate larger areas of tone and color. See "Ballroom dancers", pp. 56–9 and "Theresa", pp. 204–7.

Overpainting is the final layer of paint applied to the canvas. It can be in the form of glazes or scumbles applied over an extensive underpainting; in this case the underpainting plays a large part in the look of the finished work. See "Rose", pp. 68–70 and "Glen", pp. 208–13. Alternatively it can be a coating of opaque pigment, in which case the overpainting is all you see. See "Madonna", pp. 48–50. Between these two extremes there is a wide range of overpainting techniques from thickly impasted to smooth, enamel-like surfaces.

Painting knife technique involves applying the paint very thickly using a special trowel-shaped tool known as a painting knife. See the painting of the eagle lectern, p. 77.

Scumbling is a technique similar to glazing. But while the effects of glazing are produced by using transparent colors over lighter tones, scumbling uses lighter semi-transparent or opaque colors over darker tones. The paint is usually applied loosely so that patches of the color beneath show through. See "Firework display", pp. 188–91, where the white smoke is scumbled over the black background.

Spattering is a method of flicking paint off the thick hairs of a stiff brush (for example, a toothbrush) to create a mass of tiny irregular spots of paint.

Spraying is a way of applying paint that can produce smooth gradations of tone or soft edges. An airbrush is a useful spraying device, especially for small areas. You can use a simple spray diffuser (normally used to apply fixative), but this is not the best method, since it can involve breathing in toxic materials. For larger canvases you can use a spray gun. See "Aquarium", pp. 130–5 and "Firework display", pp. 188–91.

Squaring (or "squaring up") is a method of transferring the contours of an image to the canvas. You superimpose a grid of squares over the original, draw a similar (or larger-scale) grid on the canvas, and draw in the image square by square. See "Drawing up an image", pp. 226–7.

Stippling is a method of applying small dots of paint to the canvas. It provides more control than spattering. See "Seascape", pp. 162–5, where the sea spray is stippled.

Toned ground is a term describing an opaque imprimatura, in which the color is mixed with white to give a uniform and opaque color.

Transparent painting uses transparent colors and relies for its effects on the whiteness of the ground (as in watercolor painting) or on the various tones of the underpainting (as in glazing in oils). See "Italian glass", pp. 122–5, "Henry with a baby rabbit", pp. 196–9, and "Rose", pp. 68–70.

The opposite of transparent painting is opaque painting, in which lighter tones are produced by mixing with white.

Trompe l'oeil is illusionistic painting that deceives the observer into thinking that the objects depicted are real. See "Illusion", pp. 98–100.

Underpainting is the term for the layer or layers of paint beneath the final coat or overpainting. There are many different types of underpainting. The simplest type is tinting the ground with a colored imprimatura or with a toned ground. This can give an overall unity to whatever colors you paint on top. See "Theresa" pp. 204–7.

In grisaille or monochromatic underpainting you paint the subject in tones of a single color, thinning it to get lighter tones (see "Madonna", pp. 48–50) or using an opaque technique by mixing the color with white (see "Rose", pp. 68–70). Another form of monochromatic underpainting uses white over a dark-toned ground, such as terre verte, before glazing (see "Glen", pp. 208–13). In the two latter types, the monochromatic underpainting is a highly worked image in itself. But there are also forms of underpainting in which you block in broad areas of tone approximately. As you continue to work on the painting, subsequent layers of paint become more detailed. (See "Nightlight", pp. 126–9 and "Open country", pp. 142–5).

For acrylic painting you can use all the underpainting methods mentioned above. There are no "fat-over-lean" rules to observe and, because acrylic paint dries so rapidly, you can superimpose more layers of color more quickly than you can in oil painting. With a transparent technique, for example, you can build up great depth of tone and color by overlaying a number of thin washes (see "Venetian canal", pp. 180–3 and "Henry with a baby rabbit", pp. 196–9). This gives you a great deal of control. You can also combine transparent and opaque underpainting techniques (see "Aquarium", pp. 130–5).

Watercolor painting in its pure form is an entirely transparent medium. So it is largely a matter of building up tone and color with superimposed washes of color. But you should not overpaint extensively, otherwise you will lose the freshness of the medium.

Varnishing a painting provides it with a uniform matt or gloss surface and protects the paint from dirt and other harmful effects. Acrylic paintings can be varnished with an acrylic gloss or matt varnish as soon as they are dry. Oil paintings should be left for at least six months before varnishing. For oil paintings I prefer damar varnish, though there are also excellent synthetic resin varnishes on the market. A flat wide white bristle varnishing brush should be used.

INDEX

ACKNOWLEDGMENTS

The author would like to thank:
Clive Adams (Director, the Mostyn Art Gallery), Alan Buckingham, Nick Campbell, Theresa Campbell, Christopher Davis, Christopher Dorling, Maria-Clelia Fabris, Alan Foster (Chief Chemist, Winsor and Newton Ltd), David Garner, Tony Garzone, Joanna Godfrey Wood, Neville Graham, Glen Gregory, Alexander Hermon, Richard and Sylvia Hermon, Min Howe, Stuart Jackman, Richard Jobson, Peter Kindersley, Richard Morphet, John Perkins, David Phelps, Trudi Pollard, Colin and Jane Renfrew, J. Sainsbury plc, Patrick and Wendy Sharman, Catriona Smith, Emily Smith, Henry Smith, Southern Arts Association, Umberto and Teresy Sozzi, Anthony and Rosemary Stamp, Virgin Records, Russell Webb, Phil Wilkinson, Roger and Kathy Witney, Barbara York.

Dorling Kindersley Limited would like to thank: Alan C. Brown, Polly Dawes, Julia Harris, Kuo Kang Chen, Billy Hall, Tony and Peter Hutchings, Brian Retter (Airedale Graphics), Jim Scott, Andrew Stanger, Tim Woodcock, Richard and Hilary Bird.

Photographers
Abbreviations: b bottom, c center, l left, r right, t top.

All photographs by Ray Smith except the following:
Jacket (front) Philip Dowell
Jacket (back) Tim Woodcock and Tony Hutchings
Tony and Peter Hutchings 2t & br, 21br, 25b, 26–7, 29bl & br, 31, 34b, 35, 37b, 40, 41tl & tr, 43, 47br, 50, 53tr & br, 59t & b, 63, 67b, 70, 77bl, 81, 89, 97, 98b, 105, 106tl, 116bl, 119, 122l, 124br, 125b, 126l, 128r, 129, 136–7, 139b, 141, 142l, 144–5, 146l, 149, 150, 153, 154l, 156b, 157, 158l, 161, 162l, 165t & b, 166l, 168–9, 170l, 172–3, 174b, 175t & b, 176l, 178b, 179, 180l, 182r, 183, 184, 185b, 187, 188l, 191, 194b, 200l, 203, 204bl, 207b, 208l, 212bl & br, 213, 215b, 217, 220b, 221t & b, 222l, 224b
Tim Woodcock 9, 11, 12–13, 14–15, 16, 18, 103, 250–1.

Filmsetting by
Advanced Filmsetters (Glasgow) Limited
Reproduction, printing and binding by
A. Mondadori, Verona.

NOTE ON COLORS

The paintings in this book have been made with Winsor and Newton colors, and the manufacturer's names for these colors have been used. Alternative possibilities for some colors are listed here. Other colors are sold by different manufacturers under the names used in the book.

Winsor Red Rowney Red is similar; or you can use any comparably permanent Arylamide Red; otherwise use Cadmium Red, which is the nearest equivalent
Winsor Blue Phthalocyanine Blue, Thalo Blue, Monestial Blue
Winsor Yellow Hansa Yellow or a comparably permanent Azo Yellow
Indian Yellow Grumbacher Transparent Yellow
Winsor Green Phthalocyanine Green, Thalo Green, Monestial Green
Permanent Rose Quinacridone, Rowney Rose, Thalo Red Rose
Titanium White Superba White